Translating *Beowulf*
Modern Versions in English Verse

Translating *Beowulf*
Modern Versions in English Verse

Hugh Magennis

D. S. BREWER

© Hugh Magennis 2011

All Rights Reserved. Except as permitted under current legislation no part of this work may be photocopied, stored in a retrieval system, published, performed in public, adapted, broadcast, transmitted, recorded or reproduced in any form or by any means, without the prior permission of the copyright owner

The right of Hugh Magennis to be identified as the author of this work has been asserted in accordance with sections 77 and 78 of the Copyright, Designs and Patents Act 1988

First published 2011
D. S. Brewer, Cambridge
Paperback edition 2015

ISBN 978 1 84384 261 3 hardback
ISBN 978 1 84384 394 8 paperback

D. S. Brewer is an imprint of Boydell & Brewer Ltd
PO Box 9, Woodbridge, Suffolk IP12 3DF, UK
and of Boydell & Brewer Inc.
668 Mount Hope Ave, Rochester, NY 14620–2731, USA
website: www.boydellandbrewer.com

A CIP catalogue record for this book is available
from the British Library

The publisher has no responsibility for the continued existence or accuracy of URLs for external or third-party internet websites referred to in this book, and does not guarantee that any content on such websites is, or will remain, accurate or appropriate.

Contents

Preface	vii
Acknowledgements	ix
List of abbreviations	x
1. *Beowulf* and Translation	1
2. Approaching the Poetry of *Beowulf*	27
3. Reception, Perceptions, and a Survey of Earlier Verse Translations of *Beowulf*	41
4. Edwin Morgan: Speaking to his Own Age	81
5. Burton Raffel: Mastering the Original to Leave It	109
6. Michael Alexander: Shadowing the Old English	135
7. Seamus Heaney: A Living Speech Raised to the Power of Verse	161
8. Other Post-1950 Verse Translations	191
Epilogue	217
Bibliography of works cited	221
Index	241

Preface

When I came to Queen's University in Belfast as an undergraduate in 1966 one of our lecturers in the first year was a Mr Seamus Heaney. 1966 was the year that Heaney published *Death of a Naturalist*, though I was not aware of that at the time. Mr Heaney was a young lecturer with thoughtful and interesting ideas about modern poetry. I particularly remember him giving lectures on Eliot and Frost.

After the first year I specialized as much as possible in medieval studies on my English degree and didn't come across Heaney much. The key teachers who guided me were two very different figures but they made an effective and complementary team. One was the no-nonsense Scot John Braidwood, an old-style philologist who seemed to have a detailed knowledge of the history of every word you could think of; as well as Old English, he had a special interest in the English language in Ulster. The other was one of Tipperary's finest, Éamonn Ó Carragáin, who was equally as inspirational as Braidwood, but in a different way. Ó Carragáin's enthusiasm for *Beowulf* was exceeded only by his enthusiasm for *The Dream of the Rood*. Both men were intellectually generous, and modest, and, despite all the other delights of English language and literature, they made Old English seem to me the most exciting part of the curriculum.

Heaney has written eloquently of the influence that John Braidwood had on him as a student, a few years before me, and of how that influence eventually fed into his 1999 translation of *Beowulf*, one of the major translations to be discussed in this book. Braidwood himself was much influenced by Ritchie Girvan, whose pupil he had been at Glasgow in the period when Edwin Morgan also studied with Girvan. Morgan's translation of *Beowulf*, published in 1952, another of the major translations discussed here, is dedicated to Girvan.

Such links (I like to humour myself) give something of a personal dimension to my relationship to one strand of the story of verse translations of *Beowulf* in the second half of the twentieth century, going back to my time as a student at Queen's in the 1960s. My own social background was also similar to that of Heaney in some ways, and while I didn't have a *thole* moment exactly (see Heaney's *Beowulf*, pp. xxv–xxvi), I remember having *driv*, *childer* and *meat* moments ('drove', 'children' and 'food' in Standard English), among others, which stimulated me to think of Ulster speech in relation to Old English. Heaney's reflections about translating *Beowulf* strike a chord for me in terms of my own experience as well as interesting me in the more dispassionate context of the scholarly topic of *Beowulf* reception and appropriation.

The 1960s were also a significant time for *Beowulf* translations more generally (no personal connection imagined here): Burton Raffel's translation (1963) was another product of the 60s, as was Kevin Crossley-Holland's (1968), and in the 60s Michael Alexander (whose version of the poem came out in 1973) was studying *Beowulf* at Oxford. It is from the 60s onwards that the enterprise of translating *Beowulf* into modern English verse increasingly gains pace, particularly (as we shall see) in America. This book will examine the products of that enterprise, going back also to trace the earlier history of *Beowulf* translation into English verse, and prose, and of the reception of the poem in the wider culture. The 1960s provided my own way into *Beowulf* and *Beowulf* translation, but the story that the book traces started long before that, and is still going.

And my *Beowulf* connections continue. In that regard, I would like to thank friends and colleagues whom I have learned from and who offered advice and comments to me about *Beowulf* and its translations as I worked on this book. I am most indebted of all to my long-time colleague, font of knowledge and wisdom, Ivan Herbison, who back in the mists of time was a student of mine — and of John Braidwood. While not listing them by name, I am indebted to many others as well, friends, colleagues and recent students and seminar participants, for their suggestive ideas.

Quotations from *Beowulf* in this book are from the fourth edition of Fr. Klaeber, *Klaeber's Beowulf*, ed. Fulk, Bjork and Niles, except that I do not mark long vowels or follow the editors' convention of using superscript dots to indicate palatalized pronunciation of *c* and *g*. All other Old English poems are quoted from *ASPR*, ed. Krapp and Dobbie. Unattributed translations are my own.

Acknowledgements

As mentioned in the Preface, I am grateful to friends, colleagues and students for their suggestions and advice in connection to my work on *Beowulf* and its translations, particularly to Ivan Herbison. I would like to thank David Clark and Chris Jones for their constructive comments on earlier drafts of this book. At Boydell & Brewer I wish to thank Vanda Andrews, Rohais Haughton and my editor Caroline Palmer. And I would like to record my thanks to Queen's University Belfast for research leave and travel funding that enabled me to carry out research for *Translating Beowulf*.

I wish to thank the Librarian of the Houghton Library, Harvard University, for kind permission to quote Tennyson's translation of lines from *Beowulf* from MS Eng 952 (4) of the Houghton Library. I am grateful to Michael Alexander for kindly granting me permission to quote in full his poem '*Beowulf* Reduced', published in the poetry journal *Agenda*, © Michael Alexander. Chapters 4 and 7 of this book have drawn upon material from Hugh Magennis, 'Translating *Beowulf*: Edwin Morgan and Seamus Heaney', in Peter Mackay, Edna Longley and Fran Brearton (eds), *Modern Scottish and Irish Poetry*, © Cambridge University Press, reproduced with permission.

Every effort has been made to trace all copyright holders but if any have been inadvertently overlooked the author and publishers will be pleased to make the necessary arrangements at the first opportunity.

Abbreviations

ASPR	The Anglo-Saxon Poetic Records, ed. Krapp and Dobbie
CSASE	Cambridge Studies in Anglo-Saxon England
JEGP	Journal of English and Germanic Philology
MRTS	Medieval and Renaissance Texts and Studies
NM	Neuphilologische Mitteilungen
OED	Oxford English Dictionary, ed. Simpson and Weiner
PMLA	Publications of the Modern Language Association of America
RES	Review of English Studies

✦1✦

Beowulf *and* Translation

Introductory

Throughout its modern history the Anglo-Saxon poem *Beowulf* has inspired translations into Modern English. In the last century and a half or so, some forty verse translations have appeared in print, producing a range of different takes on the Old English poem, in everything from iambic pentameter, to jaunty ballad rhyme, to strict Old English metre, and even more prose translations have been produced.[1] Meanwhile, *Beowulf* has been a source of interest too for literary translators/adaptors in a broader sense and for other creative artists, though interestingly it has only entered into popular culture to a significant degree in recent years.[2] The present study focuses most closely on verse translations in English, particularly those produced in the last sixty years, though it also pays attention to prose translations and to previous verse translations, as well as referring to other creative adaptations.

The verse translation by Edwin Morgan (1952) is argued here to be of special significance in its own right but also as the beginning of translation of *Beowulf* into a genuinely modern poetic idiom, leading the way for many later followers down to and beyond Seamus Heaney (1999). With the exception of William Morris's uncompromisingly strange version (1895), discussed below, which creates its own – medievalizing – idiom,[3] Morgan's may be seen as the first serious sustained poetic engagement with the poem in Modern English. As explained below in Chapter 3, Tennyson had translated ten half-lines from

---

[1]   On translations of *Beowulf*, see especially Tinker, *The Translations of Beowulf*; Osborn, 'Translations, Versions, Illustrations'; Liuzza, 'Lost in Translation: Some Versions of *Beowulf* in the Nineteenth Century'.
[2]   See below, 'Epilogue'; also Osborn, 'Translations, Versions, Illustrations', pp. 350–7; Staver, *A Companion to Beowulf*, pp. 187–95; George, *Beowulf: A Reader's Guide to Essential Criticism*, pp. 115–49. On modern poetry, see especially Chris Jones, *Strange Likeness: The Use of Old English in Twentieth-Century Poetry*.
[3]   On Morris's version, see below, pp. 10–11, 57–62.

Beowulf as early as 1830 and Longfellow included translated extracts from it in a publication of 1838, but, like the majority of people generally, other poets of the nineteenth and first half of the twentieth century ignored *Beowulf*; the verse translations of the time were mostly done by scholars and amateur enthusiasts. The situation changed in the second half of the twentieth century, during which period a significant number of poets joined the scholars and the *Beowulf* enthusiasts in the enterprise of translating the poem. The version by Heaney is now the best-known translation, and the form, indeed, in which most contemporary readers experience *Beowulf*, but other later-twentieth-century versions too were also widely read in the years after their publication, and some have acquired enduring popularity, being republished over a period of decades. And the verse translation of *Beowulf* continues unabated today.

Writing from personal experience and from a specific literary and cultural context, each translator produces an individual take on *Beowulf* and presents a particular interpretation. All translation, as all reading, is interpretation, by nature always partial and incomplete, and also singular. As Kathleen Davis puts it, referring to translation in general, 'The source text for a translation is already a site of multiple meanings and intertextual crossings, and it is only accessible through an act of reading that is itself a translation.'[4] Stanley B. Greenfield shows conscious recognition of translation as being based on interpretation when he describes his own translation of *Beowulf* as 'simultaneously a poem and, by virtue of the nature of translation, an act of criticism'.[5]

At a more general level, however, it should also be borne in mind that, like all works from the past, *Beowulf* itself has changed down the years, as the scholarly agenda has changed and as the cultural climate has changed. Poststructuralism has taught us that texts are unstable and infinite anyway, whether new or old, but the interpretation and translation of works from the past in particular take place in a context of cultural relativism in which the text does not remain an objective entity. The influential student of biblical interpretation and translation Stephen Prickett writes,

> Translation, especially from one period of time to another, is not just a matter of finding the nearest equivalents for words or syntactic structures. In addition it involves altering the fine network of unconscious or half-conscious presuppositions that underlie the actual words or phrases, and which differentiate so characteristically the climate of thought and feeling of one age from that of another.[6]

Different reception contexts will do this in different ways.

---

[4] Davis, *Deconstruction and Translation*, p. 16.
[5] Greenfield, *A Readable Beowulf: The Old English Epic Newly Translated*, p. ix (the translation is discussed below, pp. 198–9). On translation as interpretation, see Steiner, *After Babel*; Venuti, *The Scandals of Translation*; Venuti writes, 'A translation always transmits an interpretation, a foreign text that is partial and altered', p. 5.
[6] Prickett, *Words and The Word: Language, Poetics and Biblical Interpretation*, p. 7.

Each translation is thus of its time and context not only in its approach to poetry but also in basic aspects of the understanding of the original poem that the translation expresses. If, in Greenfield's words, translation is an act of criticism, it is an act of criticism situated in its own time and context, an act of criticism that reflects an aspect of the instability of the source text, its instability over time. The *Beowulf* that Seamus Heaney translated in 1999 is not the same as that translated by A. Diedrich Wackerbarth in 1849 (the first full translation into English verse) or even quite the same as the versions of more recent translators. The very text of *Beowulf* has been modified in the light of advances in scholarship, including in recent decades: Michael Alexander in his revised edition of his translation (2001), published twenty-eight years after his original version, incorporates 'newly accepted readings' and adjusts his original phrasing in about forty places.[7] A broader difference between the *Beowulf* of Morgan, for example, and that of later translators concerns the whole question of the nature of the work's poetic language. As later translators would have been aware, but not Morgan, or at least not in the same way, the language of *Beowulf* is now understood to be not only traditional (which had long been recognized) but 'formulaic' in a very systematic way, being made up of patterns of recurrent phrases and phrase systems, recurrent, that is, not only in *Beowulf* itself but also in other Old English poems. And throughout a large part of its modern history translators would have known *Beowulf* as one of the great canonical monuments of English literary history, which it would not yet have been for Wackerbarth and his readers in 1849 or for other nineteenth-century translators and readers. Like all translations, translations of *Beowulf* 'age', therefore (to pick up on an observation by Umberto Eco[8]), because the historical moment and cultural context of the translator affect how he or she writes and also how he or she interprets and relates to the poem.

Verse translators of *Beowulf* make choices at the local level as part of the negotiation that the translator engages in, the 'gaining and losing' (to quote Eco again) of translation.[9] But, aware of the radical differences between Old English poetry and modern poetry,[10] they also make choices at the macro-level of their whole relationship with the poem and its poetry, engaging, consciously or not, with basic issues in translation theory. It is their attitude to these that will determine, for example, whether to go for a natural-sounding modern register (as Burton Raffel does, say) or one that is more insistently 'poetic', perhaps even archaic (as in Michael Alexander's version, for example). *Beowulf* itself is composed in the highest register

---

7   See Alexander, *Beowulf*, revised ed., p. xi.
8   Eco, *Mouse or Rat? Translation as Negotiation*, p. 144.
9   Eco, *Mouse or Rat? Translation as Negotiation*: 'negotiation', introduced on p. 6, provides the underlying principle of Eco's view of translation (as brought out in his book's title).
10 As Elizabeth Tyler points out (for example), '[if] Old English poets chose to maintain an aesthetics which took pleasure in seeking out the familiar [...] [it is] the aesthetics of the unfamiliar which governs the style of so much modern poetry' (Tyler, *Old English Poetics: The Aesthetics of the Familiar in Anglo-Saxon England*, p. 122).

available, as appropriate to the seriousness of its concerns.[11] Its language is lofty and formal, conveying delicate social nuance,[12] and it is archaic. In a recent article on the deployment of rare words in Old English poetry, with particular reference to *Beowulf*, Roberta Frank has observed, 'Anglo-Saxon poets courted the pleasures of language – the noun burnished by time, the gleaming verb, the aged but unwithered adjective', and she refers to the use of words that 'sounded old, northern, and pre-Christian to Anglo-Saxon ears'.[13] A fundamental question that arises for translators, therefore, particularly verse translators, is how are they, writing for a modern readership, to respond to words in the original that, as Frank puts it, 'lend a sheen that reveals the pastness of its multi-storied past'?[14]

Related to choice of register is the vital issue of a suitable metre, about which verse translators have to make basic decisions. Most verse translators of *Beowulf* in the past half century or so have based their metre on the (stress-based) metre of Old English, but with varying degrees of flexibility; a number of previous translators, as some modern ones, preferred syllabic metre (i.e., with a fixed number of syllables to the line). And, within the parameters of metre and register, translators devise their particular ways of approaching issues of diction and grammar, while also always having to balance what Edwin Morgan refers to as 'the care of accuracy' against the imperative of establishing 'a contact with the living verse of their time'.[15]

What should a verse translation of *Beowulf* be like? In the light of the previous discussion it will be seen that there can be no right answer to such a question. Most modern practitioners would probably agree with Morgan's principle of combining accuracy with producing 'living verse', though they would each apply that principle differently. By using the language of poetry verse translations can present the original poem anew in a way that prose cannot. Verse translations do not serve the subordinate function of aiding readers struggling with the Old English text but stand instead of the original, making it available to readers who cannot access that original, as well as to those who can (the issue of verse versus prose is explored below, later in this chapter). That being the case, as an Anglo-Saxonist I should say that, while admiring radical retakes of *Beowulf* and of other works from the past, I particularly value those translations of the poem that suggest the quality and artistry of the verse of the original, a difficult feat to achieve while producing poetry that is alive. There is no set way of doing this, and there will always be gaining and losing, but a good translation can enablingly provide for its readership a sense of what it is like to read the original.

---

[11] Cf. Edwin Morgan's comment that '[s]eriousness' is 'the [*Beowulf*] poet's most obvious characteristic and the unifying and dignifying force behind the diverse material' (Morgan, *Beowulf*, pp. xxxii–xxxiii).
[12] On the social nuances of the language of *Beowulf*, see John M. Hill, 'Translating Social Speech and Gesture in *Beowulf*'.
[13] Frank, 'Sharing Words with *Beowulf*', pp. 7 and 9, respectively.
[14] 'Sharing Words with *Beowulf*', p. 15.
[15] Morgan, *Beowulf*, pp. vi and viii.

The second chapter of this book will explore essential features of the poetry of *Beowulf* itself, thus supplying a basis for exploring the response of modern translators to those features.

Issues in Literary Translation

Why translate *Beowulf*?

Much attention has been paid in recent translation-studies writings to the theory and practice of translating literary texts, though usually with reference to modern foreign-language texts rather than 'archaic' ones. Many of the relevant issues also apply to the translation of texts from that other country, the past, however. Old English presents a particularly interesting case in that its texts are from an earlier form of the target language of its modern English translations. The English language has changed enormously since Anglo-Saxon times but some underlying common features, exploitable by translators, can still be recognized in its widely separated stages.

As it has developed in recent decades, one of the issues that translation studies has focused on is that of why particular texts are chosen for translation. Attention has been paid to the ideological, institutional and political basis of the selection and canonization of texts for translation. *Beowulf* has been one of the most frequently translated of all works from the past in the last fifty years or so, with nearly thirty translations into Modern English verse appearing in print since the Second World War, in addition to a substantial number of prose translations. This high number of translations of *Beowulf* has to do to a significant degree with the perceived importance and interest of *Beowulf* as a monument of English literature, as referred to above. The 'canon' of English literature has been acutely problematized and revised by many literary theorists, but in the larger institution of English studies, as reflected, say, in *The Norton Anthology of English Literature*, and as experienced by continuing generations of students, it lives on. In this canon as received in recent decades (as earlier), *Beowulf* has been, and continues to be, perceived as institutionally important – but not accessible to most people in the original language. *Beowulf* has been one of the 'great books' which are (to echo a phrase of King Alfred) most needful for all people to know, and so translators and publishers have sought to provide suitable versions, particularly in the potent medium of poetry. For non-specialists translations substitute for the original poem, and even students specializing in Old English are unlikely to read the whole of *Beowulf* in the original; they typically supplement their Old English edition with a translation. Many translators themselves first came across *Beowulf* as students on university Old English courses.

Translations of *Beowulf* have had a healthy potential market, then, particularly among university students, whose instructors compare versions and make their recommendations, based on perceptions of accessibility, reliability, user-friendliness and literary effectiveness. Students need translations of *Beowulf*. Some versions have proved more popular than others but by definition no version can be regarded as final or universally satisfactory and so there has been a steady stream of fresh attempts. Since its publication Seamus Heaney's version has been very much the market leader but the poetic translation of *Beowulf* continues (as described below in Chapter 8).

The translator may be participating in an economy and responding to institutional forces but, as many translators of *Beowulf* explicitly insist, their personal motivation in translating arises from their engagement with the poem itself. Translators have experienced the poetry of *Beowulf* and they wish to respond to it imaginatively, and, whether embarking on translating it without external prompting or (as in the case of Heaney) in response to a publisher's invitation, they seek to produce versions for modern readerships that convey something of the power of the original poem. In some cases dissatisfied with available existing translations, they are drawn to *Beowulf* as an interesting and challenging poem to translate, challenging but not too vast to contemplate as a manageable project.

Many translators of *Beowulf* would view their work of translation as taking place straightforwardly within the canonical world of English literature but it is interesting that the producers of some of the most high-profile versions have more complicated relationships to the English studies institution. Michael Alexander's translation, for example, may be seen as emanating from a traditional British literary-scholarly background and Roy Liuzza's from the world of current academic scholarship, but Burton Raffel writes from a very different perspective that seeks, one could say, to rescue *Beowulf* from the academic world. And the non-English backgrounds of Morgan and Heaney complicate the question of *Beowulf* as 'English' literature. Heaney's version in particular has been perceived as repositioning *Beowulf* in a new post-colonial cultural setting. Heaney's version raises in a striking way the question of whose *Beowulf* is it anyway. As argued below, it is an unsettling text with which to start off the orthodoxly canonical *Norton Anthology*.

The interest in translating *Beowulf*, however motivated, is something that Anglo-Saxonist critics must applaud in principle, not (or not only) because they value *Beowulf* for its canonical position in the institution of English studies but because they value the art and emotion of its poetry and the depth of its exploration of the significance of the heroic world in an Anglo-Saxon context; poetic translation in particular offers the possibility of some experience of this for new readers. All translation is problematic, however, and we have seen that *Beowulf* offers particular challenges to the translator. This being the case, the danger that an Anglo-Saxonist fears is that in representing the poem for a modern audience the translator will also misrepresent it. Not all users of translations worry about this danger, especially in a context of perception of the source text as inherently unstable. It is argued, indeed, that even renderings based on error can be valid and can produce exciting work.¹⁶ To the extent that the original of *Beowulf* is accessible to scholarly study and appreciation, however, I would insist from my Anglo-Saxonist perspective that a key function of its verse translations is to convey a sense of the poetry of that original, though inevitably transforming the poem in the process as all translations necessarily do.

Domesticating and foreignizing

In this context of representing the source text, one key question that has penetratingly been opened up again in the past couple of decades, particularly by Lawrence Venuti, has been that of 'foreignizing' versus 'domesticating' translations. Venuti challenges the dominance of the domesticating tradition, a dominance that in English-speaking cultures he traces back at least as far as Dryden (in fact, a domesticating approach is already there in Tyndale, and medievalists and classicists are familiar with domesticating translation and its theoretical justification in writers as various as Cicero and King Alfred, to name but two). Venuti writes,

> [T]ranslation practices in English cultures (among many others) have routinely aimed for their own concealment, at least since the seventeenth century, since John Dryden. In practice the fact of translation is erased by suppressing the linguistic and cultural differences of the foreign text, assimilating it to dominant values in the target-language culture, making it recognizable and therefore seemingly untranslated. With this domestication the translated text passes for the original, an expression of the foreign author's intention.¹⁷

The debate about the conflicting claims of 'source' and 'target' languages that Venuti here participates in was instigated by the theologian and philosopher F. E. Schleiermacher in his 1813 essay 'Ueber die verschiedenen Methoden des Uebersetzens.'¹⁸ Long anticipating Venuti's taxonomy of 'domesticating' and 'foreignizing' translations, Schleiermacher makes the classic distinction in approaches to translation between bringing the (in his case, German) reader to the original text and bringing the original text to the reader:

> [I]n the first case the translator is endeavoring, in his work, to compensate for the reader's inability to understand the original language [. . .] thus moving the reader to his own position, which is foreign to him. [. . .] The other method, however, showing the author not as he himself would have translated but the way that he as a German would have written originally in German, can hardly have any other standard of perfection than if one could claim for certain that, if the German

---

16   See, for example, Davis, *Deconstruction and Translation*, pp. 52–3.
17   Venuti, *The Scandals of Translation*, p. 31; Venuti had developed some of these ideas in his earlier monograph, *The Translator's Invisibility: A History of Translation*; other relevant recent contributions include Barnstone, *The Poetics of Translation*; Douglas Robinson, *Translation and Taboo*; Eco, *Mouse or Rat*.
18   Schleiermacher, 'On the Different Methods of Translating' ['Ueber die verschiedenen Methoden des Uebersetzens'].

readers were transformed one and all into connoisseurs and contemporaries of the author, the work itself would appear to them as now, the author having been transformed into a German, the translation does.[19]

Schleiermacher would not allow any combination of the two: 'These two paths are so very different from one another that one or the other must certainly be followed as strictly as possible, any attempt to combine them being certain to produce a highly unreliable result and to carry with it the danger that writer and reader might miss each other completely'[20] – though in practice translators can be seen as attending to both sides of the equation.

Schleiermacher's own strong preference was for the foreignizing method. As Venuti points out, however, it is the domesticating approach that has held sway, certainly in English tradition. As described influentially by Matthew Arnold, according to this approach the reader 'should be lulled into the illusion that he is reading an original work'.[21] Venuti quotes the contemporary translator Norman R. Shapiro as expressing what has been the prevailing ideal:

> I see translation as the attempt to produce a text so transparent that it does not seem to be translated. A good translation is like a pane of glass. You only notice that it's there when there are little imperfections – scratches, bubbles. Ideally, there shouldn't be any. It should never call attention to itself.[22]

The desired effect is fluency and naturalness. Fluency brings access to the translated work to a new readership, but, as Venuti stresses, it does so by effacing the essential otherness of that work and reconstituting it in the terms of the culture of the target language: 'Fluency is assimilationist, presenting to domestic readers a realistic representation inflected with their own codes and ideologies as if it were an immediate encounter with a foreign text and culture.'[23] The domesticating model is to be seen as an imperialist one, with the target language colonizing the source language.[24] Venuti accepts that domestication is inherent in all translation but argues that the translator should work to resist it by using the resources of the target language to suggest differentness and alienation:

> Translations, in other words, inevitably perform a work of domestication. Those that work best, the most powerful in recreating cultural values and the most accountable in accounting for that power, usually engage readers in domestic terms that have been defamiliarized to some extent, made fascinating by a revisionary encounter with a foreign text.[25]

---

[19] Schleiermacher, 'On the Different Methods', trans. Bernofsky, p. 49.
[20] Ibid.
[21] Arnold, *On Translating Homer*, p. 2.
[22] Quoted by Venuti, *The Translator's Invisibility*, p. 1.
[23] Venuti, *The Scandals of Translation*, p. 12.
[24] See further Chris Jones, *Strange Likeness*, pp. 128–34.
[25] Venuti, *The Scandals of Translation*, p. 5.

The poet Ciaran Carson would agree. Writing in the introduction to his 2002 translation of Dante's *Inferno*, Carson declares, 'But then some of us expect translations to sound like translations, and to produce an English which is sometimes strangely interesting. Especially translations of poetry.'[26] One could go further and argue that the language of poetry is by definition differentiated from the language of ordinary speech (thus it could be said that all of Ciaran Carson's writing is 'strangely interesting') and indeed, with Viktor Shklovsky, that it is a function of art in general to render things unfamiliar: 'The technique of art is to make objects "unfamiliar", to make forms difficult, to increase the difficulty and length of perception because the process of perception is an aesthetic end in itself and must be prolonged.'[27] Venuti's concept of 'foreignizing' translation may be seen as relating to this larger aesthetic principle of defamiliarization and the differentness of poetic language, but for Venuti the stakes are particularly high in translation since in his view to domesticate is to violate.

As in other areas of translation, the issue of domesticating versus foreignizing translation has been of concern to translators of *Beowulf* and of other Old English poems. There have been a few dramatically striking examples of foreignizing translations from the Old English, most famous among which must be Morris's translation of *Beowulf* and, a work evidently influenced by Morris, Pound's translation of *The Seafarer*,[28] while at the other extreme some translators have been assiduously domesticating in their approach: David Wright's prose version of *Beowulf*, discussed below, is a prime example. Some nineteenth-century (and later) versions of *Beowulf* are notable for a kind of (pseudo-)medievalizing with conventional archaizing diction, which might look like foreignizing at first sight but in fact accommodates the poem to models popular in the period of the translations, and may be seen therefore as another kind of domestication. One nineteenth-century verse translator, J. L. Hall, declares of his own version, 'though many archaic words have been used, there are none, it is believed, which are not found in standard modern poetry.'[29]

This kind of archaizing may be briefly illustrated by quoting a passage from Wackerbarth's version[30] (corresponding to *Beowulf*, lines 791–7, from the account of the fight with Grendel):

> THE Earl's Protector thought not meet
> The Murtherer should alive retreat,
> His caitiff Life to no one he

---

[26] Carson, *The Inferno of Dante Alighieri*, p. xix.
[27] Shklovsky, 'Art as Technique', p. 18. On Shklovsky's idea of 'defamiliarization', see further Thompson, *Russian Formalism and Anglo-American New Criticism*, pp. 68–76.
[28] For Morris's influence on Pound, see Chris Jones, 'The Reception of William Morris's *Beowulf*, pp. 198–9; and (cited by Jones) Fred C. Robinson, 'Ezra Pound and the Old English Translational Tradition', pp. 259–74.
[29] J. L. Hall, *Beowulf, an Anglo-Saxon Poem, Translated from the Heyne-Socin Text*, p. ix.
[30] Wackerbarth, trans., *Beowulf, an Epic Poem Translated from the Anglo-Saxon into English Verse*.

> Suppos'd could ever useful be.
> Then quick Beówulf's Liegeman true
> Great Weland's antient Relic drew
> For his Lord, that princely Wight,
> The Life he sought, (as there they might,)
> From Danger to protect.

Eschewing the use of imitative alliterative metre as not suiting the taste of the time, Wackerbarth adopts a form of romance verse – and romance vocabulary – familiar to nineteenth-century readers, particularly (with reference to vocabulary) those who have read their Scott: this is what romance is supposed to look like. 'I wish to get my book read', Wackerbarth declares, 'that my Countrymen may become generally acquainted with the Epic of our Ancestors wherewith they have been generally unacquainted.'[31] Wackerbarth wishes to get his book read and so adopts an easy, recognizable poetic style, though it is one that, with its breakneck narrative and obtrusive rhyme-scheme, might be thought to end up turning *Beowulf* into something resembling Chaucer's *Sir Thopas*.[32]

Genuinely foreignizing is William Morris's version of *Beowulf* (produced in collaboration with the Anglo-Saxonist A. J. Wyatt),[33] which 'medievalizes' the poem but not in a way that its readers would have come across before. The distinctive quality of Morris's register is immediately apparent at the beginning of the translation:

> WHAT! We of the Spear-Danes of yore days, so was it
> That we learn'd of the fair fame of kings of the folks
> And the Athelings a-faring in framing of valour.
> Oft then Scyld the Sheaf-son from the hosts of the scathers,
> From kindreds a many the mead-settles tore;
> It was then the earl fear'd them, sithence was he first
> Found bare and all-lacking; so solace he bided,
> Waxed under the welkin in worship to thrive,
> Until it was so that the round-about sitters
> All over the whale-road must hearken his will
> And yield him the tribute. A good king was that.[34]

The breaking rhythms and irregular syntax combine here with an insistently archaizing diction and a striking literalism in translation to produce a defamiliarizing effect. Morris chooses not to assimilate *Beowulf* to well-established patterns of poetic expression.

Morris (whose version is discussed in greater detail in a later chapter) is exceptional in the degree of his foreignizing, but the aim of bringing out the otherness of *Beowulf*, and thereby suggesting its foreignness, is by no means confined to him. Throughout the history of *Beowulf* translation, indeed, we see

---

[31] Wackerbarth, *Beowulf*, p. ix.
[32] Wackerbarth's version is discussed further, below, pp. 52–3.
[33] Morris and Wyatt, trans., *The Tale of Beowulf, Sometime King of the Weder Geats*.
[34] Morris and Wyatt., trans., *The Tale of Beowulf*, p. 179.

translators using syntax, diction and metre to 'suggest', as Roy Liuzza puts it, the original poem.[35] This foreignizing approach is notably evident in the stress-metre verse translations which began to be produced in the late nineteenth century at a time when stress metre was not characteristic of mainstream poetry; stress-based metres look much less 'foreign' today.

But, in the interest of readability, translators of *Beowulf* have generally tempered this desire to 'suggest' the original poem. As John Corbett points out, there is a conflict between the desirable aim on the part of a translator (specifically a translator of Old English) to convey the excitement and interest of the source text and 'Venuti's desire to acknowledge its otherness, through techniques of linguistic alienation': 'It is difficult to be excited by a text that is expressly designed to alienate you — you can be intrigued, yes, and intellectually satisfied, but visceral excitement is different.'[36] Many verse translations of *Beowulf* have been targeted at a popular readership of introductory-level students and general readers and have aimed at making the original work accessibly available and congenial. Like Wackerbarth, the producers of these translations wish to get their books read. Reviews of translations have often been from the point of view of the instructor, who needs a version that will maintain the interest of students.[37] The primacy of readability is indicated in the title of S. B. Greenfield's popular version, *A Readable Beowulf*, while Ruth P. Lehmann approached the translation of Old English with the limited aim 'to make a tolerable poem in its own right'.[38]

The majority of verse translations of *Beowulf* have been produced in America, where *Beowulf* features on canonical survey courses in many colleges, a trend that is now also widely established in British and Irish universities. The translation is intended to substitute for the original poem, or in some instances the translation is presented along with the original in a parallel-text layout, as in the bilingual edition of Heaney's translation.[39] Translators and their publishers have striven to present *Beowulf* in terms that their readers will understand and enjoy, with (especially in recent years) attractive layouts, supplementary information and, in some cases, handsome photographs and other illustrations. Whether they unacceptably reconstitute the original poem in their translations may be regarded as a matter of judgement in each case, as the translator negotiates between the two languages.

For Venuti all domesticating translations are 'scandalous'. Venuti insists that foreignizing, 'visible', translation is ethical, whereas domestication distorts the source text by imposing the values of the culture of the target language. These are considerations of profound significance to the whole enterprise of translation and Venuti's thinking has succeeded in bringing a new direction to translation

35 Liuzza, *Beowulf: A New Verse Translation*, p. 46.
36 Corbett, 'The *Seafarer*, Visibility and the Translation of a West Saxon Elegy into English and Scots', p. 168.
37 See further, below, pp. 132–3.
38 Lehmann, 'Contrasting Rhythms of Old English and New English', p. 121.
39 See also Chickering, trans., *Beowulf: A Dual-Language Edition*.

studies in the English-speaking world. But of course foreignizing translation inevitably distorts too: Morris's translation of *Beowulf* certainly does, as does Pound's of *The Seafarer*. Through the visibility of its disruptions and lack of fluency the foreignizing translation announces itself to be a translation but thereby cannot convey the qualities that a text had in its source culture: a text that did not sound unnatural originally is made to do so in its translated form. It has also been pointed out, by Corbett, that 'visible translation in Venuti's terms is still dependent on a hegemonic model of the English language. For visible translation to exist, there has to be a notion of a standard variety, and non-standard varieties that depart from it.'[40]

Domesticating translation appropriates the source text, accommodating it to the experience of readers of the target language and culture. We should also bear in mind, however, that all printed representations of Old English writings in the modern period, whether translations or original-language versions, appropriate their texts in radical ways. They impose the structures and procedures essential to print technology on the products of manuscript culture (which in turn may have an oral underlay), re-presenting the original texts in a form very different from that experienced by Anglo-Saxon audiences and readers. As Martin Foys has recently written, throughout the age of print Old English and other medieval scholars have 'refashioned what they represented in the light of their own ideologies and technologies of representation and reproduction'.[41] If translation is not innocent and transparent, neither is the printed edition, even the revered critical edition, which changes the appearance, layout, punctuation and even the words of the manuscript witnesses. In the modern critical edition, 'The medieval text now enters fully dressed in modern grammar and punctuation.'[42] Modern scholars are increasingly aware of the limitations of printed editions of medieval texts but they also recognize, within those limitations, the vital service that printed editions have performed, and still do. Some critics trust that salvation from the limitations of print will come in the hypertext possibilities of the still emerging digital world,[43] but electronic representations of medieval writings must also mediate, or remediate, their material, if in different ways from those of print.[44]

Editions give access, albeit (re)mediated, to the medieval text. Similarly, translation, though inevitably domesticating to a lesser or greater degree, gives a kind of access that is not otherwise available. How satisfactory that access is consid-

---

[40] Corbett, 'The Seafarer', pp. 158–9.
[41] Foys, *Virtually Anglo-Saxon*, pp. 4–5.
[42] Foys, *Virtually Anglo-Saxon*, p. 17.
[43] See, for example, McGillivray, 'Towards a Post-Critical Edition: Theory, Hypertext, and the Presentation of Middle English Works'; a note of caution is expressed by R. M. Liuzza, 'Scribes of the Mind: Editing Old English, in Theory and in Practice': see esp. pp. 272–7.
[44] The idea of remediation is developed in Bolter and Grusin, *Remediation: Understanding New Media*.

ered to be will depend on the particular translation, taken in its own context; and if the domesticating is overdone, the original poem will get lost.

Some translations of *Beowulf* incorporate distinctly 'foreignizing' elements, producing an English that is, in Ciaran Carson's phrase (quoted above), 'strangely interesting', but without alienating a modern readership. As we shall see, Burton Raffel in his version boldly domesticates *Beowulf*, evidently catering for a young and inexperienced readership in mid-twentieth-century America, but the versions of other translators, to be discussed below, including notably that of Seamus Heaney, challenge their readers with distinctive defamiliarizing features (along with a considerable degree of domestication) and, in engaging with the poetry of *Beowulf*, they each in their different ways cultivate a poetic language that is far from invisible. Such versions do not disregard accessibility but they suggest the otherness of *Beowulf*, an otherness that derives not only from its cultural remoteness but, within that remote culture, from the special traditional register of the poetry of *Beowulf*, which was both 'familiar' and distinctively different from natural speech even in its own period. Even in its Anglo-Saxon context there is a strong element in the poetry of *Beowulf* of 'visibility', and of, if not the foreign, certainly that which is out of the ordinary. In responding to this, translators make use of different kinds of non-standard Modern English and they exploit aspects of the 'strange likeness' (to allude to the title of Chris Jones's recent book[45]) between features of Old English and potential features of Modern English, involving stress patterns, word formation (especially compounding), alliterative play and sentence structure.

Prose and Verse

Kemble, and Translation as an Aid to Study

As well as the verse translations, of course, many prose translations of *Beowulf* have also been produced. Very often, though not always or not only, they are intended to be aids to studying the original text, and such translations mostly lack the element of imaginative engagement with the poetry of the Old English that can be achieved in verse versions. A pattern for prose translations of *Beowulf* was set by the first person to translate the whole poem into Modern English, John Mitchell Kemble, who produced his translation in 1837 as part of the second volume of his (second) edition of *Beowulf*, intending it to be used along with the text of the original poem. Kemble describes his translation as follows:

> The translation is a literal one; I was bound to give, word for word, the original in all its roughness: I might have made it smoother, but I purposely avoided doing so, because had the Saxon poet thought as we think, and expressed his thoughts

---

[45] Jones is in turn alluding to a phrase from Geoffrey Hill: 'Not strangeness, but strange likeness', Geoffrey Hill, *Mercian Hymns*, XXIX.

as we express our thoughts, I might have spared myself the trouble of editing or translating the poem. A few transpositions of words, &c. caused principally by the want of inflections in New English [. . .] are all that I have allowed myself, and where I have inserted words I have generally printed them in italics.⁴⁶

Kemble highlights here the differentness of *Beowulf* and he sets his face against producing an overly fluent version, preferring, he declares, to render the original literally, 'in all its roughness'. The translation accompanied his edition of *Beowulf* and is clearly intended to supplement the text of the original rather than to substitute for it. A sample from the translation (corresponding to *Beowulf*, lines 499–510a) illustrates Kemble's approach:

> Hunferth the son of Eglaf spake, *he* that sat at the feet of the Lord of the Scyldings; he bound up a quarrelsome speech: to him was the journey of Beowulf, the proud sea-farer, a great disgust; because he granted not that any other man should ever have beneath the skies, more reputation with the world than he himself: 'Art thou the Beowulf that didst contend with Breca on the wide sea, in a swimming match, where ye for pride explored the fords, and out of vain glory ventured your lives upon the deep water?'⁴⁷

This may be compared to the original Old English text of the passage (lines 499–510a):

> Unferð maþolode,   Ecglafes bearn,
> þe æt fotum sæt   frean Scyldinga,
> onband beadurune. Wæs him Beowulfes sið,
> modges merefaran, micel æfþunca,
> forþon þe he ne uþe   þæt ænig oðer man
> æfre mærða þon ma middangeardes
> gehedde under heofenum   þonne he sylfa:
> 'Eart þu se Beowulf,   se þe wið Brecan wunne
> on sidne sæ   ymb sund flite,
> ðær git for wlence   wada cunnedon
> ond for dolgilpe   on deop wæter
> aldrum neþdon?'⁴⁸

In his translation of this passage Kemble parallels the word order and asyndetic syntax of *Beowulf* and tolerates cumbersome expression, seeking to convey the literal sense of the Old English words. Later prose translators might not all agree with Kemble about the 'roughness' of *Beowulf* but they tend to follow him in sticking closely to the literal surface meaning of the Old English text, perceiving

---

⁴⁶ Kemble, *A Translation of the Anglo-Saxon Poem of Beowulf*, p. l.
⁴⁷ It is convenient to select these particular lines for illustration, since they are also used by Tinker in *The Translations of Beowulf*; quotation of versions of these lines below from prose translations not covered by Tinker is intended to facilitate comparison for readers who may also wish to consult Tinker.
⁴⁸ Kemble sets out the text in short lines but his edition of these lines is not significantly different from that quoted here (from *Klaeber's Beowulf*). On Kemble's edition, see further pp. 51–2, below.

that readers need the translation to help them to understand the language of the original. Even more literal was the version by Benjamin Thorpe published in 1855 in a parallel-text format, in which the translation, though reading like prose, is (alongside Thorpe's edited text) chopped up into short lines.[49] I quote Thorpe's translation of the beginning of the Unferth altercation (lines 1002–6 in Thorpe's lineation), with his Old English text beside it:

Hunferð maþelode,	Hunferth spake,
Ecgláfes bearn,	Ecglaf's son,
þe æt fótum sæt	who at the feet sat
freán Scyldinga;	of the Scyldings' lord;
onband beadu-rúne.	unbound a hostile speech.

Kemble doesn't mention it in his account of his translation, which concentrates on his principle of faithfulness to the original, but his version is notably archaizing, as is the version by Thorpe.[50] In the quoted passage Kemble uses the old past-tense form *spake*, the second-person-singular present-tense forms *art* and *didst* and the early Modern English syntactical formulations *granted not* and *didst contend*, and he displaces the adverbial phrases *to him* and *beneath the skies* away from their natural position in Modern English sentence structure; in contrast with modern usage he also accompanies *disgust* with the indefinite article and deploys the unidiomatic phrase *for pride*. The archaizing goes against his aim of preserving the 'roughness' of the original, since such archaizing brings associations of highly developed literary convention, but generally the style suggests something of the otherness of *Beowulf*. Kemble keeps literal but also fashions what he considers to be a fitting kind of literary English. Like many of his successors, he assumes that a register that archaizes to some degree is appropriate for the Old English poem, even in a version in Modern English prose. Other translators would take the archaizing further.

Some twentieth-century prose translations

The dust jacket of C. L. Wrenn's 1950 revision of the translation of *Beowulf* by John R. Clark Hall (originally published in 1901) – 'Clark Hall' being one of the most enduringly popular of all translations of the poem – declares that this version 'will serve the double purpose of providing the general reader with a just idea of the matter of the poem, and furnishing the professional student with the material and guidance necessary for the early stages of his study of the original.'[51] In the 'Prefatory Remarks' to the volume, J. R. R. Tolkien writes that 'the presentation of a translation into plain prose of what is in fact a poem, a

---

[49] Thorpe, ed. and trans., *The Anglo-Saxon Poems of Beowulf, The Scôp or Gleeman's Tale, and The Fight at Finnesburg*.
[50] Thorpe's version was also criticized at the time for its Latinate diction: see below, p. 64.
[51] John R. Clark Hall, *Beowulf and the Finnesburg Fragment*, dust jacket.

work of skilled and close-wrought metre (to say no more)' needs defence.'⁵² He goes on to provide such a defence, insisting, '"Clark Hall" revised or unrevised, is not offered as a means of judging the original, or as a substitute for reading the poem itself. The proper use of a prose translation is to provide an aid to study.'⁵³ Tolkien adds, in words that Kemble would have agreed with, 'a good translation is a companion to honest labour.'⁵⁴ Prose translations are utilitarian companions for students, and in this utilitarian context literary correspondence takes second place to fidelity to the sense. In Tolkien's view, 'Perhaps the most important function of any translation used by a student is to provide not a model for imitation, but an exercise for correction.'⁵⁵

Hall would also go on to publish a verse translation of *Beowulf*, in 1914.⁵⁶ His prose translation is literal in its approach but notable too for its incorporation of archaic features. In the original edition of the prose version the account of Beowulf's exchange with Unferth begins as follows (*Beowulf*, lines 499–510a):

> Then Unferth, the son of Ecglaf, who sat at the feet of the lord of the Scyldings, spoke, and gave vent to secret thoughts of strife, – the journey of Beowulf, the brave sea-farer, was a great chagrin to him, for he grudged that any other man under heaven should ever obtain more glory on this middle-earth than he himself.
>
> 'Art thou that Beowulf who strove with Breca, contended with him in the open sea, in a swimming-contest, when ye two for vainglory tried the floods, and ventured your lives in deep water for idle boasting?'

There is no *spake*, *granted not* or obtrusive displacement of adverbials, as in Kemble, but *thou* and *ye* are here, *grudged that* is mannered and *for vainglory* parallels Kemble's *for pride*. Hall's version recalls that of Kemble in other translation choices as well and in aspects of its general register, though the overall effect is smoother and Clark Hall is more uniform in its use of Modern English syntax.

Wrenn's 1950 revised version of Clark Hall makes some corrections in the light of subsequent scholarship and introduces minor rewordings throughout. Wrenn generally proceeds with a light touch and his revision retains a somewhat archaic feel, though the archaism is toned down, with the most egregious oddities in diction purposefully removed. As Tolkien notes, for example, *ten timorous trothbreakers together* (line 2846) is wisely emended to *ten cowardly traitors together*.⁵⁷ Tolkien could also have drawn attention to such instances as *to*

---

52 Tolkien, 'Prefatory Remarks on Prose Translation of "Beowulf"', p. ix.
53 Tolkien, 'Prefatory Remarks', p. x.
54 Tolkien, 'Prefatory Remarks', p. xi.
55 Tolkien, 'Prefatory Remarks', p. xvi. As mentioned below (p. 50), the very first translation of *Beowulf*, by Thorkelín (1815) (into Latin), was immediately corrected in the collations of his edition with the original manuscript made by Conybeare and Madden (in 1817 and 1824, respectively).
56 On this, see below, pp. 65–6.
57 Tolkien, 'Prefatory Remarks', p. xv.

find out in what sort the Ring-Danes had quartered in it after their beer-carouse (lines 116–17), changed to *to find how the Ring-Danes had disposed themselves in it after their ale-drinking*; *carking care* (line 190), changed to *the trouble of this time*; and *must needs flee thence under the fen-fastnesses* (line 820), changed to *had to flee thence among the fen-fastnesses* (though Wrenn retains *fen-fastnesses*). Typical rewordings are *dwelt* for *sojourned* (line 9), *courts* for *castle* (line 13) and *men* for *folk* (line 24).

In the quoted passage Wrenn does away with the dash after *secret thoughts of strife*, starting a new sentence instead, and he corrects Hall's punctuation when he changes the comma after *was a great chagrin to him* to a semi-colon, but he makes no further alterations. In the immediately succeeding ten lines there are a number of changed expressions but these are mostly instances of scholarly reinterpretation or of tightened-up translation: *swam* (line 512) is changed to *journeyed*, which is closer to the Old English *reon*, literally 'rowed'; *meted out the sea-paths* (line 514) becomes *passed over the paths of the sea*, picking up on the sense of 'traverse' for the verb *mæton*, as given in Klaeber's glossary, but also rendering the Old English more straightforwardly – while at the same time providing a more stately rhythm; *battled with your hands* (line 514) becomes *made quick movements with your hands*, a correction of Hall's interpretation of *brugdon*; *glided over the ocean* (line 515) becomes *sped over the ocean*, clarifying the sense of *glidon*. An apparent stylistic change is the alteration of *he had the greater strength* (line 518) to *he had greater strength*, but this too can be seen as a correction: there is no instrumental demonstrative in the original. It is notable that Wrenn keeps unchanged Hall's mannered *Ye two toiled in the water's realm seven nights* (lines 516–17), including adoption of the medieval usage of 'night' to refer to day (as reflected elsewhere in standard Modern English only in the relic *fortnight*).

For Tolkien the Modern English of prose *Beowulf* translations should be 'harmonious' and should avoid 'colloquialism and false modernity'.[58] This conviction provides the rationale for an elevated register incorporating archaizing features, such as he finds in Wrenn's 'Clark Hall': 'If you wish to translate, not rewrite *Beowulf*, declares Tolkien, 'your language must be literary and traditional: not because it is now a long while since the poem was made, or because it speaks of things that have since become ancient; but because the diction of *Beowulf* was poetical, archaic, artificial (if you will), in the day that the poem was made.'[59] Here Tolkien does argue for literary correspondence between source and translation: the translation is doing more than conveying (to revert to an earlier quotation from Tolkien) 'the matter of the poem, and furnishing the professional student with the material and guidance necessary for the early stages of his study of the original'; it is doing so in an appropriate style that suggests qualities of the Old English.

---

58 'Prefatory Remarks', pp. xv–xvi.
59 'Prefatory Remarks', p. xvii.

Tolkien makes his remarks in introducing Wrenn's 'Clark Hall' but it is also interesting to consider them with reference to his own prose translation of an extract from *Beowulf*, the part referred to as the 'Finnsburh Episode'. The translation is printed in Alan Bliss's posthumous edition of lectures on *Beowulf* by the great man at Oxford in the 1920s and 1930s.[60] In fact Tolkien also produced a prose translation of the whole of *Beowulf*, as well as a verse translation of about a fifth of the poem, both of which remain unpublished, however, and currently unavailable for study.

Tolkien's translation of the 'Finnsburh Episode' extract begins (corresponding to *Beowulf*, lines 1063–74),

> There was song and music together before Healfdene's war-captain; harp was played, ever and anon, a tale was duly told. Then Hrothgar's bard, in performance of his office, recounted a thing for the entertainment of those in hall upon the benches, [told how life's ending came to] the sons of Finn.
>
> When the sudden peril came upon them, the doughty Healfdene, Hnæf of the Scylding house, was fated to fall in the *Freswæl*. Indeed no cause had Hildeburh to praise the Jutish loyalty: without fault of hers she was in that clash of shields bereft of those she loved, child and brother; they fell by doom, wounded with spears; an unhappy woman was she.

Tolkien provides a mostly literal translation, though he has the (from today's perspective, startling) confidence to supply what he argues to be a missing line. The translation is not meant to stand on its own but is intended to be used along with the Old English text and the accompanying copious interpretative notes, which were originally written as lecture notes (and which offer justification for a number of controversial textual decisions and interpretations). The language is 'literary and traditional' with some archaizing features in its diction (*doughty*, *doom* and, a few lines later, *aforetime*; *recounted a thing* also has an archaic feel, as suggested by the most similar usage cited in the *OED*, 'telle us som moral thyng', in Chaucer's *Pardoner's Prologue*), in its word order (*no cause had Hildeburh* and *she was in that clash of shields bereft*) and in its phrasing (the omission of articles in *harp was played* and *in hall*), but Tolkien's writing is not quaint or overly mannered. It is notable that in his translation of the companion piece to the 'Finnsburh Episode', the 'Finnsburh 'Fragment' (also printed in *Finn and Hengest*), Tolkien resists any temptation to translate the second-person-singular pronoun as *thou/thee* (second-person-singular forms happen not to occur in the 'Episode').

As stated above, Tolkien's translation is mostly literal. Nonetheless, on stylistic grounds he allows himself some latitude in it, doubtless comforted by the fact that his readers can also access the original text: indeed in Bliss's edition the Old English and the translation are printed in parallel-text format. The opening lines of the Old English passage, as edited by Tolkien, are as follows:

---

[60] Tolkien, *Finn and Hengest: The Fragment and the Episode*.

Þær wæs sang ond sweg   samod ætgædere
fore Healfdenes   hildewisan,
gomenwudu greted,   gid oft wrecen.
Ðonne healgamen   Hroþgares scop
æfter medobence   mænan scolde [. . .]

A more verbally accurate translation of these lines would be 'There there was song and music along with each other together before Healfdene's battle-leader, the wood of joy was touched, the tale often told. Then Hrothgar's bard had to recount entertainment in the hall along the mead-benches . . .' This is more verbally accurate than Tolkien but it is hardly literary prose. Tolkien is balancing the desirability of writing literary prose against the principle of literalness and it is interesting that where a possible conflict arises he comes down on the side of literary prose. Thus in the first line he sacrifices the locative force of Þær and removes the tautology of *samod ætgædere*. In the third line he clarifies the meaning of the compound *gomenwudu*, spells out the idea of 'playing' implicit in *greted* and moves the equivalent of *oft* out of its original phrase into a kind of *apo koinou* position (i. e., it might be taken as referring to the preceding or succeeding phrase, or to both),[61] rhetorically elaborating the adverb in the process (*oft* becomes *ever and anon*); and at the same time as moving *oft* he introduces a new explanatory adverb (*duly*) in its place: Tolkien was clearly striving here to avoid a bathetic rendering of the potentially lame-looking phrase *gid oft wrecen*, 'the tale (was) often told', and was willing to modify the sense to do so. In translating the fourth and fifth lines he inserts the explanatory phrase *in performance of his office*, which has no direct equivalent in the original, and assimilates the abstract noun *healgamen* to modern usage by supplying a concrete referent (*a thing*) and a human audience (*of those*): *a thing for the entertainment of those in hall upon the benches*; here he also shifts the qualifier 'hall' to a new place in the sentence, where it refers to the listeners (*those in hall*) rather than the entertainment (*healgamen*). In these lines too he drops the element of duty conveyed by *scolde* ('had to'); this verb is presumably the source of the adverb *duly* introduced a few lines earlier but if so it indicates the freedom with which Tolkien approaches the passage, despite his insistence on the requirement of literalness in prose translation. Something rather more complex than literal translation is going on in his rendering of this passage. Tolkien may see prose translation as merely 'a companion to honest labour' but he wants to write well in an appropriate literary style and his translation is carefully crafted.

This balancing of the principle of literalism against the desirability of writing literary prose is apparent in utilitarian translations from Kemble to Hall to Wrenn and Tolkien and on down to later versions aimed at aiding students studying the text of *Beowulf*. Among such versions are the much-used translations of G. N. Garmonsway, in *Beowulf and its Analogues*, completed by Jacqueline Simpson (1968), and S. A. J. Bradley, in his collection *Anglo-Saxon Poetry* (1982).

---

[61] On *apo koinou* constructions, see Mitchell, 'Apo koinou in Old English Poetry?'.

These translators work hard in their prose versions to help students translating *Beowulf*, and in my own experience many students value the translations particularly for this purpose. Both writers also seek to make *Beowulf* readable, however. Garmonsway's style comes out in his version of the introduction to the debate between Beowulf and Unferth (*Beowulf*, lines 499–505):

> Unferth, son of Ecglaf, who sat at the feet of the lord of the Scyldings, spoke thus, unloosing secret words to stir up strife. The venture of Beowulf, the gallant seafarer, caused him great displeasure, for he would not willingly grant that any other man on earth had ever performed more glorious deeds beneath the heavens than he himself.[62]

Garmonsway's language is accessible but dignified, a heightened form of Modern English, and his rhythm is carefully controlled, the second sentence in particular having a steady cumulative sweep. In *Beowulf and its Analogues* the translation of *Beowulf* is accompanied by translations of a range of supplementary material, allowing analogues to be accessed in Modern English rather than in their original languages.

Bradley seeks, as he declares in his preface to *Anglo-Saxon Poetry*, to interest readers who are encountering the poetry only through his translation. In the preface he expresses the hope that his translation of Old English poems will lead readers to go to the originals: 'In helping its readers to an appreciation and enjoyment of Anglo-Saxon poetry in its Old English form it is hoped that this book will prove to be of some transitional aid.'[63] Bradley's translation aims to serve a double purpose, as is highlighted in the cover-blurb of the first edition: 'The translations attempt a style acceptable to the modern ear yet close enough to aid parallel study of the Old English text.'

Bradley's account of the beginning of the altercation between Beowulf and Breca (lines 499–505) illustrates his approach – a utilitarian one but in a register that is acceptable as fluent literary Modern English:

> Unferth, Ecglaf's son, who sat at the feet of the lord of the Scyldings, spoke out and unloosed provocative imputations. To him the enterprise of Beowulf, the courageous seafarer, was a great insult because he did not allow that any other man on earth might ever gain more glories beneath the heavens than he himself.

Like Garmonsway's, which it recalls in some of its translation choices, this translation is close to the original in sense and even, where possible, in word order. It lacks something of the dignity of Garmonsway's diction but it reads well, being written in natural sounding, though distinctly Latinate, language. Notable words and phrases are *unloosed* (also found in Garmonsway), an example of somewhat elevated diction; *provocative imputations*, strikingly Latinate; *enterprise* (also in Garmonsway), prosaic-sounding compared to *sið*; *a great insult* is much more current in its expression than *a great disgust* or *a great chagrin* (as seen in other

---

[62] Garmonsway and Simpson, trans., *Beowulf and its Analogues*, pp. 15–16.
[63] Bradley, trans., *Anglo-Saxon Poetry*, p. viii.

translations) but is less resonant perhaps than Garmonsway's *a great displeasure*. Both these versions achieve readability, though this is at the expense of losing the immediacy and the rhythmical and syntactical abruptness of the Old English and a sense of the formulaicity of its verse. The reader gets an appreciation of the surface meaning and content of the Old English poem but gets little sense of the feel of its poetry.

Particularly notable among twentieth-century prose translations of *Beowulf* is that of David Wright. Wright's 1957 translation, though eventually superseded by Michael Alexander's verse one, was a popular Penguin Classics title, much reprinted. Wright expresses his literary ambitions when he writes that he has set out to produce 'a readable version in contemporary English prose and to bring out those qualities of the original which in other translations, it seems to me, have been either overlooked or overlaid'.[64]

Wright, following the example of E. V. Rieu translating Homer for Penguin Classics,[65] argues that prose is more appropriate than poetry for translating *Beowulf*. Tolkien had insisted that prose translation of poetry needed a defence and found that defence in its limited utilitarian function. Likewise, Wright's 'successor' on the Penguin list, Michael Alexander, took the opposite view from Wright, asking readers who might find his own translation too free 'to consider whether a literal prose version of a verse epic is, properly, a translation'.[66] In his second edition in 2001, Alexander is more circumspect: here he asks readers 'to consider whether literal prose does not too freely discard the potential advantages of verse'.[67] On reflection, Alexander allows that prose translations can be useful, 'and more than useful – the English of Garmonsway's version [of *Beowulf*] has dignity and rhythmical shape', but he insists on the unique potential of poetry translated as poetry:

> Most prose translations, however, are drab, and make it a virtue to fall so short that the translation cannot be confused with the real thing. A poetic translation is an attempt to offer an equivalent poem to those who cannot read the original.[68]

Wright produced his translation not for students studying the text of *Beowulf* but, in line with the educative principles of Penguin Classics, for the general reader: he was bringing *Beowulf* to a readership that couldn't access the poem in

---

64 Wright, *Beowulf: A Prose Translation with an Introduction*, p. 21.
65 See further below, pp. 158–9.
66 Alexander, *Beowulf* (1972 ed.), p. 49.
67 Alexander, *Beowulf* (2001 ed.), pp. lv–lvi.
68 *Beowulf* (2001 ed.), p. lvi. In the introduction to his translated collection, *The First Poems in English* (2008), Alexander recalls that in the introduction to its predecessor, *The Earliest English Poems*, he had boldly declared that he had never understood the point of translating poetry into prose; he adds sardonically, 'this was before I had read some of the verse translations of Old English poetry' (p. xxx). Interestingly, he himself included a couple of passages translated into prose in the third edition of his *The Earliest English Poems* (as mentioned further below, p. 140, n. 27).

the original but would be interested in knowing this literary classic in translation. His choice of prose as the medium for his translation was a considered one. He argues that, like the *Iliad* and the *Odyssey* but unlike the *Aeneid* and *Paradise Lost*, *Beowulf* is a 'primary epic', in which the most important thing is the story:

> In the *Aeneid* and *Paradise Lost* the story is a peg on which the poet hangs his poem, while in Homer and *Beowulf* the poem is the story, and vice versa. Therefore to render the *Iliad*, the *Odyssey*, or *Beowulf* into prose is not only feasible but in some ways more desirable than to translate them into verse. Verse which is not poetry obscures the story, and therefore the poem, without providing an adequate substitute for the style of the poem.[69]

The idea that the story is the essence of *Beowulf* was soon seen by critics to be no longer tenable, which is one reason why Wright's translation was superseded. His major justification for translating into prose disappears once his view of *Beowulf* as 'story' is rejected. His argument about 'verse which is not poetry' may be valid but the whole point about the most engaging verse versions of *Beowulf* is that they are verse which is poetry.

In his translation Wright opts for what he calls a 'middle style' between the 'queer jargon' of archaism, which he saw as a feature of previous translations, and the 'equally wrong' approach of colloquialism. He writes, 'The argument against the middle style is that in comparison with the original it seems colourless. With this I do not entirely disagree: in any case, better no colours than faked ones.'[70] In adopting contemporary English prose his aim is not to try to represent the poetry of *Beowulf* but to maintain the interest of his readers.[71] Thus he carefully 'domesticates' the translation to suit the experience of his modern audience. As a brief example of the domesticating approach adopted by Wright, here is his version of lines 499–505:

> Unferth, son of Ecglaf, who occupied a place of honour near the feet of the Danish king, spoke up. The enterprise of Beowulf greatly annoyed him, because he could not bear the thought that any living man might win more distinction than himself. So he broached a thorny topic.

The smooth hypotactic syntax, prosaic diction (*occupied, enterprise, annoyed*) and use of idiomatic modern phrasing (*spoke up, broached a thorny topic*) are among the domesticating features of the passage. The approach of Wright is radically unlike that of Tolkien's 'companion to honest labour'. He provides a substitute version of the poem rather than an aid to translation and in doing so he is happy to write in a neutral style that assimilates *Beowulf* to modern literary experience and completely disregards its own poetry and poetics. Only the story remains.

E. Talbot Donaldson takes a more 'foreignizing' line in his translation (1966), another of the most widely read renderings of the poem, particularly after being

---

[69] Wright, *Beowulf*, pp. 21–2.
[70] Wright, *Beowulf*, p. 24.
[71] Wright, *Beowulf*, p. 25.

adopted in *The Norton Anthology of English Literature*. Donaldson achieves admirable accuracy but also hopes 'that the reader unfamiliar with Old English [such as the target reader of the *Norton*] may derive from this translation some real sense of the poem's extraordinary qualities',[72] an ambitious aim for a prose version. Since the translation *is* in prose the aim can be realized only to a limited extent but Donaldson fashions a syntax and diction that seek to preserve from the original its 'extraordinary richness of rhetorical elaboration alternating with – often combined with – the barest simplicity of statement'.[73] Donaldson's writing comes across as somewhat ponderous but achieves a dignified tone. With regard to his somewhat elevated register he has been praised for not being afraid to use 'unreal' English.[74] His rendering of lines 499–505 is as follows:

> Unferth spoke, son of Ecglaf, who sat at the feet of the king of the Scyldings, unbound words of contention – to him was Beowulf's undertaking, the brave seafarer, a great vexation, for he would not allow that any other man of middle-earth should ever achieve more glory under the heavens than himself.

Syntactical flexibility is in evidence here, with asyndetic coordination, more use of apposition than is normal in Modern English prose and displacement of one of the appositional phrases, *the brave seafarer*, away from its correlative to a position in which (strictly) it is stranded in terms of grammatical concord. The passage is formal in expression and carefully worded, with *unbound words of contention* and *a great vexation* standing out as instances of epic-sounding diction, and *middle-earth* (less familiar in popular consciousness in 1966 perhaps than it is today) evoking Anglo-Saxon ways of thinking; and there is a notable rhythmic resonance, particularly in the extended causal clause that brings the sentence to a conclusion. Within the limitations of prose, Donaldson's is a worthy and accurate version which, balancing accessibility and a sense of otherness, manages to give some suggestion of the quality of the original poem. It should be said that it does not suggest the excitement of the original poem, however, and it was viewed by teachers as dull (and was eventually displaced by Seamus Heaney's translation in the *Norton Anthology*). Robert Boenig, Anglo-Saxonist and discontented user of Donaldson in the *Norton*, complains that the translation 'has convinced generations of sophomores that *Beowulf* is a dull poem'.[75]

With regard to the 'queer jargon' of earlier prose translations, Wright particularly singles out the version by J. R. Clark Hall, which had been endorsed by Wrenn and Tolkien as a useful companion to the study of *Beowulf*.[76] Hall is no more extravagant than some other translators in his archaizing, however, such as Thomas Arnold (1876) and John Earle (1892), and some degree of archaizing is

---

[72] Donaldson, *Beowulf*, pp. xiv–xv.
[73] Donaldson, *Beowulf*, p. xii.
[74] Crane, '"To Thwack or Be Thwacked": An Evaluation of Available Translations and Editions of *Beowulf*', p. 327.
[75] Boenig, 'The Importance of Morris's *Beowulf*', p. 12.
[76] Wright, *Beowulf*, p. 23.

the norm.[77] And it is worth pointing out in concluding this section that the use of 'queer jargon' in nineteenth-century and early-twentieth-century prose translations of *Beowulf*, though very evident, in most versions pales in comparison to what we find in verse (to be discussed more fully in a later chapter).

It is also interesting that even those who claim to be eschewing archaism seem drawn to it anyway. Chauncey B. Tinker, who sees his 1902 prose translation as 'an attempt to make as simple and readable a version of the poem as is consistent with the character of the original', and who declares, 'Archaic forms, which have been much in favor with translators of Old English, have been excluded',[78] still ends up with a somewhat archaizing feel to his translation, as in his version of lines 499–505:

> Unferth, the son of Ecglaf, who sat at the feet of the lord of the Scyldings, spoke, and stirred up a quarrel; the coming of Beowulf, the brave seafarer, vexed him sore, for he would not that any other man under heaven should ever win more glories in this world than he himself.

This is basically Modern English and very unlike *Beowulf* in syntax and diction, but 'vexed him sore' and 'he would not that any other man' sound like archaisms to me. In Tinker, as in many other prose translations, we get a wash of comforting archaizing but no sense of what Chris Jones refers to as the 'shock of the old'.[79] An opposing approach is that of Wright, who presents *Beowulf* in straightforward modern literary prose: 'better no colours than faked ones'. Despite serving generations of appreciative readers in other ways, neither approach captures much of the literary quality of *Beowulf* itself. Which brings us to poetry.

This chapter has touched on some larger issues in translation, with particular reference to *Beowulf*, including the reasons why *Beowulf* has been so popular with translators, the debate about 'domesticating' and 'foreignizing' translations, and the question of verse versus prose. One of the most eloquent responses to this last question was given by John Keats, of course, after reading Chapman's Homer. The power of verse is compellingly conveyed by Keats when he describes

---

[77] Arnold (Thomas Arnold 'the Younger') follows the word-for-word approach of Kemble: 'Unferth spake, the son of Ecglaf, who sat at the feet of the master of the Scyldings; he unbound the secret counsel of his malice. The expedition of Beowulf, the valiant mariner, was to him a great cause of offence; for that he allowed not that any other man on the earth should ever appropriate more deeds of fame under heaven than he himself' (Arnold, trans., *Beowulf, a Heroic Poem of the Eighth Century*); Earle waxes more literary, producing modern prose but with frequent archaism: 'Unferth made a speech; he who sate at the feet of the Scyldings' lord, broached a quarrelsome theme – the adventure of Beowulf the high-souled voyager was great despite to him, because he grudged that any other man should ever in the world achieve more exploits under heaven than he himself' (Earle, trans., *The Deeds of Beowulf, Done into Modern Prose*).
[78] Tinker, Beowulf, *Translated out of the Old English*, p. 5.
[79] See Chris Jones, *Strange Likeness*, p. 6.

the new 'wide expanse' that Chapman's translation opened out for him. In 'On First Looking into Chapman's Homer' he writes,

> Then felt I like some watcher of the skies
>   When a new planet swims into his ken;
> Or like stout Cortez, when with eagle eyes
>   He stared at the Pacific – and all his men
> Look'd at each other with a wild surmise –
>   Silent upon a peak in Darien.

Such excitement is possible, if rarely achieved, in verse translations of poetry, but is quite beyond the capacity of prose renderings. The question remains, however, to what extent Keats was reading Homer when he read Chapman's Homer.[80]

The next chapter will turn to the Old English poem itself, pointing to key aspects of its poetry and poetics that verse translators have to engage with. *Beowulf* will be characterized as a poem both deeply traditional and deeply original, composed in a distinctively poetic language and highly reflective in its treatment of its story. The third chapter will explore the ways *Beowulf* has been received and perceived in the modern era and in this context will consider in more detail approaches to translating it into verse in the first hundred years in which verse translations were produced, down to 1950. Then, building on that chapter and the previous two, in subsequent chapters I will examine the varying ways in which modern verse translators (post-1950) respond to and re-present *Beowulf* in modern poetic form.

---

[80] Matthew Arnold pronounced, 'Chapman, like Pope, merits in himself all respect, though he too, like Pope, fails to render Homer' (*On Translating Homer*, pp. 26–7).

✦2✦

Approaching the Poetry of Beowulf

The present chapter takes us back to *Beowulf* itself, presenting a discussion of its poetry and poetics in the historical context of the larger tradition to which the poem belongs. Having briefly explored key poetic features of *Beowulf* in general terms, it will go on to focus on two specific illustrative passages from the poem (lines 1–11 and 867b–74). In subsequent chapters we will be considering the responses of modern verse translators to the features covered in this chapter and we will also be looking at versions of the illustrative passages in some translations.

Aspects of the Poetry and Poetics of *Beowulf*

Beowulf is viewed in the modern criticism of Old English poetry, as it has developed in the last seventy years or so, as a work of great artistry, originality and depth. It is 'solid and dazzling', in Seamus Heaney's memorable phrase,[1] as critics continue to demonstrate through close study.[2] It is also, however, a work of a highly traditional kind, participating at all levels in what has insightfully been referred to as 'the aesthetics of the familiar'.[3] It stems from the oral culture of the Anglo-Saxons and their continental ancestors: it is traditional in its metrical and syntactic structures, its 'word-hoard' of poetic vocabulary and its formulaic patterns of phrasing; and it is traditional too in the themes that it deals with and in the value-system that motivates its action. *Beowulf* is the work of a Christian

---

[1] Heaney, *Beowulf*, 'Introduction', p. xii (references to Heaney's 'Introduction' follow the pagination of the Faber edition, 'Introduction', pp. ix–xxx).

[2] Among a wealth of critical writings on the poetry of *Beowulf*, key and influential items that stand out include Bonjour, *The Digressions in Beowulf*; Brodeur, *The Art of Beowulf*; Irving, *A Reading of Beowulf*; Niles, *Beowulf: The Poem and its Tradition*; Fred C. Robinson, *Beowulf and the Appositive Style*; Irving, *Rereading Beowulf*; Orchard, *A Critical Companion to Beowulf*; Tyler, *Old English Poetics: The Aesthetics of the Familiar in Anglo-Saxon England*; see also Fulk, ed., *Interpretations of Beowulf*.

[3] The phrase comes from the title of Elizabeth Tyler's monograph, referred to in the previous note.

poet and its written transmission would have been in a Christian context, but it is a 'heroic' poem, set in the pre-Christian warrior society of the Germanic heroic age, that imagined past in which, as in the Homeric age, heroes achieved fame in carrying out great deeds against formidable opponents, in accordance with the ideals of glory, honour and personal loyalty.

Seamus Heaney, author of the most popular translation of *Beowulf* currently in use, is struck by the remoteness of this poem from modern life,[4] and he strives to relate it to the world of his own experience. In a parallel fashion, scholars struggle to understand what *Beowulf*, a poem itself about a remote past, might have meant to an Anglo-Saxon audience, and indeed what its Anglo-Saxon audience – or audiences – might have been.[5] The poem is preserved uniquely in a manuscript from the early eleventh century but is likely to have had a considerable transmission history before that, having been composed perhaps two or three centuries earlier but also being subject to textual change in the course of that transmission; we have no external reference to the poem in the Old English period.[6]

Whatever the date of its composition, *Beowulf* comes from long after the period of its setting. Looking back, as it does, it is remarkable in the sustained reflectiveness of its treatment of its heroic themes; it is of the tradition that tells about the heroic age but apart from that tradition in outlook and understanding.[7] This apartness gives it its tone; it is as much an elegiac meditation as a narrative poem. The subject matter of *Beowulf* has been seen to concern contrasting experience,[8] but in its stance too *Beowulf* is a poem of apparent oppositions or

---

[4] See Heaney, *Beowulf*, p. xii.
[5] Among important recent discussions relevant to these issues are Howe, *Migration and Mythmaking in Anglo-Saxon England*; Clemoes, *Interactions of Thought and Language in Old English Poetry*; Niles, 'Reconceiving *Beowulf*: Poetry as Social Praxis' and *Old English Heroic Poems and the Social Life of Texts*, pp. 13–71 ('Locating *Beowulf* in Literary History').
[6] *Beowulf* is preserved in London, British Library, Manuscript Cotton Vitellius A. xv: see Kiernan, *Electronic Beowulf*, containing digital facsimiles, transcription, edition, etc. On the dating of *Beowulf*, see Chase, ed., *The Dating of Beowulf*; Bjork and Obermeier, 'Date, Provenance, Author, Audiences'; Frank, 'A Scandal in Toronto: *The Dating of Beowulf* a Quarter Century On'.

On the issue of textual change in the course of transmission, see Lapidge, 'The Archetype of *Beowulf*'; drawing upon Katherine O'Brien O'Keeffe's seminal study *Visible Song: Transitional Literacy in Old English Verse*, Lapidge notes, 'Anglo-Saxon scribes, in the process of copying Old English verse, very frequently interfered with what they were copying by substituting metrically (and often lexically) acceptable words and phrases into the copy-text which lay before them' (pp. 36–7). Similarly, Tyler emphasizes the degree to which intervening scribes or reciters are 'participating in the ongoing composition of the poem' (*Old English Poetics*, p. 6); see also Pasternack, *The Textuality of Old English Poetry*, esp. pp. 1–32.
[7] On the Old English heroic tradition, see my chapter, 'Germanic Legend and Old English Heroic Poetry'.
[8] See especially Tolkien, '*Beowulf*: The Monsters and the Critics'; also Bonjour, *The Digressions in Beowulf*; Brodeur, *The Art of Beowulf*; Shippey, 'Structure and Unity'; Orchard, *A Critical Companion*, 'Style and Structure', pp. 57–97.

contradictions – between the outlook of the poem itself and the heroic values of the tradition in which it participates, and between what we might refer to, if a little anachronistically, as 'tradition' and 'the individual talent': the poem uses a traditional verse form with exceptional artistry, showing verve, inventiveness and intelligence, and it deploys the traditional form to address profound issues in human experience, 'about human nature and its ancestry', as Michael Alexander eloquently expresses it.[9]

Beowulf is composed, of course, in the formal metre handed down by tradition that is ubiquitous in Old English poetry, in which each line is made up of two half-lines, and each half-line has two stressed and a variable number of unstressed syllables, according to a system of rules that allows for a range of different configurations of stressed and unstressed syllables in the half-line (usually classified as five 'types', as first identified by Eduard Sievers).[10] The other essential feature of Old English metre is that the two half-lines are bound together by alliteration. This metrical scheme is supported by the 'word-hoard' of poetic diction, including a wealth of synonyms and near-synonyms that allow the same idea to be fitted into a range of alliterative contexts. As well as *mann* and *wer*, for example, Beowulf shares with Old English poetry in general the following 'poetic' words for 'man': *beorn*, *eorl* (used in a more restrictive sense in prose), *guma* (cf. also, in Beowulf, *dryhtguma*, 'retainer, warrior', *seldguma*, 'hall-retainer'), *hæleð*, *rinc* (cf. also the compounds *beadorinc*, 'battle-warrior', *guðrinc*, 'battle-warrior', etc.) and *secg*; the ordinary word *wiga*, 'warrior', is also used, both as a simplex and as the second element of a compound word (*æscwiga*, '[ash-]spear-warrior', *byrnwiga*, 'mailed warrior', etc.).

This metrical structure underlies the strongly aural quality of Old English poetry, giving it power and solidity. Lines have a strong caesura and discrete phrases stand out strongly in relation to each other, at the same time as being linked together through alliteration: 'the iron / flash of consonants / cleaving the line' (as referred to by Heaney in his poem 'Bone Dreams'[11]). The structure encourages patterns of phrasal parallelism and phrasal contrast, including abrupt opposition and the use of parenthetic interjections – highlighted in modern editions of Old English poems by the frequent appearance of dashes (or brackets) – and narrative has a markedly exclamatory quality. In the hands of a gifted poet, the metrical structure can be used with subtlety and deftness, with half-lines of different patterns being brought together in varying combinations:

---

9 *Beowulf: A Verse Translation*, revised ed., p. xii.
10 Sievers, 'Zur Rhythmik des germanischen Alliterationsverses' (1885), introducing the concept of the Sievers 'five types' of half-line metrical structure. The five types identified by Sievers are A (/ x / x), B (x / x /), C (x / / x), D (/ / \ x), E (/ \ x /) (where / indicates a stressed syllable, \ a lightly stressed syllable, and x one or more than one unstressed syllable), with minor variations allowable particularly within types D and E; later theorists refined Sievers's scheme, developing the idea of 'light' verses (with only one stressed element) and 'heavy' verses (with three stressed elements).
11 Heaney, 'Bone Dreams', in his collection *North*, pp. 27–30, at p. 28.

one student of Old English metre refers to the *Beowulf* poet's 'careful avoidance of any regularity of rhythm'.[12] And the formal structure can be embellished by other – non-structural – sound effects, such as rhyme, paronomasia, cross-alliteration (with two sets of alliteration in the same line), and alliterative play extending over more than one line.

Oral and aural

A suggestive passage in *Beowulf* shows the oral poet of Germanic tradition at work, while itself illustrating some of the poetic features it refers to:

> Hwilum cyninges þegn,
> guma gilphlæden, gidda gemyndig,
> se ðe eal fela ealdgesegena
> worn gemunde, word oþer fand
> soðe gebunden; secg eft ongan
> sið Beowulfes snyttrum styrian
> ond on sped wrecan spel gerade,
> wordum wrixlan. (lines 867b–74a)

[At times a thegn of the king, a man laden with eloquence, mindful of songs, who remembered a multitude of stories from the whole range of ancient tradition, found new [other] words, properly bound together. The man began again artfully to treat of Beowulf's exploit and skilfully to relate an apt tale, to vary his words.]

I will return to technical features of this passage a little later. For the moment, it is offered as an image of the poetic tradition in which *Beowulf* participates. In accordance with the rules of metre the words are 'properly bound together' (*soðe gebunden*), and they are 'artfully' (*snyttrum*) arranged, with attention to variation in expression (*wordum wrixlan*). It is notable that the passage appears to give a considerable amount of detail about poetic composition but is actually quite unspecific, using language that is qualitative rather than precise in the character of its description. In this respect it is typical of the generalizing tendencies of *Beowulf* and Old English poetry as a whole, absorbing the individual into the framework of tradition.

Beowulf portrays an oral culture, a culture in which knowledge and story live in memory and utterance rather than in writing, as in the passage just quoted. It also displays features in its *form* that have been identified as distinctive of oral literature.[13]

The *Beowulf* poet adopts the stance of the oral *scop*, 'minstrel', in his narrative voice, speaking in the first-person plural from the perspective of a shared tradition – 'Hwæt, we Gar-Dena [. . .] / [. . .] þrym gefrunon' (lines 1–2; 'Listen, we

---

[12] Lehmann, 'Broken Cadences in *Beowulf*', p. 1.
[13] See my article, 'Audience(s), Reception, Literacy', drawing upon the classic study of Ong, *Orality and Literacy: The Technologizing of the Word*; see also Orchard, 'Oral Tradition'.

have heard of the glory . . . of the Spear-Danes . . .') – or, more usually, in a non-individualized first-person singular, as a speaker with special knowledge of that tradition – 'Ne hyrde ic cymlicor ceol gegyrwan' – (line 38; 'I have not heard of a ship more fittingly prepared'). The poem's narrative voice is exclamatory and communal, and the narration and speeches are rich in gnomic and proverbial-sounding lore, its sententious utterances assuming assent from the community for whom and to whom the narrator speaks: 'Swa sceal geong guma gode gewyrcean' (line 20; 'So must a young man bring it about by generosity . . .').

The *Beowulf* poet adopts the stance of the *scop* but in fact this narrator and this audience are a fiction. As *Beowulf* – the text – is read, or read out, the narrator is absent and the homogeneous audience that the poem constructs becomes part of the poem rather than being part of the real world of its reception. *Beowulf* gives the impression of being the oral utterance of a *scop*, using the traditional medium of heroic poetry to pass on things he has heard about, but its relationship to the tradition is more complex: *Beowulf* is a literate work, which offers a meditation on its heroic world rather than itself coming directly from such a world.[14]

The language of poetry

I have suggested that the relationship between the *Beowulf* poet and the tradition to which his poem belongs is a complex one. The poetry of *Beowulf* is traditional but it is also highly distinctive, this distinctiveness being an important aspect of the interplay between individuality and tradition. Alliteration, for example, is integral to the structure of the metrics of *Beowulf* but is also insistently used by this poet with striking artfulness, as are other aspects of the play of sound in the poem.[15] And the interplay between individuality and tradition is equally evident in *Beowulf* at the level of vocabulary, which is based on the traditional 'word-hoard' of poetic words but can be brilliantly creative in the use of that word-hoard. In particular, *Beowulf* is exceptionally rich in poetic compound words, a far higher proportion of which are unattested elsewhere than is the case with any other surviving Old English poem. The potent exploitation of poetic simplex words is also in evidence.[16]

Compound words contribute to one of the characteristic features of Old English poetic syntax, the elaborate use of variation and repetition. This is a syntax which in weaving patterns of apposition, parallelism, recapitulation and juxtaposition exploits grammatical characteristics of the Old English language. In Old English (unlike the Present-Day English of modern translators), word endings rather than, or as well as, word order indicate the relationship between words in a sentence

---

14   On the 'absent author', see Bäuml, 'Varieties and Consequences of Medieval Literacy and Illiteracy'.
15   See especially Orchard, *A Critical Companion*: 'Style and Structure', pp. 57–97, 'Words and Deeds', pp. 169–202.
16   See Frank, 'Sharing Words with *Beowulf*.

and so, especially in poetry, there is greater flexibility in constructing interweaving patterns of grammatically related phrases. Indeed, just as there is a special poetic vocabulary in Old English verse – 'almost [...] a language within a language', as Michael Alexander has referred to it[17] – so too a distinctive poetic syntax has been identified. Having studied the 'rules' of word order in the poetry, one recent commentator on Old English poetic syntax goes as far as to declare, 'For the Anglo-Saxons, the language of poetry may have been something analogous to a foreign language or a second native language, which they had to learn separately from their "first" language.'[18] The syntax of poetry shows distinctive differences from that of prose and, we may assume, of ordinary speech.[19]

The grammatical characteristics of Old English poetry, often accompanied by the kinds of sound patterns mentioned above, are seen in a particularly developed form in *Beowulf*, facilitated by the poet's remarkable inventiveness in compounding. The next section of this chapter aims to show some of these features in action: before turning to the modern versions and their approaches to translation, I now wish to examine a couple of passages from *Beowulf* which illustrate its poetry and poetics.

Two Passages from *Beowulf*

Beowulf, lines 1–11

The much-analysed opening lines of the poem provide one such convenient example:

> Hwæt, we Gar-Dena   in geardagum,
> þeodcyninga   þrym gefrunon,
> hu ða æþelingas   ellen fremedon.
>   Oft Scyld Scefing   sceaþena þreatum,
> monegum mægþum   meodusetla ofteah,
> egsode eorlas,   syððan ærest wearð
> feasceaft funden.   He þæs frofre gebad:
> weox under wolcnum,   weorðmyndum þah,
> oð þæt him æghwylc   þara ymbsittendra
> ofer hronrade   hyran scolde,
> gomban gyldan.   Þæt wæs god cyning.

These powerful and resonant lines present a carefully wrought introduction to the first half of the poem and begin to touch on major preoccupations that will

---

[17] Alexander, *The Earliest English Poems*, 'Introduction', p. 11.
[18] Momma, *The Composition of Old English Poetry*, p. 193.
[19] For key recent contributions, see Momma, *The Composition of Old English Poetry*; Donoghue, 'Word Order and Poetic Style: Auxiliary and Verbal in *The Metres of Boethius*'; Blockley, *Aspects of Old English Poetic Syntax*; many relevant issues are also discussed in Mitchell, *Old English Syntax*.

be explored in the later narrative. Lines 1–52 of *Beowulf*, usually referred to as the 'Prologue', and the first numbered section or 'fitt' (lines 53–114), may be seen as a meditation on the steady passage of great events remembered from long ago, focusing on *þrym*, 'acts of glory', and *ellen*, 'deeds of valour', but also on the passing of time, mutability. It is a meditation that is begun in this opening sequence, which introduces the ancient past of the poem and covers the achievements of a great Danish king, Scyld Shefing. The rest of the Prologue completes the account of Scyld's life and describes his impressive ship funeral, itself an emblem of the themes of *þrym* and *ellen* on the one hand and mutability on the other. The first fitt will trace the story of Scyld's successors down the generations to the time of King Hrothgar and the immediate events of the poem's story.

In line with the traditionality of the poet's approach, *Beowulf* begins with a conventional formal call to attention of an imagined physical audience, *Hwæt*, literally meaning 'What' but usually rendered as 'Listen' or 'Indeed'; older translators have 'Behold' or 'Lo', which sound unidiomatic today but could be said to reflect the archaic aspect of the diction of *Beowulf*. We might grammatically translate the rest of the opening sentence as 'We have heard of the glory [with the direct object *þrym*, 'glory', and verb *gefrunon*, 'heard', delayed to the end of the second line] in days of yore of the kings of the people (*þeodcyninga*) of the Spear-Danes (*Gar-Dena*), how the noblemen accomplished [deeds of] valour (*ellen*).' There is notable grammatical parallelism between *Gar-Dena* and *þeodcyninga* and it would also be possible indeed to take *þeodcyninga* as being in apposition to rather than dependent on *Gar-Dena*: 'we have heard of the glory of the Spear-Danes, the kings of the people', the 'Spear-Danes' thus being identified with the kings of the people. The extremely light punctuation of Old English poetry manuscripts means that syntactical ambiguity is often a possibility. Such ambiguity has to be resolved in oral performance – and in translation – but can remain unresolved 'on the page'.²⁰

Line 3 constitutes an expansion on the opening exclamatory statement while at the same time in *ellen fremedon*, 'accomplished [deeds of] valour', it provides grammatical parallelism (reinforced by the *-on* rhyme) to *þrym gefrunon*. It might also be possible to translate *ða æþelingas* as 'then noblemen' rather than 'the noblemen', thus recapitulating or varying *on geardagum*, 'in former days'.²¹ This first sentence provides a grand *Arma virumque cano*-type statement (to refer to the opening words of Virgil's *Aeneid*) of concerns covered by the poem, stressing

---

²⁰ Punctuation, paragraphing and other key layout elements in editions of Old English poems are usually (silently) the contribution of the editor(s), a circumstance that is receiving critical attention in current research: see esp. Fred C. Robinson, 'Mise en page in Old English Manuscripts and Printed Texts'; Liuzza, 'Scribes of the Mind: Editing Old English in Theory and in Practice'. The punctuation of Old English texts was a particular concern in the work of Bruce Mitchell in recent decades, beginning with his 1980 article 'The Dangers of Disguise: Old English Texts in Modern Punctuation'.
²¹ As argued by Howlett, *British Books in Biblical Style*, p. 506; Orchard, *A Critical Companion* (p. 59), finds this idea plausible.

the themes of the glory and courage of the Danish kings and people, all set in a remembered past. The voice of the narrator, speaking to and for an implied community, is characterized by certainty and directness of expression, the sense arranging itself around key simplex nouns (*þrym, ellen*) supported by verbs in the indicative mood. The key nouns are abstract but used in a concrete sense, as action words: *þrym* suggests glorious *actions*, *ellen* valorous *deeds*. The language is restrained and dignity is conveyed in this opening sentence by the parallelism, poetic word order – with inversion and suspended resolution –, poetic vocabulary (*geardagum*, 'days of yore', *þeodcyninga*, 'people-kings') and compound words (*Gar-Dena, geardagum, þeodcyninga*).

The sense of dignity and restraint is maintained in the rest of the passage. We might render the second sentence as follows: 'Often Scyld Scefing, in troops of enemies, deprived [with again the resolution provided by the verb (*ofteah*) delayed] many tribes of their mead-benches (*meodusetla*), terrified/inspired awe in warriors,' in which the 'mead-benches', synecdochically representative of the hall, the focus and symbol of social life in the heroic world, epitomize the (lost) autonomy and self-esteem of the enemy tribes conquered by Scyld, and *egsode eorlas*, 'terrified warriors' or 'inspired awe in warriors', is an appositive phrase presenting a kind of variant on or development of the preceding line. The sentence now modulates into a subordinate clause, 'since the time when he was first found destitute'. The adjective *feasceaft*, which I have translated 'destitute' but more literally means 'having few things', is an instance of the figure of litotes or understatement, common in Old English, alluding contrastingly to Scyld's mysterious arrival among the Danes as an unknown orphan.

The third and final sentence of our passage elaborates the contrast between the destitute boy and the great king he is to become. Beginning with further understatement, the account of Scyld continues, 'He experienced comfort (*frofre*) for that: he prospered (*weox*, literally 'waxed') under the clouds [i.e., in the world], thrived in worldly honours (*weorðmyndum*), until each one of the neighbouring tribes [the Old English is actually less abstract here than my translation, having *ymbsittendra*, 'those situated, or sitting, around'], over the whale's road, had to obey him, give him tribute; that was a good king.' The closing exclamation is offered as a truth, which everyone will agree with. It is understood to be justified by the preceding sequence, which exploits verbal variation and cumulation in its account of Scyld's achievements: the sequence consists of three principal verbs (*gebad*, 'experienced'; *weox*, 'prospered'; *þah*, 'thrived'), of which the latter two (near synonyms) present manifestations of Scyld's success, explaining *how* he 'experienced comfort for that'. These principal verbs lead to the climactic *oð þæt*, 'until', clause, in which *hyran*, 'obey, listen to', and *gomban gyldan*, 'pay, or yield, tribute', are again examples of variation.

The passage is conceived as a single unit, the essential mode of which is exclamatory. It is made up of three sentences that are broadly symmetrical in structure, each beginning with a measured declarative statement or sequence of statements, including therein an element of variation; this larger part of the sentence is then modified in each instance by a brief subordinate clause, the latter balancing or completing the sentence's theme. In the first sentence the subordinate clause is an adverbial 'how' clause; in the other two the subordinate clauses are temporal ('since' and 'until'), these three conjunctions, *hu*, *syððan* and *oðþæt*, being significantly among those used most frequently in the poem, in keeping with its generally contrastive and additive syntactic mode.

The language of these opening sentences is carefully wrought, but it is also formulaic. Alliterating phrases used here occur elsewhere in *Beowulf* and in other Old English poems in comparable metrical environments.[22] To give just two examples from our passage, *in geardagum*, 'in days of yore' (line 1b) appears again in *Beowulf* at lines 1354 and 2233 (as *on geardagum*); the phrase *in/on geardagum* also occurs in *Christ and Satan* (ASPR I, 135–58), line 367, *Christ I* (ASPR III, 3–15), line 251, *The Wanderer* (ASPR III, 134–7), line 44, and the related formulation *æfter geardagum*, 'after days of yore', also appears (*The Phoenix* [ASPR III, 94–113], line 384). And the yoking of *þeodcyninga*, 'people-kings', and *gefrunon*, 'heard' (line 2), is reflected later in *Beowulf* at line 2694, *Ða ic æt þearfe gefrægn þeodcyninges*, 'Then I heard that at the need of the king of the people';[23] elsewhere *þeodcyning* not only collocates with *gefrignan* (Riddle 67 [ASPR III, 231], line 1) but it also does so with *þrym* (*Genesis A* [ASPR I, 3–87], line 1965) (cf. *Beowulf*, line 2) and with *þearfan* (*Judgement Day II* [ASPR VI, 58–67], line 162) (cf. *Beowulf*, line 2694).

In such instances the *Beowulf* poet is tapping into the rich ready-made resources provided by the poetic tradition. It is also notable, however, that some of the phrases that recur in the poem are not found in other surviving poems. The formula *monegum mægþum* is an example of one that does not turn up elsewhere. This might be due simply to the smallness of the surviving corpus of Old English poetry – if we had more poetry we might find examples of *monegum mægþum* and its variants. It is also possible, however, that the *Beowulf* poet has formulations that are his own, just as key elements in his vocabulary are his own (see below): he is using formulaic language in a 'generative' way. Thus, *ærest* is linked with *syððan* in other poems (*Genesis A*, line 2776; *Elene* [ASPR II, 66–102], line 116) and with *weard* (Riddle 83 [ASPR III, 236], line 5) but the Beowulfian phrase *syððan ærest weard* (lines 6b, 1947b) is unparalleled. The word *cyning* occurs over two hundred times in surviving Old English poetry but the expression *þæt wæs god cyning* is unique to *Beowulf*, where it is used three times (lines 11b, 863b, 2390b); phrases belonging to the system represented in the *Beowulf* formula do, however, appear in other poems: *Þæt is æðele cyning*, 'that is a noble king' (*Andreas* [ASPR II, 3–51], line 1722b), *þær is riht cyning*, 'where there is a true king' (*Guthlac A* [ASPR III, 49–72], line 682b).

---

[22] For a listing of all repeated formulas in *Beowulf*, see Orchard, *A Critical Companion*, pp. 274–314.
[23] At line 2694 *gefrægn* is lacking in the manuscript but it is universally inserted by editors.

In his use of formulaic language in these opening lines therefore the *Beowulf* poet may be seen using tradition but varying it and extending it. *Gar-Dena*, 'Spear-Danes' (line 1), is an instance from a system of ways of referring to the Danes that the poet makes use of, with no parallels elsewhere in the poetry, though the formulaicity of this phrase is obvious. Words like *Gar-Dena* are on one level little more than poetic tags and the choice of whether to call the Danes Spear-Danes (lines 1, 601, etc.) or Bright-Danes (lines 427, 609) or Ring-Danes (lines 116, 1279, 1769) or North-Danes (line 783) or East-Danes (lines 392, 616, 828) or South-Danes (lines 463, 1996) or West-Danes (lines 383, 1578) seems to be purely down to the requirements of alliteration. At the same time, however, such diction, even if it must appear uninspired, serves to confirm the poet's participation in tradition.

Throughout the whole passage, then, the traditional nature of the language is strongly in evidence. The vocabulary in this discursive passage is mostly not distinctive, though it will become more so later, just as the certainties of the communal outlook will become more problematical. The opening *Hwæt* locates the poem in traditional narrative; the poetic compound nouns, apart from *Gar-Dena* and the conventional-looking *meodosetla*, are familiar from elsewhere in Old English poetry (in *meodosetla ofteah* it is the juxtaposition rather than the words themselves that is remarkable: the hall is supposed to be a place of social joy, not violence);[24] in adopting the kenning (a kenning being an allusive metaphorical phrase) *ofer hronrade*, 'over the whale's road' (for the sea), also found in two other poems, the poet draws on a standard technique of Old English poetry.[25] At this beginning stage of *Beowulf* the poet is situating his narrative in the heroic world and emphasizing the relationship of the poem to a larger tradition.

The passage is composed, of course, in the formal metre of Old English poetry, as described above (p. 29). It is made up predominantly of 'type A' half-lines, according to the Sievers system, giving a sense of steady development in the narrative.[26] The regularity of lines 5–11 is particularly apparent: here we see a sequence of lines beginning with type A, this pattern being interrupted only by the light verses at lines 9 and 10; within the sequence there are two consecutive lines of AB structure (lines 6 and 7) enveloped by two of AE structure (lines 5 and 8).

---

[24] For *geardagum* and *þeodcyninga*, see above, p. 35; occurrences of *weorðmynd* in the plural can be found in *Christ I* (ASPR III, 3–15), line 378, *Alms-Giving* (ASPR III, 223), line 3), *Judith* (ASPR IV, 99–109), line 342, *Guthlac A* (line 463), as well as elsewhere in *Beowulf* (line 1752).

[25] *Andreas* (line 821, on *hronrade*) and *Genesis A* (line 205, *geond hronrade*). On the possible close relation of these poems to *Beowulf*, see Orchard, *A Critical Companion*, p. 167. The use of kennings is characteristic of Old English (and Old Norse) poetry generally; cf. *hwæles eðel*, 'whale's homeland' (*Andreas*, line 274, *The Seafarer* [ASPR III, 143–7], line 60, *The Death of Edgar* [ASPR VI, 22–4], line 28), also for the sea.

[26] On the effect of the different half-line types on narrative pace, see Raw, *The Art and Background of Old English Poetry*, pp. 87–122; Scragg, 'The Nature of Old English Verse', pp. 60–3.

The basic metrical framework is enriched by some non-structural alliteration, although, in line with the restraint we have been observing in other aspects of the passage, this kind of embellishment is less insistent than in many other parts of the poem. Still, at the level of non-structural alliteration we see here an example of cross-alliteration (line 1: g and d)[27] and we also see considerable use of double alliteration (lines 2, 5, 6, 7, 8, 9, 11) and instances of alliterative play across lines (lines 1–2, *gefrunon, fremedon*; lines 5–6, *-setla, syððan*; lines 11–12, *cyning, cenned*, the last pair serving to link our passage with the next narrative unit of the poem). Rhyme effects are evident in the *-on* of *gefrunon* and *fremedon* at the end of lines 2 and 3 (these two lines sandwiched between ones ending in *-um*: *geardagum, þreatum*), the *-de* of *hronrade* and *scolde* in line 10, and the *-an* of *hyran, gomban* and *gyldan* in lines 10 and 11.

Beowulf, lines 867b–74

As a second, contrasting, passage illustrative of the art of the *Beowulf* poet, I wish to return to the extract quoted earlier, describing the traditional poet at work. In this passage, which is *about* the skill of the poet, the *Beowulf* poet takes the opportunity to pull out a few stops, exhibiting in it some of the technical features mentioned in his depiction of poetic composition.[28]

Here is the passage again:

> Hwilum cyninges þegn,
> guma gilphlæden,   gidda gemyndig,
> se ðe eal fela   ealdgesegena
> worn gemunde,   word oþer fand
> soðe gebunden;   secg eft ongan
> sið Beowulfes   snyttrum styrian
> ond on sped wrecan   spel gerade,
> wordum wrixlan;   welhwylc gecwæð

Here we notice double alliteration in lines 868, 872 and 874 and alliterative play across lines at lines 869–70 (*-fela, fand*), 871–3 (three consecutive lines of *s* alliteration, with additional play on *b* [*gebunden, Beowulfes*] and on *w* [*-wulfes, wrecan*]) and 873–4 (in which the initial sound of *wrecan*, as well as connecting with *Beowulfes*, anticipates the *w* alliteration of line 874). Paronomasiac and rhyme-like effects are also in evidence. Thus, there is play on *eal* and *eald* at line 869, *worn* and *word* at line 870, and *sped* and *spel* at line 973. At line 870

---

[27] On the alliteration of gutteral g (*Gar-*) and palatal g (*gear-*) in line 1, see Orchard, *A Critical Companion*, p. 60; cf. also *gomban gyldan* (line 11). Orchard is surely correct in seeing this 'archaic' alliteration as 'utterly traditional' rather than as evidence for an early date for the poem (as he points out [ibid.], the distinction between the two pronunciations of g apparently arose in the eighth century).

[28] On this passage, see further Eliason, 'The "Improvised Lay" in *Beowulf*'; Creed, '". . . Wél-hwelć Gecwæþ . . .": The Singer as Architect'; Nolan and Bloomfield, '*Beotword, gilpcwidas*, and the *gilphlædan* Scop of *Beowulf*'.

gemunde echoes the earlier *gemyndig* (line 868) and is also linked by rhyme-effect to *gebunden* (line 871); and towards the end of the passage (lines 871–4) four out of six half-lines end in *-an* (*ongan, styrian, wrecan, wrixlan*).

It is notable that this aural play of sound and word highlights key ideas in the passage, to do with memory, tradition, words and the skill of the poet. Such ideas are also highlighted through the use of words unique to this passage. The vocabulary of the passage is grounded in traditional poetic diction (*guma, worn, secg, sið*) but also contains terms found only here – *gilphlæden, ealdgesegena* – and words found in phrasal combination only here – *soðe gebunden, snyttrum styrian, spel gerade*. The key ideas are also brought out through sentence structure, in which cumulation of epithets and variation are prominent. The passage is made up of two sense units, the first of which tells that a thegn composed words, stressing at length this man's eloquence and mastery of tradition, while the second goes on to highlight the artistry of his new *spel*, 'tale', about Beowulf's exploit. As is brought out by this grammatical structure, in the depiction of the oral poet at work no distinction is made between composition and performance: it is only in performance that the oral poem is realized.

Metrically the passage is made up predominantly of type A half-lines (*gidda gemyndig, worn gemunde*, etc.), as was the case with our previous passage, but, supplying rhythmical variety, there is more use here of types D and E, with their patterns of secondary stress, especially in the second sense unit: *guma gilphlæden* (D), *word oþer fand* (E), *secg eft ongan* (E), *sið Biowulfes* (D), *welhwylc gecwæð* (E).

In this virtuoso passage sound, sense and grammar combine in a self-conscious display of the craft of the *Beowulf* poet in what is itself an evocation of the craft of 'the poet'. This observation brings us back to the question of the relationship of *Beowulf* itself to the originally oral poetic tradition in which it participates, which I discussed earlier. I hope that consideration of these lines, along with that of the other passage we have looked at, may serve to give a sense of the richness and art of the poetry of *Beowulf*, which modern poets must somehow come to terms with in their translations. Needless to say, if we had examined other passages in *Beowulf*, this would have brought out other aspects of the poetry of this many-faceted work.

Conclusion

As mentioned above, we will be returning to these two passages in subsequent chapters, to consider how they are treated by some modern poets in their translation of the Old English. An essential point about the poetry of *Beowulf* that I have concentrated on in this chapter is that it is at once traditional and strikingly original. In its originality *Beowulf* exploits the possibilities of tradition but it also transcends tradition, standing outside the pre-Christian heroic world it describes and complicating – while respecting – the value-system of its people.

In looking back at *Beowulf* from their modern perspective, translators are addressing a poem therefore that comes from a distant phase of language and culture and that even within that phase represents a special register which is handled with particular craft and sophistication by the *Beowulf* poet. The most successful (in my view) poetic translations discussed in the following chapters are conscious of these considerations but they, and others, disagree about how to respond to the challenge of creating an appropriate register in representing the Old English poem in Modern English. What most verse translators strongly agree upon is what they see as their primary aim, which is to produce poetry that lives. The balancing act will be to do so while at the same time doing appropriate justice to the poetry of *Beowulf*.

☦3☦

Reception, Perceptions, and a Survey of Earlier Verse Translations of Beowulf

Subsequent chapters will focus particularly on verse translations of *Beowulf* from Edwin Morgan's on, covering the period from the 1950s down to the present. There were plenty of attempts at rendering *Beowulf* in English verse before Morgan, of course, and I wish to give an overview of these before coming to the more recent period. In the present chapter I will sketch in something of the earlier larger reception history of *Beowulf* in the modern era and trace some inherited and changing perceptions of it, with particular reference to the history of its translation into verse. I have already referred to some of the translations from the nineteenth and early twentieth centuries in a previous chapter, focusing on ideas of translation theory and approach. At the risk of some duplication of material, I consider verse translations again in the present chapter but as well as taking account of the features of the translations just mentioned I will also emphasize the understandings of and attitudes to the poem that animate them. Invaluable groundwork has been done by Andreas Haarder, Tom Shippey and others on material covered in this chapter and, though their focus was not primarily on translation, my debt to these scholars will be clearly evident below and is gratefully acknowledged.[1]

Beowulf in the Nineteenth Century, and up to 1914

The beginnings of significant knowledge of *Beowulf* date only from the turn of the eighteenth-to-nineteenth century, and the poem remained largely the preserve of scholars throughout most of the nineteenth century, achieving more widespread interest and popularity only towards the end of the century and particularly in

---

[1] Haarder, *Beowulf: The Appeal of a Poem*; Shippey and Haarder, ed., *Beowulf: The Critical Heritage*; see also Frantzen, *Desire for Origins: New Language, Old English, and Teaching the Tradition*; J. R. Hall, 'Anglo-Saxon Studies in the Nineteenth Century: England, Denmark, America'.

the twentieth century. Translations of the poem have contributed importantly to the ongoing development of that interest and popularity, which have been increasingly evident in recent decades and are probably at their height today. But getting *Beowulf* better known was one aim of translations from the start.

The early recovery and translation of *Beowulf*

The single surviving manuscript containing *Beowulf* had been acquired by the sixteenth-century antiquarian Laurence Nowell and later became part of the collection of Sir Robert Cotton (1571–1631), whence it made its way into the possession of the British Museum (founded in 1753) as manuscript Cotton Vitellius A. xv. Despite the vicissitudes of history (including damage to the edges of all the pages of the manuscript due to a fire in 1731), *Beowulf* had been preserved down the centuries. But it remained unread and to a significant degree unreadable: Old English prose was well understood in seventeenth- and eighteenth-century England, but verse was a different matter. And the eighteenth century in particular was not fertile ground anyway for the study of Old English literature, as Allen Frantzen, among others, has documented; Frantzen refers to the hostility to Anglo-Saxon antiquities in this period, reflecting the view, 'common in the eighteenth century, that Anglo-Saxon England was a barbarous place with a barbarous civilization only lifted to respectability by the Norman Conquest'.[2] Joseph Ritson, antiquarian and editor of ballads and metrical romances, is typical of the age when he dismisses the Anglo-Saxons as 'for the most part, an ignorant and illiterate people' and declares that 'it will be vain to hope for proofs, among them, of genius, or original composition, at least in their native tongue.'[3] Ritson described Old English verse as 'a rhymeless sort of poetry, a kind of bombast or insane prose, from which it is very difficult to be distinguished'.[4]

In 1786 *Beowulf* came to the attention of the Icelander Grímur Jónsson Thorkelín, archivist of the Danish court in Copenhagen. Among the few before Thorkelín who had noticed *Beowulf* was Humphrey Wanley, who includes reference to it in his great 1705 catalogue of early English manuscripts and who prints therein a mostly correct transcription of lines 1–19 and 53–73 of the poem. Wanley couldn't make much sense of *Beowulf* but he worked out that it was written in verse and hazarded a description of it as being about a Danish hero who fought against kings of Sweden.[5] *Beowulf* was next mentioned by Thomas Wharton in his *History of English Poetry* (1776), but only in passing in a footnote at the beginning of the work. Echoing Wanley, Wharton writes, 'The curious reader is also

---

[2] Frantzen, *Desire for Origins*, p. 192.
[3] Ritson, quoted by Shippey, 'Introduction', Shippey and Haarder, *Beowulf: The Critical Heritage*, p. 3.
[4] Quoted by Isaac D'Israeli (1841), *Amenities of Literature, Consisting of Sketches and Characters of English Literature*, I, 53.
[5] Wanley, *Librorum Veterum Septentrionalium, qui in Angliae Bibliothecis extant*.

referred to a Danish Saxon poem, celebrating the wars which Beowulf, a noble Dane, descended from the royal stem of Scildinge, waged against the kings of Swedeland.'[6]

It was the reference to the hero as Danish that particularly interested Thorkelín and stimulated him to have two transcriptions of the manuscript text made, the second carried out by himself.[7] On the basis of these transcriptions, full of errors as they were, Thorkelín produced the first edition of the poem, finally publishing it in 1815. Thorkelín himself reports that he had had to start work on this project again when all his materials on it were destroyed in the bombardment of Copenhagen in 1807, by British forces.[8] Wackerbarth, the first translator of all of *Beowulf* into English verse (1849), comments sympathetically – and patriotically – on this disaster: he laments that Thorkelín's edition 'was ready for Publication in 1807, when the inexplicable Policy of the Danish Government gave Rise to a War with England, and in the ever to be regretted Bombardment of Copenhagen that followed, the Antiquarian's House, and the literary Property he had been for thirty Years diligently collecting perished in the Flames'.[9] Recent scholarship suggests, however, that the delay in the publication of Thorkelín's edition was due more to his own incompetence as a scholar. In the view of the most recent commentator, Magnús Fjalldal, given Thorkelín's scholarly inadequacies, his edition was 'a predictable disaster'.[10]

Thorkelín's edition abounds in instances of mistaken morpheme division and wrong letters: according to the calculation of J. R. Hall, there is an average of one letter-error every 1.7 long lines.[11] And, undeterred by his lack of knowledge of Old English poetry, Thorkelín accompanies his edited text with a floundering parallel translation into Latin (set out in short lines which follow the Old English half-lines), the first translation of the whole poem. The translation aims at word-for-word literalism, though, as he admits in his preface, Thorkelín found the task of translating the poem taxing indeed:

> I have tried to render our poet and his circumlocutions word for word, in which matter if anywhere I have not satisfied the reader, I hope that he will kindly pardon me, as I have inevitably been tormented by the very great confusion of the letters

---

[6] See Shippey, 'Introduction', in Shippey and Haarder, *Beowulf: The Critical Heritage* (p. 3).
[7] See Kiernan, *Electronic Beowulf*, for digital facsimiles. Thorkelín's transcriptions, though error-strewn, are of key importance for constructing the text of the poem, since the state of the edges of the manuscript pages deteriorated significantly in the period after the transcriptions were made.
[8] Thorkelín, *De Danorum rebus gestis seculi III & IV: Poëma Danicum dialecto Anglosaxonica*; for an English translation of Thorkelín's preface to his edition, see Bjork, 'Grímur Jónsson Thorkelín's Preface to the First Edition of *Beowulf*: translation by Taylor Close and Robert E. Bjork at pp. 298–315.
[9] Wackerbarth, *Beowulf*, p. xi.
[10] Fjalldal, 'To Fall by Ambition – Grímur Thorkelín and his *Beowulf* Edition', p. 321.
[11] J. R. Hall, 'Anglo-Saxon Studies in the Nineteenth Century', p. 245.

and by the rough variation in the meaning of words, which is ambiguous, erratic and often in turn self-contradictory.[12]

Opinions of Thorkelín's translation have been almost unanimously condemnatory, from Kemble, who finds 'some gross fault' within every five lines, to Wackerbarth, who declares it to be 'certainly worse than useless', to Marijane Osborn, who comments that it is 'often mistaken'.[13] Thorkelín's version is significant, however, as the first complete translation of *Beowulf*. His edition and translation instigated the concentrated study of the poem, but they were produced by an ill-equipped scholar in the days before Germanic philology and at a time when a basic understanding of Old English poetry and poetics was lacking – and this shows. Thorkelín's translation was also not aided by his own faulty transcription of the manuscript text. Indeed it is the unsatisfactory nature of Thorkelín's text that especially militates against his producing an adequate translation.

Thorkelín's edited version and translation of the opening eleven lines of the poem are as follows:

Hwæt wegar Dena	Quomodo Danorum
In geardagum	In principio
Þeod cyninga	Populus regum
Þrym gefrunon	Gloriam auxerit,
Hu þa æþelingas	Quomodo principes
Ellen fremedon.	Virtute promoverit.
Oft Scyld Scefing	Sæpe Scyldus Scefides
Sceaþen þreatum	Hostes turmis,
Monegum mægþum	Multis nationibus
Meodo setla ofteah	Dignas sedes auferens
Egsode. Eorl	Terruit. Dux
Syþþan ærest wearþ	Postquam fiebat,
Feasceaft funden	Miseris obviis
He þæs freofre gebad.	Solatium mansit.
Weox under weolcnum	Crevit sub nubibus,
Weorþmyndum þeah	Honore viguit,
Oþ þæt him æghwylc	Donec ille quilibet
Þara ymbsittendra	Accolarum
Ofer hronrade	Ad cetorum vias
Hyran scolde	Suum cogeretur

[12] Thorkelín, *De Danorum rebus gestis*, p. xix: 'Poëtam nostram eiusqve periphrases verbum ad verbum reddere conatus sum, qva in re, si ubivis lectori non satisfecerim, eum spero benevole condonaturum fore mihi, cui cum maxima characterum confusione, et significationis vocum ambiguæ, vagæ, et sibi sæpe invicem oppositæ salebrosa varietate conflictari necessum fuit.'

[13] Kemble, *The Anglo-Saxon Poems of Beowulf, The Travellers Song and The Battle of Finnesburg*, pp. xxix–xxx; Wackerbarth, *Beowulf*, p. xi; Osborn, 'Translations, Versions, Illustrations', p. 341. Shippey is less categorical: '[Thorkelín's] half-line by half-line translating method makes his intended meaning hard to follow, though I do not find it as bad as is described by Cooley 1940 and Osborn 1997' ('Introduction', p. 11, referring to Cooley, 'Early Danish Criticism of *Beowulf*, and Osborn, 'Translations, Versions, Illustrations').

Goban gyldan
Þæt wæs god cyning.

Tributum solvere.
Ille fuit bonus Rex.

By way of comparison, it may be helpful to quote (again) the corresponding lines from *Klaeber's Beowulf*, and to supply as literal a translation as is feasible in Modern English:

> Hwæt, we Gar-Dena   in geardagum,
> þeodcyninga   þrym gefrunon,
> hu ða æþelingas   ellen fremedon.
> Oft Scyld Scefing   sceaþena þreatum,
> monegum mægþum   meodosetla ofteah,
> egsode eorlas,   syððan ærest wearð
> feasceaft funden.   He þæs frofre gebad:
> weox under wolcnum,   weorðmyndum þah,
> oð þæt him æghwylc   þara ymbsittendra
> ofer hronrade   hyran scolde,
> gomban gyldan.   Þæt wæs god cyning.

[Listen, we have heard of the glory in days of yore of the kings of the people (*þeodcyninga*) of the Spear-Danes (*Gar-Dena*), how the noblemen accomplished [deeds of] valour. Often Scyld Scefing deprived troops of enemies, many tribes, of their mead-benches (*meodusetla*), terrified/inspired awe in warriors; he experienced comfort for that: he prospered under the clouds, thrived in worldly honours (*weorðmyndum*), until each one of the tribes situated around, over the whale-road, had to obey him, give him tribute: that was a good king.]

An English version of Thorkelín's Latin translation might read,

> How in the beginning the people of the kings increased the glory of the Danes, how they [the people] advanced the princes in valour. Often Scyld son of Scef terrified enemies with his troops, taking away the worthy seats from many tribes. After he became ruler, he awaited consolation from the miseries that lay in his path. He grew great under the clouds, flourished in honour, until each and every one of those dwelling near was driven to the roads of the whales to pay tribute to him. He was a good king.

Thorkelín's translation errors here are due partly to the deficiencies of his Old English text, in which some letters are misread (ð is also silently changed to þ) and morphemes are not correctly divided (instances of the latter being *wegar*, in which the first-person pronoun which in the Old English is the subject of the opening sentence is not identified; and *þeod cyninga*, which is not recognized to be a compound; Thorkelín mis-transcribes *gomban* as *Goban* but still manages to supply the right sense), and the errors are due partly to failure to understand the basic meaning and use of Old English words (examples are *gefrunon*, 'heard', translated 'auxerit', 'increased'; *meodo*, 'mead', clearly taken to be a 'meed' word; and *hwæt*, translated as a variant of *hu*). In his preface Thorkelín had referred to the meaning of words being ambiguous in *Beowulf*, a quality that is very much reflected in his own translation here as well, in which, for example (as in the

Old English), the genitives of the opening clause could be construed in several different ways.

Thorkelín is not properly equipped to edit and translate the poem but tries his best anyway. He gets into deeper trouble as he proceeds after this opening passage, mistaking the *blæd*, 'renown, glory', of Beowulf spreading widely for his blood flowing profusely (*Sanguine late scaturiente*), turning the gnomic passage at lines 20–3 into an apostrophe ('Thus you ought to bring it about by ready gifts of treasure, O king, offered to your fathers, so that in after times young men may become accustomed to follow their leaders, when wars come': 'Ita debes cimeliorum / O Rex efficere / Præsentibus donis / Patribus (oblatis) tuis, / Ut juvenes / Post assuefiant / sequi duces, / Ubi bella venerunt'),[14] and, confused by the mention of Beowulf at line 18, taking the description of Scyld's ship funeral to be an account of the voyage to Denmark of the hero and his *virorum cohors*, 'troop of men' (*virorum cohors* translating *hringed stefna*, 'ringed-prow'), a troop which is 'ready for action and eager for the journey' (*expedita et itineris avida*).

It is the Danishness of *Beowulf* that particularly interests Thorkelín, as he makes clear in his patriotic preface to his edition and translation. The preface begins,

> Among all the monuments of the ancient Danish world which time, the devourer of things, has bequeathed to us, the admirable epic concerning the Scyldings now properly published stands out. For we have here the well-watered sources from which can be drawn forth knowledge of religion and of poetry and the sequence of the achievements of our people in the third and fourth centuries.[15]

As well as initiating the scholarly study of *Beowulf*, Thorkelín thus also begins the enterprise of nationalistic appropriation of it which was to be a popular one among nineteenth-century scholars. I will refer to this appropriation in a later section; for the present we might note that Thorkelín values *Beowulf* not for its literary qualities but for what it tells us about the past. Concerning its literary qualities, his statement about the 'rough variation in the meaning of words,

---

[14] Thorkelín's Old English text reads (*Beowulf*, lines 20–3), 'Swa sceal maþma / Gode gewircean / Fromum fegiftum / On fæder þina / Þæt hine on ylde / Eft gewunigen / Wil gesiþas / Þonne wig cume.' Compare *Klaeber's Beowulf*:

    Swa sceal geong guma   gode gewyrcean,
    fromum feohgiftum   on fæder bearme,
    þæt hine on ylde   eft gewunigen
    wilgesiþas,   þonne wig cume.

We might translate the latter, 'Thus must a young man bring it about by his goodness/liberality, by generous gifts of treasure while under the protection of his father, that his dear companions may remain with him in his old age, when war comes.'

[15] Thorkelin, p. vii: 'Inter omnia monumenta veteris orbis Danici, quæ tempus edax rerum nobis requivit, admirabile de Scyldingis Epos publici nunc iuris factum eminet. Habemus enim hic irriguos fontes, unde religionis poëseosqve notitia, et gentis nostræ rerum seculis III et IV gestarum series deduci possit.'

which is ambiguous, erratic and often in turn self-contradictory' is as much as he has to offer.

Thorkelín's edition and translation was followed by a translation of the poem into Danish by N. F. S. Grundtvig, a free paraphrase in a rhyming ballad metre.[16] Grundtvig, a wide-ranging scholar with strong nationalistic and religious convictions, was keenly interested in Danish history and antiquities and hoped that his translation would be of value as a 'text-book in patriotism.'[17]

Ten years before the publication of Thorkelín's edition, Sharon Turner, having independently discovered the poem, had initiated the history of *Beowulf* translation when he bravely included word-for-word renderings into English of selected passages from it (set out in short lines) in his summary of the poem in the fourth volume of his *The History of the Anglo-Saxons* (1805); in the same volume he also quotes some forty lines from *Beowulf* and other Old English poems in the original language and adds comments on Old English metre.[18]

Turner viewed Anglo-Saxon poetry as reflecting a 'rude' state of poetical genius and taste,[19] but he came to recognize that *Beowulf* was an important literary monument, characterizing it as 'a specimen of an Anglo-Saxon poetical romance': he declares in the 1820 (third) edition of his *History*, 'It is the most interesting relic of the Anglo-Saxon poetry which time has spared to us', adding, 'and, as a picture of the manners, and as an exhibition of the feelings and notions of those days, it is as valuable as it is ancient.'[20] In his second edition (1807) of the *History* he includes the beginning of the poem among the translated extracts (this passage is not in the first edition):

> What have we not in the world,
> in former days,
> heard of the glory
> of the Theod-kings?
> How the ethelings
> in strength excelled!

[16] Grundtvig, *Bjowulf's Drape*.
[17] See Tinker, *The Translations of Beowulf*, pp. 22, 25.
[18] Turner, *The History of the Anglo-Saxons*, IV (1805), 398–408, 414–17; on metre, he declares, 'It appears to me that the only rule of the Saxon versification which we can now discover is that the words are placed in that peculiar rhythm or cadence which is observable in all the preceding extracts' (p. 416). Later he would write that in their poetry the Anglo-Saxons 'used no rules at all' (*History of the Anglo-Saxons*, 3rd ed., III, 301).
[19] 'In no country can the progress of the poetical genius and taste be more satisfactorily traced than in our own. During that period which this work attempts to commemorate, we find it in its earliest state. It could indeed have been scarcely more rude to have been at all discernible' (Turner, *The History of the Anglo-Saxons*, 3rd ed., III, 299).
[20] Turner, *The History of the Anglo-Saxons*, 3rd ed., III, 326; quoted by Frantzen, *Desire for Origins*, p. 194; for a longer extract, see Shippey and Haarder, *Beowulf: The Critical Heritage*, pp. 161–6. On the growth of interest in Anglo-Saxon poetry at the beginning of the nineteenth century, see Payne, 'The Rediscovery of Old English Poetry in the English Literary Tradition'.

> Oft the scyld of the race of Scefa,
> from hosts of enemies,
> from many tribes,
> the mead of the seats withdrew.

Turner has difficulty with these lines (not understanding *Gar-Dena*, for example, and introducing a negative: the *na* of *Dena*?) but he makes a better stab than Thorkelín: he recognizes the first-person-plural pronoun, for example, and gets the meaning of *gefrunon* right. And his revised version of these lines in the 1820 edition of the *History*, written after he had consulted Thorkelín's edition, is a further considerable improvement:

> How have we of the Gar-Danes,
> in former days,
> of the Theod-kings,
> the glory heard?
> How the ethelings
> Excelled in strength!
> Oft the scyld-scefing
> from hosts of enemies,
> from many tribes,
> the mead-seats withdrew.[21]

Here Turner is still unable to cope with the opening exclamatory *Hwæt* and has to improvise with *Scyld Scefing* but the overall meaning corresponds reasonably to that of the original. Soon, however, he goes badly wrong, like Thorkelín mistaking the ship funeral of Scyld for an account of the 'embarkation of Beowulf and his partizans', who are setting out to travel to Denmark. Even in 1805 when translating the half-line *blæd wide sprang* (line 18b) he avoids Thorkelín's error of interpreting *blæd* as 'blood', translating the half-line instead 'The fruit wide sprang', though he wrongly (if understandably) assumes that the Beowulf to whom this phrase applies is the hero of the poem.

Short extracts from *Beowulf* were translated into English by Ebenezer Henderson in 1818, closely following Thorkelín's Latin version.[22] Then in 1826 came the first translation of selected portions of the poem into English verse, interspersed with plot summary, by John Josias Conybeare.[23] Conybeare adopts blank verse as his poetic form:

> List! We have learnt a tale of other years,
> Of kings and warrior Danes, a wondrous tale,
> How æthelings bore them in the brunt of war.[24]

---

[21] *The History of the Anglo-Saxons*, 3rd ed., III, 327.
[22] Henderson, *Iceland; or the Journal of a Residence in that Island during the Years 1814 and 1815*, II, 329–30; reprinted in Shippey and Haarder, *Beowulf: The Critical Heritage*, pp. 156–7.
[23] Conybeare, *Illustrations of Anglo-Saxon Poetry*; the work was published posthumously, Conybeare having died in 1824.
[24] *Illustrations*, p. 35.

Conybeare aims at literary fluency and elegance rather than word-for-word literalness. After his translation and summary he prints the Old English text of the translated passages accompanied by a literal rendering into Latin: for the opening three lines of the translation, as quoted above, he has

Hwæt we Gar-Dena	Aliquid nos de Bellicorum Danorum
In gear-dagum	In diebus antiquis
Þeod cyninga	Popularium regum
Þrym gefrunon,	Gloria accepimus,
Hu ða Æðelingas	Quomodo tunc principes
Ellen fremedon.	Virtute valuerint.[25]

In his verse translation rather than striving for literalness he seeks to convey the story of the poem and to bring extended passages from it to life in poetic Modern English. As Roy Liuzza has explained, his use of blank verse brings a classical feel to the translation and renders the original poem acceptable to an early-nineteenth-century audience, with Conybeare accommodating it to the taste of his readers by recasting it so as to release it from what he refers to as the 'barbarisms and obscurity of the language' and the 'shackles of a metrical system at once of extreme difficulty, and, to our ears at least, totally destitute of harmony and expression'.[26] For Conybeare, *Beowulf* is worthy of being brought to the attention of his contemporaries, however: in it can be found 'many of those which have in all ages been admitted as the genuine elements of poetic composition'.[27] The translation was praised by Isaac D'Israeli, father of Benjamin, in 1841 – 'Conybeare's poetical version remains unrivalled' – though D'Israeli also draws attention to the extent of the recasting involved in Conybeare's approach to this 'primitive' poetry: 'But if a literal version of primitive poetry soon ceases to be poetry, so likewise, if the rude outlines are to be retouched, and a brilliant colouring is to be borrowed, we are receiving Anglo-Saxon poetry in the cadences of Milton and the "orient hues" of Gray.'[28]

Also evident in the translation is Conybeare's uncertain grasp of the sense of the Old English, reflective of the state of knowledge of the language of the poem at this time, though his understanding is an advance on that of Thorkelín and Turner: he even hits on the import of the opening *Hwæt* (though not translating it properly in his Latin literal version).[29]

---

[25] *Illustrations*, p. 82. We might translate Conybeare's Latin as follows: 'We have heard something concerning the glory of the kings of the people of the warlike Danes in ancient days, how the princes then were strong in their courage.'
[26] Conybeare, *Illustrations*, pp. 80–1; quoted by Liuzza, 'Lost in Translation', pp. 285–6.
[27] *Illustrations*, p. 81.
[28] D'Israeli, *Amenities of Literature*, I, 57.
[29] In the notes that accompany his Old English text and Latin translation Conybeare comments on *Hwæt we* (p. 82): 'There is a little abruptness, if not obscurity, in this sentence; the same use of "Hwæt" will be found in Canto 24, l. 3 [line 1652]. It somewhat resembles the *H ōn* of Hesiod' (i.e., an exclamation calling for silence).

Conybeare's treatment of narrative is illustrated in his rendering of the passage in which Beowulf first hears news of Grendel's attacks:

> Such tidings of the Grendel and his deeds
> The Goths' high chief, the thane of Higelac, learn't;
> He that was the strongest of the sons of men.
> And soon that noble soldier bad array
> A goodly ship of strength. The hero spoke
> His brave intent, far o'er the sea-bird's path
> To seek the monarch at his hour of need.[30]

Conybeare may be regarded as the first English popularizer of *Beowulf* (for an educated readership, of course), carefully tailoring it to suit his own taste and that of his readership. As Tom Shippey notes, his *Illustrations* was 'the source from which British readers continued to draw their knowledge of the poem for some time'.[31]

Thorkelín's edition of *Beowulf* was immediately perceived to be highly inadequate. Conybeare collated Thorkelín's edited text with the manuscript in 1817 and corrected it extensively (he also corrected the translation), going on to use this collation, which was itself far from free of errors, for his *Illustrations of Anglo-Saxon Poetry*. Error-tracking collations of Thorkelín's edited text and the *Beowulf* manuscript were also made by Frederic Madden (1824), N. F. S. Gruntvig (1831) and Benjamin Thorpe (1830), the latter providing the basis for Thorpe's own later edition of the poem (1855).[32] Thorkelín's edition was finally superseded by the much more scholarly edition of John Mitchell Kemble (1833), the pioneering exponent of Germanic philology in England.[33] Kemble's edition is dedicated to 'James Grimm' and applies the principles of the new language science. Of the unfortunate *editio princeps* Kemble writes scathingly, 'not five lines of Thorkelín's edition can be found in succession, in which some gross fault, either in the transcript or the translation, does not betray the editor's utter ignorance of the Anglo-Saxon language'.[34] He also takes a sideswipe at the translations of Turner and Conybeare on the way past: 'Even the works of Mr. Turner and Professor Conybeare, although in some respects immeasurably superior to Thorkelín's, are marked with mistranslations and false readings of no light kind.'[35] Kemble's edition was based on his own transcription of the poem. J. R. Hall notes that whereas Thorkelín has nearly 300 letter-errors in the first 500 long

---

[30] *Illustrations*, p. 38, corresponding to *Beowulf*, lines 194–201.
[31] Shippey, 'Introduction', p. 27.
[32] See J. R. Hall, 'Anglo-Saxon Studies in the Nineteenth Century', p. 246; for Conybeare's and Madden's collations, see Kiernan, *Electronic Beowulf*. On Thorpe's edition (and translation), see above, p. 15.
[33] Kemble, ed., *The Anglo-Saxon Poems of Beowulf, The Travellers Song and The Battle of Finnesburg*; on Kemble's edition, see J. R. Hall, 'The First Two Editions of *Beowulf*'.
[34] Kemble, *The Anglo-Saxon Poems*, pp. xxix–xxx.
[35] *The Anglo-Saxon Poems*, p. xxx.

lines of *Beowulf*, Kemble has only twenty-one, a mark of the advance in editing that his edition represents.[36]

Kemble was a philologist and also a leading representative of the 'Saxonism' of the earlier nineteenth century, following Turner in embracing values and traditions associated with the Anglo-Saxon world.[37] For Kemble, as for Turner, the Anglo-Saxon period was an originary one: 'the childhood of our own age, – the explanation of its manhood'.[38] *Beowulf* might be 'rude' but it presents 'a very faithful picture' of that originary period.[39]

As philological study advanced, Kemble's edition would itself soon be superseded by others, of which the most influential were produced in Germany, which was of course very much the centre of gravity of philology in the nineteenth century and the setting for a veritable industry of scholarship. In 1863 appeared Moritz Heyne's authoritative edition, soon to become a standard and much reprinted and revised down the generations; Heyne's edition circulated along with others from such heavyweights as Grein (1857–8, 1867), Ettmüller (1875), Holder (1881–4) and, after the turn of the century, Holthausen (1905–6).[40] Ettmüller and Grein were also the first translators of *Beowulf* into German (in 1840 and 1857, respectively), both adopting alliterating stress-based metre as their medium.[41]

Kemble's revised edition of his *Beowulf* (1835–7) included a close translation of the poem into English prose, the first full translation into English; I provided a short quotation from this in Chapter 1.[42] Kemble intended his translation as an aid in interpreting *Beowulf* and aimed at literalness. To refer again to a passage from him quoted earlier, 'I was bound to give, word for word, the original in all its roughness', he wrote; 'I might have made it smoother, but I purposely avoided doing so.'[43] We saw earlier that, though literal in his approach, Kemble also strove to write literary prose, with a lightly archaizing style. The literary

---

[36] 'Anglo-Saxon Studies in the Nineteenth Century', p. 248.
[37] See Young, *The Idea of English Ethnicity*, pp. 33–7.
[38] Kemble, *The Saxons in England*, I, v.
[39] Kemble, *The Saxon Poems*, p. xxxii.
[40] Heyne, ed., *Beowulf. Mit ausführlichem Glossar*; Grein, ed., *Bibliothek der angelsächsischen Poesie*, I, 255–341, and *Beovulf nebst den Fragmenten Finnsburg und Valdere*; Ettmüller, ed., *Carmen de Beovulfi Gautarum regis rebus praeclare gestis atque interitu*; Holder, ed., *Beowulf*; Holthausen, ed., *Beowulf nebst dem Finnsburg-Bruchstück*.
[41] Ettmüller, trans., *Beowulf. Heldengedicht des achten Jahrhunderts*; Grein, trans., *Beowulf*. These translations were followed by versions by Simrock, *Beowulf. Das älteste deutsche Epos* (1859, in alliterating stress-metre), Heyne, *Beowulf. Angelsächsisches Heldengedicht* (1863, in iambic pentameter) and others (see Tinker, *The Translations of Beowulf*). Translations were also produced in French (Botkine, *Beowulf*, Épopée Anglo-Saxonne, 1877, in prose), Italian (Grion, 'Beovulf: poema epico anglosassone del vii secolo', 1883, in imitative metre), Swedish (Wickberg, *Beowulf, en fornengelsk hjältedikt*, 1889, in imitative metre) and Dutch (Simons, *Béowulf, Angelsaksisch Volksepos*, 1896, in iambic pentameter).
[42] See above, p. 14.
[43] Kemble, *A Translation of the Anglo-Saxon Poem of Beowulf*, p. l.

quality of the writing is already apparent in the opening lines of his translation, which hardly come across as rough (though the sentences are not well-formed classical ones):

> Lo! We have learned by tradition the majesty of the Gar-Danes, of the mighty kings in days of yore, how the noble men perfected valour. Oft did Scyld the son of Scéf tear the mead-thrones away from the hosts of his foes, from many tribes; the earl terrified them, after he first was found an outcast. He therefore abode in comfort, he waxed under the welkin, he flourished with dignities, until each one of the surrounding peoples over the whale's path, must obey him, must pay him tribute: That was a good king!

This reads well and in terms of sense it represents a striking advance on previous English translations. Apart from the troublesome *eorl* (line 6 of *Beowulf*), taken here to refer to Scyld, the translation is essentially a reliable one, based on a good text.

English verse translation in the nineteenth century

A number of other literal student-directed translations into English prose, intended as ancillary to the study of the original, but also archaizing in their style to some degree, appeared in the course of the nineteenth century, by Thorpe (1855), Arnold (1876) and Earle (1892);[44] Thorpe's and Arnold's translations accompanied their editions of the poem, while Earle's was a free-standing scholarly translation informed by the substantial progress in the textual study of *Beowulf* achieved by German scholars in the later nineteenth century. Further prose translations would appear in the opening years of the twentieth century, by J. R. Clark Hall (1901), Tinker (1902) and Child (1904).[45] As scholarly work on *Beowulf* developed and the poem consolidated its place as a university teaching-text, there was a steady demand for serviceable translations, which continued to improve in their accuracy and understanding of the poem and its poetics as the scholarship that they reflected advanced. They were not going to do much, however, to bring *Beowulf* into wider public consciousness.

Targeting a wider audience, English verse translation of *Beowulf* (i.e., of the whole poem, as opposed to extracts) began in 1849 with A. Diedrich Wackerbarth's version, in a ballad-like rhyming syllabic metre. In using a ballad-like metre Wackerbarth was taking a different tack from the classicizing Conybeare but, like Conybeare, he was appealing to the literary taste of the day. The result of his style of verse, however, is to give a completely false impression of the poetry of *Beowulf*, as he himself seems to have been uncomfortably conscious of: in his preface to the translation he writes,

---

[44] Thorpe, ed. and trans., *The Anglo-Saxon Poems*; Arnold, ed. and trans., *Beowulf, a Heroic Poem of the Eighth Century*; Earle, trans., *The Deeds of Beowulf*.
[45] J. R. Clark Hall, trans., *Beowulf and the Fight at Finnsburg*; Tinker, trans., *Beowulf*; Child, *Beowulf and the Finnesburh Fragment*.

Some may ask why I have not preserved the Anglo-Saxon alliterative Metre. My Reason is that I do not think the Taste of the English People would at present bear it. I wish to get my book read, that my Countrymen may become generally acquainted with the Epic of our Ancestors wherewith they have been generally unacquainted [. . .]. Still, if the literary Bent of this Country should continue for some few Years longer the Course it has of late Years pursued, it will be time to give this Poem to the English People in English alliterative Metre, and I shall be thankful to see it done.[46]

Wackerbarth, Professor of Anglo-Saxon at the Catholic college St Mary's, Oscott,[47] based his translation on the edition of Kemble – 'this accurate and beautiful Edition cannot be too highly valued'[48] – which gave him a sounder text to work with than had been available previously. He began work soon after Kemble's edition came out but he explains that he proceeded very slowly with the translation 'on account of the Difficulty of the Work, and the utter Inadequacy of any then existing Dictionary'; he writes, 'I still however wrought my Way onward, under the Notion that even if I should not think my Book, when finished, fit for Publication, yet that the MS. would form an amusing Tale for my little Nephews and Nieces.'[49] This last remark suggests Wackerbarth's perception of the level of literature represented by *Beowulf*.

Wackerbarth sought an easy entertaining style, as did Lumsden in the next verse translation (1881), also in rhyming syllabic metre,[50] both of them turning *Beowulf* into metrical romance but neither, in doing so, having much impact in terms of raising the popular profile of the poem. Here is Wackerbarth in jaunty full swing, wreaking havoc on the sinister passage (lines 99–104) in which Grendel first comes to attack Heorot:

> Thus gallantly the Comrades fared,
>   Till one both stark and fell,
> Dark Deeds to perpetrate prepared, –
>   A ghastly Foe from Hell:
> And Grendel hight that Demon gaunt;
>   The Marches were his lonely Haunt,
> The Moor and Fen and Fastness' height
>   He held subjected to his Might.

The critic and clergyman Stopford Brooke, who himself included translated extracts from *Beowulf* in his *History of Early English Literature* (1892),[51] colour-

---

46 Wackerbarth, *Beowulf*, pp. ix–x.
47 Wackerbarth, an Anglican priest who converted to Catholicism, dedicated his translation to Nicholas Wiseman, soon to be Archbishop of Westminster and Cardinal; on Wackerbarth's life, see F. L. E., 'Obituary, Francis Diedrich Wackerbarth' (Wackerbarth adopted the name Athanasius on being received into the Catholic Church: hence the 'A.' in the byline of his *Beowulf* translation).
48 Wackerbarth, *Beowulf*, p. xii.
49 Wackerbarth, *Beowulf*, p. viii.
50 Lumsden, trans., *Beowulf, an Old English Poem*.
51 Brooke, *The History of Early English Literature*, I, 17–131.

fully dismisses this kind of verse translation. Discussing his own approach (and also rejecting prose translation), he writes,

> Translations of poetry are never much good, but at least they should always endeavour to have the musical movement of the poetry, and to obey the laws of the verse they translate. A translation made in any one of our existing rhyming metres seemed to me as much out of the question as a prose translation. None of these metres resemble those of Anglo-Saxon poetry, and, moreover, their associations would modernize old English thought. An Anglo-Saxon king in modern Court dress would not look more odd and miserable than an Anglo-Saxon poem in modern rhyming metre.[52]

Here Brooke, writing for a general audience rather than for scholars, and addressing some of the issues of translation theory and practice highlighted above in Chapter 1, advocates a 'foreignizing' approach, an approach that seeks to bring the reader to the poetry of the original rather than, like Wackerbarth and Lumsden, and indeed Conybeare with his blank verse,[53] the other way around. For Brooke, bringing the reader to the poetry means eschewing prose – 'A prose translation even when it reaches excellence, gives no idea whatever of that to which the ancient English listened'[54] – and using a kind of verse that 'resembles' that of the Old English. He still strives to make his translation readable, however.

Among the passages translated by Brooke is that describing the funeral of Scyld (lines 32–40a, 50b–2):

> There at haven stood, hung with rings, the ship,
> Ice-bright, for the outpath eager, craft of Æthelings!
> So their lord, the well-beloved, all at length they laid
> In the bosom of the bark, him the bracelet-giver, –
> By the mast the mighty king. Many gifts were there,
> Fretted things of fairness brought from far-off ways! –
> Never heard I of a keel hung more comelily about
> With the weeds of war, with the weapons of the battle,
> With the bills and byrnies [. . .]
> None of men can say,
> None of heroes under heaven, nor in the hall the rulers,

---

[52] *The History of Early English Literature*, I, ix. In the same year another verse translator of *Beowulf*, J. L. Hall, would ask, 'Is it proper, for instance, that the grave and solemn speeches of Beowulf and Hrothgar be put in ballad measures, tripping lightly and airily along?' (J. L. Hall, *Beowulf, an Anglo-Saxon Poem*, p. viii).
[53] Brooke rejects blank verse as a medium for translating Old English poetry, 'as it is weighted with the sound of Shakespeare, Milton, or Tennyson, and this association takes the reader away from the atmosphere of early English poetry' (*The History of Early English Literature*, I, x); cf. Isaac D'Israeli's comments on Conybeare's selections in iambic pentameter, above, p. 49.
[54] *The History of Early English Literature*, I, x; Brooke continues (ibid.), 'The original form is destroyed, and with it our imagination of the world to which the poet sang, of the way he thought, of how he shaped his emotion.'

For a truthful truth, who took up that lading.⁵⁵

This contrasts radically with the rhyming of Wackerbarth and successfully takes over some of the features of Old English poetry – the compounding, the appositive syntax, a diction that is both stylized and inventive, a strong rhythmical-alliterative structure – but the verse comes across as pedestrian and limited in its expressive capacity. Here *comelily* and *for a truthful truth* are particularly feeble. Brooke writes, 'I felt myself then driven to invent a rhythmical movement which would enable me, while translating literally, to follow the changes, and to express, with some little approach to truth, the proper ebb and flow of Anglo-Saxon verse.'⁵⁶ This was a worthy aim but, eloquent preacher though he reputedly was,⁵⁷ Brooke was not equipped to bring it to fruition. It is interesting, however, to see him and other late-nineteenth-century translators struggling to find a suitable verse medium for their versions of *Beowulf*, beginning to recognize the need to adopt a stress metre in an age in which syllabic metre dominated.

The first full Modern English translation of *Beowulf* to make use of a stress-based metre was that of James M. Garnett (1882), a few years before Brooke's translated extracts. Garnett's was also the first translation to be published in the United States and it was much reprinted in the decades after its first publication.⁵⁸ The verse lines of the translation are made up of two half-lines, each having two accented syllables. Garnett instigates the tradition in English of using imitative metre for the translation of *Beowulf*, a tradition that would become the dominant one in future years. He does not imitate the alliterative component of Old English metre, however, employing alliteration only occasionally – as an effect rather than for structural purposes.

Garnett presents a version of *Beowulf* in verse but, unusually, combines this form with an emphatically literalist approach to the translation, following the Old English indeed in a word-for-word manner. His use of accentuation is unobtrusive, and the translation recalls Kemble's literal prose version of the poem. Again, as a sample, I quote the beginning of the Unferth episode (lines 499–505):

> Hunferth then spoke, the son of Ecglaf,
> Who at the feet sat of the lord of the Scyldings,
> Unloosed his war-secret (was the coming of Beowulf,
> The proud sea-farer, to him mickle grief,
> For that he granted not that any man else
> Ever more honor of this middle-earth
> Should gain under heaven than he himself).

---

55 *The History of Early English Literature*, I, 38.
56 *The History of Early English Literature*, I, x.
57 See Webb, 'Brooke, Stopford Augustus (1832–1916)'.
58 Garnett, trans., *Beowulf: An Anglo-Saxon Poem, and The Fight at Finnsburh.*

Garnett aims to get the best of both worlds, thereby hoping to aid the student working with the Old English text but also to interest the general reader. The result is a curious kind of overwrought prose-poetry in a curious kind of English, with much disruption of normal modern English word order, frequent lack of clarity in expression and – as with other translators – an evident fondness for archaizing diction. Tinker complains that 'it is hard to read the lines as anything but prose,'[59] a comment that has considerable justification, though there is a distinctive underlying rhythmic structure to the lines which may be seen as qualifying the writing as verse, of a cumbersome kind. Garnett accepts that his translation 'lacks smoothness' but he perceives the original as lacking smoothness as well and thinks that his verse gives 'a better idea of the poem than a mere prose version would do'.[60] He adds, 'While it would have been easy, by means of periphrasis and freer translation, to mend some of the defects chargeable to the line-for-line form, the translation would have lacked literalness, which I regarded as the most important object.'[61] In terms of our discussion in the opening chapter, Garnett offers a translation which in its literalness is also foreignizing.

A decade later J. L. Hall published another verse version, the second to be published in America.[62] Like Garnett's version (which Hall praises[63]), Hall's adopts a stress metre but softens the strangeness of this for his readers by accompanying it with a syllabic metrical effect. He writes in his preface, 'In order to please the larger class of readers, a regular cadence has been used, a measure which, while retaining the essential characteristics of the original, permits the reader to see ahead of him in reading';[64] he goes on to observe that his cadences 'closely resemble those used by Browning in some of his most striking poems.'[65] Hall is generally freer than Garnett in his approach to translation, not attempting the kind of literalism that we have seen in the latter translator. Hall's verse is also insistently alliterative, the first of its kind among (complete) *Beowulf* translations in English: Wackerbarth would perhaps have been 'thankful to see it done'.

Hall's translation (submitted at Johns Hopkins for the degree of PhD) was addressed to the scholar but also to the member of that 'larger class of readers', the student of English literature, 'giving him, in modern garb, the most ancient epic of our race'.[66] Hall's approach is illustrated in a vivid passage from the fight with Grendel (lines 813–19a; p. 29, lines 21–7 in Hall's lineation):

> But Higelac's hardy henchman and kinsman
> Held him by the hand; hateful to other
> Was each one if living. A body-wound suffered

---

[59] Tinker, *The Translations of Beowulf*, p. 86.
[60] Garnett, *Beowulf*, p. xi.
[61] Ibid.
[62] See n. 52, above.
[63] J. L. Hall, *Beowulf*, p. viii.
[64] Hall, *Beowulf*, p. vii.
[65] Hall, *Beowulf*, p. viii.
[66] Hall, *Beowulf*, p. vii.

> The direful demon, damage incurable
> Was seen on his shoulder, his sinews were shivered,
> His body did burst. To Beowulf was given
> Glory in battle.

The translation, comparable in technique to that of Brooke, adopts a somewhat foreignizing approach, achieved through the use of alliteration, inversion of word order and heightened diction, but Hall manages to combine this approach with a reasonable degree of readability, though the expression is often strained and curious, as in the translation of lines 196–9a (Hall, p. 8, lines 6–10):

> So Higelac's liegeman,
> Good amid Geatmen, of Grendel's achievements
> Heard in his home: of heroes then living
> He was stoutest and strongest, sturdy and noble.
> He bade them prepare him a bark that was trusty.

This passage also nicely illustrates Hall's use of 'cadence'.

The last translation of *Beowulf* into English verse in the nineteenth century was that of William Morris. In his self-consciously medievalizing translation of 1895 Morris too employs both a stress-based metre and structural alliteration, but he carries the foreignizing approach much further than any previous translator.[67] Morris's version is unlike any other, hitting the reader between the eyes in suggesting the otherness of *Beowulf*. It does so, it has to be admitted, at the expense of making *Beowulf* into something of a lumbering oddity, awkward and unwieldy. The opening lines (quoted at greater length above) give a flavour of Morris's style:

> What! We of the Spear-Danes of yore, so was it
> That we learn'd of the fair fame of the kings of the folks
> And the Athelings a-faring in framing of valour.

Morris's translation was praised in some quarters when it first came out. For Theodore Watts, writing in the *Athenaeum*, Morris's 'sympathy with the Old English temper is nothing less than marvellous'.[68] Watts takes up a familiar theme when he declares that the translation 'will seem uncouth to the general reader whose ear is familiar only with the quantitative scansion of classic movements and the accentual prosody of modern rhyme and blank verse', but for Watts such criticism is misplaced: 'But if the business of the translator is to pour the old wine into the new bottles with as little loss as possible of its original aroma, Mr Morris's efforts will have been crowned with entire success.'[69]

Few critics since, however, have found much to say in favour of Morris's *Beowulf*. Edwin Morgan's verdict is perhaps the harshest, describing it as 'disas-

---

[67] Morris and Wyatt, trans., *The Tale of Beowulf, Sometime King of the Weder Geats*.
[68] [Watts,] unsigned review, p. 386.
[69] [Watts,] unsigned review, p. 385.

trously bad, uncouth to the point of weirdness, unfairly inaccurate, and often more obscure than the original (hardly in fact a translation at all, since Morris "worked up" a prose paraphrase passed to him with increasing misgiving by the scholarly A. J. Wyatt).[70] Morgan presents a jaundiced survey of existing translations down to his own day, not having a good word to say about any of them, but his severest words are for Morris. Marijane Osborn is more understated but hardly less sympathetic in her criticism when she comments on the lines 'Ye twain in the waves' might / For seven nights swink'd. He outdid thee in swimming': 'This passage is relatively successful compared to many others in this version, the poet merely being led into "swink'd" by the alliterative "swimming"'.[71] Morris scholars have largely ignored the translation, though Jack Lindsay pauses to refer to it as 'one of his least successful productions'; Fiona MacCarthy declares, 'Few people have had a good word to say for Morris's *Beowulf* (least of all in Oxford). I will not attempt one. It is Morris at his most garrulous and loose.'[72]

A number of recent articles, by Robert Boenig, Roy Liuzza and Chris Jones,[73] and an earlier one, by P. M. Tilling,[74] adopt more sympathetic attitudes to Morris's version. Boenig argues for its importance for Morris's development as a writer of prose romance (though it was one of the very last things Morris wrote) and insists on the appropriateness of archaizing effects in its vocabulary and syntax – 'for the original poem attempts in its own way to archaize'[75] – and he praises the translation's balance of accuracy and poetic excitement. Liuzza and Jones consider Morris's *Beowulf* in the context of its cultural setting and of Morris's perception of the original poem. Jones brings out aspects of the language ideology of the time, referring to 'nativist' pro-Anglo-Saxon views in the nineteenth century, while Liuzza, noting that Morris had shown himself perfectly capable of translating Icelandic sagas in a direct and straightforward way, sees Morris in his *Beowulf* translation as 'apparently trying to recreate the experience of reading *Beowulf* in the depth of its history, across the centuries that separate it from us'. He observes, 'In effect he was trying to make distance itself into an aesthetic category, to respect and recreate the strangeness of the reading encounter with an ancient poem.'[76] Liuzza acknowledges the bizarreness of the translation, however, and finds it 'almost unintelligible in places', and even Boenig admits that there are 'problems' with it.[77]

---

[70] Morgan, *Beowulf*, p. vii.
[71] Osborn, 'Translations, Versions, Illustrations', p. 349.
[72] Lindsay, *William Morris: His Life and Work*, p. 365; MacCarthy, *William Morris: A Life for our Time*, p. 649.
[73] Boenig, 'The Importance of Morris's *Beowulf*'; Liuzza, 'Lost in Translation'; Chris Jones, 'The Reception of William Morris's *Beowulf*'.
[74] Tilling, 'William Morris's Translation of *Beowulf*: Studies in his Vocabulary'.
[75] 'The Importance of Morris's *Beowulf*', p. 11.
[76] 'Lost in Translation', p. 293.
[77] 'Lost in Translation', p. 291; 'The Importance of Morris's *Beowulf*', p. 7.

Both Boenig and Liuzza were anticipated in some of their conclusions by Tilling, though the latter takes a different line from Liuzza in his consideration of Morris's saga translations ('using consciously archaic words [. . .] reasonably accurate, but often difficult to read').[78] Tilling analyses the principles and methods of the *Beowulf* translation, with particular reference to vocabulary, and shows that Morris was trying to recreate the text as closely as possible for his modern readers: the translation 'cannot be judged a complete success', admits Tilling, but it 'repays study because it is a serious attempt, by a literary figure of some consequence, to convey to his readers something of the nature of the text, as well as the meaning, of a great poem from their culture'.[79]

With regard to the point about Morris's saga translations, it is useful to quote a short extract from his version of *Volsunga Saga*, on which he collaborated with Eiríkr Magnússon. The passage is from the climax of the Sigmund–Signy story, where Sigmund and his son Sinfjotli arrive at the stronghold of King Siggeir, husband of their sister Signy, intending to kill the king in an act of vengeance. The avengers are accidentally discovered in their hiding place by one of the two young sons of Siggeir and Signy, who

> beholds withal where two men are sitting, big and grimly to look on, with overhanging helms and bright white byrnies; so he runs up the hall to his father, and tells him of the sight he has seen, and thereat the king misdoubts of some guile abiding him; but Signy heard their speech, and arose and took both the children, and went out into the porch to them and said:
> 'Lo ye! These younglings have bewrayed you; come now therefore and slay them!'
> Sigmund says, 'Never will I slay thy children for telling of where I lay hid'.
> But Sinfjotli made little enow of it, but drew his sword and slew them both, and cast them into the hall at King Siggeir's feet.[80]

In this vigorous and graphic passage the translation is literal, to the extent indeed of unidiomatically preserving the shifting tenses of the original, and the diction is archaic and stilted. The passage is hardly 'straightforward' but neither is it difficult to read. Similar stylistic features are apparent in the Morris/Magnússon translation of *Grettis Saga*, as illustrated, for example, by a short extract from the account of Grettir's fight with Glam, another vigorously descriptive passage, and of course a famous analogue to the Beowulf-and-Grendel episode in *Beowulf*:

> Now Glam gathered up his strength and knit Grettir towards him when they came to the outer door; but when Grettir saw that he might not set his feet against that, all of a sudden in one rush he drave his hardest against the thrall's breast, and spurned both feet against the half-sunken stone that stood in the threshold of the door, so that his shoulders caught the upper door-case, and the roof burst

---

78 Tilling, 'William Morris's Translation of *Beowulf*', p. 165; on Morris's translations from Old Norse, see further Quirk, 'Dasent, Morris and Principles of Translation'; see also Swannell, 'William Morris as an Interpreter of Old Norse'.
79 'William Morris's Translation of *Beowulf*', p. 174.
80 Morris and Magnússon, trans., *Völsunga Saga*, p. 304.

asunder, both rafters and frozen thatch, and therewith he fell open-armed aback out of the house, and Grettir over him.

Bright moonlight was there without, and the drift was broken, now drawn over the moon, now driven from off her; and, even as Glam fell, a cloud was driven from the moon, and Glam glared up against her. And Grettir himself says that by that sight only was he dismayed amidst all that he ever saw.[81]

Notably here, in a move that eschews strict literalness, Morris 'feminizes' the word moon, which in Old Norse is a neuter noun.

And Morris's (and Magnússon's) translations of Old Norse heroic poetry reflect the same kind of approach as the prose translations, as in the opening two stanzas of *The Song of Atli*:

> In days long gone
> Sent Atli to Gunnar
> A crafty one riding,
> Knefrud men called him;
> To Giuki's garth came he,
> To the hall of Gunnar,
> To the benches gay-dight,
> And the gladsome drinking.
>
> There drank the great folk
> 'Mid the guileful one's silence,
> Drank wine in their fair hall:
> The Huns' wrath they feared,
> When Knefrud cried
> In his cold voice,
> As he sat on the high seat,
> That man of the southland.[82]

Morris medievalizes his language and preserves the laconicism of the original, though he does not imitate closely its metrical form with its structural alliteration and insistent stress pattern. In his verse and prose translations from the Old Norse, done about twenty-five years before the *Beowulf*, Morris like other romantically influenced nineteenth-century translators, combines medievalizing with fluency.

In the *Beowulf* he carries the medievalizing further and boldly sacrifices fluency in pursuit of otherness. One other passage for comparison may serve to suggest the distinctiveness of the *Beowulf* translation. Morris also produced a verse translation of the *Aeneid*, the first edition of which appeared in 1875. Virgil's famous opening lines are Englished as follows:

> I sing of arms, I sing of him, who from the Trojan land
> Thrust forth by Fate, to Italy and that Lavinian strand
> First came: all tost about was he on earth and on the deep

---

[81] Morris and Magnússon, trans., *Grettis Saga*, pp. 89–90.
[82] Morris and Magnússon, trans., *The Song of Atli*, p. 446.

> By heavenly night for Juno's wrath, that had no mind to sleep:
> And plenteous war he underwent ere he his town might frame
> And set his Gods in Latian earth, whence is the Latin name,
> And father-folk of Alba-town, and walls of mighty Rome.
> Say, Muse, what wound of godhead was whereby all must come,
> How grieving, she, the Queen of Gods, a man so pious drave
> To win such toil, to welter on through such a troublous wave:
> – Can anger in immortal minds abide so fierce and fell?[83]

Morris is experimenting here too, notably in the length of his iambic line, which is heptameter, but he is experimenting in a manner far removed from what we find in his *Beowulf* of twenty years later. There is a poetic archaizing going on in the diction of his '*Aeneids*' (illustrated here particularly in *drave* and *fell*) and much poetic inversion of normal word order is apparent, but the register is insistently classical, the style is sweeping, with a notable cultivation of run-on lines, and the sentences are extended and hypotactic in structure.

Here, by contrast, is Morris's version of the hero's altercation with Unferth in *Beowulf*:

> Spake out then Unferth that bairn was of Ecglaf,
> And he sat at the feet of the lord of the Scyldings,
> He unbound the battle-rune; was Beowulf's faring,
> Of him the proud mere-farer, mickle unliking,
> Whereas he begrudg'd it of any man other
> That he glories more mighty the middle-garth over
> Should hold under heaven than he himself held:
> 'Art thou that Beowulf who won strife with Breca
> On the wide sea contending in swimming,
> When ye two for pride's sake search'd out the floods
> And for a dolt's cry into deep water
> Thrust both your life-days? No man the twain of you,
> Lief or loth were he, might lay wyte to stay you
> Your sorrowful journey, when on the sea row'd ye.'[84]

The archaizing is even more pronounced here, as is the manipulation of word order, and integral to the verse form is the insistent percussive rhythm with structural alliteration that, combined with these other features, gives the writing its strange uniqueness.

William Morris's translation of *Beowulf* was too uncompromising to contribute significantly to increasing interest in or understanding of *Beowulf* in the larger culture of the time, but it represents a striking experiment in literary medievalism even by the standards of the arch-medievalizer Morris, and it must be seen as a major artistic engagement with the Old English poem. Boenig ends his article finding himself wishing that Morris's *Beowulf* were available in paperback for contemporary readers so that he could use it with his students reading *Beowulf*

---

[83] Morris, *The Aeneids of Virgil*, p. 1.
[84] *The Tale of Beowulf*, p. 194.

in translation at the end of the twentieth century: 'They would thus come closer to encountering the original poem.'[85] One senses that using this translation to teach *Beowulf* today might not quite have the effect that Boenig desires. The translation teaches us a lot, though, about Morris's developing medievalism and about the literary context in which it was produced.

Perceptions of *Beowulf*

Wackerbarth referred to giving *Beowulf* to the English people. As mentioned above, however, the poem remained largely the preserve of scholars throughout most of the nineteenth century, as was the case with Old English literature in general. For example, in the popular anthology *Choice Specimens of English Literature*, published in 1864, *Beowulf* does not appear and indeed, in what is a volume of 526 pages, there are only three pages of Old English texts – twenty-three lines from the poem *Genesis (A)* and two short prose extracts.[86]

Among literary figures in the first half of the nineteenth century, *Beowulf* was discussed by Isaac D'Israeli, and a few lines of it had been translated by Tennyson (friend of J. M. Kemble) as early as 1830, who later would produce a translation of *The Battle of Brunanburh*.[87] Tennyson's translation of lines from *Beowulf* survives in a notebook held by the Houghton Library of Harvard University, reproduced here:

> Him the eldest
> Answered.
> The army's leader
> His wordhoard unlocked
> We are by race
> Gothic people
> And Higelac's
> Hearth ministers
> My father was
> To folk known[88]

Clearly using Conybeare's *Illustrations of Anglo-Saxon Poetry*, Tennyson has produced a literal word-for-word translation of the Old English passage (corresponding to lines 258–62 of *Beowulf*). In Conybeare he read,

Him se yldesta	*Ille senior*
Answarode,	*Respondebat,*
Werodes wisa	*Exercitus dux*
Word hord onleac.	*Orationis thesaurus reserabat.*
'We synt gumcynnes	*'Nos sumus ortu*
Geata leode,	*Gothica gens,*

---

[85] 'The Importance of Morris's *Beowulf*, p. 12.
[86] Smith, ed., *Choice Specimens of English Literature*.
[87] 'Battle of Brunanburh', ed. Ricks, *The Poems of Tennyson*, III, 18–23.
[88] MS Eng 952 (4), Houghton Library, Harvard University.

And Higelaces
Heorð geneatas.
Wæs min fæder
Folcum gecyðed.'

Et Higelaci
Familiares ministri.
Erat pater meus
Viris cognitus.'[89]

Tennyson is guided by Conybeare's Latin in some of his translation choices – *army's leader, ministers* – but he is certainly engaging with the Old English text itself and indeed reflects the original more directly than does Conybeare in using such words as *eldest, wordhoard, hearth* and *folk*. The translation is no more than a brief exercise but is worth considering here as the first Englishing of lines from *Beowulf* by a major literary figure. It would be fifty years before Tennyson returned to translating Old English poetry in his 'Battle of Brunanburh', a translation of great verve and imagination – in the view of Christopher Ricks, 'probably the best verse-translation of any Anglo-Saxon poetry'[90] – and a likely influence on William Morris.

Isaac D'Israeli, much influenced by Turner, has a dozen pages on *Beowulf* in the first volume of his three-volume *Amenities of Literature* (1841), in which he views it as a metrical romance coming from a primitive period of 'semi-civilisation', compares it to the works of Homer and presents a leisurely summary of its content down to the scene of Beowulf's dispute with Unferth. *Beowulf* may be primitive but for D'Israeli its hero 'appeals to nature and excites our imagination.[91] D'Israeli lost his eyesight as he worked on the *Amenities* and was assisted in writing it by his son Benjamin, who also brought out a new edition of the book in 1859, after the death of Isaac.[92]

Sixteen years after the publication of D'Israeli's *Amenities*, under the title 'A Primitive Old Epic', a prose summary of *Beowulf* appeared in the pages of *Household Words*, a popular weekly magazine edited ('conducted') by Charles Dickens.[93] There was no by-line to the piece but, as suggested by Nicholas Howe, the writer must have been Henry Morley, who was a staff-writer at the magazine at the time (and the most prolific contributor to its pages) and also an enthusiastic student of literary history.[94] Howe's suggestion is borne out by the fact that the *Household Words* summary is used verbatim by Morley in Volume I of his later

---

[89] Conybeare, *Illustrations*, p. 89. Note also Conybeare's verse translation of the same passage:
Him answering straight, the chieftain freely oped
The treasury of his speech: 'Our race and blood
Is of the Goth, and Higelac our lord:
My sire was known of no ignoble line.' (*Illustrations*, p. 40)
There is no sign of influence of this version in Tennyson's translation.
[90] Ricks, *Tennyson*, p. 292. See also Alexander, 'Tennyson's "Battle of Brunanburh"'; Irving, 'The Charge of the Light Brigade: Tennyson's *Battle of Brunanburh*'.
[91] D'Israeli, *Amenities of Literature*, I, 80–92, 'Beowulf; the Hero-Life', quotations at pp. 44 and 92, respectively.
[92] Disraeli, *Amenities of Literature*, 'Beowulf: the Hero-Life', I, 51–8.
[93] 'A Primitive Old Epic'.
[94] Howe, '*Beowulf* in the House of Dickens'.

English Writers, and he draws upon some of its wording again in his more reflective account of *Beowulf* in his *Sketches of Longer Works in English Verse and Prose* in the Cassell's Library of English Literature series.[95]

For Morley *Beowulf* might be an epic but it is also primitive. He introduces the summary of it as follows:

> The Celtic bards withdrew to the fastnesses of Britain, and with the conquering Saxons came the Gleemen, whose first songs related to the Sagas of the North. One primitive epic they brought with them, the tale of Beowulf, is the oldest story of which there is any trace in our literature, or in that of any kindred tongue. A lively picture of past customs, and a record of past manners of thought, it has been preserved for us in a single manuscript, now much defaced by fire, which seems to have been written in this country about eight hundred years ago.[96]

Morley goes on to acknowledge his indebtedness to Thorpe's edition and translation: 'Our version is much indebted for its faithfulness, always indirectly, often most directly, to Mr Thorpe's excellent edition of the Anglo-Saxon poem, to which a translation is attached, having the one fault, that it is into English of a Latin form.'[97] In the ensuing summary, though the prologue is omitted, the Danish part of the poem is covered in considerable detail (covering ten columns of print), to the extent of often reading like a paraphrase; the Geatish part is treated only perfunctorily (one column).

Morley was bringing the poem to the attention of a wide audience, as Wackerbarth and his verse-translating successors also sought to do, but it hardly entered into public consciousness to a significant degree. Morley, a leading figure in the rise of English studies, who later became Professor of English Language and Literature at King's College London and then at University College London,[98] also published a more detailed summary of the poem (as mentioned above) in his *Sketches of Longer Works in English Verse and Prose*, and he paid significant attention to *Beowulf* and other early literature in his historical survey *English Writers*. In the former of these popularizing works he intersperses his prose summary with passages in imitative verse (though without structural alliteration); in the latter he includes a survey of the history of the study and translation of *Beowulf* down to his own time of writing.[99]

But it was not until the criticism of writers like Bernhard ten Brink (translated from the German) and Stopford Brooke at the very end of the century and after, that we see the beginnings of the wider appreciation that *Beowulf* was

---

[95] Henry Morley, *English Writers*, pp. 253–64; *Sketches of Longer Works in English Verse and Prose*, pp. 1–14.
[96] *Household Words*, 17, 459.
[97] Ibid.
[98] D. J. Palmer notes, 'To Henry Morley belongs the distinction of being the first to devote an academic career in England solely to English Studies' (Palmer, *The Rise of English Studies*, p. 50).
[99] *English Writers*, pp. 265–78. On Morley as a 'populariser of literature', see Hunter, 'Morley, Henry (1822–1894)'.

later to achieve. Brooke, while regretting that 'the poem is lamentably destitute of form' (a common critical perception until much later) and that its dialogue is 'without much imagination', included detailed treatment of *Beowulf* in his *History of Early English Literature* and provided extensive selections from the poem in translation (in an archaizing alliterative metre, as we have seen).[100] Ten Brink declares that *Beowulf* is not a national poem or an epos, since '[s]uch poems arise only among nations that victoriously maintain ideals of higher culture against inimical forces', but he goes on to insist, 'If *Beowulf* is no national poem and no epos in the strict sense, taking matter and composition into account, yet, as regards style and tone, character and customs, it is both in a high degree. [...] A great wealth of poetic feeling is revealed in this poem.'[101] *Beowulf* gets an entry in the *Encyclopædia Britannica* for the first time in 1910 (by Henry Bradley).[102]

In this context of growing appreciation of *Beowulf* John R. Clark Hall produced his two translations, a prose one in 1901 and a verse one in 1914.[103] In the introduction to the prose translation, he declares *Beowulf* to be a poem 'of no mean order' but it is also 'the poem of a nation's childhood',[104] in which the poet shows 'crudity and clumsiness and want of resource in handling the material' and tells his story 'very much as a child would tell it.'[105] Hall is equally half-hearted about the literary qualities of *Beowulf* in the introduction to his verse translation:

> The poem of *Beowulf* is of the highest interest to English people [...]. Apart from this, and from its value as a unique source of information as to the social conditions of our ancestors in their continental home before they migrated hither, it has sufficient literary merit to be well worth reading for its own sake. It is very uneven, to be sure – it sinks every now and then to the level of the dullest prose, and has the prolixity which is characteristic of a primitive and leisurely age – but for the most part it is thoroughly good stuff.[106]

Ameliorating the perceived crudity and clumsiness of the original, Hall's verse translation aims at 'the smoothness necessary to make the poem attractive to

---

100 Brooke, *The History of Early English Literature*, I, 17–131 (quotations at p. 102). On Brooke, see esp. Haarder, *Beowulf: The Appeal of a Poem*, pp. 111–16.
101 Ten Brink, *History of English Literature*, I, *To Wyclif*, p. 28.
102 Bradley, '*Beowulf*', *Encyclopædia Britannica* (11th ed.); see Shippey, 'Introduction', *Beowulf: The Critical Heritage*, p. 67.
103 On these, see above, pp. 15–6.
104 J. R. Clark Hall, *Beowulf* (prose), p. xx; cf. Kemble's characterization of Anglo-Saxon history in general: 'The subject is a grave and solemn one : it is the history of the childhood of our own age, – the explanation of its manhood' (Kemble, *The Saxons in England*, I, v).
105 J. R. Clark Hall, *Beowulf* (prose), pp. xvii, xviii. The perceived childishness of *Beowulf* is also reflected in Wackerbarth's view of his translation of it as representing 'an amusing Tale for my little Nephews and Nieces' (quoted above, p. 53). Turner had compared the style of Old English poetry to the kind of language evident in the efforts of 'our children' (*The History of the Anglo-Saxons*, 3rd ed., III, 160).
106 J. R. Clark Hall, *Beowulf* (verse), p. ix.

modern ears',[107] and so though adopting a four-stress line he largely dispenses with alliteration:

> Lo! We have heard tell how mighty the kings
> of the Spear-bearing Danes were in days that are past,
> how these men of high birth did valorous deeds.

He also criticizes previous translations for being too archaic in diction, but he himself, among numerous other examples of archaism, refers to Scyld, who 'took mead-benches oft / from parties of foemen' (lines 4–5) and who 'waxed under the welkin' (line 8). Overall, the translation reads as laboured and uninspired, which is hardly untypical of the bigger picture of early translations of *Beowulf*.

Before this period of wider appreciation when *Beowulf* was getting (albeit highly qualified) praise from literary critics, it was essentially scholars and their students who had knowledge of the poem. As we have seen, they were painfully conscious of the roughness of its poetry but they were interested in it as presenting, in Sharon Turner's words, 'a picture of the manners' and 'an exhibition of the feelings and notions' of the ancient past. One of the early reviewers of Thorkelín, the Germanist William Taylor, writing in 1816, reflects this perception when he describes *Beowulf* as a 'curious production' throwing light on 'the manners and spirit of the Gothic north', a poem which 'may no doubt be applied to the discovery of historical truth'. Taylor waxes lyrical at the end of his piece when he extols *Beowulf*, in words that it is hard to resist quoting, as 'the most brilliant coruscation of the boreal dawn of literature'.[108]

And in the period of romantic 'nation forging' of the nineteenth century (to appropriate Linda Colley's suggestive phrase[109]), scholars saw *Beowulf* as a foundational monument. As Allen Frantzen says of its early reception, 'Early scholars saw *Beowulf* as a record of English Germanic origins and mined it for evidence of the heroic civilization that distinguished the Anglo-Saxon past.'[110] The cultural appropriation of *Beowulf* was by no means confined to English writers. Thorkelín had entitled his edition of *Beowulf*, *Poema Danicum dialecto Anglosaxonica*, 'A Danish Poem in Anglo-Saxon Dialect', thereby seeking to claim the poem for his adopted homeland.[111] He regarded *Beowulf* as a Danish poem translated into

---

[107] J. R. Clark Hall, *Beowulf* (verse), p. x.
[108] [Taylor,] *The Monthly Review*; reprinted in Shippey and Haarder, *Beowulf: The Critical Heritage*, pp. 132–6 (quotations at p. 136).
[109] Colley, *Britons: Forging the Nation 1707–1837*.
[110] Frantzen, *Desire for Origins*, p. 195.
[111] Sharon Turner was quick to retort, '[Thorkelín] is not entitled to claim it as a Danish poem; it is pure Anglo-Saxon; and though I grant that the Anglo-Saxon language is very like that of the old Icelandic poetry which has survived, yet it is a similarity with great idiomatic and verbal differences. It is by no means identity' (*The History of the Anglo-Saxons*, 3rd ed., III, 326–7, n. 2).

Anglo-Saxon, perhaps by King Alfred, with Christian references creeping in as part of the process of translation.[112]

German scholars and translators assumed that *Beowulf* belonged to the national heritage of Germany and embraced it with increasing fervour. Thus, for Heinrich Leo, Anglo-Saxon was 'a *German* dialect in the strictest sense of the word'.[113] Leo's 1839 study of *Beowulf* was entitled *Beowulf, das älteste deutsche, in angelsächsischer Mundart erhaltene, Heldengedicht*, '*Beowulf*, the oldest German heroic poem, preserved in Anglo-Saxon dialect',[114] and the view that *Beowulf* is the oldest German epic is also reflected in the titles of the translations of Simrock (1859) and von Wolzogen (1872), *Das älteste deutsche Epos* and *Das älteste deutsche Heldengedicht*, respectively.[115] Tom Shippey writes of the project of German philologists to construct 'a national ancestral culture' and comments that in nineteenth-century German treatments of *Beowulf* one can see patriotism turning increasingly to aggressive nationalism; and racism is not far away'.[116]

Beowulf also struck a nationalistic chord in England, at least for the select constituency that knew about it. Shippey notes that among English commentators there is little of the fervour of German pronouncements and he suggests that 'the comparative lack of nationalist feeling shown by English scholars can be attributed to the nineteenth-century suppression of specifically English sentiment in the interest of an ideology of British unity'.[117] There was plenty of English sentiment around, however, and, in this context, English scholars were proud of their *Beowulf*, introducing a distinctly nationalistic note into some of their discussions of it. In 1820 Turner expressed his chagrin that *Beowulf* had not been first printed in England: 'our antiquarian patriotism may be blamed that, when so much labour and money have been applied to print, at the public expence, so many ancient remains, and some of such little utility, we should have left this curious relic of our ancestors to have been first printed by a foreigner, in a foreign country'.[118] As J. R. Hall notes, in 1824 Frederic Madden too lamented the fact that the only edition of *Beowulf* that had by then been published was 'by a *foreigner*'.[119] Isaac D'Israeli, noting that the Danes, among whom 'the patri-

---

[112] J. R. Hall, 'The First Two Editions of *Beowulf*', p. 242. For a brief overview of nationalist appropriations of *Beowulf* in the nineteenth century, see also David, 'The Nationalities of *Beowulf*: Anglo-Saxon Attitudes'.
[113] Leo, *Altsächsische und angelsächsische Sprachproben*, p. xi ('eine deutsche Mundart im engsten Sinne des Wortes'), quoted by Eric Stanley, *The Search for Anglo-Saxon Paganism*, p. 8.
[114] Leo, ed., *Beowulf, das älteste deutsche, in angelsächsischer Mundart erhaltene, Heldengedicht*.
[115] Simrock, trans., *Beowulf. Das älteste deutsche Epos*; von Wolzogen, trans., *Beovulf (Bärwelf). Das älteste deutsche Heldengedicht*.
[116] Shippey, 'Introduction', pp. 37, 71; see further John Hill, '*Beowulf* Editions for the Ancestors'.
[117] Shippey, 'Introduction', p. 74.
[118] Turner, *The History of the Anglo-Saxons*, 3rd ed., III, 326.
[119] J. R. Hall, 'Anglo-Saxon Studies in the Nineteenth Century', p. 435.

otism of literature is ardent', had claimed *Beowulf* as their own, expressed gratitude to Kemble for producing an English edition of the poem: 'Mr Kemble has redeemed our honour by publishing a collated edition, afterwards corrected in a second with a literal version.'[120]

Wackerbarth described *Beowulf* as 'the Epic of our Ancestors' (as quoted above) and later John R. Clark Hall (also quoted above) spoke in similar terms. For Henry Morley, *Beowulf*, along with Cædmon's 'Paraphrase' (the biblical poems of the Junius Manuscript), represents worthily the beginning of English literature: '[These] two noblest pieces of First-English are also the most ancient, and stand worthily at the beginning of a literature that represents, without a break, the life and labour of the people of this country for twelve hundred years.'[121] Stopford Brooke declares, 'The poem is great in its own way, and the way is an English way. The men, the women, at home and in war, are one in character with us. It is our Genesis, the book of our origins.'[122] The fact that Brooke was born near Letterkenny in County Donegal is no impediment to his embracing an English identity in which he perceives *Beowulf* to be intimately implicated. For Brooke, Beowulf himself epitomizes the ideal of manhood that has been found throughout English history. Beowulf might have been a Geat but his poem is English – 'we may fairly claim the poem as English'[123] – and Beowulf's qualities 'represent the ancient English ideal, the manhood which pleased the English folk even before they came to Britain; and because, in all our history since Beowulf's time, for 1200 years or so, they have been repeated in the lives of English warriors by land and sea whom we chiefly honour.'[124] Brooke particularly compares Beowulf to Lord Nelson: 'Gentle like Nelson, he had Nelson's iron resolution.'[125]

Referring to Old English poetry more widely, Brooke discerns in it 'that steady consistency of national character, that clinging through all difficulty to the aim in view, that unrelenting curiosity, that desire to do better what has been done.'[126] Brooke's pronouncements represent classic expressions of the racial myth of Englishness which flourished in the nineteenth century.[127] As noted above, he himself was born in Ireland, a biographical detail that illustrates the aspect of

---

[120] D'Israeli, *Amenities of Literature*, I, 91; D'Israeli goes on (ibid.) to express his views about Kemble's translation, criticizing its literalness: 'Such versions may supply the wants of the philologist, but for the general reader they are doomed to read like vocabularies.'
[121] Morley, *Sketches of Longer Works*, p. 14.
[122] Brooke, *English Literature from the Beginning to the Conquest*, p. 83.
[123] Brooke, *The History of Early English Literature*, I, 25.
[124] *The History of Early English Literature*, I, 31.
[125] *The History of Early English Literature*, I, 29; see also his *English Literature from the Beginning to the Norman Conquest*, p. 63.
[126] Brooke, *The History of Early English Literature*, I, vii.
[127] See MacDougall, *Racial Myth in English History: Trojans, Teutons, and Anglo-Saxons*; MacDougall points to four postulates of this myth in its most highly developed form: the inherent superiority of Germanic peoples, both in character and in their institutions; the Germanic origin of the English people; the unparalleled freedom of English political and religious institutions, which is inherited from Germanic forefathers; the burden of world

inclusiveness that has been seen to characterize constructions of Englishness in the last third of the century. As Robert Young puts it, 'Englishness became something inclusive, defined not in terms of autochthonous origins attached to a particular place, and only very generally in terms of origin.'[128] Brooke can invoke 'a common racial and cultural origin in the Anglo-Saxons,'[129] with which he can identify culturally, defining himself as English and celebrating *Beowulf* as a foundational expression of essential English qualities.

American investment in things Anglo-Saxon began with Thomas Jefferson and continued with the teaching of Old English in a few universities from the 1820s. Jefferson didn't know *Beowulf* but he idealized the pre-Norman age and he considered that the American colonists were the 'true heirs of the Anglo-Saxon heritage of constitutional liberty'.[130] He even proposed having images of Hengist and Horsa, mythic founders of Anglo-Saxon England, on the Great Seal of the United States.[131] The 'father of the University of Virginia', as his epitaph has it, Jefferson wrote a grammar of Old English and included 'Anglo-Saxon' on the curriculum that he designed for the new university, thus initiating the history of Old English as an academic subject in America.[132]

Influenced by German philological scholarship but looking to early England for America's racial heritage, American scholars increasingly embraced the study of Old English as the nineteenth century went on, so that 'by the end of the century America had developed a strong tradition of Anglo-Saxon scholarship'.[133] Unlike most of their British contemporaries, American literary figures also took an interest: as J. R. Hall summarizes, 'Henry Wadsworth Longfellow composed a long essay on Anglo-Saxon literature, David Thoreau ventured to capture its spirit in verse, James Russell Lowell praised its "homespun" diction, and Walt Whitman celebrated it – along with himself.'[134]

It is worth pausing particularly on Longfellow, who in that 'long essay on Anglo-Saxon literature' (published in 1838) wrote on *Beowulf* at some length and translated almost seventy lines of it (all of Fitt 3) into verse.[135] For Longfellow, *Beowulf*

leadership that the English bear since they, 'better than any other Germanic people, represent the traditional genius of their ancestors' (p. 2).
[128] Young, *The Idea of English Ethnicity*, p. 172.
[129] Young, *The Idea of English Ethnicity*, p. 180.
[130] Bernstein, *Thomas Jefferson*, p. 24.
[131] See J. R. Hall, 'Mid-Nineteenth-Century American Anglo-Saxonism: The Question of Language', p. 133.
[132] On Jefferson and Old English, see further Hauer, 'Thomas Jefferson and the Anglo-Saxon Language'; Frantzen, *Desire for Origins*, pp. 203–7.
[133] J. R. Hall, 'Anglo-Saxon Studies in the Nineteenth Century', p. 448; see also Frantzen, *Desire for Origins*, pp. 207–13.
[134] Hall, 'Anglo-Saxon Studies in the Nineteenth Century', p. 448.
[135] [Longfellow,] 'Anglo-Saxon Literature', pp. 104–6; for the translation from *Beowulf*, see also *The Poetical Works of Henry Wadsworth Longfellow*, pp. 739–40.

is like a piece of armor; rusty and battered, and yet strong. From within comes a voice sepulchral, as if the ancient armor spoke, telling a simple, straight-forward narrative. [. . .] The style, likewise, is simple, – perhaps we should say, austere.[136]

Longfellow describes the passage he translates, in which Beowulf hears the news of Grendel's attacks and travels to Denmark, as having 'a high epic character'.[137] Warming to his subject, he exclaims, 'We can almost smell the brine, and hear the sea-breeze blow, and see the mainland stretch out its jutting promontories, those sea-noses (sæ-næssas), as the poet calls them, into the blue waters of the solemn main.'[138]

The translation begins,

> Thus then much care-worn
> the son of Healfden
> sorrowed evermore,
> nor might the prudent hero
> his woes avert.
> The war was too hard,
> too loath and longsome,
> that on the people came,
> dire wrath and grim,
> of night-woes the worst.
> This from home heard
> Higelac's Thane,
> good among the Goths,
> Grendel's deeds. (corresponding to lines 189–95)

Longfellow keeps close to the literal meaning of the Old English as he understands it (which is reasonably well), half-line by half-line. In doing so, he fears that his readers 'will see very little poetry in all this' but he urges them to follow the exhortation of Kemble, whose edition is among the publications he is reviewing, to judge *Beowulf* not by modern standards but those of the times it describes, viewing it as a 'rude but very faithful picture of an age [. . .] brave, generous and right-principled'.[139]

As mentioned above, the first full verse translations of *Beowulf* published in America were those of Garnett (1882) and J. L. Hall (1892). Garnett's version was aimed at 'the general reader' and for the 'aid of students of the poem'; Hall's, as noted earlier, was addressed to scholarly readers but also sought to interest the student of English literature, 'giving him, in modern garb, the most ancient epic of our race'.[140] These translations cater for a readership of students studying *Beowulf* and at the same time reflect a construction of American literary history

---

[136] Longfellow, 'Anglo-Saxon Literature', p. 102.
[137] Longfellow, 'Anglo-Saxon Literature', p. 104.
[138] Ibid.
[139] Longfellow, 'Anglo-Saxon Literature', p. 106.
[140] Garnett, *Beowulf*, Preface to Second Edition, p. xv; Hall, *Beowulf*, p. vii (see Tinker, *The Translations of Beowulf*, pp. 84, 95).

and American identity that places *Beowulf* at its beginning. *Beowulf* is the most ancient epic of 'our race'.

An American translation of *Beowulf* in literary prose was published by Tinker in 1902, 'as an attempt to make as simple and readable a version of the poem as is consistent with the character of the original',[141] followed by another by C. G. Child in 1904, and in 1909 Francis Gummere brought out his popular verse translation, based on a version of Old English metre, with alliteration, and abounding in archaism and poetic diction, a translation which is still available in print today and on the internet.[142] The opening lines give a flavour of his register and diction:

> LO, praise of the prowess of people-kings
> of spear-armed Danes, in days long sped,
> we have heard, and what honor the athelings won!
> Oft Scyld the Scefing from squadroned foes,
> from many a tribe, the mead-bench tore,
> awing the earls. Since erst he lay
> friendless, a foundling, fate repaid him:
> for he waxed under welkin, in wealth he throve,
> till before him the folk, both far and near,
> who house by the whale-path, heard his mandate,
> gave him gifts: a good king he!

Gummere in his stiff and mannered version is among those who have Scyld waxing under welkin (line 8), and later, as Scyld's funeral approaches, we read that 'In the roadstead rocked a ring-dight vessel' (line 32).

The Harvard Classics (1910) edition of Gummere's translation has an introductory note which refers to the Anglo-Saxons as 'our Teutonic ancestors', reflecting the perception about identity and origin widely evident in other American writers: 'When our Teutonic ancestors migrated to Britain from the Continent of Europe', states Gummere, 'they brought with them the heroic songs in which their minstrels were accustomed to celebrate the deeds of their kings and warriors.'[143] Some seventy years earlier Longfellow had written of 'our Saxon

---

[141] Tinker, trans., *Beowulf, translated out of the Old English*, p. 5.
[142] Child, trans., *Beowulf and the Finnsburh Fragment*; Gummere, trans., *The Oldest English Epic*. In a previous article, Gummere had rejected the claims of blank verse for translating *Beowulf* – too grand for a 'primitive' epic like *Beowulf* – and of syllabic rhyme – it carries us 'far back into the glories of our national past' but 'is easy and garrulous where *Beowulf* is breathless and rough' (Gummere, 'The Translation of *Beowulf*, and the Relations of Ancient and Modern English Verse', pp. 53, 48); cf. the comments of D'Israeli and Brooke on blank verse translations, above, nn. 49 and 53, respectively. On American translations, see further John Hill, '*Beowulf* Editions for the Ancestors', pp. 67–9.
[143] Gummere, trans., *Beowulf* (Harvard Classics ed.), p. 1.

forefathers in England',[144] and throughout the nineteenth century 'Anglo-Saxonism' is a significant theme in American culture.[145]

Twentieth-Century Perspectives

The twentieth century saw a marked and progressive increase in the amount of attention devoted to *Beowulf* by scholars on both sides of the Atlantic Ocean and saw too the widespread adoption of the poem on university teaching programmes, where it was taught both as 'language' and, increasingly, as 'literature'. The sheer number of translations produced over the century is one indicator of the prominence of the poem on degree courses.[146] *Beowulf* and its offshoots have also become increasingly, especially approaching the present day, the object of interest in wider popular culture. For what it is worth, a 2007 googling of 'Beowulf' turned up some 4,920,000 hits (ranging from the good to the bad and the ugly), rocketing to 16,700,000 in 2008, after the release of the Robert Zemeckis film *Beowulf*. By way of comparison there were 4,590,000 hits for 'Chaucer', 1,490,000 for 'Gawain', 1,130,000 for 'Aeneid' and 5,010,000 for 'Iliad'.[147] As noted recently by Eileen Joy and Mary Ramsey, 'For all the talk of the supposed marginalization of Old English studies within the American and British academies, *Beowulf* continues to fascinate students, scholars and artists alike.'[148]

Joy and Ramsey go on to refer to Terry Eagleton's recent insistence that *Beowulf* 'ultimately retains its pride of place in English studies mainly due to its function, from the Victorian period forward, as the cultural tool of a troubling nationalist romance with an archetypal and mythological past'.[149] We have seen in the previous section evidence of the validity of Eagleton's perception of the political role of *Beowulf* throughout its modern history, a political role that Tom Shippey too highlights when he writes, surveying the 'critical heritage' of *Beowulf*, 'one has to say that the poem itself at all times appeared as a source of potential authority

---

[144] Longfellow, 'Anglo-Saxon Literature', p. 93.
[145] Robert Young notes indeed that the racial designation 'Anglo-Saxon' 'was originally used predominantly in North America, and introduced into English precisely to describe the English abroad, the diasporic population' (*The Idea of English Ethnicity*, p. 181), adding, '"Anglo-Saxon" referred to indeterminate English people, of any kind, in any place' (ibid.). On American Anglo-Saxonism, see Horsman, *Race and Manifest Destiny: The Origins of American Racial Anglo-Saxonism*; J. R. Hall, 'Mid-Nineteenth-Century American Anglo-Saxonism: The Question of Language'; VanHoosier-Carey, 'Byrhthoth in Dixie: The Emergence of Anglo-Saxon Studies in the Postbellum South'.
[146] See Osborn, Updated Bibliography to Tinker, *The Translations of Beowulf*, pp. 155–79; Bjork and Niles, *A Beowulf Handbook*, 'Works Cited, Translations', pp. 379–81.
[147] I should point out that nearly 250,000 of the 'Beowulf' hits in these searches were specifically with reference to the Beowulf-cluster software operating system.
[148] Joy and Ramsey, 'Introduction: Liquid *Beowulf*, p. xxx.
[149] Joy and Ramsey, 'Liquid *Beowulf*, p. xxx, referring to Eagleton, 'Hasped and Hooped and Hirpling: Heaney Conquers *Beowulf*, p. 16.

and power'.[150] But it is an oversimplification to assume that, because the poem has been appropriated in the cause of national and literary grand narratives, it is therefore inextricable from such narratives. Heaney's treatment of it, for one, problematizes this interpretation, as I hope to show below, and other translators appropriate *Beowulf* in interesting and different ways. Recent artistic and popular adaptations are not interested in *Beowulf* as a monument of English literature; and within academia the poem has been put to new uses. In Joy and Ramsey's striking phrase, *Beowulf* has become 'liquid', and it was also perhaps more liquid in some ways in the past than critics like Eagleton have been willing to credit. To quote Joy and Ramsey again, referring to significant strands in contemporary *Beowulf* scholarship, Old English scholars 'have argued for situating Old English studies within contemporary theoretical paradigms that would help us to investigate how, in [John D.] Niles's words, literary works such as *Beowulf* "shape the present-day culture that calls them to mind as past artefacts"'.[151]

Liquid or not, *Beowulf* was a source of great industry for scholars in the twentieth century and continues to be so in the twenty-first. With reference to the progressive increase in the scholarship of the poem referred to above, in a recent survey Allen Frantzen counted 223 publications on *Beowulf* in the 1800s but 1303 in the 1900s down to 1972 (using the Greenfield–Robinson *Bibliography*,[152] the cut-off date of which is 1972) and he charts a further 110% increase between 1972 and 1997 (using the *Anglo-Saxon England* annual bibliographies).[153] Things haven't been slowing down since 1997 either.

A turning point in the criticism and appreciation of the poem came with the publication of J. R. R. Tolkien's lecture '*Beowulf*: The Monsters and the Critics' in 1936, in which Tolkien focused on the poem as literature rather than, as most scholars had up until then, as an interesting historical document but one with embarrassing childishness in its story, structure and poetic execution.[154] This view, which we have seen expressed by late-nineteenth-century commentators, was still the accepted one when Tolkien wrote. It is expressed famously by one of the major authorities of the early twentieth century, W. P. Ker, in a passage which Tolkien quotes in his essay. Ker pronounced,

> In construction [*Beowulf*] is curiously weak, in a sense preposterous; for while the main story is simplicity itself, the merest commonplace of heroic legend, all about it in the historical allusions, there are revelations of a whole world of tragedy, plots different from that of *Beowulf*, more like the tragic themes of Iceland.[155]

---

[150] Shippey, 'Introduction', p. 74.
[151] Joy and Ramsey, 'Liquid *Beowulf*, p. xxxi, quoting Niles, 'Introduction: *Beowulf*, Truth, and Meaning', p. 9.
[152] Greenfield and Robinson, *A Bibliography of Publications on Old English Literature*.
[153] Frantzen, 'By the Numbers: Anglo-Saxon Scholarship at the Century's End', pp. 483–6.
[154] On the perceived childishness of *Beowulf*, see above, p. 65.
[155] Ker, *The Dark Ages*, p. 253.

For Ker, 'The fault of *Beowulf* is that there is nothing much in the story', and 'It is too simple'.[156]

The literary critic Frank Kermode recalls his time studying *Beowulf* in the period before the Tolkienian literary turn took effect:

> The interests of the teachers were exclusively philological and antiquarian. *Beowulf* provided them with a great variety of complicated scholarly problems, and it was in these that they wanted to involve their students. They rarely found it necessary or desirable to speak of *Beowulf* as a poem, and when they did so they were quite likely to say it was not a particularly good one.[157]

It is a mark of this turning point and of the changing agenda in approaches to *Beowulf* that the biggest increase in studies of the poem in the twentieth century (down to 1972) as compared to the nineteenth was in the area of 'literary interpretations' – 306 as compared to sixteen[158] – of which three-quarters (244) were published after 1940. Tolkien's publication also contributed to the consolidation of *Beowulf*'s canonical reputation, persuasively identifying it as literature worth studying. Kermode exclaims, 'It would not be easy to think of a parallel to this occasion, a professorial lecture that changed a generation's attitude to a document of national and historical importance.'[159]

A key earlier publication had been Friedrich Klaeber's article 'Die christlichen Elemente im *Beowulf* (1911–12), which argued influentially that the Christian elements of *Beowulf* were not interpolated or superimposed onto a pure pagan original[160] but were an integral part of the very fabric of the poem.[161] Klaeber also produced what has perhaps been the most influential twentieth-century edition of the poem, the third edition of which was the standard edition in the United States from its publication in 1936 until very recently; 'Klaeber' has now been re-edited and updated in a revised version.[162]

Klaeber (1863–1954) migrated to the United States and spent much of his career there (though retiring to Germany in 1931). After the heyday of Germanic philology, the twentieth century also witnessed another kind of migration, as the centre of gravity of *Beowulf* studies, and of Old English studies more generally, shifted away from Germany, first to Britain but increasingly to North America, where many more Anglo-Saxonists now live and work than anywhere else:

---

[156] *The Dark Ages*, pp. 252 and 253.
[157] Kermode, 'The Modern *Beowulf*', p. 2.
[158] Frantzen, 'By the Numbers', p. 483.
[159] Kermode, 'The Modern *Beowulf*', p. 2.
[160] Cf. the title of Ettmüller's 1875 edition of the poem: *Carmen de Beovulfi Gautarum regis rebus praeclare gestis atque interitu, quale fuerit ante quam in manus interpolatoris, monachi Vestsaxonici, inciderat*. Ettmüller sets out to present Beowulf as it was 'before it fell into the hands of an interpolator, a West Saxon monk'.
[161] Klaeber, 'Die christlichen Elemente im *Beowulf*'; for a summary, see Klaeber, *Beowulf and the Fight at Finnsburg*, pp. xlviii–li ('The Christian Coloring').
[162] Klaeber, ed., *Klaeber's Beowulf*, ed. Fulk, Bjork and Niles; on the earlier editions of 'Klaeber', see Fulk, 'The Textual Criticism of Frederick Klaeber's *Beowulf*'.

the membership directory of the International Society of Anglo-Saxonists for 2006–7 listed, out of a world-wide total of 566 members, 249 members based in the United States and Canada, 135 in the United Kingdom and Ireland, and 41 in Germany, with another five in German-speaking parts of Switzerland and one in Austria (leaving 135 in other countries). And it is in America that translations of *Beowulf* have particularly proliferated.

'Almost everyone has heard of *Beowulf*', wrote the prose translator David Wright in 1957.[163] Wright's claim obviously overstates things but was true enough when applied to educated readers in the English-speaking world. And with *Beowulf* firmly established as a canonical teaching text on both sides of the Atlantic, being studied both in the original language and, particularly in America, also in translation, we get a stream of modern English versions of every type in the twentieth century, bringing us down to the translations of Morgan and his successors discussed in the subsequent chapters of this book.

Differing readerships, and two 1940s verse translations

In a survey published in 1970–1, J. K. Crane distinguishes translations of *Beowulf* as aimed at four quite different audiences: the first group of translations he identifies are 'those intended for the general reader interested in "reading", not "studying", the poem'. Crane continues,

> The second category of reader is the non-specialist student who could be expected to both read [*Beowulf*] and examine its artistry, yet who would have no knowledge of Anglo-Saxon to assist him in the latter regard. [. . .] The third group is the specialist, the reader with an Anglo-Saxon background who is attempting to rectify for himself the disparities between the original and *any* translation. [. . .] And finally, in the fourth division are the Morgan and Raffel translations in which the attempt is rather to create a new work of art than preserve and make available an old one.[164]

Crane pragmatically identifies broad categories of readership that translators write for (and, we might add, that publishers seek to market to). These categories are useful to use in a shorthand way, though there are problematic assumptions underlying them, with surely considerable overlap between them. Crane is right in seeing the fourth type as potentially 'more self-sustaining' (as he puts it) than the others,[165] the others being limited by their utilitarian aims. On the other hand, the examples of the fourth type that Crane cites could also be viewed as ideal representations of the first type. Certainly their authors regard themselves as making available the old poem *as well as* creating a new one, and their

---

[163] Wright, *Beowulf*, p. 9.
[164] Crane, 'To Thwack or Be Thwacked', p. 320.
[165] Ibid.

readers seek a 'version' of the original, reflecting something of the qualities of that original.

The two translations I wish to refer to before bringing this chapter to a close are from the 1940s, the period just before Morgan's translation. They may be viewed as setting the scene for his translation and as representing versions of the *status quo* to which he reacted. The first of them, by Charles W. Kennedy (1940),[166] belongs fairly securely to Crane's second category, being aimed at the student studying *Beowulf* in translation, and indeed Crane praises it as the best in this category 'for bringing home the peculiar qualities of Anglo-Saxon poetry'.[167] Kennedy's translation is accompanied by an extensive introduction containing much literary-critical discussion designed to bring out the student's appreciation of the poem. The translation was published in America and achieved considerable popularity, being reprinted down to 1978.

Kennedy aims his version of *Beowulf* at students. He also has the objective, however, of writing 'authentic modern verse':

> It has been my endeavor to translate the poem faithfully into authentic modern verse, and to avoid if possible that lack of spontaneity of spirit and flow of narrative that is a besetting snare of the translator. I have employed the four-beat alliterative measure, but without any attempt at strict adherence to the conventional types of Old English half-line.[168]

The metrical form leads to a heavily alliterating style with insistent half-line structure and to an iambically/anapestically tending rhythm that is often very obvious – Crane remarks that 'occasionally it degenerates into "Night Before Christmas" banter';[169]

> He throve under heaven in power and pride,
> (no lineation, corresponding to *Beowulf*, line 8)

or

> A ring-prowed ship
> Straining at anchor and sleeted with ice,
> Rode in the harbor, a prince's pride.
> (corresponding to *Beowulf*, lines 32–3)

This is surely too rhythmically pronounced to work as modern poetry. And though Kennedy achieves a sense of seriousness and drama in many passages, the expressiveness of his phrasing is interspersed with quaintness and, as with 'endured it ill' in the following quotation, with stiffness:

> Then an evil spirit who dwelt in the darkness
> Endured it ill that he heard each day

---

[166] C. W. Kennedy, trans., *Beowulf: The Oldest English Epic*.
[167] 'To Thwack or Be Thwacked', p. 228.
[168] Kennedy, *Beowulf*, p. vii.
[169] Crane, 'To Thwack or Be Thwacked', p. 228.

The din of revelry ring through the hall,
The sound of the harp, and the scop's sweet song.
(corresponding to *Beowulf*, lines 86–90)

Edwin Morgan particularly takes Kennedy to task for describing his translation as being in 'authentic modern verse' while employing a considerable amount of archaic diction:

Would that phrase [i.e., 'authentic modern verse'] at that date [1940], if it meant anything at all, cover such words and expressions as: *Lo!, I ween, smote him sore, what time . . ., blithesome band, 'twas a weary while, wretched wight, wove his words in a winsome pattern, 'neath, o'er, guerdon, oft, sire, no whit, bills and byrnies, when his soul must forth . . .*? Such diction is certainly alien to 'modern' verse practice, and what authenticity can there be in the use of terms which were trite and *passé* by 1600?[170]

The translation is far from convincing in 'bringing home the peculiar qualities of Anglo-Saxon poetry', but Kennedy's version was as good as it got before Morgan's own translation. And it played a part in making *Beowulf* interesting enough to read in the original, as one of today's highly respected scholar/translators has personally testified: Marijane Osborn writes that Kennedy's version 'was the form in which I first read *Beowulf*, and I remember being swept along through the narrative.'[171]

The other translation that I wish to mention, finally, belongs to Crane's first category, being 'intended for the general reader interested in "reading", not "studying", the poem'. This is the translation by Mary Waterhouse, published in England in 1949, in blank verse. This translation did not make much of an impression in poetic circles or among Anglo-Saxonists, but it is relevant to refer to it here, as it was the most recent one when Morgan brought out his version.[172]

Waterhouse justifies her bold choice of blank verse as her poetic medium largely in negative terms: the various imitative approaches adopted by previous translators haven't worked. In translating 'for the modern ear', she seeks in her version to escape 'that air of flippancy or frivolity which imitative versions in modern English give'; these imitative versions are also, unlike the original, frequently

---

170 Morgan, *Beowulf*, pp. ix–x.
171 Osborn, 'Translations, Versions, Illustrations', p. 358.
172 Waterhouse, trans., *Beowulf in Modern English*. Contemporary reviewers damned the translation with faint praise: Stanley Rypins declared it to be 'a reflection rather of scholarly competence than of poetic sensibility' and opined that in her choice of blank verse as her metre Waterhouse 'handicaps herself unnecessarily with a crippling burden' (review, p. 421); J. N. Scannell described it as 'a competent and workmanlike volume' but was of the view that 'Beside the poetic grandeur of the original Miss Waterhouse's verse is, inevitably, flat and prosaic' (review, pp. 300 and 301); more positive was R. M. Lumiansky, who liked Waterhouse's choice of metre and welcomed the translation as 'an accurate, highly readable version of the poem' (review, p. 248). G. Storms felt that Waterhouse's 'execution is, in the main, pleasant and reliable' (review, p. 141).

'overburdened with alliteration'.[173] Waterhouse's valid criticisms of existing translations cause her to look elsewhere for a model to follow: 'These considerations led to the choice of blank verse as the medium, taking it as the modern heroic line and therefore the equivalent of the older one'.[174] In using blank verse, she intends to provide 'a clear and straightforward version of the poem, free from archaisms, real or spurious, alike of word, phrase, or verse form'.[175]

Waterhouse has a certain logic on her side when she identifies blank verse as a kind of 'modern' (understood in its broadest sense) equivalent of Old English metre. But of course the adoption of blank verse brings a whole series of historical associations and connotations that profoundly alter the register and feel of the poem. Blank verse may be, or (more correctly) may have been, a kind of default mode of English verse but it is far from being a neutral medium. In Waterhouse's version we get a polished, classicized *Beowulf*. In the view of one reviewer it presents a 'pleasant and reliable' image of the original poem,[176] but in being pleasant and reliable it also distorts:

> Lo, of the Spear Danes' might in days of old
> And of the kings of men we have heard tell.
> How princes then their deeds of glory wrought.

This has dignity and formality but it turns *Beowulf* into a 'poetic' poem from the golden treasury of (post-medieval) English verse. And, as Edwin Morgan insists, 'blank verse is no longer a living medium for extended writing'.[177]

Morgan was also quick to point out that the language of Waterhouse's version is far from modern. He is just as scathing in attacking her translation as he had been with Kennedy's. Noting her claim that she is providing a clear and straightforward translation that is free from archaisms, he exclaims,

> The amount of self-deception underlying this assertion may be judged from the following select list: *Lo!, thou/thee/ye, 'neath, o'er, 'twixt, 'tis/'twas/'twill, no wise, full oft, whoso, hath/doth, venture grim, the twain* [. . .]

And he goes on for another five lines giving further examples.[178]

Waterhouse's choice of metre does not come off and the accompanying diction is distinctly unmodern in many respects, as is the syntax (as the elaborate inversion of word order in the quotation above illustrates). It is interesting that this last translation of the first half of the twentieth century reverts to the metre adopted by Conybeare at the very beginning of the translation of *Beowulf* into English verse more than a hundred and twenty years earlier. The obvious drawbacks of this metre are firmly pointed out by Morgan, some of whose criticisms

---

[173] Waterhouse, *Beowulf in Modern English*, p. ix.
[174] Ibid.
[175] Ibid.
[176] See n. 172, above.
[177] Morgan, *Beowulf*, p. xii.
[178] Morgan, *Beowulf*, p. x.

of blank verse in *Beowulf* translations had long been anticipated by commentators of earlier generations.[179]

Though plenty of pedestrian work was also produced in the second half of the twentieth century, *Beowulf* generally fared better with its translators in this period than it had previously. In particular, in a context in which *Beowulf* itself, without patronizing qualification about its roughness, its childishness or its lack of classical proportions, was recognized at last as a great poem which could speak to modern audiences, translators focused on in the following pages would, in their varying ways, produce poetic versions of *Beowulf* that were convincingly modern – something that none of those considered in this chapter managed to achieve.

---

[179] See especially Gummere, 'The Translation of *Beowulf*' (1886); see n. 142, above.

✦4✦

Edwin Morgan: Speaking to his Own Age

Edwin Morgan had a clear aim in mind when he published his translation of *Beowulf* in 1952.[1] As he brings out in the manifesto-like 'Introduction' to the translation and indicates in its very title, *Beowulf: A Verse Translation into Modern English*, he wanted to produce a version of *Beowulf* in the living medium of modern English poetry, a version that, while properly guided by its author's commitment to 'the care of accuracy',[2] is written for the reader of poetry and that works as poetry. As he worked on *Beowulf*, Morgan had already produced or was working on translations into Modern English of the Anglo-Saxon poems *The Ruin*, *The Seafarer* and *The Wanderer* and some Old English riddles;[3] slightly later (1953) he produced a translation of a twenty-two line passage from *Beowulf* into Scots.[4]

Dating from early in what was to be a long and distinguished literary career (Morgan was thirty-three in 1952), Morgan's version of *Beowulf* must be seen as being on a different level poetically from any translation of the poem that had been produced up until that time and a very significant piece of work in its own right. Only Morris's version approaches it in the depth of its engagement with the Old English poem and Morris had gone for a distinctly unmodern register. As the analysis below brings out, Morgan's translation did not fully achieve his aim in writing it, but it is a work of great critical interest and taken in the context of its time it represents a key milestone in the history of *Beowulf* transla-

---

[1] Morgan, trans., *Beowulf: A Verse Translation into Modern English*. As Morgan indicates in his 'Introduction' (p. xxxiv), the translation is based on the text of Klaeber's third edition.
[2] Morgan, *Beowulf*, p. vi.
[3] Morgan, *Collected Poems*, pp. 31, 31–4, 34–7, 37–9, respectively; these poems had been intended for publication in 1952 in Morgan's collection *Dies Irae*, which due to financial problems of the publisher (Lotus Press) never appeared. With reference to Anglo-Saxon studies, note also Morgan's poems 'Harrowing Heaven, 1924' and 'The Grave' (*Collected Poems*, pp. 30, 39–40; from *Dies Irae*), 'Grendel' (*Collected Poems*, pp. 427–8; from 'uncollected poems', 1976–81), 'Cædmon's Second Hymn' and 'New Old English Riddles' (*Themes on a Variation*, pp. 92, 93–4).
[4] 'Auld Man's Coronach', translating *Beowulf*, lines 2444–62a, the lament of an old man for his hanged son; see further below, pp. 86–7.

tions. The writing of the young Morgan shows imagination and flair, with some dazzling effects, and it succeeds in producing a lively and gripping narrative. Most crucially, Morgan's *Beowulf* makes available to a new readership something of the power and resonance of the original poem.

'The Translator's Task in *Beowulf*'[5]

Stressing the importance of vigour as a quality essential to poetic translation, Morgan offers his version of *Beowulf* as one which, according to his 'Introduction' to the translation, 'aims to interest and at times to excite the reader of poetry without misleading anyone who has no access to the original.'[6] He finds the field of translation in general to be 'thickly cluttered with the mere monuments of industry – dry, torpid, and unread',[7] with *Beowulf*, in particular, faring badly at the hands of its translators. As a modern poet, he is appalled at the quality of the existing published verse translations (of which there had been fifteen since 1849) as poetry. He pulls no punches in his unqualified dismissal of these, and he sets out in his version self-confidently to present *Beowulf* for the first time in the terms of contemporary verse, as opposed to what he refers to as the 'linguistic crinkum-crankum and mock-epopeanism' of the versions produced previously to his own.[8]

Previous translations

'Not one [of the existing translations of *Beowulf*]', writes Morgan, as he gets into the stride of his broadside attack in the Introduction, 'has succeeded in establishing itself as a notable presentation, even for its own period, of a great original. [...] Nothing has been found [...] in these *Beowulf* translations to interest either the practising poet or the cultivated reader of poetry.'[9] He is particularly scathing about translations produced since the end of the First World War, since they came from a time of great vitality for English poetry but showed not the slightest sign that they did so. 'The most notable fact about the post-1918 versions', he writes, 'is that they fail to establish a contact with the poetry of their time, and therefore fail to communicate.'[10] He means they fail to communicate as poetry.

This is the fault of the translators and not of the original poem, which Morgan considers to be a great one, if also remote. He demonstrates that the post-1918 versions follow those of the preceding period in cultivating archaism and quaint-

---

[5] The title is that of the first section of Morgan's 'Introduction' to his translation of *Beowulf* (p. v).
[6] Morgan, *Beowulf*, p. vi.
[7] *Beowulf*, p. v.
[8] *Beowulf*, p. xii.
[9] *Beowulf*, p. vii.
[10] *Beowulf*, p. viii.

ness in diction and in many cases adopting as their prosodic medium either blank verse or rhyming syllabic metres, though he points out that some – unsuccessfully, in his view – also used forms of stress metre based on Old English metre. Archaism is a 'tiresome and usually thoughtless (and hence often ludicrous) tone-raising device,'[11] rejected in twentieth-century poetry but ubiquitous in *Beowulf* translations,[12] and the favoured prosodic mediums for translators of *Beowulf* have the effect of 'a metrical archaizing';[13] the result tends to be 'flat, dull, and mechanical' in the case of blank verse,[14] and, in the case of rhyming syllabic metres, produces a 'trite, trivial and even rollicking effect,'[15] wholly inappropriate to the rhythmical variety and subtlety of the original and to the seriousness that Morgan takes to be 'the most obvious characteristic' of the Old English poem.[16]

Of course, most of the people who had attempted verse translations of *Beowulf* had not been recognized poets but were scholars or 'amateurs' of one kind or another. The one poet as such (among many other things) who had translated *Beowulf* was William Morris, who produced what is universally acknowledged to be a very strange version indeed, in a verse form that imitates that of Old English but carries archaism to an extreme degree. Morgan, out of sympathy with Morris's experimenting medievalism, is unsparing in his condemnation of this translation, which is (to refer again to a passage quoted earlier) 'disastrously bad, being uncouth to the point of weirdness, unfairly inaccurate, and often more obscure than the original (hardly, in fact, a translation at all, since Morris "worked up" a prose paraphrase passed to him with increasing misgiving by the scholarly A. J. Wyatt)'.[17]

Morgan rejects blank verse and rhyming syllabic metres as inappropriate in a living modern poem and adopts instead an 'imitative' stress metre for his translation, very different from that of Morris, however. Morgan's metre is based loosely on the four-stress line of Old English poetry, and makes flexible use of alliteration. Morgan points out in his 'Introduction' that although most previous translators of *Beowulf* had shown little interest in stress metre (and those that had had used it as an archaizing device), modern poets, including T. S. Eliot and W. H. Auden, had been successfully experimenting with stress metre from the 1920s and 1930s on, achieving through it a wide range of effects and moods.[18]

---

[11] Ibid.
[12] Morgan finds it legitimate to use archaisms occasionally, for special effect ('Introduction', p. x).
[13] Morgan, *Beowulf*, p. xiii.
[14] Ibid.
[15] *Beowulf*, p. xv.
[16] *Beowulf*, pp. xxxii–xxxiii.
[17] *Beowulf*, p. vii; also quoted above, pp. 57–8.
[18] Morgan does not provide proper consideration of the 'imitative' stress-metre version of *Beowulf* by Charles W. Kennedy, however (*Beowulf: The Oldest English Epic, Translated into Alliterative Verse*), which is not archaizing in the manner of other stress-metre versions. Morgan notes the unfavourable view of Kennedy's metre expressed in the review by Garmon-

As contributory factors towards this development, he cites the reaction against verslibrism, the desire to combine natural speech-rhythms with a feeling of pattern, the influence of Hopkins (a poet that he himself greatly admired)[19] and a renewed interest in Old and Middle English poetry.[20] Thus, in adopting a form of stress metre for his own poem, he places himself in this context of current developments in English poetry, as well as consciously responding to the rhythm and 'craggy solidity'[21] of *Beowulf* itself. Chris Jones aptly refers to the metre of Morgan's *Beowulf* as 'a blank verse version of the Old English accentual line'.[22] Since the appearance of Morgan's version, the vast majority of English verse translations of *Beowulf* have been in some form of stress metre, with alliterative effects incorporated to varying degrees.

Speaking to his own age

Morgan wants his *Beowulf* to be read, and appreciated, by 'the cultivated reader'. He translates out of a 'passionate sympathy with the alien poet',[23] as he puts it, and his sensitive understanding of the art of *Beowulf* is apparent, but he approaches *Beowulf* in the first place as a modern poet. For a translation of the Anglo-Saxon poem to succeed, Morgan insists, it must be 'couched in terms acceptable to one's poetic co-readers and co-writers';[24] and he goes on to spell out his conviction that 'the translator's duty is as much to speak to his own age as it is to represent the voice of a past age; these are, indeed, equal tasks.'[25] Chris Jones picks up on the elements of this negotiation when he writes that Morgan 'moves the idiom of the poem towards the twentieth century, while at the same time refraining from obliterating the value of its difference.'[26]

This is to be a new kind of translation of *Beowulf*, then, something to be considered seriously as poetry, produced by a writer at the forefront of developments in high literary culture and with a sophisticated awareness of technical issues concerning modern prosody. Morgan's translation also has the intention, therefore, or the effect, of bringing *Beowulf*, whose confinement to the realms of philology, history and medievalism had been borne out by the treatment of its previous verse translators, into the ambit of creative literature, where Morgan felt that it rightly belonged. Having discovered the power and excitement of the poetry of *Beowulf* as an undergraduate student studying Old English at Glasgow

---

sway (p. 34), who disliked the use of alliterative metres in modern translations, but he does not himself examine Kennedy's verse (see Morgan's 'Introduction', pp. xxvii–xix).

[19] See Chris Jones, 'Edwin Morgan in Conversation', p. 49.
[20] Morgan, *Beowulf*, p. xix.
[21] *Beowulf*, p. xvi.
[22] *Strange Likeness*, p. 143.
[23] Morgan, *Beowulf*, p. v.
[24] *Beowulf*, p. xi.
[25] Ibid.
[26] *Strange Likeness*, p. 147.

with Ritchie Girvan,[27] Morgan brought the imagination, craft and individuality of an informed practitioner of contemporary English poetry to bear on the translation of the Old English poem, in a way that no previous translator had been in a position, or had been inclined, to do. Morgan's version is a *Beowulf* not conceived as a popular work aimed at the general reader or at the disciple of medievalism but one written for the 'cultivated' readership of modern English poetry.

Morgan does not ease the path of the reader by providing much in the way of supplementary material. Line numbers are supplied and there is a glossary of proper names but no introduction to the poem in its context, no explanatory notes and little in the way of signposting of narrative development by means of headings, and no marginal annotation. Morgan does divide up the poem into sections but these are very large units indeed (e. g., lines 194–1250, 'Beowulf and Grendel'), which do not help the reader to negotiate the complexity of the poem's narrative detail; the manuscript division of the text of *Beowulf* into 'fitts', or sections, ranging in length from forty-three to 142 lines, is ignored. Morgan presents his modern text starkly as a poem, inviting his readers to respond to it in its own terms.

Scottish literary contexts

At the time he produced his translation of *Beowulf* (he had started on it soon after he got his degree in 1947, his undergraduate studies having been interrupted by the Second World War),[28] Morgan was working in Glasgow in a literary context in which questions of identity and language politics were being hotly debated.[29] In his *Beowulf*, however, as in most of his other work, he looks out beyond this immediate context, writing for a wider audience and not striving for a self-consciously Scottish inflection in the language of his poetry. In 1953 he produced a translation of a passage from *Beowulf* into Scots, but in the translation of the complete poem into English (and published in England) he is placing himself in the wider context of poetry in English. He was fully aware then, as

27 Morgan discusses studying with Ritchie Girvan (to whom he dedicated his translation of *Beowulf*) and describes the undergraduate English course he followed at the University of Glasgow in the 1930s and 1940s (interrupted by the war), in Chris Jones, 'Edwin Morgan in Conversation': Girvan was 'a scholar of the old school, an old grammarian' (p. 47); Morgan studied Old English throughout the four years of his degree: the course 'wasn't modern at all you see, even the literature – of course the language side wasn't at all modern' (p. 50). In an earlier interview, Morgan spoke of the attraction that Old English poetry had for him at university: 'The poetry appealed to me very, very strongly. I liked both the melancholy side of it, the elegiac side of it, which is pretty strong, but also the heroic side of it. It was the first really convincing heroic poetry that I read as a student' ('Nothing is Not Giving Messages', interview with Robert Crawford, in Morgan, *Nothing is Not Giving Messages*, pp. 118–43, at p. 121).
28 Chris Jones, 'Edwin Morgan in Conversation', p. 48.
29 See Nicholson, *Edwin Morgan: Inventions of Modernity*, pp. 14–30.

later, of issues of English cultural supremacy that weighed heavily on Scottish writers: 'the Scots have, and have long had, to worry about their relation and attitude to England', he would write;[30] and in translating *Beowulf* he knew he was appropriating a great monument from the edifice of English literary history. He was appropriating it, however, on behalf of modern English poetry rather than for a more local constituency, though in doing so he was making a statement to that constituency.

Morgan always resisted pigeonholing. As one critic writes, 'What sets him apart is his apparent refusal to forge a settled poetic identity and this despite the fact that he has material at his disposal which could have been used in this way.'[31] He had engaged in the debate going on when he returned from the war about whether Scottish poets should write in Scots or in English and had advocated a permissive attitude rather than the kind of dogmatic approach insisted upon by Hugh MacDiarmid and others. Contributing to a heated discussion on the subject in the correspondence columns of *The Glasgow Herald* in 1946, Morgan stressed that the choice of language should be made with attention to the preferred audience that the poet has in mind and that poets should be free to write either in 'a Scots mixture' or in 'a northern variant of the standard language', enriching and rejuvenating it from their own experience.[32] His own choice was for the latter, not only because of his preferred audience but also because he wished to place himself in the wider tradition of poetry in English, which for his purposes was more enabling than Scots.

Morgan's Scots translation of a passage from *Beowulf* (lines 2444–62a), 'The Auld Man's Coronach',[33] describing the grief of an old man whose son has died on the gallows, is an intimate and deeply lyrical piece of work, capturing the sense of numbed desolation of the Old English elegiac mood, to produce a compelling free-standing short poem. It is very much a reworking of the Old English lines, and it does not seek to transport the reader to ancient Germania but to present emotion with dignity (as suggested by the Scottish-Gaelic word *coronach* itself, meaning 'lamentation') and also with idiomatic immediacy. The translation is down-to-earth in its language, significant elements of which are everyday words deriving directly from Old English, though not in use in the standard language,[34] and subdued in its rhythmical effects; it feels unforced and idiomatic. It is also highly poetic in expression, however. Its rhetorical features, most notably repetition, omission of the verb 'to be', inverted word order and looseness of syntax,

---

[30] Edwin Morgan, 'The Beatnik in the Kailyard', p. 65; quoted by Nicholson, *Edwin Morgan: Inventions of Modernity*, p. 15.
[31] Gregson, 'Edwin Morgan's Metamorphoses', p. 149.
[32] *Glasgow Herald*, 26 November, 1946, letters page. See further Nicholson, *Edwin Morgan: Inventions of Modernity*, p. 21.
[33] The text of the poem is reproduced in Chris Jones, *Strange Likeness*, pp. 169–70.
[34] Examples are *dowie*, 'sorrowful', *thole*, 'suffer', *maun*, 'must', *minds*, 'remembers', *daws*, 'dawns'. Among words from Old Norse are *toom*, 'empty', and *whidders*, 'gusts'.

serve to emphasize the emotion and to lend dignity to the expression of that emotion, as in the opening lines:

> Waesome, waesome the hert that is his,
> Faither wha sees his only laudie
> Waive i the widdie on gallows tree.

Though free in approach, Morgan is restrained in his additions. Most striking perhaps is his filling out of the Old English image of the father remembering every morning the *ellorsið*, 'journey elsewhere' (line 2451), of his son:

> He minds him on ilka morn that daws
> But his son has stravaig'd to the morn-come-never.

The verse is underlain throughout by a steady four-stress metrical structure, based on Old English metre, with pronounced caesura and an alliteration that is unobtrusive but highlights key images and thoughts. There is little sense of forward movement in the dirge-like poetry, as reflects the all-encompassing emotion. The closing lines work to a climax with reference to the old man's desires, which turns out, however, to be only the bleakness of 'Naethin ava'.

Published in *The Glasgow Herald*, 'The Auld Man's Coronach' is aimed at a Scottish readership and draws upon the rich associations of vernacular literary language to produce a powerful and moving poem, in which the Old English has been imaginatively 'domesticated'. It is a mood piece rather than a developed narrative work, however, and Morgan did not seek to extend the use of Scots with reference to more complex or intractable material in Old English (or other languages). Chris Jones is surely right when he declares, with reference to 'The Auld Man's Coronach', 'For Morgan, Scots is a medium associated with domestic emotion and folk and oral culture[;] it therefore provides the appropriate tenor here, but not for most of *Beowulf*, with its higher register, more closely associated with "official" cultural authority'.[35]

For his *Beowulf* Morgan uses Standard English, and a Standard English not conspicuously 'northern' in character; there are some but not many obvious signs of a specific regional idiom.[36] Morgan's translation is remarkable, however, not

---

[35] *Strange Likeness*, p. 170. See further, Mairi Robinson, ed., *The Concise Scots Dictionary*, s. v.
[36] In line with Scottish vernacular practice is Morgan's consistent preference of the conjunction *till* (never *until*) in the translation (line 9, etc.) and the use of *hid* as a past participle (line 161) and of *throve* (line 8) and *pled* (line 1994) as the past tenses of *thrive* and *plead* respectively, though *throve* is also perhaps also formal, with suggestions of the archaic; also consistent with Scottish usage is the deployment of the verbs *gally*, 'frighten' (line 1429), and *sheen*, 'shine, polish' (line 2257); and Morgan's use of the (originally Norwegian) word *kraken*, 'sea-monster' (line 422, etc.), may also reflect Scottish linguistic influence. On Scots morphology and vocabulary, see especially Aitken, 'Scottish Speech: A Historical View with Special Reference to the Standard English of Scotland'; Charles Jones, *The English Language in Scotland: An Introduction to Scots*; Charles Jones, ed., *The Edinburgh History of the Scots Language*; Mairi Robinson, ed., *The Concise Scots Dictionary*.

only for the quality of its language but also for the vigour of its rhythmical effects, based on a four-stress metrical structure that derives ultimately from that of Old English itself, and it has been suggested that this metrical structure may provide a link with Morgan's Scottish background. This structure, with its in-built alliteration, had been inherited and developed by, among others, Scots poets of the later Middle Ages, including a favourite of Morgan's, William Dunbar, whose alliterative verse is strongly percussive. Morgan's poetic output resembles that of Dunbar in other ways, most notably in its sheer 'restless variety'[37] and formal experimentation – Dunbar was also a poet who resisted pigeonholing – but in particular the influence of Dunbar and other medieval Scottish poets is likely to have reinforced the appeal of stress-rhythm for Morgan and to have given him an increased sense of its rhythmical possibilities. Morgan insists that experimentation with stress metre is a feature of modern poetry anyway but it is a feature that he finds particularly natural in his own Scottish context. In the 'Introduction' to his *Beowulf* he speaks of 'a generally renewed interest in Old and Middle English non-syllabic poetry',[38] but this interest was also specific to himself (as are the other factors he enumerates in the relevant passage; see above, p. 84).

Colin Nicholson reminds us that it was six months before his *Beowulf* came out that Morgan published his essay entitled 'Dunbar and the Language of Poetry', in which the argument 'suggests a northern pedigree for his own modernisation of Anglo-Saxon script'.[39] In that essay Morgan writes that the practice of Dunbar and other medieval Scots poets 'proves that the older tradition was very pervasive and very congenial to the Scottish spirit and [Dunbar and other Scottish poets] pay it that debt of exemplification which is often more revealing than their addresses to Chaucer'.[40] He declares that 'the effects in Dunbar belong to something permanent in the spirit of the language'.[41] It is perhaps in Morgan's 'exemplification' of aspects of medieval Scots poetry (itself influenced by the Old English tradition with which Morgan is engaging) that we may observe a Scottish-influenced inflection in Morgan's *Beowulf*. Even here, however, we should note that alongside Morgan's appreciation of the Scottish Dunbar is his admiration for the alliterative poetry of later medieval England, notably in *Sir Gawain and the Green Knight*, *Pearl* and *Piers Plowman*.[42]

---

[37] The phrase is from McCarra, 'Edwin Morgan: Lives and Work', p. 4.
[38] Morgan, *Beowulf*, p. xix.
[39] Nicholson, *Edwin Morgan*, p. 46. The reference is to Morgan's 1952 academic article 'Dunbar and the Language of Poetry'.
[40] 'Dunbar and the Language of Poetry', p. 139; quoted by Nicholson, *Edwin Morgan*, p. 46.
[41] 'Dunbar and the Language of Poetry', p. 157.
[42] As expressed in *Nothing is Not Giving Messages*, p. 122, and in Jones, 'Edwin Morgan in Conversation', p. 50.

Morgan's *Beowulf*: 'Energy in Order'

In that same article on Dunbar, Morgan offered a definition of poetry as 'the manifestation of energy in order'.[43] This provides an apposite description of his approach in his translation of *Beowulf*; we have already noted (above, p. 82) his emphasis on the necessity of 'vigour' in poetic translation. The phrase 'energy in order' captures suggestively that combination of compelling verve and formality that characterizes much of Morgan's writing in his *Beowulf*, producing effects that engage and often surprise the reader.

'Energy in order' in a particular passage

Energy in order is most obvious in scenes of lively action and description, such as in the following sequence of two carefully elaborated sentences (in which the Danish warriors trace the journey of the mortally wounded Grendel back to his mere after his fight with Beowulf):

> Ungrievous seemed
> His break with life to all those men
> Who gazed at the tracks of the conquered creature
> And saw how he had left on his way from that place –
> Heart-fatigued, defeated by the blows of battle,
> Death-destined, harried off to the tarn of krakens –
> His life-blood-spoor. There the becrimsoned
> Waters were seething, the dreadful wave-sweep
> All stirred turbid, gore-hot, the deep
> Death-daubed, asurge with the blood of war,
> Since he delightless laid down his life
> And his heathen soul in the fen-fastness,
> Where hell engulfed him. (lines 841–53)

This is a passage in which the narrative sweeps steadily onwards but the narrative movement is also complicated by intricate grammatical development and abrupt oppositions, dense imagery and varied rhythmical effects and is coloured by an insistently mannered diction, features that can be seen as reflecting aspects of the Old English. The sense of onward sweep is achieved through the ending of sentences and clauses in mid-line and the use of enjambment and cumulative sentence structure, a sentence structure in which declarative statement is followed by a complex of qualifying material; the other features mentioned above lend interest and variety to the narrative.

The cumulative sentence structure, with pervasive use of apposition and variation and based on strongly differentiated half-lines, is closely modelled on that of the Old English (though Morgan skates over the Old English phrase *deaðfæge deog* (line 850), 'doomed to death, he hid himself', which interrupts the flow of

---

43 'Dunbar and the Language of Poetry', p. 138.

the second sentence in the original with a change of grammatical subject from the waters to Grendel; Morgan reconceives *deaðfæge* as *death-daubed* and has no equivalent to *deog*). Within this structure, striking compound words – *heart-fatigued, life-blood-spoor, gore-hot, death-daubed*, and so on – provide strong images, as do other carefully chosen epithets; particularly notable among the latter are *becrimsoned, seething* and *all stirred turbid*, these at the centre of a dense and emotive passage describing the waters of the mere.

The descriptive words are mostly monosyllabic and provide lively patterns of rhythm, heightened but not dominated by alliterative effects, most noticeably in the compound pairings *death-destined, death-daubed* and *fen-fastness*. The only words in the entire passage of more than two syllables are the mannered-looking *ungrievous* (translating *No* [. . .] / *sarlice*, 'not at all . . . grievously' [lines 841–2]), *becrimsoned* (translating *on blode*, 'in blood' [line 847]) and *delightless* (translating *dreama leas*, 'without joys' [line 850], an Old English phrase that expresses an elegiac idea familiar in the poetry[44]).

The corresponding Old English passage is also rich in emotive vocabulary (and in compound nouns and adjectives) but it mostly uses traditional language and generalized images to convey the hopelessness of Grendel and the gruesomeness of the scene. Morgan's epithet *heart-fatigued*, for example, is highly expressive in its very originality, but the corresponding word in *Beowulf* itself, *werigmod*, 'weary-minded, weary in mind' (line 844), is a familiar and unspectacular elegiac word in Old English poetry, appearing in five other poems, as well as elsewhere in *Beowulf*.[45] Similarly, the phrase corresponding to Morgan's striking *gore-hot*, *haton heolfre*, 'with hot gore' (line 849), is not particularly remarkable; it makes use of a common poetic word for 'blood, gore', which occurs elsewhere (including in *Beowulf*) in collocation with *hat*, 'hot'.[46] On the other hand, the Old English phrase corresponding to *he had left* [. . .] / *His life-blood-spoor* (lines 844–7) presents a dense and graphic image that stretches traditional language in an exciting way rather than making use of ready-made phrasing on this occasion: the original poem has *feorhlastas bær*, literally 'carried his life-tracks/life-steps'

---

[44] Cf. *Genesis A* (ASPR I, 3–87), lines 40, 108; *Christ and Satan* (ASPR I, 135–58), line 167; *Daniel* (ASPR I, 111–32), line 557; *Christ III* (ASPR III, 27–49), line 1627; *Beowulf*, line 1720.

[45] See *Andreas* (ASPR II, 3–51), line 1366; *The Phoenix* (ASPR, III, 94–113), line 428; *The Wife's Lament* (ASPR III, 210–11), line 49; *Metrical Psalms* (ASPR V, 3–150), 68:3, line 1; *Guthlac A* (ASPR III, 49–72), line 255; cf. *werigferhð*, 'weary in mind' (*Judith* [ASPR IV, 99–109], lines 249, 290; *Andreas*, line 1400; *The Whale* [ASPR III, 171–4], line 19). The compound *werigmod* also occurs elsewhere in *Beowulf*: 'Oferwearp þa werigmod wigena strengest', 'weary-minded, the strongest of warriors stumbled' (line 1543), which is translated by Morgan in the sequence, 'Then the foot-soldier, strongest of warriors, / Exhausted in spirit, slipped and fell' (lines 1543–4), with a different phrase sought out to render *werigmod* this time (viz. 'exhausted in spirit').

[46] For *haton/hatan heolfre*, see also *Andreas*, lines 1241, 1247, *Beowulf*, line 1423; in translating the latter occurrence ('Flod blode weol [. . .] / hatan heolfre', 'The flood welled with hot gore', lines 1422–3), Morgan changes the syntax, expressing *hatan*, 'hot', by means of the verb *boiled*: 'Waves welled blood [. . .] / Boiled with crimson' (lines 1422–3).

(line 846), i.e., 'left traces of his life-blood as tracks as he made his way'; it would also be possible to interpret *feorh*, 'life', as referring to Grendel's soul and/or to the vanishing traces of his life. In this suggestive phrase, highlighted by being delayed to the very end of the sentence – a device reflected in Morgan's translation – the Old English poet creates a compound noun based on the familiar enough *-lastas*, '-tracks', word-formation pattern, but the first element, *feorh*, is an arresting choice and the combination of *feorhlastas* with the verb *bær*, 'carried', also unexpected, provides a rich metaphor.[47] Morgan's mannered tripartite compound concisely captures the meaning here, with Grendel as a hunted animal, though the curiousness of *spoor* distracts from the immediacy of his image.

The use of words like *spoor* is among the most striking features of the passage. Other words that stand out here as mannered or curious are *Ungrievous*, *krakens*, *becrimsoned*, *seething*[48] and *delightless*. Such words may not be archaic but, with the exception of the weird and wonderful *krakens* as a term for sea-monsters,[49] they are clearly poeticisms. *Kraken* makes a number of other appearances in the translation, always translating the Old English *nicor*, 'sea-monster' (lines 422, 575, 1411). The use of this mannered vocabulary has a defamiliarizing, foreignizing effect in a poem that has an underlying modern register, distancing the reader from the narrative. Through the use of such language Morgan gives a sense of the poetic language of the original and of its lofty literary tone, creating (as Chris Jones puts it) 'a texture of lexical alterity',[50] but this jars somewhat with his idea of writing in the language of contemporary poetry, which he insists so strongly upon in his 'Introduction'. Morgan's use of poetic vocabulary is accompanied in the passage by occasional recourse to inverted word order, also a conventional poetic device. Thus we get *Ungrievous seemed / His break with life* and *he delightless laid down his life*, in both of which instances the inverted word order highlights unusual items of vocabulary, the three-syllabled *Ungrievous* and *delightless*.

'Poetic' features of the translation

Features of our passage are characteristic of the translation as a whole, not least the use of mannered vocabulary, including some archaisms or poeticisms, and

---

[47] Other compounds of the *-lastas* pattern include *feðelastas*, 'footsteps, footpath' (*Beowulf*, line 1632; *Judith*, line 138), *fotlastas*, 'footprints, track' (*Beowulf*, line 2287), *widlastas*, 'far-wandering tracks' (*Andreas*, line 677; cf. *widlastum*, *Wulf and Eadwacer* [ASPR III, 179–80], line 9), *wræclastas*, 'paths of exile' (*Christ and Satan*, line 120; *The Wanderer* [ASPR III, 134–7], line 5; etc.).

[48] Elsewhere Morgan employs the oxymoronic phrase *wintry seethings* (line 516, translating *wintrys wylmum*, 'the surgings/floods of winter').

[49] According to the *OED*, a *kraken* is '[a] mythical sea-monster of enormous size, said to appear off the coast of Norway'; pedantic readers will note that such beasts would not live in tarns.

[50] Jones, *Strange Likeness*, p. 141.

inverted word order. Notable archaisms/poeticisms are the 'sea'-words *main* (lines 49, 1862), *brine-* (in the kenning, invented by Morgan,[51] *brine-hold*, line 517) and *deep* (line 849); *throve* as the past tense of *thrive* (line 8), *thrived* being the more usual form in twentieth-century British English, though *throve* may reflect Scottish usage; *give us fair forwarding!* (line 269, translating *wes þu us larena god*, 'be good/generous in your advice to us'); *make petition* (line 352, translating *þu bena eart*, 'you are a petitioner/ask'); *doom* (line 1266), meaning 'judgement'; *fiend* (line 2074), meaning 'enemy' (translating *-grom*, 'fierce one'); *sheen* (line 2257) as a verb, meaning 'shine' (probably known to Morgan as a Scottish usage) (translating *bywan*, 'polish'); *hoary* (line 2553), for 'grey' (translating *har*, 'grey'); *laved* (line 2721, translating *gelafede*, 'poured water on, washed'), and *couch* (line 3034; cf. also *hall-couch*, line 1241), for 'bed' (translating *hlimbed*, 'bed of rest'). Among other curious and mannered items of vocabulary are *worldly excelling* (line 17, translating *woroldare*, 'worldly honour'), *folk-queen* (line 640, translating *folccwen*, 'queen of the people'), *cynosure* (line 641, translating *freolicu*, 'noble'), *roamer* (line 703, translating *-genga*, 'walker, traveller'), *dalesman* (line 750, translating *hyrde*, 'guardian, keeper'), *insatiablest* (line 1122, translating *gifrost*, 'most greedy'), *unlax (fists)* (line 1335, translating *heardum clammum*, 'hard grips'), *moveless* (line 2586, translating *aldorleasne*, 'lifeless'), *ferventest* (line 1668, translating *hatost*, 'hottest'), *venture* (line 2132, in the phrase *venture out my flesh*, translating *ealdre geneðde*, 'should risk my life'), *unloath* (line 2489; no real equivalent in the Old English), *unslothful* (line 2564, translating *unslaw*, 'not blunt'), *unfriended* (line 2612, translating *wineleasum*, 'friendless'), *seldom swearer* (line 2738, translating *ne me swor fela / aða*, 'I did not swear many oaths'), *pledgefastness* (line 2922, translating *treowe*, 'good faith'), *feast-faring* (line 3026, translating *hu him æt æte speow*, 'how he got on at his meal'), *maculate* (line 3041, translating *-fah*, 'stained, variegated').

Poetic inversion of word order is also a device widely used in the translation. Instances exemplifying different patterns of inversion cultivated by Morgan are *this one spirit / [. . .] his malice began* (lines 100–1), *Progenitor he was* (line 111), *Long was the time* (line 146), *of the Creator they knew nothing* (line 180), *him every counsellor / Happily remembers* (lines 265–6), *not with a sword shall I silence him* (line 679), *He had the last of the dead man devoured* (line 744), *Much must he learn* (line 1060), *I from all these things / [. . .] may draw rejoicing* (lines 2739–40). The reference at lines 107–8 to *the everlasting Lord / Destining for the death of Abel killed* (translating the finite clause *þone cwealm gewræc / ece drihten, þæs þe he Abel slog*, 'the eternal Lord avenged the killing after he slew Abel') combines displacement of *killed* with a curious intransitive use of *[d]estining*, to produce a phrase mannered to the point of being unintelligible.[52]

---

[51] Elsewhere Morgan has the term *swan's-way* (line 200), following Old English *swanrade*, 'swan's road'; though hyphenated, *swan's-way* is not strictly a compound word.

[52] Note also the cumbersome multiple inversions of lines 2656–9, resulting in extreme convolution: *Certain is my knowledge / That not his deserts dating from of old / Could allow him alone out of the Geatish host / To suffer sorrow and to fall in fight.*

Another poetic device favoured by Morgan is the omission of the verb 'to be', particularly in exclamations: note *king worth the name!* (line 11), *No ship in fame more fittingly furnished* (line 38, which also has inverted word order), *no settling with money* (line 156), *my name, Beowulf* (line 343), *Now no delay* (line 386), *wretched his future* (line 805). And also 'poetic' is Morgan's use of exclamatory 'O', as in *O treasure-giver* (line 2070), and his widespread use of repetition, encompassing both exact verbal repetition and also patterns of anaphora and similar rhetorical figures. In the category of exact repetition are *flourish, flourish* (line 1218), *miseries, miseries* (line 2004), *it is few, it is few* (line 2150), *He circled and circled* (line 2296), *rejoiced, / Rejoiced* (lines 2298–9), *near, near was death* (line 2728); expressions making use of other patterns of repetition include *too strong, too long, and too malignant!* (line 134), *Great-framed, greatheart* (line 198), *death-wood, death-shafts* (line 398), *brief use, brief love* (line 2240), *helmet on helmet* (line 2763), *Threatened and rethreatened* (line 2938), *This is the hatred and this is the hostility* (line 2999). Neither these kinds of repetition nor verbless clauses, as mentioned above, are features of *Beowulf* itself (though, of course, *Beowulf* is rich in other kinds of repetition).

Another kind of repetition can be seen in Morgan's cultivation of doublets and alliterative pairings, some but by no means all prompted by similar pairings in the original. Examples are *demon and damned* (line 163, translating *helrunan*, 'one skilled in the mysteries of hell'), *bitted and bridled* (line 1399, translating *gebæted*, 'bridled/equipped with a bit'), *desired and despaired* (line 1604, translating *wiston and ne wendon*, 'wished and did not expect'), *force and fierceness* (line 2349, translating *eafoð ond ellen*, 'strength and courage'), *heroes and horseman (sleep)* (line 2457, translating *ridend swefað, / hæleð in hoðman*, 'horsemen sleep, heroes in their graves', lines 2457–8) and *hatred and hostility* (line 2999, translating *sio fæhðo ond se feondscipe*, 'the feud and the enmity').

These 'poetic' aspects of Morgan's style are very conspicuous and their presence is pervasive in the translation. They contribute to the translation's sense of formality, elevation of tone and unusual complexity of style, though some of them have the effect of making the verse look 'conventional' and mannered – even, in places, bathetic.[53] They succeed in suggesting the otherness of *Beowulf* but they do not quite accord with the idea of distinctively modern diction which Morgan insists on so strongly in his Introduction. In practice Morgan combines the modern with strikingly unmodern effects.

Vocabulary and rhythm

'Poetic' words are only one kind of heightened diction deployed in the translation. Morgan's vocabulary is also fresh and inventive, with much use of unex-

---

53   As in the overdone *too strong, too long, and too malignant!* (line 134), or the inconsequential *and he shed his tears; / And grey was his head* (lines 1872–3), or the oxymoronic *How common is the rareness* (line 2030).

pected words and expressions, ranging from unpoetic-looking abstract terms, such as *authority* (line 79; Old English *geweald*, 'control'), *assumptions*, used with reference to armour (line 437; no equivalent in the Old English) and *war-ability* (line 2349; Old English *eafoð ond ellen*, 'strength and courage'), to the zeugma of expressions like *doom-swept away / To Grendel and horror* (lines 477–8, translating *hie wyrd forsweop / on Grendles gryre*, 'fate swept them away into the terror of Grendel'), *Shot wide of the target, shot death to his kinsman* (line 2439, translating *miste mercelses ond his mæg ofscet*, 'missed the target and shot dead his kinsman') and *maculate with glitter and horror* (line 3041, translating *gryrefah*, 'terrible in its variegated colouring'), and the startling *Kobolds and gogmagogs, lemurs and zombies* (line 112, translating *eotenas ond ylfe ond orcneas*, 'giants and elves and monsters'); Morgan seems to have regretted the latter line – 'I knew I was pushing it a bit there!'⁵⁴ – but in its exotic and uncanny associations it may be seen as presenting an appropriately dizzying combination of weird creatures.

Just before this we find *miscreations* (line 111, translating *untydras*, 'monstrous offspring'), and elsewhere Morgan makes use of such striking and vivid expressions, many of them sharpening the imagery of the original, as *drenched with crimson*, referring to Heorot (line 486, translating *blode bestymed*, 'made wet with blood'), *on the skin of the abyss* (line 510, translating *on deop wæter*, 'in deep water'), *blaze valour's power* (line 659, translating *mægenellen cyð*, 'make known mighty valour'), *enlaired* (line 1008), in the sequence *Where the body enlaired and in bed locked fast / Sleeps after its feast* (translating *þær his lichoma legerbedde fæst / swefeþ æfter symle*, 'where his body, secure in its bed, sleeps after the feast'),⁵⁵ *dangerous defiles* (line 1410, translating *enge anpaðas*, 'narrow single-track paths'), *throbbings of care* (line 1993, translating *sorhwylmum*, 'surgings of grief'), *tidewater of death* (line 2269, translating *deaðes wylm*, 'surge of death'), *flame's panoply* (line 2309, where the Old English has the unadorned *fyr*, 'fire'), *belch glowing flakes*, referring to the dragon (line 2312, translating *gledum spiwan*, 'spew flames'); at line 450 *Threads the waste dales* (with reference to Grendel) provides a particularly arresting reworking of the Old English *mearcað morhopu*, 'stains his moor-retreat'.⁵⁶

Morgan also makes pointed use of Latinate and romance vocabulary, as in the very opening line, *How that glory remains in remembrance*. He cultivates words and phrases such as *progenitor* (line 111), *rite of decorum* (line 359), *candidates* (line 368), *Proffering princely cups* (line 622), *deploy* (line 874), *sumptuous* (line 1489), *inscribed with the genesis* (line 1688), *testament and abundance* (line 2235), *chivalry* (line 2255) and *payment for the profusion of princely treasures* (line 2843). These contribute to the formality and dignity of expression that characterizes the trans-

---

⁵⁴ Jones, 'Edwin Morgan in Conversation', p. 49.
⁵⁵ Here the sound of *leger-* ('place of lying') is picked up in *enlaired*, providing a new metaphor (also contributed by Morgan is the metaphor *locked*, in an inverted phrase).
⁵⁶ One wonders whether Morgan originally might have meant to write *treads* instead of *threads*; if so, he retained the latter reading.

lation, as do other resonant expressions – *epic fury* (line 777), *sagas of the dead* (line 870), *vigilant for fame* (line 3182), and so on – and as do lofty-sounding passages with flowing rhythm: at some moments of particular seriousness or reflection smooth iambic and trochaic rhythmical effects are evident, as in *In any other man beneath the sun* (line 752), *The strangers sat / Sick at heart and stared across the sky* (lines 1601–2), *Quenched the thirst of swords in Friesland* (line 2357), *Over the streams of darkness from lands far away* (line 2808). Such patterns of rhythm are in striking contrast to the vigorous stress-patterns found in passages of vivid action or description – *Combat unatonable, conduct bitterly awry* (line 2441), *Ghastly, maculate with glitter and horror* (line 3041), and so on – or in lyrical sequences; a notable example of the latter comes at lines 1133–6, where the coming of spring is excitingly evoked:

> till another season
> Visited the world, as it must, with days
> Gloriously adazzle in vigil for their hours
> For ever without fail.

The dancing rhythm of these lines of strong imagery, set off by intricate alliterative patterning and tumbling enjambment, aptly conveys the energy of spring. The third line is particularly lively, to the extent of becoming tenuously comprehensible before being vaguely resolved in the liturgical-sounding *For ever without fail* of the closing half-line of the sentence (ending in mid-line); *vigil* and *hours* too may be seen as contributing unexpected liturgical associations to these sparkling but somewhat elusive lines.[57]

Vigorous rhythmical effects are also achieved by the abrupt juxtaposition of epithets: *beautiful, huge* (line 1663), *dusk's fiend, frightful* (line 2074), *Tremendous, marvellous* (line 2086), *adventurer, unfriended* (line 2612), *the victor, the darer* (line 2756). In these appositive pairings the second epithet is often in unexpected or contradictory relationship to the first, rather than confirming or extending the meaning of the first, a feature too of some of Morgan's compound words.

---

57   The corresponding lines from *Beowulf* are as follows (lines 1133b-6a):
         oþ ðæt oþer com
     gear in geardas,   swa nu gyt deð,
     þa ðe syngales   sele bewitiað,
     wuldortorhtan weder.
[until another year came to the dwelling-places, as yet it does now, those times of gloriously bright weather that continually observe their proper seasons.]
In translating a passage from *Beowulf* extremely difficult to convey the full sense of (and fully to understand), Morgan's *in vigil* is prompted by *bewitiað*, 'observe, keep watch', and *Gloriously adazzle* by *wuldortorhtan*, 'gloriously bright'; *for their hours* is daring as a translation for *sele*, 'times, proper times, seasons', and *For ever without fail* is an expansion of *syngales*, 'continually', by means of which Morgan suggests the feeling of providential inevitability of the original.

Compound words

The use of compound words is one of the great strengths of Morgan's translation and such words are central to the register cultivated in it. In the interview with Chris Jones, Morgan acknowledged that the use of compounds was one of the features that might seem to distance his translation from the modern register, but distancing can work to good effect and anyway there are plenty of compounds in the modern register of such poets as Hopkins and Pound. Morgan comments with reference to his own practice, 'In fact the compound words were criticised in some reviews – they were felt not to fit in with the modern idea of how you write the language, but they seem to be very much a part of Old English and therefore a part of English.'[58] In his use of compounds, as in his cultivation of elaborate patterns of variation,[59] Morgan is properly pushing the boundaries of modern poetry and at the same time producing in his language, in accordance with Benjaminian (and indeed foreignizing) principles, 'the echo of the original'.[60]

Compound words offer conciseness and density of meaning and their rhythmical and imaginative possibilities are richly exploited by Morgan, making an important contribution to the vigour of his writing. Some of the compounds are routine enough, as they are in the Old English, like *battle-chief* (line 263, translating *ordfruma*, 'leader in battle'), *fire-tempered* (line 305, translating *fyrheard*, 'hardened by fire') and *mead-house* (line 484, translating *medoheal*, 'mead-hall'), but the compounds often bring unlikely nouns and adjectives together in vividly descriptive pairings, creating (to quote Chris Jones) 'new strangeness out of the analogy with the old'.[61] Examples are *sin-forced (feud)* (line 153, translating *fyrene ond fæhðe*, 'sin and feud'), *foam-throated* (lines 218 and 1909, closely imitating *fami(g)heals*, 'foamy-necked') and *doom-swept* (line 477, translating *hie wyrd forswop*, 'fate swept them away'), or unlikely pairs of nouns, as in *flood-fall* (line 1516, translating *færgripe flodes*, 'sudden grip of the flood'), *malicework* (line 2317, translating *nið*, 'malice, destruction') and *rain-brunt* (line 3116, translating *isernscure*, 'shower of iron', i.e., 'shower of iron-headed arrows'); in *panic horror* (line 769), which I take to be a compound noun despite the absence of the hyphen, the second element refines and heightens the meaning of the first (providing a

---

[58] Jones, 'Edwin Morgan in Conversation', p. 49. The importance of compound words in Old English poetry would have been impressed on Morgan by his teacher at Glasgow, Ritchie Girvan. As Girvan states in his book *Beowulf and the Seventh Century: Language and Content*, the compound word was sought by Anglo-Saxon poets for its 'emotional value, and the presence of sounding compounds is throughout the mark of the poetic style' (p. 4).
[59] For an example of particularly insistent variation, see lines 1503–5.
[60] Benjamin, 'The Task of the Translator', p. 79. Benjamin goes on to endorse the view of Rudolf Pannwitz, whom he quotes: 'The basic error of the translator is that he preserves the state in which his own language happens to be instead of allowing his language to be powerfully affected by the foreign tongue' (p. 82).
[61] *Strange Likeness*, p. 140.

wonderful translation of the highly ironic *ealuscerwen*, 'sharing out of ale', which really means 'distress, terror').

Descriptive vividness is also apparent in less original-looking combinations, such as (noun plus adjective) *sea-keen* (line 33, translating *utfus*, 'eager to set out [to sea]'), *wave-scudding* (line 1907, translating *wegflotan*, 'wave-floater', i.e., 'ship') and *flood-buoyed* (line 1908; no equivalent in the Old English) and (noun plus noun) *wave-swell* (line 464, translating *yða gewealc*, 'rolling of the waves') and *shield-clash* (line 2039, translating *lindplegan*, 'shield-play'). Other compound patterns include noun plus verb, as in *rope-rigged* (line 1906, translating *sale fæst*, 'made fast with rope'); adjective plus adjective, as in *thick-thronging (retinue)* (line 400, recasting the original's reference to 'many' [*manig*] warriors); adverb plus adjective, as in *far-gathered (trappings)* (line 37, translating *madma fela / of feorwegum*, 'many treasures from distant parts'); and adverb plus noun, as in *far-sailors* (line 254, translating *feorbuend, / mereliðende*, 'far-dwellers, sea-farers').

Such formulations, incorporating rhythmical and (occasionally) alliterative play, reflect Old English practice, but Morgan also goes in for tripartite compounds, a rare feature in Old English poetry. Tripartite compounds provide strong patterns of stress and particularly dense imagery, and Morgan's employment of them can produce exciting – even Hopkins-like – effects. We have already noted his creation of *life-blood-spoor* (line 847). Other tripartite compounds in his translation of *Beowulf*, many of which are alliterative, include *treasure-hoard-guardian* (line 887, translating *hordes hyrde*, 'guardian of the hoard'), *winter-wave-bound (boat)* (line 1132, translating *winter yþe beleac*, 'winter locked up the waves', a finite clause), *death-evil-fated* (line 2077, translating *feorhbealu fægum*, 'deadly evil for the fated one'), *at the sea-swell-verge* (line 2412, translating *holmwylme neh*, 'near the surge of the sea'), *fire-surge-flashing (dragon)* (line 2670, translating *fyrwylmum fah*, 'shining with surgings of fire'), *fire-wave-fury* (line 2819, translating *hate heaðowylmas*, 'hot hostile flames') and *knife-stroke-broken* (line 2904, translating *sexbennum seoc*, 'weakened by sword-wounds').

Syntax and the narrative voice

The use of compound words also helps Morgan to preserve the cumulative sentence patterns of the Old English poem, with their power and intensity, as in the passage discussed above (pp. 89–91), or their sinuous meandering.[62] Abrupt oppositions and interjections, characteristic of the original poem, are also in evidence, some of which are pointed up on the page by the use of dashes. Morgan is not shackled by the sentence structures of the original, however, and often introduces syntactical changes. Such changes include the creation of tripartite compounds, as just mentioned, and the frequent substitution of present participles for finite verbs in passages of brisk narration, as in *seizing thirty /*

---

[62] Note, for example, the meandering quality of the long sentences at lines 1572–84, the structure of which closely follows that of the Old English.

Soldiers (lines 122–3, translating *genam / þritig þegna*, 'he seized thirty thegns'), *waging his enmity* (line 152, translating *heteniðas wæg*, 'he bore enemy-malice'), *brandishing with force* (line 235, translating *þrymmum cwehte*, 'he brandished it with force'), and the substitution of adverbial, adjectival and nominal phrases for finite clauses, as in *in rite of decorum* (line 359, translating *cuþe he duguðe þeaw*, 'he knew the custom of the company'), *doom-swept away* (line 477, translating *hie wyrd forsweop*, 'fate swept them away') and *thieves of the dead* (line 3027, translating *wæl reafode*, 'plundered the slain'). Among other syntactical changes made by Morgan are the introduction of rhetorical questions, as at lines 162–3, *what man's knowledge / Can map the gliding-ground of demon and damned?*, a sequence that also incorporates other grammatical restructuring (translating *men ne cunnon / hwyder helrunan   hwyrftum scriþað*, 'men do not know to where the one skilled in the mysteries of hell glided/made his way on his roamings'); the change of a metaphor to a simile at line 311 (similes not being a common feature in the densely metaphorical tradition of Old English poetry), *Like a lantern illuminating many lands* (translating *lixta se leoma ofer landa fela*, 'the light shone over many lands'); and the filling out of a concise phrase by means of a finite clause: *trouble was needed* (line 1638, translating *weorcum*, 'with difficulty').

The example of a rhetorical question being substituted for a declarative statement cited above – *what man's knowledge / Can map the gliding-ground of demon and damned?* – also illustrates the final kind of syntactical change that I wish to mention, and in some ways the most significant. This change is not only a syntactical one but is also reflective of Morgan's whole approach to translating *Beowulf* and re-presenting the Anglo-Saxon epic as a modern poem. This change is the general removal of the communal character of the narrative voice and the consequent displacement of the poem from a world of tradition, with a strong oral dimension, a tradition which the Old English poet had participated in and transcended, to a culture in which the poet writes as an individual for individual readers, writes in a self-conscious way primarily 'for the page' (as Morgan put it in his interview with Chris Jones).[63] This change may have been reinforced by the lectures of Ritchie Girvan: it is interesting that in his book on *Beowulf* Girvan plays down the oral aspect of the poem and sees it very much as a work to be read.[64]

Morgan, with *man* in the singular (*what man's knowledge*), appeals in the rhetorical question to an indefinite world beyond the narrative, while the original

---

[63] Jones, 'Edwin Morgan in Conversation', p. 49.
[64] Girvan writes (*Beowulf and the Seventh Century*, p. 13), '[*Beowulf*] could never have been recited in hall in its complete form, and it cannot easily be divided into sections suitable for delivery there. Moreover, it is too leisurely, and lacks the packed dramatic intensity which is characteristic of the [shorter Germanic] lays and had evidently a special appeal. Finally, the fact that it has numbered sections which are evidently old, and probably original, strongly suggests a literary composition in the strict sense.' The critical consensus today would be that *Beowulf* is a 'literate' work but one very suitable for oral recitation; see especially Orchard, 'Oral Tradition' and *A Critical Companion*, pp. 57–97.

poem refers to 'men' as members of a group. A similar rhetorical question had been introduced at lines 51–2:

> Who can say with truth, whether counsellor in hall,
> Or warrior on earth – where this freight was washed?

This translates:

> Men ne cunnon
> secgan to soðe,   seleræ dende,
> hæleð under heofonum,   hwa þæm hlæste onfeng. (lines 50b–2)

[Men do not know how to tell with truth, hall-counsellors, heroes under the heavens, who received that freight.]

Again (and despite the reference to the counsellor in hall and warrior on earth), the question and the use of the indefinite singular remove the communal perspective, a communal perspective reinforced in the original by the deployment of the formulaic phrase *Men ne cunnon*. The Old English had also expressed the destination of the 'freight' in personal terms (*who received that freight*), thus inviting a spiritual interpretation, while Morgan recasts this in the passive voice (*where that freight was washed*).

This removal of the communal perspective is apparent in the very opening lines of Morgan's translation, in which the first-person-plural declarative statement *Hwæt, we Gar-Dena* [. . .] , inviting assent from the implied audience that the statement constructs, is replaced by the exclamation of an omniscient but impersonal narrator:

> How that glory remains in remembrance,
> Of the Danes and their kings in days gone,
> The acts and valour of princes of their blood! (lines 1–3)

And Morgan's version doesn't say in *whose* remembrance the glory of the Danes remains, a sense of impersonality being conveyed by this circumstance as well.

Similarly at line 38 the communal first-person-singular clause *ne hyrde ic cymlicor   ceol gegyrwan*, 'I have not heard of a ship more splendidly prepared', becomes an impersonal, and passive, exclamation: *No ship in fame more fittingly furnished*. And the formulaic phrase *mine gefræge*, 'as I have heard tell', is either ignored or recast in impersonal terms. The phrase occurs six times in *Beowulf* and Morgan always removes the first-person perspective in his translation. The occurrences are at lines 776 (Morgan, no equivalent), 837 (Morgan, *as minstrels retell*), 1955 (Morgan, *as his fame speaks*), 2480 (Morgan, *As fame related*), 2685 (Morgan, *men say*) and 2837 (Morgan, *by all accounts*).

At line 2200 Morgan does use the phrase *in days nearer ours* (translating *ufaran dogrum*, 'in later days')[65] and he is not consistent in depersonalizing the alternative first-person formulaic phrase expressing traditional knowledge, *ic [. . .] gefrægn*, 'I have heard' (the negative variant *ne gefrægn ic*, 'I have not heard', appears at line 1027): note the occurrences at lines 74 (Morgan, *we are told*), 575 (Morgan, *never have I heard* – but spoken by Beowulf), 1027 (Morgan, *Not [. . .] have I heard*), 2484 (Morgan, *I believe*), 2694 (Morgan, *as I believe*), 2752 (Morgan, *I know*) and 2773 (Morgan, *We are told*). Despite the inconsistency in Morgan's practice in these latter incidences, an overall pattern of depersonalizing and de-communalizing the narrative is apparent in the translation, a pattern that reflects Morgan's aim of making his version a modern poem. In effecting this change Morgan jettisons an important dimension of the original, which he finds incompatible with the modern idiom in which he seeks to work. More generally, his translation also lacks a sense of the traditional formulaic language of *Beowulf* (which scholars had not really explored anyway by the time he was writing). One of the features of the traditional and communal dimension of *Beowulf* was that it had supplied a feeling of intense emotional involvement in the story, which is not available in the same way in the more detached approach of Morgan.

Morgan's lack of empathy with or interest in traditional features of the poetry of *Beowulf* may be seen as consonant with his wariness about issues of tradition in general. As Kevin McCarra notes, he 'is on record as disliking ideas of history and tradition [. . .]. What he rejects in notions of heritage is the implication that the past is forcing the poet in a particular direction.'[66] He responds to the 'music' of *Beowulf*[67] but is determined to translate that music into a new idiom. In doing so he, inevitably, radically changes the character of the narrative voice.

Two Passages for Consideration

Morgan's *Beowulf*, lines 1–11

The opening sentences of Morgan's translation read as follows:

> How that glory remains in remembrance,
> Of the Danes and their kings in days gone,
> The acts and valour of princes of their blood!
>   Scyld Scefing: how often he thrust from their feast-halls
> The troops of his enemies, tribe after tribe,
> Terrifying their warriors: he who had been found
> Long since as a waif and awaited his desert
> While he grew up and throve in honour among men

---

[65] Cf. also *one of our kind* (line 713, translating *manna cynnes / sumne*, 'one of the race of men').
[66] McCarra, 'Edwin Morgan: Lives and Work', pp. 3–4.
[67] Morgan, *Beowulf*, p. xxviii.

Till all the nations neighbouring about him
Sent as his subjects over the whale-fields
Their gifts of tribute: king worth the name![68]

Morgan retains the opening sentence of three interconnected lines but changes it from a declarative statement to an awe-filled *how* exclamation and removes the communal perspective, as mentioned above. Morgan's ideal of vigour is evident elsewhere in the translation but he sacrifices it here in the attempt to convey awe and dignity. There is little sign in this sentence, or in the passage as a whole, of the graphic imagery or arresting compounds which I drew attention to in the preceding section, and exciting patterns of rhythm are not in evidence.

The mostly abstract romance and Latinate vocabulary of the opening sentence contributes to this feeling of awe and dignity but the solidity and impact of the words of the original are lacking: in the original the verb *fremedon*, 'performed, carried out', emphasizes the activity involved in *þrym*, 'glory', and *ellen*, '(acts of) valour', and *gefrunon*, 'heard', links that activity to living poetic tradition. The succinct *in days gone* (rather than the easy stock phrase *in days gone by*) effectively conveys a sense of mutability but the formal-sounding alliterating phrase *remains in remembrance* suggests duty, perhaps, rather than engagement with the great events passed on in memory; the hendiadys of *acts and valour*, divorcing the two concepts, results in a weaker formulation than in the original, and *princes of their blood* while high-sounding is not precise in its meaning. Morgan does not closely imitate the structure of the original sentence, in which the grammatical resolution of the opening clause is delayed until the end of the second line (*gefrunon*), but line 3 in his version is an appositive expansion of the idea of *glory*, just as the closing 'how' clause in the Old English expands on *þrym*, a concise noun phrase being substituted for the finite clause in the translation; and Morgan's mannered word order, notably in the separation of *Of the Danes* from its governing noun *glory*, might be said to reflect the poetic word order of the *Beowulf* sentence, though it is hardly in the idiom of modern verse.

Morgan's three-line opening sentence is followed by a more sweeping one which takes us down to the end of the quoted passage (eight lines). As in the original, this second sentence becomes more specific about the glory and valour mentioned in the first, focusing on the figure of Scyld Scefing. It leads on consecutively from the first, and itself appears strongly consecutive in structure. The subject, *Scyld Scefing*, is introduced in a free-standing verbless exclamation, with the rest of the sentence providing the descriptive justification for the exclamation; the sentence also ends with a verbless exclamation, *king worth the name!*, which rounds it off, emphatically bringing the sentence back to the celebratory note on which it had begun. The *who* clause beginning at line 6 turns out to be the basis of the rest of the sentence, for the following temporal clauses are dependent on it, with the result that the sentence seems to run on and on with

---

68 For the corresponding Old English lines, see p. 32, above.

subordinate material before being given renewed focus by the closing *king worth the name!*

As well as beginning and ending with these exclamatory phrases, the whole sentence is, like the first, a *how* exclamation. This parallelism contributes to the cumulative structure of the passage overall and enhances continuity. *How* exclamations, however, are reminiscent of pre-twentieth-century poetic traditions rather than suggesting a distinctively modern kind of language.

The sense of grammatical consecutiveness in the second sentence is signalled on the page by the use of colons, and the sense of temporal consecutiveness is conveyed by the sequence of temporal markers, *had* (line 6) and *Long since* (line 7) specifying a past in the past and *While* (line 8) and *Till* (line 9) expressing development, while the frequentative expressions *often* (line 4) and *tribe after tribe* (line 5) suggest a sense of the relentlessness of Scyld's military success (cf. Old English *Oft*, line 4, and *monegum*, line 5). After the initial assertion of *thrust from their feast-halls* (line 4), the sentence moves from the passiveness of *had been found* (line 6) and *awaited* (line 7) to the images of dominion with which it ends. The relationship of the elements in *While he grew up and throve*, however, – particularly the *and* – is confusing: presumably Scyld grew up awaiting his desert and then 'throve' in honour: the thriving constituted the desert he had awaited.

The Old English lines corresponding to Morgan's second sentence are made up of a sequence of active verb phrases, strongly set off by the half-line framework of the verse. There is consecutiveness but the sense proceeds by means of short, sharply juxtaposed phrases. Morgan's version is smoother, more discursive, and more sweeping. He turns the abrupt finite clause *egsode eorlas*, 'he terrified the warriors' (line 6), into a participial phrase, *Terrifying their warriors*; changes the more direct *syððan* clause just after this (also line 6) to a qualifying *who* (relative) clause; links by means of *and* his equivalent to the contrastive phrase *he þæs frofre gebad*, 'he experienced consolation/solace for that' (line 7), to the preceding reference to Scyld's destitution:

> He who had been found
> Long since as a waif and awaited his desert (lines 6–7);

and he interrupts the phrase *Sent* [. . .] / *Their gifts of tribute* with the discursive *as his subjects over the whale-fields* (line 10), which replaces the original's image of irresistible power (*hyran scolde*, 'had to obey', line 10) with one of status (*subjects*); the discursiveness here contributes too to the sense of onward flow in these lines. *Sent* also comes across as less oppressive and humiliating than *gomban gyldan*, 'give tribute' (line 11), in which the submission is by no means long-distance; likewise, *gifts of tribute* suggests a voluntary acknowledgement of Scyld in contrast to the bald *scolde*, 'had to', of *Beowulf* itself.

The ferocity of Scyld is thus to an extent played down in Morgan's version. Even the word *thrust* in the phrase *thrust from their feast-halls / The troops of his enemies* is somewhat generic in its associations, whereas *meodosetla ofteah*, 'took away [from many enemies] their mead-benches' (line 5), is more obviously violent. Morgan's version draws on the symbolic significance of the hall as representative of the tribe's security and autonomy but presents a less nakedly destructive image than the Old English.

The verb *thrust* is one of a number of words in the passage that contribute a markedly literary feel to the writing. Other such words are *remembrance, throve, waif* and the kenning *whale-fields*. These are not archaic words (*whale-fields* indeed is Morgan's own invention) but they represent a kind of heightened poetic register, distancing the reader from the narrative and distancing the language of the poem from that of ordinary speech, while at the same time fitting *Beowulf* into poetic modes of expression more recognizable to a post-medieval (though not specifically modern) readership.

Another literary-sounding phrase is *awaited his desert*, briefly referred to above. This is not only much vaguer and weaker than the original *he þæs frofre gebad* (line 7) – and, as in line 8, Morgan's use of *and* (*and awaited his desert*) introduces an element of coordination not present in the original – but is also an inaccurate rendering of the Old English, which means literally 'he experienced consolation/solace for that'. Morgan changes the sense from one of fulfilment to one of patience or expectation. In the Old English, Scyld did not await his desert while he grew up but he experienced consolation for his initial destitution in that he prospered under the clouds (*weox under wolcnum*, line 8: *weox* literally means 'grew' but by extension 'prospered').

Morgan's *Beowulf*, lines 867–74

For these lines Morgan has

> Then a king's retainer,
> A man proved of old, evoker of stories,
> Who held in his memory multitude on multitude
> Of the sagas of the dead, found now a new song
> In words well linked: the man began again
> To weave in his subtlety the exploit of Beowulf,
> To recite with art the finished story,
> To deploy his vocabulary.[69]

By the time he gets to these lines Morgan is well into his stride. This is a fairly straightforward passage by Morgan's standards; it is fluent and unfussy and gives the impression of being thoughtfully composed but with little in the way of obvious poetic effects. Morgan is concerned to get across a sense of the tone and descriptive quality of the evocative Old English depiction of the poet and his artistry but he does not attempt to imitate the virtuosity of the Old English lines. Alliteration here is light, the rhythm generally smooth and there is an absence of

---

[69] For the corresponding Old English lines, see p. 37, above.

Morgan's trademark compound words. Like the Old English, his version gives a lively impression of the technique of traditional poetry without actually going into specific detail, the vocabulary being generic rather than precise: *words well linked, subtlety, with art, deploy*. The one wrong note is in the prosaic closing phrase *To deploy his vocabulary*, which sounds banally inadequate.

The translation is mostly alert and confident, however. Grammatically it follows the sentence structure of the original but Morgan is not literal-minded in his response to imagery and phraseology and his version of the Old English lines is flowing and natural-sounding: *Then* rationalizes *Hwilum*, 'at times'; *evoker of stories* nicely reworks *gidda gemyndig*, 'mindful of tales'; *held in his memory* is a resonant paraphrase of *gemunde*, 'remembered'; *multitude on multitude* is a fluent rendering of the tricky *ealfela* [. . .] *worn*, 'multitude of very great number'; *sagas of the dead* imaginatively extends the meaning of *ealdgesegena*, 'ancient oral traditions'; *now* is a helpful addition, reinforcing the movement of the passage from description of the man and his art to focusing on his new act of composition in the 'present' (the colon in line 871 also reinforces this movement); *weave* sharpens *styrian*, 'recite'; *finished* offers an intelligent interpretation of *on sped*, 'successfully' (i.e., in Morgan's interpretation, 'got to the end of'). Morgan is misled by Klaeber's gloss of *gilphlæden* (Klaeber: 'covered with glory') into translating *guma gilphlæden*, 'a man laden with eloquence', as *A man proved of old*, and the unfortunate *deploy his vocabulary*, as well as being grating, does not capture the potential of *wordum wrixlan*, 'vary his words', a phrase richly suggestive of a key characteristic of Old English poetry, and one indeed reflected in Morgan's version of these lines (in the three phrases in apposition referring to the retainer at the beginning and in the three lines beginning with *To* at the end).

Generally, however, Morgan's response to the Old English lines is sensitive and assured, producing an interesting if unspectacular passage in his translation. It is evocatively descriptive without unduly holding up the progress of the narrative.

Morgan's *Beowulf*: Contexts and Reception

Beowulf still belonged very much to the territory of philologists in the mid twentieth century. Though some poets had been attracted particularly by the sound and rhythm of Old English poetry, notably Pound and Auden,[70] most people interested in modern poetry would have seen little reason to be interested in *Beowulf*. Many of those who had studied *Beowulf*, 'a sort of dinosaur in the entrance hall of English Literature' as Michael Alexander referred to it,[71]

---

[70] See Chris Jones, *Strange Likeness*, pp. 17–67, 68–121.

[71] *Beowulf* (1973 ed.), p. 10. Alexander went on to add, 'Until recently those who wished to study English at university were only allowed to proceed after a minute examination of the epidermis of this sacred monster – or rather of its front end, for the last third of the poem

and other Old English poetry at university had been put off by the difficulty of the language and the dryness of their lecturers' (philological) approach. The world of contemporary poetry seemed to be a world very different from that of philology and, to quote Alexander again, 'Some of the mud that was so zealously slung at the old "crib and gobbet" approach seems to have stuck, very unfairly, to the image of the unoffending poem.'[72] Within Old English studies, Tolkien had published his seminal critical article on *Beowulf* but the key literary studies of the poetry of *Beowulf* still lay ahead.

Hostility to the world of philology is epitomized in Kingsley Amis's 1950s poem '*Beowulf*', for example, which can still make an Anglo-Saxonist wince.[73] Amis is caustically dismissive of *Beowulf* and its hero and of the approach of philological scholars, which he cleverly parodies in the poem. Beowulf the hero and philology are conflated in Amis's unsympathetic perspective – 'Must we then reproduce his paradigms?', he exclaims at the end of the poem – and both are presented as irrelevant to the concerns of (modern) literature.

Not long afterwards Brigid Brophy and associates, expressing the same outlook as Amis, would famously consign *Beowulf* to the ranks of books 'we' could do without: 'Boring and unattractive as a story, pointlessly bloodthirsty but – we are always told – fundamentally Christian, *Beowulf* is a fine example of primitive non-art' and it 'should now be handed over to the historians or left to be picked apart by linguistic scholars'.[74] In fact *Beowulf* was already pretty much the preserve of historians and linguists and, as noted below, despite the efforts of Morgan, would continue to be so in the middle decades of the twentieth century.

Morgan had encountered some antipathy to Old English among his fellow students as an undergraduate but his own experience of and response to it were different, and different too from that of metropolitan intellectuals like Amis and Brophy: 'I was one of the few who positively liked Anglo-Saxon', he later said. 'It was generally thought to be a hard part of the course and wasn't very popular. But I liked it and fairly soon I suppose got into the way of being able to read the language and to enjoy it.'[75] As someone who also belonged to that parallel universe of contemporary poetry, Morgan saw himself as equipped to make what he felt to be a great poem available in a form 'acceptable to one's poetic co-readers and co-writers',[76] something he felt to be well worth doing. It is interesting that, like Alexander and Heaney after him, he was working in a non-metropolitan context, away from the circles of Amis and Brophy. In practice his translation did little to change perceptions (Amis and Brophy were writing after his transla-

was rarely used as a translation exercise' (ibid.). In the different climate in which he produced his 2001 edition, Alexander dropped this discussion from his revised Introduction.
72 Ibid.
73 Amis, *Collected Poems 1944–1979*, p. 18.
74 Brophy, Levey and Osborne, *Fifty Works of English Literature We Could Do Without*, p. 1.
75 Morgan, *Nothing is Not Giving Messages*, p. 121.
76 Morgan, *Beowulf*, p. xi.

tion came out) or to alter the 'lang–lit' divide that continued to be a feature of English studies in many British, particularly English, academic institutions in the twentieth century. The British intellectual climate at the time was not very favourable, and indeed the main readership of the translation turned out to be in America, not the readership that Morgan originally had in mind; the translation was widely used on college literature courses there at a time when in Britain and Ireland *Beowulf* was typically not being taught in translation, only in Old English. Symbolic of Morgan's indifference to the idea of a lang–lit divide was his dedication of his modern poem to an Old English scholar, Girvan.

Morgan's translation of *Beowulf* into 'proper' modern poetry was a pioneering attempt. His version is not always convincing in its response to the original text, as I have suggested, and his technique does not always fit the bill in this ambitious undertaking – ambitious especially for a young poet working to develop his craft and find his own voice. It is important, however, to acknowledge the significance of Morgan's enterprise in bringing *Beowulf* into the world of modern poetry, producing a version of it for a sophisticated modern readership. It is also important to acknowledge the extent of his success in this enterprise. His translation takes *Beowulf* seriously and works to recreate it as a modern poem. It presents a gripping narrative with admirable pace and atmosphere, in a form that is interesting poetically, if uneven in its execution. The translation shows vigour but also dignity and gracefulness.

Morgan's version was generally not enthusiastically received, however, in the period after its publication. An early review by Ben Kimpel, published in *Poetry*, gives it only a 'C-minus'. Kimpel refers to Morgan as 'a conscientious artisan' and remarks in half-hearted praise that there is 'nothing offensive in his diction';[77] he declares that *Beowulf* must find a great poet if 'the thrill which the best Old English poetry can give' is to be conveyed; he ends his review by observing, 'Mr. Morgan correctly realized that the field was open for the great poet; it still is.'[78]

More positive was the assessment of the editor of *Poetry Review*, John Smith, who reviewed the paperback version that came out in 1962, selecting it indeed as his 'Editor's Choice' for the relevant number of the journal. Smith finds in Morgan's version 'something of the feel of the time and place as well as the language [of the original]' and he draws attention to the 'remarkable consistency and apparent ease' of the translation.[79] For Smith, Morgan's *Beowulf* 'has the power to give readers considerable pleasure', though at the same time he thinks that the translation is too often 'merely "ordinary"' and that the verse is rhythmically monotonous in places.[80] The Old English scholar and critic Edward Irving (writing in 1966) is lukewarm in his response to Morgan's version: he notes with tempered approval that 'much of the time it sounds like poetry' and declares

---

[77] Kimbel, 'Mr. Morgan's *Beowulf*: C–', pp. 46, 47.
[78] 'Mr. Morgan's Beowulf: C–', p. 48.
[79] [Smith,] 'Editor's Choice', p. 107.
[80] 'Editor's Choice', p. 108.

that '[t]he verse rarely sinks below a certain level of interest and expressiveness', but, considering the views that Morgan expresses in his Introduction, he judges the translation to be 'more conservative and more pallid than might have been expected'.[81]

In his survey of translations of *Beowulf* in print in the 1960s, J. K. Crane gives a damning verdict on Morgan's version, referring to its 'unnatural phraseological patterns', which 'hinder comprehension and mutilate metrics'.[82] Crane finds Burton Raffel's version (to be discussed in the next chapter) to be much superior; 'Morgan's, by contrast, staggers', he writes, adding that it 'offends the ear more than most others'.[83] On the other hand, the poet and critic Kenneth Rexroth (writing after Raffel's version had come out) praised Morgan's translation as the most elegant he knew.[84] And the leading Anglo-Saxonist Eric Stanley, writing after Michael Alexander's translation had also appeared, declared Morgan's to be 'the most satisfactory of all the attempts to reduce *Beowulf* to Modern English verse'.[85] Showing a perceptive understanding of Morgan's approach, Stanley comments, 'Morgan is literal enough for us to know what words of his render each half line of the poem, and good enough for us to feel that some new grace has been given to many ancient lines'.[86]

Burton Raffel himself was a reviewer of Morgan's *Beowulf*, producing a brief notice in *College English* when the paperback version came out (which was the year before the publication of Raffel's own translation) and discussing it at greater length in an article in *Yale Review* a couple of years later;[87] he also refers to Morgan's translation in subsequent publications.[88] In the *College English* review Raffel grants that Morgan's translation 'is at least reasonably clear and clean' but he states that it is 'not successful poetry'. In the *Yale Review* piece he refers to Morgan as 'not perhaps a good poet' and to his 'failure to create good poetry';[89] indeed in this essay he distinguishes between his own approach to translation, that of a poet, and the approach of Morgan, 'a scholar-critic',[90] thereby dismissing Morgan as not really a poet at all.

Even some of the more sympathetic critics mentioned above failed to appreciate the poetry of Morgan's *Beowulf*, which we have seen to be varied, graceful,

[81] Irving, 'Reviews of Recent Translations', p. 69.
[82] Crane, '"To Thwack or Be Thwacked"', p. 334.
[83] Ibid.
[84] Rexroth, 'Classics Revisited – IV: *Beowulf*', p. 27.
[85] Stanley, 'Translation from Old English', p. 70.
[86] 'Translation from Old English', p. 71.
[87] Raffel, 'Review of *Beowulf*, trans. Edwin Morgan'; 'On Translating *Beowulf*'.
[88] Raffel, *The Forked Tongue*, pp. 24–70 and *passim*; see also Raffel, *The Art of Translating Poetry*, *passim*.
[89] 'Review of *Beowulf*, trans. Edwin Morgan' p. 587; 'On Translating *Beowulf*', p. 541 (*The Forked Tongue*, p. 66). In the latter discussion, while insisting on Morgan's failure to create good poetry, Raffel does have something good to say about his translation: 'his is on the whole a dignified version, written quite plainly out of deep and intelligent respect for the *Beowulf* poet' (ibid.).
[90] 'On Translating *Beowulf*', p. 532 (*The Forked Tongue*, p. 58).

intelligent and at times exciting. Kimpel, Crane and Raffel miss the qualities of the translation altogether, while others I have referred to are perhaps looking for something more flowing and easy-to-read, more student-orientated, perhaps, than what Morgan offers. Morgan invites the reader to savour intricacies of diction and rhythm rather than always sweeping on ahead with the narrative. It is understandable that readers primarily interested in the narrative could feel dissatisfaction with Morgan's version and look for a rendering that they might perceive as less 'fussy'. After Morgan it was certainly felt that there was room for further attempts at recreating the poem in modern English verse. It is to the first of these further attempts that we turn in the next chapter, moving across the Atlantic Ocean from Britain to America as we do so.

✦5✦

Burton Raffel:
Mastering the Original to Leave It

Burton Raffel's translation of *Beowulf* appeared in 1963, eleven years after that of Edwin Morgan. Raffel would go on to be a prolific and admired translator of poetry (and prose) from many languages, ancient and modern, but, as was the case with Morgan, his translation of *Beowulf* comes from early in his literary career. It is the confident and energetic work of a young writer, and it comes indeed from a time that was one of ostensible confidence and optimism in the larger dominant culture as well. Like Morgan, having previously done translations of other Old English poems,[1] Raffel had moved very soon afterwards to the much more ambitious undertaking of translating *Beowulf* (using Klaeber's third edition as his basic text).[2] Since then, of course, both poets have had long and distinguished careers, though moving in very different directions.

Raffel on Raffel

Raffel has written much in explanation and justification of his translation of *Beowulf* in particular and of his approach to translation in general.[3] He insists in his *Yale Review* essay 'On Translating *Beowulf*' on the creative subjectivity of the poet-translator, who 'needs to master the original in order to leave it'.[4] The poet-translator must not be trapped by the original but must be guided by 'the necessity of self-expression' and by an 'inner voice':[5] 'The greatest sin a translator

---

[1] See Raffel, trans., *Poems from the Old English*.
[2] See Raffel, *Beowulf*, p. xx (where he also refers to his 'extensive use' of the edition by Dobbie (*ASPR*) and also to consulting Wrenn's 1953 edition); on Raffel's correspondence with the scholars Robert P. Creed and Jess B. Bessinger, Jr while he was working on his translation, see below, p. 133, n. 41.
[3] As well as 'On Translating *Beowulf*', *The Forked Tongue* and *The Art of Translating Poetry*, see Raffel's essay 'Translating Medieval European Poetry'.
[4] 'On Translating *Beowulf*', p. 533 (*The Forked Tongue*, p. 59).
[5] 'On Translating *Beowulf*', pp. 545, 546 (*The Forked Tongue*, p. 70).

can commit, accordingly, is to fail to breathe life into his recreation. He can never breathe life into it if he is unable to force himself away from the original, and far enough away so that he can be close in spirit and yet be free to *create* in the new linguistic medium.'[6] The letter killeth, but the spirit giveth life, so to speak.

Morgan, for example, is viewed by Raffel as too closely tied to the original, too academic, and not free enough in recreating the original in new terms. As I have mentioned (see above, p. 107), Raffel distinguishes between his own approach to translation, that of a poet, and the approach of Morgan, 'a scholar-critic'. This is insensitive to the art of Morgan, whose version, though more 'self-abasing' (to use Chris Jones's term in relation to Morgan's stance as a poet) than that of Raffel, is effective as poetry in a different but perfectly legitimate way.[7] Raffel's comments give an excellent insight into his own approach, however. He is unapologetic about taking liberties with the original in the name of poetry. He is refreshingly unstuffy in his attitude to the translator's task – he even emphasizes that a translation must inevitably distort.[8] The danger is, of course, that too free an approach will not worry enough about the distortion and thus will misrepresent the original. This is what some commentators, particularly Old English scholars, have accused Raffel of in his *Beowulf*. Marijane Osborn sums up this view when she writes of the Raffel translation, 'This rendering into an extremely free imitative verse is probably, as Raffel claims, the liveliest translation of *Beowulf*. My misgivings echo those of many reviewers: in its freedom this translation often misrepresents the poem.'[9] Osborn also refers to Raffel's version as a 'loose (and provocative) translation into modern poetry.'[10] Edward Irving, who generally approves of Raffel's version, speaks of 'a certain recklessness' in the translation and suggests that '[h]e is often guilty of "luridizing" his original in an exaggerated and not very tasteful way, sometimes in a seriously misleading way.'[11]

Raffel had experimented with translating Old English verse before he produced his version of *Beowulf* and he would produce other translations from Old English in the future.[12] As in his previous Old English work, he uses a four-beat line in his *Beowulf* but, as he explains in his Introduction to the translation,

---

[6] 'On Translating *Beowulf*', pp. 533–4 (*The Forked Tongue*, p. 59).
[7] On the 'self-abasing' character of Morgan's poetry, see Chris Jones, 'Edwin Morgan', where Jones writes of Morgan's 'tendency to self-abasement in service of the poem' (p. 163) and of his 'sublimation of the artist's personal concerns to the greater requirements of the art form' (p. 162).
[8] 'On Translating *Beowulf*', p. 533 (*The Forked Tongue*, p. 59): 'there must be distortion, to a greater or lesser degree, simply by definition'.
[9] Osborn, 'Translations, Versions, Illustrations', p. 358.
[10] 'Translations, Versions, Illustrations', p. 342.
[11] Irving, 'Reviews of Recent Translations', p. 70; Raffel responds, objecting to Irving's criticisms, in a letter printed in *The Forked Tongue*, pp. 140–1. Elsewhere, however, Raffel himself admits to something very like Irving's 'certain recklessness' when he writes, acknowledging that good translation is 'an act of hubris', that the good translator is a 'risk-taker' ('Translating Medieval European Poetry', p. 35).
[12] Raffel, *Poems from the Old English*; *Poems and Prose from the Old English*.

'I have felt it advisable, even obligatory, to alliterate much more freely [than in the earlier translations], occasionally as the Old English alliterates, more usually in irregular patterns developed *ad hoc*.'[13] Here we see Raffel's practice changing as he responds to the challenges offered by the epic poem. He has not changed his 'personal credo' with regard to making translations, however, and in the Introduction to his *Beowulf* he repeats a passage from the Introduction to his earlier collection, *Poems from the Old English*: 'The translator's only hope is to re-create something roughly equivalent in the new language, something that is itself good poetry and that at the same time carries a reasonable measure of the force and flavor of the original. In this sense a recreation can only be a creation.'[14] These comments from *Poems from the Old English* are very much consonant with ideas of Raffel we have seen expressed above. Later he would write, 'What the translator of medieval poetry must do [. . .] is to convey to *his* audience not the bare words of his original text but the *meaning* of those words' (Raffel's emphases).[15]

In *Poems from the Old English* Raffel declares too that at times he has omitted Old English metaphors from the translations and indeed that he has added images not in the original poems.[16] Strategies of this kind are by no means unique to Raffel – they are also widely practised by Morgan, for one, and it has been insisted indeed, by Valentine Cunningham, that such 'pleonasm' is an essential characteristic of all translation[17] – but Raffel carries them further than many other translators and he makes a special point of drawing attention to them, in line with his principle of 'leaving' the original poem. For Raffel, this kind of radical approach, which he would refer to later as the 'interpretive' approach,[18] is what defines a poetic translation. Rather than being tied too closely to the original the translator of a poem like *Beowulf* must keep the bigger picture in mind: 'The translator of medieval verse is transmitting an entire culture, a dead worldview, with all its dead customs and turns of phrase – cast in molds of dead verse form and verse movement.'[19] In doing so, the translator must be bold, and boldness is certainly one of the key qualities of Raffel's translation.

---

[13] *Beowulf*, p. xxii.
[14] *Beowulf*, p. xxi; *Poems from the Old English*, p. xxvi (2nd ed., p. 12).
[15] 'Translating Medieval European Poetry', p. 35.
[16] *Poems from the Old English*, p. xxviii (2nd ed., p. 14).
[17] Cunningham, 'Interlinearversitility, or, The Anxieties of Translating'; see also Cunningham's essay, 'Thou Art Translated: Bible Translating, Heretic Reading and Cultural Transformation', especially pp. 115–18.
[18] In his 1988 volume *The Art of Translating Poetry* (pp. 110–28), Raffel identifies four broad types of translation: *formal* translation, largely for scholarly rather than literary purposes; *interpretive* translation, the type he himself practises, aimed primarily at a general audience which reads for literary reasons; *expansive* (or 'free') translation, as practised by Christopher Logue, for example, in his translations of the *Iliad*; and *imitative* translation, 'which in plain truth I think just barely translation at all' (p. 110), as in the *Imitations* of Robert Lowell. He seems to consign Morgan to the ranks of the formal translators, along with Stanley B. Greenfield and others (see pp. 118–21).
[19] 'Translating Medieval European Poetry', p. 35.

Raffel in Practice

Burton Raffel's translation of *Beowulf* represents the Old English poem in a highly accessible and readable form. Raffel's approach is geared towards engaging the modern reader – the 'general reader' – in a vivid and exciting narrative concerned with heroic exploits and their significance, and doing so in a way that that reader can understand and appreciate. Clarity, logic and progression are hallmarks of the treatment of narrative in Raffel's translation, producing a satisfying impression of narrative connectedness. The narrative itself has pace and variety and is marked above all by a strong sense of forward momentum, as the reader is swept along by its stirring action and speeches. Raffel strives not to distract from this by the obtrusive use of poetic effects or mannered diction, and he shuns archaism and formulaic language, adopting an idiom that is dignified but also, for the most part, modern and natural-sounding. His version of *Beowulf* is lively and reads well; it makes a very different impression indeed from that given by *Beowulf* itself, however, since the Old English poem is not known for the qualities I have just highlighted.

Narrative momentum

The sense of forward narrative momentum is achieved in a number of ways. The metrical structure adopted by Raffel itself contributes a suitable framework for narrative. The four-beat metre provides a steady rhythm but is not intrusive and, though there are examples of vigorous alliteration, particularly in passages of exciting action, alliteration is mostly light throughout, hardly noticeable in many sequences of straightforward narrative. An example of insistent alliteration comes in the account of Beowulf's victory in combat over Grendel, a climactic scene, of course, when the hero

> stopped
> The monster's flight, fastened those claws
> In his fists till they cracked, clutched Grendel
> Closer. (lines 759–62)

In a passage such as that describing the discovery of the dragon's treasure, on the other hand, a significant enough narrative juncture but not a big moment in the poem, alliteration, while there in the background, does not divert attention from the 'facts' of the story and thereby make the scene seem more important than it is:

> a man stumbled on
> The entrance, went in, discovered the ancient
> Treasure, the pagan jewels and gold
> The dragon had been guarding, and dazzled and greedy
> Stole a gem-studded cup, and fled. (lines 2213–17)

Narrative momentum is maintained in this sentence constructed around a series of action verbs – *stopped, went in, discovered, stole, fled* –, with no overly distracting metrical embellishments, and indeed only light descriptive colouring.

Building on this metrical structure, Raffel uses enjambment very extensively indeed. In particular, a distinctive characteristic of his run-on lines is his preference for phrases beginning at the end of one line and being completed at the beginning of the next, as in *stumbled on / The entrance* and *ancient / Treasure* in the passage just quoted. Such phrases moving the reader briskly on from one line to the next are everywhere in the translation, from *cut / For themselves* (lines 2–3), *every / Land* (lines 4–5) and *Ruler / Of glory* (lines 16–17) in the opening lines, to *ever / Lived* (lines 3180–1) and *no man / So open* (lines 3181–2) at the end.

Line boundaries are thus smoothed out by Raffel, with syntax over-riding metrical division and the last word of the line having a pronounced linking function. The last word of the line often also bears considerable thematic importance, with 'strong' words being placed in this position. At the end of lines Raffel sometimes repeats words that have occurred in this position previously in the same passage, as in the sequence on the fight with Grendel, from which I quoted above, in which a number of lines end with the key word *claws* (lines 738, 746, 748, 760, 763 [741 has the rhyming end-word *jaws*]). Elsewhere there may be wordplay relating the endings of different lines, or thematic links between final words. Thus, for example, there is a sequence of lines at lines 127–30 ending *morning, laments, joyless, mourning*, combining wordplay and thematic connection; a thematic connection is apparent in the final words of lines 176–81, *Hell's, Hell, God, Lord*, leading to *Hail* at the end of line 186; similarly at lines 54–62 we have lines ending *father, men, son, children, daughter* (cf. lines 372–3, ending *father, daughter*); in a graphic passage at lines 815–20 key narrative words are placed at the end of the line: *pain, shoulder, split, Beowulf, escaped, den*; and at lines 847–9 we find *boiling, heat, swirling*. While such effects are not obtrusive, they tighten the sense of narrative and thematic connection between lines, moving the attention of the reader away from the structure of the individual line. Other patterns apparent across the ends of lines include (delayed) rhyme (e. g., lines 104–7, *slime, crime*; 1409–10, *steep, deep*) and contrast of meaning (e. g., lines 487–8, *fewer, more*; 1254–5, *hall, hell*).

The structuring of sentences overall works to enhance the sense of forward momentum and narrative connectedness. Instead of the abrupt opposition and apposition of the original, which interrupt progression, Raffel favours smooth syntax and clearly defined sentence development. Especially notable is his use of present participles where the Old English has either finite verbs or no direct equivalent. Present participles deployed in this way are a staple feature of modern literary narrative (but not of that of Old English poetry), and they are widely in evidence in Raffel's translation, as, for example, in the passage in which Hrothgar's coastguard challenges Beowulf and his warriors when they arrive from Geatland. Raffel has

> He came riding down,
> Hrothgar's lieutenant, spurring his horse,
> Needing to know why they'd landed, these men
> In armor. Shaking his heavy spear
> In their faces he spoke. (lines 231–6)

The closing part of this gives a straightforward, and entirely typical, example of the substitution of a present participle for a finite verb; here Raffel renders the two discrete clauses of the original – *þrymmum cwehte / mægenwudu mundum, meþelwordum frægn*, 'strongly he shook his mighty spear, asked with formal words' (lines 235–6) – as one combined image (making use of one of his line-straddling phrases), consisting grammatically of a premodifying present participle and a verb phrase. The note of aggressiveness in *In their faces* is one that Raffel reads into the Old English account.

Present participles are also brought in in the first part of the quotation. The first of them, *riding*, is an idiomatic enough equivalent to *ridan*, 'to ride', in the Old English (line 234); *spurring his horse*, however, is Raffel's descriptive addition, and *Needing to know* represents a concise recasting of the Old English finite clause *hine fyrwyt bræc / modgehygdum   hwæt þa men wæron*, 'curiosity pressed him in the thoughts of his mind as to what these men were' (lines 232–3). These participles provide an element of smooth and logical narrative progression, in contrast to the abrupt effect of the sequence of separate half-lines in the original. They also add interest to the account of the episode, imparting a sense of urgency through the consecutive relationship of these two phrases (without linking *and*) and emphasizing the point of view of the coastguard; point of view is also emphasized in the deictic reference to '*these* men / In armor'.

The coastguard goes on (lines 242–3) to contrast the openness of the approach of Beowulf and his men with the furtiveness of previous incomers, who had intended harm against the Danes. Unlike the Geats, these invaders had come *sneaking ashore / From their ships, seeking our lives and our gold*. Narrative momentum is again achieved here through the use of present participles. The Old English has *þe on land Dena   laðra nænig / mid scipherge sceðþan ne meahte*, 'so that in the land of the Danes no enemies could do harm with their ship-army'. Raffel turns this into two parallel present participle phrases, linked by rhyme (*sneaking, seeking*) as well as alliteration. The sense of furtiveness is supplied by Raffel and that of intentionality enhanced in this atmospheric translation, and Raffel renders the non-specific verb *sceðþan*, 'harm', with the concrete *seeking our lives and our gold*.

At lines 220–1 Raffel introduces a present participle where there is no directly equivalent finite verb in the original. The recasting is a bit more complicated in this instance but as elsewhere Raffel is binding two distinct Old English clauses (though with different subjects) – *wundenstefna   gewaden hæfde, / þæt ða liðende land gesawon, / brimclifu blican*, 'the curved-prowed (ship) had advanced, so that the travellers saw land, the sea-cliffs shining' (lines 220–2a) – into an integrated image: *Standing in the round-curled prow they could see / Sparkling hills*. The introduction of the detail of the sailors standing in the prow, by means of a present participle premodifying the principal clause, achieves a smooth and coherent narrative flow. Just after this in the same sentence *rejoicing* / [. . .] *they quietly ended / Their voyage* (lines 222–4) exemplifies the same stylistic trait, the Old English having þa wæs sund liden, / eoletes æt ende, 'then was the water crossed, the voyage at an end' (lines 223b–4a). The added participles bring out the coherence of the scene being depicted, as well as, in the case of *rejoicing*, adding emotive detail (further descriptive detail is added in *quietly*).

Urgency is apparent in the cumulative sequence of present participles at lines 153–7, in a passage that ponders the misery that Grendel causes to the Danes: *keeping the bloody feud / Alive, seeking no peace, offering no truce, accepting no settlement* [. . .] *and paying* [. . .]. The Old English has a series of finite verbs – *wan*, 'fought', *wæg*, 'carried on', *wolde*, 'wished to' (lines 151–8) – and is appositive in structure. Raffel converts these verbs into a cumulative series of present participles, giving a strong sense of forward momentum, with the rhetorical force of the sequence emphasized by the repetition of the adjective *no* (four times) and the absence of the conjunction *and*.

Cumulation, exemplified in this passage and in others quoted above, is itself one of Raffel's characteristic techniques that contribute to this strong sense of forward momentum in his writing. He makes use of cumulative sequences not only of present participles, as here, or in a passage near the end of the poem describing a military pursuit, where in contrast to the appositive statements of the original –

> Þa wæs æht boden
> Sweona leodum,   segn Higelaces
> freoðowong þone   forð ofereodon (lines 2957b–9)

[Then pursuit was given to the people of the Swedes, the banners of Hygelac overran the place of refuge] –

the army is depicted as

> sweeping across the field,
> Smashing through the walls, waving Higlac's
> Banners as they came. (lines 2958–60)

Raffel also has cumulative sequences of finite verbs, as in the sequence *stopped, went in, discovered, stole, fled* mentioned earlier, or in a later breathless account of battle, in which the warrior Efor, it is reported,

> Caught the Swedish king, cracked
> His helmet, split his skull, dropped him,
> Pale and bleeding, to the ground, then put him
> To death with a swift stroke. (lines 2486–9)

By contrast, the corresponding passage in the original poem is made up of a series of discrete clauses, with changes of subject, and the relatedness of the actions is left implicit:

> þær Ongenþeow   Eofores niosað;
> guðhelm toglad,   gomela Scylfing
> hreas hildeblac;   hond gemunde
> fæhðo genoge,   feorhsweng ne ofteah. (lines 2486–9)

[there Ongentheow approached Eofor; the war-helmet split apart, the old Scylfing fell, battle-pale; his hand remembered enough feuds, did not withhold the mortal blow.]

And, as well as of finite verbs and participles, cumulative sequences of adjectives are also a feature of Raffel's translation. The agony of the Danes as they are oppressed by Grendel is

> harsh
> And unending, violent and cruel, and evil. (lines 192–3)

The corresponding Old English has a series of adjectives but also makes use of phrases in apposition, and the half-line structure is very apparent:

> wæs þæt gewin to swyð,
> laþ ond longsum,   þe on ða leode becom,
> nydwracu niþgrim,   nihtbealwa mæst. (lines 191b–3)

[that struggle was too harsh, grievous and long-lasting, which came upon the people, cruel distress, the greatest of night-evils.]

According to Raffel, Beowulf, as he prepares to fight Grendel, is

> wakeful,
> Watching, waiting, eager to meet
> His enemy, and angry at the thought of his coming. (lines 707–9)

The corresponding Old English is a dense single clause:

> ac he wæccende   wraþum on andan
> bad bolgenmod   beadwa geþinges. (lines 708–9)

[but he, watching in anger for the enemy, awaited the outcome of the combat, enraged in his mind.]

Cumulation is also a feature of *Beowulf* itself, of course, but its use there is predominantly descriptive, whereas in Raffel's translation the emphasis is primarily on action. This emphasis on action is illustrated particularly in passages of description in the original which Raffel has converted into passages of action. In *Beowulf* Wealhtheow's statement of her belief in the loyalty of the Danish noblemen is expressed adjectivally:

Her is æghwylc eorl oþrum getrywe,
modes milde, mandrihtne hold;
þegnas syndon geþwære, þeod ealgearo. (lines 1228–30)

[Here each nobleman is true to the other, mild of mind, loyal to his lord; the thegns are united, the people fully prepared.]

In Raffel's version this loyalty is expressed as action:

All men speak softly, here, speak mildly
And trust their neighbors, protect their lord,
Are loyal followers who would fight [. . .] (lines 1228–30)

Similarly, a description of the violence of battle which is expressed in the Old English by means of a single verb supported by adjectival material –

þonne heoru bunden, hamere geþruen,
sweord swate fah swin ofer helme
ecgum dyhttig andweard scireð. (lines 1285–7)

[when the ornamented sword, forged by the hammer, the sword stained with blood, strong in its edges, cuts through the boar-crest over the opposing helmet]

–

is recast, and supplemented, by Raffel as an asyndetic cumulative series of action participles:

Smashing their shining swords, their bloody,
Hammer-forged blades onto boar-headed helmets,
Slashing and stabbing with the sharpest of points. (lines 1285–7)

And action is also emphasized in passages of reported speech, where Raffel omits introductory speech verbs, launching directly into the speeches themselves. Thus:

Finn offered them,
Instead of more war, words of peace:
There would be no victory, they'd divide the hall [. . .] (lines 1084–6)

And again:

He and the brave Hengest would live
Like brothers [. . .] (lines 1099–100)

The Old English is more formal, and less immediate, in introducing these speeches:

ac hig him geþingo budon,
þæt hie him oðer flet eal gerymdon [. . .] (lines 1085b–6)

[but they offered them an agreement, that they would completely clear another hall for them . . .]

> aðum benemde
> þæt he þa wealafe   weotena dome
> arum heolde [...] (lines 1097b–9a)

[declared with oaths that he would treat the survivors of the calamity with honour, in accordance with the judgement of his counsellors.]

The omission of these verbs imparts urgency and immediacy to the presentation of speeches, bringing readers straight to their substance and to the actions that the speeches are concerned with, and highlighting the point of view of the speakers.

In these ways Raffel's treatment of narrative produces an accessible and readable version of the Old English poem, establishing and retaining the interest of the modern reader. In maintaining this interest, Raffel also makes widespread use of rhetorical features, though not of an overly poetic kind. There is much use of anaphora and other kinds of repetition, adding dignity to the narrative: *If he can, / If he can* (lines 444–5), *whoever, whatever* (line 942), *Would stop, would break* (line 966), *soldier after soldier* (line 1113), *Eight horses [. . .] ./ Eight steeds* (lines 1036–7), *What I said I will do, I will do* (line 1706), *Prosperity, prosperity, prosperity* (line 1735); another kind of repetition occurs in the cumulation of *-ing* participles mentioned above, a further example of which is the description of the dragon, no longer *Glowing in the dark sky, glorying / In its riches, burning and raiding* (lines 2833–4). Other favoured rhetorical tropes of Raffel's include zeugma (lines 243, *seeking our lives and our gold*; 743–4, *death / And Grendel's great teeth came together*; lines 1199–1200, *saved / Its tight-carved jewels, and his skin*; etc.), exclamation (line 1, *Hear me!*; line 489, *How she wept!*; line 766, *a miserable journey for the writhing monster!*; etc.), and personification, particularly of death (lines 743, 975, 1007, etc.) but also of fate (lines 734, 2400) and life (line 792).

Speeches are marked in the translation by the use of ceremonious exclamatory language, as in *But to table* (line 489), *Let your sorrow end!* (line 1385), which can sound stilted. In speeches too Raffel cultivates a kind of heroic brevity and directness, as in *Nor will I* (line 435), *The truth / Is simple* (lines 532–3), *He could not* (line 2855), though, like the narrative, speeches can also contain elaborated, if sometimes laborious wordplay: 'Hergar', says Hrothgar,

> had died and dying made me,
> Second among Healfdane's sons, first
> In this nation. (lines 468–70)

Examples of such wordplay in the narrative include *fearing / The beginning might not be the end* (lines 133–4) and *a brave / Man on an ugly mission* (lines 3028–9).

Raffel produces an accessible and readable translation of the Old English poem. On the other hand, many of the distinctive qualities of that poem have had to be jettisoned in the process. With the emphasis on forward momentum, the *Beowulfian* feature of discrete half-line phrases standing out strongly in relation to each other is smoothed out. Repetition and variation are not significantly in evidence in Raffel's version, and in contrast to the appositional technique of the original poem, connections between sentence elements are explicitly signalled in the translation.

'Directness and clarity'

In his 'Afterword' to Raffel's *Beowulf*, R. P. Creed refers to the 'directness and clarity' of the translation, an apt characterization indeed, but one which also highlights the un*Beowulfian* quality of Raffel's writing.[20] Though certain rhetorical features are in evidence as we have just seen, the language of Raffel's translation is generally natural-sounding and unostentatious. The phrase *bright-tongued boasts* (line 640, a descriptive expansion of the Old English *gilpcwide*, 'boast-speech') is a rare obvious poeticism and one of a relatively small number of compound words that Raffel includes, and *sea-road* (line 239, a close translation of *lagustræte*) is a rare kenning. Raffel works to make his writing interesting, as we have seen, but he mostly avoids such arresting expressions, in line with the emphasis on accessibility to the general reader and on narrative momentum, as referred to above.

Thus, he simplifies the original where he deems it helpful, cutting out unnecessary detail and indirectness of expression. The Spear-Danes, Ring-Danes, West-Danes and so on of the original become simply the *Danes* or *Danish* (line 1, 391, etc.), or the name is dropped altogether (e.g., lines 116, 383), and the dynastic name Scylding, which occurs forty-five times in *Beowulf*, does not appear, as is the case with a host of other potentially confusing names; even Hildeburh becomes another nameless woman in Raffel's version: she is simply *Finn's wife, Hnaf's sister* (line 1171). The names themselves are in many cases simplified in their spellings (though not the main ones like *Beowulf*, *Grendel* and *Hrothgar*, which are too well known to change), to make them look less alien to modern experience – *Shild, Herot, Higlac*, and so on.

Simplification also includes stylistic features, such as the replacement of litotes with more categorical formulations, as at line 3128, *the Geats were not troubled with scruples* (Old English *lyt ænig mearn*, 'little did anyone mourn', line 3129); the removal of irony, as at line 768, *Danes shook with terror* (Old English *Denum eallum wearð* [. . .] *eorlum ealuscerwen*, 'that was some sharing-out of ale for the Danes', lines 767b–9a); the recasting of negative statements as positive, as at line 1469, *Unferth was afraid* (Old English *selfa ne dorste*, 'he himself did not dare', line 1468), and again in the same passage (lines 1471–2), *Beowulf and fear / Were strangers* (Old English, *Ne wæs þæm oðrum swa*, 'it wasn't so for the other one [Beowulf]', line 1471); also, like Morgan, Raffel largely dispenses with the use of the first-person narrator, considering this presence, which is such a definitive

[20] 'Afterword' (Raffel, trans., *Beowulf*), p. 124.

element of heroic narrative, to be intrusive and irrelevant to the modern reader: at lines 39–40, for example, he has *No ship / Had ever sailed* for the Old English *Ne hyrde ic cymlicor ceol gegyrwan*, 'I have not heard of a ship more handsomely prepared' (line 38). This removal of the first-person narrator is one of the transformations by means of which Raffel takes *Beowulf* out of the tradition in which the original poem places itself, a formulaic and stylized tradition, and presents it in a modern idiom as the creation of a modern poet.[21]

Raffel provides much clarifying information as he goes along, glossing, explaining and rewording, to ensure that the reader knows exactly what is happening in the story and who is doing what. Thus, when describing Grendel, for example, rather than translate *feond on helle* (line 101) literally as 'a fiend in hell' or the like, he makes sure that the reader understands that Grendel does not literally live in hell but that he *made his home in a hell / Not hell but earth* (lines 103–4). The metaphor *isernscure*, 'shower of iron', used in *Beowulf* at line 3116 of arrows being fired in battle, is explicated as *arrows falling in iron / Showers* (lines 3116–17). A similar clarification of an Old English image, in a passage in the translation that is remarkable for its lively play of sound and sense, comes in the account of the approach of Beowulf and his men to Hrothgar's hall:

> They arrived with their mail shirts
> Glittering, silver-shining links,
> Clanking an iron song as they came. (lines 321–3)

This is an alert and poetically expressive rendering, picking up on the image of singing in the original and recasting it appropriately in a way that clarifies the Old English image. The original has (lines 321b–3a)

> Guðbyrne scan
> heard hondlocen;   hringiren scir
> song in searwum.

[The battle-mail-coat shone, hard, with hand-forged links, the bright ring-mail sang on the armour.]

---

[21] On Morgan's removal of the first-person narrator, see above, pp. 98–100. With reference to his exclusion of the first-person narrator, Raffel himself wrote, '[W]hen I see a *hyrde ic* or a *mine gefræge* I drop them, uniformly, not because they are formulaic expressions to which I have any objection, in the OE, or indeed to which I have any relevant feelings, in the OE, but solely because they are not expressions which fit into the tone and texture of the modern English equivalent which, as a poet, I feel I want to attempt to create' (*The Forked Tongue*, p. 26 [letter to J. B. Bessinger]). Note that Raffel makes use of a communal first-person plural in referring to God's oversight of the world: *the ancient beginnings of us all* (line 91), *as He walks through our world* (line 181). In the corresponding Old English passages there is no such first-person-plural dimension; Raffel's introduction of it serves to relate the people in the poem to the reader, whereas in the Old English the sense of their remoteness from 'us' is maintained. On Raffel's use of first-person-plural forms in specifically Christian references, see below, p. 123; see also below, p. 129–30, on the first-person forms at the very beginning of the translation.

Also by way of clarification, at lines 147–8 Raffel reminds readers that Hrothgar is *king / Of the Danes*; he localizes Geatish action against the Franks as taking place *along their river / Rhine* (lines 2914–15), not mentioned in the original; and he inserts names of characters where the reader might lose track of who is being referred to in a particular passage (where the reference is left implicit in the original). For example, at the first introduction of Beowulf into the narrative the hero's name is withheld in *Beowulf* itself, not occurring at all in the relevant scene (lines 194–319) and eventually appearing only at line 343. In *Beowulf* instead of the name Beowulf we get *Higelaces þegn*, 'Hygelac's thegn' (line 194), and *se goda*, 'the good man' (line 205), and are informed that the leader's father was Ecgtheow (lines 262–3). Raffel specifies at once that this is Beowulf we are hearing about and he strategically inserts the name into his account of the relevant scene as he goes along (lines 184, 204, 259, 306). Similarly, other personal names, not present at the corresponding points in the original, are inserted for purposes of clarification: random examples are *Unferth* (line 1469), *Hrothgar* (line 1791), *the Geats* (line 3128).

In speeches Raffel provides a sense of immediacy and structural tightness by inserting narrative signposts and pithy connectives: *And there's more* (line 587), *But of Grendel* (line 2070), *I ought to / Go on* (lines 2071–2). And he also amplifies the detail of the original, filling out images and metaphors. Where Hrothgar's horse is 'bridled' in *Beowulf* (*gebæted*, line 1400), in Raffel it is *brought, saddled / And bridled* (lines 1399–1400); where in *Beowulf* the 'last survivor' brings 'an amount of treasure worthy of being hoarded, of plated gold' (*hordwyrðne dæl, / fættan goldes*, lines 2245b–6a), in Raffel he brings *The precious cups, the armor and the ancient / Swords* (lines 2242–3); the 'Geatish woman' (*Geatisc meowle*) at Beowulf's funeral becomes *a gnarled old woman* (line 3150); Beowulf's understated reference to Grendel not wishing to leave Heorot empty-handed – *No ðy ær ut ða gen   idelhende / [. . .] gongan wolde*, 'he did not at all wish to go out from there empty-handed', lines 2081–3) – is amplified by Raffel in graphic terms: Grendel *meant to leave us / With his belly and his pouch both full* (lines 2082–3). At lines 1794–5 Raffel amplifies the original by developing an extended metaphor for sleep. *Beowulf* has

> sona him seleþegn   siðes wergum,
> feorrancundum   forð wisade.

[At once a hall-servant showed forth [to his bed] the one weary from his exploit, the one who had come from afar.]

In Raffel, with the equivalent of *feorrancundum* being applied to the 'country' of sleep, not to Beowulf, this becomes

> A Danish servant
> Showed him the road to that far-off, quiet
> Country where sleep would come. (lines 1794–6)

A particularly vivid extended image, amplifying that of the original poem, comes at lines 974–7, where Raffel describes how the mortally wounded Grendel fleeing from Heorot

>   Ran
> With death pressing at his back, pain
> Splitting his panicked heart, pulling him
> Step by step into hell.

This is a vigorous filling-out of the less detailed and somewhat abstract account in *Beowulf*:

> no þy leng leofað   laðgeteona
> synnum geswenced,   ac hyne sar hafað
> in niðgripe   nearwe befongen,
> balwon bendum. (lines 974–7)

[no longer will the hostile assailant live, weighed down with sins, but pain has tightly seized in its malicious grip, in destructive fetters.]

In this last passage from Raffel it is also notable that the element of human interest is developed, as the feelings of Grendel are strongly emphasized. Elsewhere too the feelings of characters are brought out more than in the original. When Beowulf returns to Geatland, Higlac in his anxiety to hear about his adventures is *unable to stay silent* (line 1983), a humanizing addition. Emotions are foregrounded in the depiction of personal relationships: Hengest had to stay with Finn, *Whom he hated* (line 1129); the original is less direct and does not personalize the relationship, saying only that Hengest had to stay 'very unwillingly' (*eal unhlitme*). Just before this, Raffel has Finn declare that he and Hengest would live *Like brothers* (line 1100), whereas in the original he swears, in more reserved terms, to 'act honourably' (*arum heolde*, line 1099) towards Hengest and his followers.

Where feasible Raffel in his domesticating treatment also relates the content of the story to modern experience and more familiar literary traditions. He uses idiomatic language to bring the narration to life, drawing upon phrases as varied as *wagging tongues* (line 1105), *ate / And drank like kings* (lines 1232–3), *weird and wonderful* (line 1649), *slim chances* (line 1873), *right there* (line 3093). Some such accommodations to modern experience jar perhaps, as when he has Hrothgar and Hrothulf 'toasting' each other (line 1015), or when he equates status in the heroic world with wealth rather than with the power that wealth can bring (as when Wiglaf gets the 'wealthiest Geats', line 3111 [no equivalent in the Old English], to bring wood for Beowulf's funeral).[22] Anachronistically, the strongholds of the Danes become a castle (line 53), à la later medieval literature, and the barrow of the dragon and the burial mound of Beowulf become towers, an

---

[22] Note also line 25, where Raffel has *wealth is shaped with a sword*, in a vivid recasting of the original, 'so must a man prosper (*geþeon*)'.

image that Raffel uses insistently and that, with reference to the dragon's 'tower', he elaborates enthusiastically:

> A stone tower built
> Near the sea, below a cliff, a sealed
> Fortress with no windows, no doors. (lines 2243–5)

The corresponding passage in *Beowulf* speaks of a *beorh*, 'barrow' (line 2241), *wæteryðum neah, / niwe be næsse, nearocræftum fæst*, 'near the waves of the water, new by the headland, secure in its devices for preventing access' (lines 2242b–3).[23]

Raffel also uses amplification to emphasize the Christian outlook of the people in *Beowulf* and of the poem's narrative voice. The question of the 'Christian colouring' of *Beowulf* has been a familiar one in scholarship down the years.[24] In addition to a number of biblical allusions, characters in the poem refer to a single benevolent God and the narrator speaks from a Christian, or at least Judaeo-Christian, perspective. The religious dimension of the poem is distinctly enhanced in Raffel's treatment, with references to God being expanded and particularized in Christian terms and with the inclusive first-person-plural pronoun being used to convey a sense of shared belief in which the reader too by implication participates. The *Fæder alwalda*, 'father who is ruler of all', of line 316, for example, mentioned by the coastguard, becomes in Raffel *the Lord our God*; the *mihtig God*, 'mighty God', acknowledged by Hrothgar (line 1725) becomes *Our eternal Lord*; Beowulf's unadorned reference to 'God' helping him (line 1658) is rendered more specific in Raffel's *our Father in heaven*. Raffel expands the narrator's reference (line 1059) to the Lord ruling all mankind 'as still he does now' (*swa he nu git deð*) into a more sustained and spiritual religious image:

> Then and now
> Men must lie in their Maker's holy
> Hands, moved only as He wills.[25] (lines 1057–9)

---

23 On Raffel's rejection of 'barrow' and other possibilities as a translation of *beorh*, see his *The Art of Translating Poetry*, pp. 174–6; he considers that *barrow* would remind modern people too much of 'wheel-barrows', and he sees *tower* as 'lexically not entirely accurate, nor historically entirely accurate, but having I would argue both the right aesthetic associations and at the same time also meeting the other claims quite sufficiently well' (p. 176).

24 The seminal article on this scholarly theme is Klaeber's 'Die christlichen Elemente im *Beowulf*'; see also Klaeber's section 'The Christian Coloring' in the third edition of his edition of *Beowulf* (pp. xlviii–li). Important recent contributions are Irving, 'Christian and Pagan Elements', and Cavill, 'Christianity and Theology in *Beowulf*'.

25 Note here the capitalization of the initial letter of the pronoun referring to the deity as well as of the relevant noun. Morgan, Raffel, Alexander and Heaney all capitalize such nouns, and all but Morgan also capitalize the pronouns. The issue of the capitalization of initial letters of nouns referring to the deity is one that has divided editors of *Beowulf*. The original manuscript does not normally capitalize sacred (or other) names, of course, thereby leaving open the question of the degree of 'Christian colouring' in their use. Editors have to capitalize or not, and whichever decision they take will affect interpretation. Among those

Similarly, the narrator's already strongly Christian comment (lines 180–1) that the ancient Danes did not know God –

> metod hie ne cuþon,
> dæda demend, ne wiston hie drihten God (lines 180b–1)

[They did not know the ruler, the judge of deeds, nor did they recognize the Lord God] –

is further heightened in Raffel's lyrical evocation of God's care for the world: he depicts the Danes as

> knowing neither God
> Nor His passing as He walks through our world, the Lord
> Of heaven and earth. (lines 180–2)

In the account of the funeral of Beowulf at the very end of the poem the reference to life leaving the body –

> þonne he forð scile
> of lichaman læded weorðan (lines 3176b–7)

[when he must be led forth from his body] –

is transformed by Raffel into an image of the soul going to heaven: at this time the lord

> leaves
> His body behind, sends his soul
> On high. (lines 3176–8)

In his treatment of religion, as in other aspects of his approach, Raffel amplifies, clarifies and simplifies, with the result that his version is more insistently and more consistently Christian than the original, both in its narrative voice and in the sentiments of the people in the poem. And although we have seen that Raffel plays down the dimension of traditional narration in his version, with its associations of shared communal values (cutting out first-person-singular formulas, for example), he assumes another kind of community of outlook of speaker and audience, that based on Christian belief.

'The necessity of self-expression'

In many of the features of Raffel's translation I have been discussing, the original is being supplemented or amplified in the interest of enhancing the sense of

---

who capitalize nouns referring to the deity are Klaeber (but note that the fourth-edition editors capitalize only 'God', not other words for the deity), Wrenn-Bolton and Jack; such words appear uncapitalized in the *ASPR* edition and in Mitchell and Robinson. None of these editors capitalizes the relevant pronouns.

narrative momentum, of providing clarification and directness – emotive as well as 'factual' – and generally of maintaining the interest of the reader. Raffel has no compunction about using such 'pleonastic' strategies (to use Valentine Cunningham's phrase),[26] seeing these interventions as part of what he must do as a poet to make *Beowulf* into a work that speaks directly to the modern reader. And in some of the instances touched on above he is clearly going further than supplementing and amplifying: he is bringing in entirely new ideas and details, in line with his philosophy of 'leaving' the poem in order to recreate it. In cultivating pleonasm of this kind Raffel trusts in his instinct as a poet, and he embraces the poet's 'necessity of self-expression' as providing the only means of bringing to life the work from the distant past and thereby accommodating it to the understanding of the modern reader.[27]

Among the multitude of added 'factual' and emotive descriptive details in the translation we might note the following diverse examples: the emotive (if anachronistic) classification of Shild's funeral ship as a *fighting / Ship* (line 32); the reference to the *body* (line 34) of Shild at the time of his funeral, implying a distinction between soul and body not made here in the original poem; the description of the swords among the treasure in Shild's funeral ship as *hooked* (line 38) (a curious epithet in a Germanic context), where the Old English has 'battle-weapons' (*hildewæpnum*, line 39); the suggestive reference to the *silence* (line 121) of Herot as Grendel makes his first night-attack; the comparison of the road to Herot to a *Roman road* (line 321), presumably suggested by the reference in the Old English to this road being 'paved with stone' (*stanfah*); the mention of the coastguard *whipping / His horse* (lines 1892–3; cf. *spurring his horse* [line 232], as mentioned above) as he hurries to meet the Geats (in the Old English he 'rode', *rad* [line 1893], to meet them).

The added descriptive detail often consists of the insertion of a single emotive epithet (or two, as in *dry and barren* [desert, line 1213]), as in *miserable* (Danes, line 15), *dripping* (with blood, line 419), *glowing* (with courage, line 480), *flooded* (with fear, line 753), *rattling* (benches, line 775) and *grating* (boards, line 776), *dropping down* (misery, line 929), *bubbling* (blood, line 1122), *foaming* (cup, line 1193), *staggering* (under a heavy weight, line 1635), *bobbing* (ship, line 1896), *booming* (sea, line 1918), these and many other suggestive and colourful descriptive elements being added to the more restrained and terser narration of the original.

Whole phrases and clauses are also added, however, elaborating images not present in the original. Thus, Beo's warriors were *wound round his heart / With golden rings* (lines 20–1), where the Old English simply refers to his generous gift-giving. When Shild's ship is cast out to sea it is reported that no one knows

---

[26] See above, n. 111. On 'Adding and improving' in translation, see also Eco, *Mouse or Rat?*, pp. 50–6; as Eco observes, 'It happens occasionally that, in order to avoid a possible loss, one says more than the original – and perhaps to say more means to say less, because the translator fails to keep an important and meaningful reticence or ambiguity' (p. 50).

[27] On the 'necessity of self-expression', see above, p. 109.

whose hands / Opened to take that motionless cargo (lines 51–2; cf. also lines 894–5), in which the suggestive elements of hands opening and *motionless* are the translator's additions, the original having the understated image *hwa þæm hlæste onfeng*, 'who received that cargo' (line 52). The Old English relates that Hrothgar's retainers 'eagerly obeyed' him (*georne hyrdon*, line 66), a point that Raffel converts into a vivid image of personal commitment: they *Swore by his sword* (line 66). There is nothing corresponding at all to Raffel's description of Grendel as *spawned in that slime* (line 104) or *Conceived by a pair of those monsters, [. . .] murderous creatures* (lines 105–6); indeed the murderousness of Grendel's mother is very much in question in *Beowulf* and later it is said disturbingly that people 'know of no father' of Grendel or 'whether any such mysterious spirits (*dyrnra gasta*) had been born before' (lines 1355–7).

Some of Raffel's most suggestive added images have to do with death, stressing particularly the darkness of death. He speaks of Herdred following his father *into darkness* (line 2202; no equivalent in the Old English). He writes that in the fight with the dragon Beowulf *stared at death* (line 2587; no equivalent in the Old English) but was unwilling to make the journey of death –

> a journey
> Into darkness that all men must make, as death
> Ends their few brief hours on earth. (lines 2589–91)

The Old English lacks a journey metaphor at the corresponding point and the (rather Shakespearean) mention of the few brief hours of life is also Raffel's contribution, considerably developing the powerful, and concise, gnomic observation of the original poem: *swa sceal æghwilc mon / alætan lændagas*, 'so must every man give up his transitory (loaned) days' (lines 2590b–1a). Elsewhere among metaphors of death, Raffel writes of Grendel killing a sleeping warrior:

> Death
> And Grendel's great teeth came together,
> Snapping life shut. (lines 743–5)

The image is unparalleled in the original. And in a vivid evocation of mortality he refers to the owners of ancient treasure as having been *hurled to the grave* (line 2266), where the Old English has the restrained statement that baleful death has 'sent forth' (*forð onsended*) many.

Other images of darkness, as well as those concerned with death, provide atmospheric descriptive detail for Raffel. There is the *crashing darkness* (line 2006) of the fight between Beowulf and Grendel, the *darkness / And dreams* (lines 2210–11) of the dragon's sleep, the *darkness* (line 2219) of the night of the dragon's attack.

To finish off this section by citing a few more examples of striking images contributed by Raffel, we might note his description of the moon when it *Hangs in skies the sun had lit* (line 413) (no mention of sun or moon in the Old English, lines 413–14). In a passage of graphic description Beowulf boasts that in his swimming match with Breca when he was attacked by monsters he *smashed* / *The monsters' hot jaws* (lines 577–8) (no mention of jaws, hot or otherwise, in the Old English). Similarly, in a visually strong image of Grendel, Beowulf imagines *his claws and teeth / Scratching at my shield, his clumsy fists / Beating at my sword blade* (lines 680–2) (*Beowulf* itself refers abstractly to Grendel's *niþgeweorca*, 'deeds of enmity' [line 683]); and in other images of Grendel he is shown to *gnaw the broken bones / Of his last human supper* (lines 735–6) (here *supper* is prompted by *ðicgean*, 'partake of' [line 736] but the Old English has nothing about gnawing on bones); and it is related that he *growled in pain* (line 87) when he heard the music of Herot (*Beowulf* says only that he *geþolode*, 'endured', it). These vivid descriptive details about Grendel, supplied by Raffel, indicate the monster's animal nature and ferocity but they also serve to categorize him, making him more 'definable' and comprehensible than he is in the original. Raffel helps the reader to understand, but *Beowulf* does not necessarily mean us to understand.

Two Passages for Consideration

Raffel's *Beowulf*, lines 1–12

> Hear me! We've heard of Danish heroes,
> Ancient kings and the glory they cut
> For themselves, swinging mighty swords!
> How Shild made slaves of soldiers from every
> Land, crowds of captives he'd beaten
> Into terror; he'd traveled to Denmark alone,
> An abandoned child, but changed his own fate,
> Lived to be rich and much honored. He ruled
> Lands on all sides; wherever the sea
> Would take them his soldiers sailed, returned
> With tribute and obedience. There was a brave
> King![28]

One is immediately struck by the vigorousness of the writing in this exclamatory passage, which is direct and clear in expression and enthusiastically (if disconcertingly so, given the brutality of what is being described) celebratory in tone. Raffel immediately grabs the attention of the reader and maintains momentum throughout. The narration is vivid, with key ideas highlighted in strong encapsulating phrases – *the glory they cut, swinging mighty swords, beaten / Into terror, With tribute and obedience*. The passage is tightly organized as one sense unit, developed over a series of clearly connected clauses and sentences, culminating in the final exclamation towards which the whole sequence has moved, an exclamation that is succinctly expressed in line 11b of the original but that in Raffel's version spills over into the following line. Connectedness is suggested by the

---

[28] For the corresponding Old English lines, see p. 32, above.

use of a dependent participle in *swinging* in the opening sentence and by the insertion of *How* (transferred from the final clause of the first sentence in the original) at the beginning of the second sentence, thereby continuing the exclamation of the first sentence and also providing a sense of explanation of the opening generalization. Other elements contributing to the connectedness of the passage are the explicatory *but* signalling Shild's change of fate, and the colon in the third sentence, a visual cue indicating to the reader the illustrative function of what follows.

A firm sense of narrative momentum is provided by these linking devices and by other features of the passage. Instead of the abrupt half-lines of the original we get a more discursive forward movement, with steady but not intrusive alliteration; Raffel employs phrases that are generally longer than in the original, some of them straddling lines (seven lines out of the first eleven have enjambment), and he uses straightforward, undistracting, language, lacking in poeticisms. The highly wrought diction of the original with its compounds and formulas is simplified and sharpened: abstract becomes concrete (as in *swinging mighty swords*, a pleonastic rendering of the unspecific *ellen fremedon*, 'performed [deeds of] valour'); poetic words become 'ordinary' ones and there are no compounds (*Gar-Dena*, 'Spear-Danes', is streamlined to *Danish*, for example, with *heroes* added by way of amplification); active verbs are used to bring out the energy and determination of Shild and the other 'Ancient kings' (*the glory they cut / For themselves, swinging mighty swords, beaten / Into terror, changed his own fate*, etc.); possible obliqueness is straightened out (depriving enemies of their mead-halls becomes making slaves of them, and Raffel specifies that it was to *Denmark* that Shild came as a child, whereas the original does not spell this out). Only the exclamation *Hear me!* (to which I will return below) perhaps strikes an unnatural note.

Raffel's approach is aimed at drawing the reader in, producing in the process, however, a kind of poetry that is in key respects most unlike that of *Beowulf*. Raffel is producing a recreation of *Beowulf* in a modern idiom of course, not an exact imitation, and so the qualities of his verse will necessarily be different from those of the original poem. His approach to translation is such that his version of these opening lines has vigour and reads fluently but his language, in its very natural-soundingness, lacks the power and resonance found in the majestic corresponding passage of *Beowulf*.

In its full-blooded recreation of the original the translation also ends up effecting a kind of 'cultural' transposition of the ancient Danish world, which might be considered problematic. Cultural transposition is evident in the deployment of the word *soldiers* to refer to the Danish warriors and in the notion that Shild grew *rich*, with the unhistorical implication that this should be seen as a good thing for its own sake. These may be seen as somewhat jarring individual notes but they also reflect a cultural transposition that is going on at a more general level throughout this opening passage. In the passage Raffel has replaced the definitive tribal dimension of the original with one that suggests a kind of centralized aggressive militarism. Gone is the mention of the local neighbouring tribes that Scyld and his warriors defeat in face-to-face battles, with Scyld in among the troops of his enemies (*sceaþena þreatum*); in their stead we see armies being sent out with the purpose of expanding a powerful empire. Despite the sequence of active verbs in the passage, only in *swinging mighty swords* is there an impression of the personal involvement of the kings in battle. Raffel presents Shild and the Danes as oppressors crushing the weak, with Shild making slaves of his enemies and bringing home crowds of captives, having, chillingly, beaten them into terror. The translation emphasizes the ruthlessness of Shild and the Danes as a terrorizing[29] force of empire rather than their triumphant emergence as a dominant tribe among their neighbours.

This transposition may provide Raffel with a way of enlivening the picture of the violent early Germanic world and accommodating it to the understanding of modern readers but if so it only succeeds in emphasizing the otherness of the world of the poem in an unsympathetic way, with the result that it must be difficult for the thinking reader to identify with the Danes or to share the narrator's enthusiasm for their ruthless ways. The use of the word *brave* in praise of Shild at the end of the passage may reflect anxiety about the image of the Danes and may be an attempt to ameliorate it. The adjective does not provide a faithful sense of the meaning of Old English *god*, 'good', in this context since the preceding sequence has stressed the power and success of Shild, not his bravery. *Brave* may be in part prompted by considerations of alliteration but also may be intended as an unproblematic praise-word for a military leader. Edwin Morgan's *king worth the name!* captures the sense of the original better but in the context of Raffel's foregrounding of Shild's brutality (which is played down in Morgan's translation) might look particularly callous.[30]

Key to the issue of the reader's attitude to the Danes and their doings is the question of the nature and stance of the narrator in this opening passage. In most of the translation the presence of a narrator is not strongly felt. We have seen that first-person formulations are usually dropped and that the communal perspective is generally played down; the traditional narrator is recast to become something more like the omniscient narrator. At the very beginning of the poem, however, the first-person narrator *is* in evidence, as indicated by the opening phrase *Hear me!* (first-person singular) and by the second phrase *We've heard of* (first-person plural), utterances which together suggest the presence of an individual narrator speaking for and in a community, in which the reader too is incorporated. The very beginning of the poem thus has the effect, confusingly, of both absorbing the 'reader/listener' into the outlook of the narrator and distancing him or her from what is being described, because of course most

---

[29] Note that *egsode*, which Raffel translates as 'he'd beaten into terror', also has the sense of 'awe' as an aspect of its meaning.
[30] A supplementary explanation for Raffel's choice of *brave* to translate *god* might be that he has found it as one of the possible meanings listed under *god* in Klaeber's glossary (as it is also in Wrenn's) and has thus found legitimation for using it here.

modern readers/listeners do *not* know about the Danish heroes they are being reminded of; nor, as I have intimated, are they likely to be as uncritical of them as they are presented here, as the narrator clearly expects them to be. There are no signs that Raffel wishes to subvert the narrative voice or have it interpreted ironically – the narrator will soon recede as a presence anyway – and so the contradictory signals in these opening lines remain unresolved.

This passage at the beginning of the poem is lively and attention-grabbing therefore, but there are aspects of Raffel's treatment of the Old English that undermine his no-nonsense approach, raising what appear to be unintended uncertainties of interpretation and attitude for the reader. The opening exclamation *Hear me!* may itself be seen as containing the seeds of the problems of the passage. It draws readers into the poem but at the same time distances them from the narrative voice, since they are not really in the situation assumed by this utterance. It may also prompt the distracting question of who this *me* is. And while we have seen that the language of the passage is generally natural-sounding, *Hear me!* is oddly unidiomatic and stilted as an expression, a factor that also has a distancing effect for the reader. It sounds vaguely ceremonious but it is not easy to associate it with any recognizable modern register. If anything, *Hear me!* sounds ostensibly like the expression of a petition rather than a call for attention, which it is presumably intended to be.

Raffel's *Beowulf*, lines 867–74

> And sometimes a proud old soldier
> Who had heard songs of the ancient heroes
> And could sing them all through, story after story,
> Would weave a net of words for Beowulf's
> Victory, tying the knot of his verses
> Smoothly, swiftly, into place with a poet's
> Quick skill, singing his new song aloud
> While he shaped it [. . .][31]

This is a fine example of Raffel's fluent discursive writing, showing a more consistent sureness of touch, in my view, than our previous passage. Here we have a rhythmically and syntactically smooth sequence that nicely illustrates the translator's approach of making the narrative interesting enough to engage the reader while not distracting from that narrative with obvious fancy poetic effects. Resting on its foundation of steady alliteration (almost all of which is non-plosive), the verse moves forward evenly in a clearly presented narrative development within the single sentence that makes up the passage, a sentence that Raffel has formed by joining together two juxtaposed sense units in the original into one unified sentence, the second half of which is arranged around the thematically key present participles *tying* and *singing*. Within the sentence

[31] For the corresponding Old English lines, see p. 37, above.

Raffel's characteristic enjambment, linking lines together, is in evidence, and the sentence itself is also connected to the preceding and succeeding material by means of the conjunction *and*, so that the whole larger sequence sweeps forward coherently in a controlled and measured way.

As elsewhere, Raffel's language is straightforward and natural-sounding. There are no compound nouns or adjectives and no instances of mannered diction. With the exception of one word (*Victory*), the passage is composed entirely of monosyllables and dissyllables. The language is straightforward but the choice of word and phrase is deft. The spontaneous nature of Germanic oral composition is evoked well, for example, by *Quick skill, singing his new song aloud* and, particularly perhaps, *While he shaped it*, and the breadth of the traditional poet's repertoire is brought out in *could sing them all through* and *story after story*.

The passage also illustrates Raffel's technique of amplification of the original, supplying suggestive descriptive additions. The *cyninges þegn*, 'king's thegn' (line 867), of the original becomes *a proud old soldier*, a description that helps to personalize this figure and suggest his wealth of knowledge and experience (though, as elsewhere, *soldier* seems not to hit the right note); other amplificatory touches are supplied in *songs of the ancient heroes* (Old English *ealdgesegena*, 'ancient tradition', line 869), *Victory* (Old English *sið*, 'experience', line 872), *singing his new song aloud* (Old English *wrecan spel*, 'recite a tale', line 873; 'singing' words are not used at all in the corresponding passage in the original). The distinctive metaphor that Raffel introduces in this passage is the image of poetry as weaving a net of words and of the poet tying the knot of his verses together. This is an appropriate and perceptive instance of Raffelian pleonasm, prompted by the suggestion of tying together in *soðe gebunden*, 'truly bound together' (line 871), and that of intricacy in *snyttrum*, 'skilfully' (line 872). Here, alert to the possible associations of the original, Raffel produces a fine poetic image, expressive without being fussy, and consonant with the imagery of *Beowulf*.

As is true generally, Raffel's verse in the passage does not resemble that of Old English but the passage is composed with notable fluency and skill, qualities that are very fitting in a passage about the art of the Germanic oral poet.

A Poem for Modern Readers

Burton Raffel's translation of *Beowulf* is a work of its time and place, that of the America of the middle decades of the twentieth century, a time and place of confidence and cultural optimism, if also of perceived external threat. Reflective of this self-confident outlook, the translation presents for the interested general reader – in practice Raffel has a predominantly college readership in mind – a lively and essentially uncomplicated version of the Old English epic. The translation also reflects Raffel's – and, he perceives, his readers' – impatience with academic and poetic fussiness, evincing straightforwardness in interpretation and expression. What rhetorical colouring there is is accessible and unostentatious.

This bold and unpedantic approach to the translation of the venerable Old English classic enables Raffel to produce a version of *Beowulf* that is interesting and easier to read and understand than many other versions, including (it should be said) *Beowulf* itself. In his boldness Raffel simplifies, clarifies and amplifies, even confidently bringing in new imagery where he deems it appropriate. Such additions are legitimate in principle, reflecting (to draw on comments of R. P. Creed on Raffel) the translator's task of opening out and displaying more fully hints enclosed in the language of the original.[32] Raffel's additions, which are based on his firm belief in the visionary power of the 'poet', may not always reflect faithfully the world of *Beowulf*, as we have seen, but they can also be very enabling for the reader, bringing the original to life in exciting ways.

It is not so much in what he adds as in what he has to leave out that Raffel's translation exhibits limitations as a version of *Beowulf*. In making his translation a poem for modern readers Raffel produces something very different from the great original. His version is accessible but does not really illuminate the poetic art of *Beowulf* or provide a sense of its place in a tradition. The impetus towards clarification and simplification also works against subtlety and complexity, closing down possible ambiguities and uncertainties of interpretation and giving the modern reader a work less unfamiliar and challenging than the original poem. All translations offer particular readings of their originals, of course, but Raffel's confident recreation is especially insistent in doing so, remaking the poem in a no-nonsense way that he sees as appealing to his intended primary readership of the mid-ish twentieth century. Raffel's instinct is to bring *Beowulf* straightforwardly into the ken of the modern reader rather than to try to capture the qualities of its intricate and stylized poetry or to highlight the possible tensions that can be discerned in its meaning, or indeed to bring out the alterity of the poem from modern experience. In the classic Schleiermacherian paradigm of approaches to translation (as mentioned above, p. 7–8), it is clear that Raffel's translation of *Beowulf* represents the second of the two polarities, as outlined in Schleiermacher's seminal lecture: 'Either the translator leaves the author in peace as much as possible and moves the reader toward him; or he leaves the reader in peace as much as possible and moves the writer toward him.'[33] In Venuti's terms, Raffel's approach is very much that of 'domestication'.[34]

Raffel's translation found favour particularly with U.S. college instructors and their students. At a time when Old English literature was normally being

---

[32] Creed, 'Foreword' to Raffel, *Poems from the Old English*, p. xi (referring to other Old English translations by Raffel, but the point is equally applicable to his *Beowulf*): 'The Old English scholar may be ready to chide Mr. Raffel for his "addition" [of an image of *hands* in his translation of *The Husband's Message*] when he suddenly sees the *rightness* of these "hands" and turns his chiding into praise for the poet who has *opened out, displayed more fully*, the hint enclosed in the image *agrof* (Creed's italics).

[33] Schleiermacher, 'On the Different Methods of Translating', trans. Bernofsky, p. 49.

[34] See above, p. 7.

taught only in the original language in British and Irish universities and on the European continent, there was a significant market for translations for the 'great literature' and Old English-through-translation courses common in America. Some such courses used anthologies, most famously the 'Norton' (from 1962), which included E. Talbot Donaldson's prose translation of *Beowulf* from the 1966 edition, while others made use of separate translations, including Morgan's and Raffel's; a number of other translations in verse and prose were also produced from the 1960s on, to be taken up on college courses.[35] In this context, it is notable that, as in other notices (see above, p. 107), Edwin Morgan's translation gets short shrift in an American teaching-orientated handbook published in 1984: in one essay in that volume it is criticized as 'a dull and frequently awkward translation', while Raffel's version is praised for its liveliness and is seen as 'more aesthetically satisfying than translations of a more academic flavor';[36] another contributor to the same collection reports that she uses Raffel's version on her course, 'because he is a poet whose verse moves'.[37] This assessment coincides with that of Edward Irving nearly two decades earlier: 'To my knowledge, [Raffel's] is the only translation which students enjoy and which they find exciting.'[38] J. K. Crane's article, mentioned previously, which finds Raffel greatly superior to Morgan, is also written from a teaching perspective.[39]

Robert P. Creed, writing the glowing 'Afterword' to Raffel's version, explicitly refers to students as readers of Raffel's translation. Ignoring Morgan's version, he declares,

> It used to be necessary to insist to college sophomores that Homer was a great poet and not a writer of pseudo-archaic prose. Until now it has been necessary to insist that *Beowulf* is a great poem – neither a piece of puzzling prose nor a singsong composed by children skipping rope. Raffel has changed that. All one has now to do is to open this *Beowulf* at any point and begin reading aloud.[40]

Raffel had consulted Creed, as a leading Anglo-Saxonist, about translation issues in the course of his work on *Beowulf*.[41]

Raffel manifestly succeeded in his aim of making *Beowulf* accessible to modern readers. His version established itself as a popular verse translation, particularly in America, and brought generations of readers to *Beowulf* in translation. It provided only a partial take on the poem, however, and the degree to which it succeeded in fulfilling Raffel's artistic purpose of conveying 'in reasonable measure

---

35   See below, pp. 196–215.
36   Short, 'Translations of *Beowulf*', p. 11.
37   Kliman, 'Teaching *Beowulf* in Translation to Undergraduates', p. 62.
38   Irving, 'Reviews of Recent Translations', p. 69.
39   See above, p. 107.
40   Creed, 'Afterword' (Raffel, trans., *Beowulf*), p. 123.
41   Raffel reproduces his correspondence with Creed in his *The Forked Tongue*, pp. 52–7; he also corresponded intensively at this time with J. B. Bessinger, Jr: see *The Forked Tongue*, pp. 24–52.

the force and flavor of the original' must be seen as questionable.[42] The experience of reading Raffel's version is nothing like that of reading *Beowulf* itself. In the coming decades, other translators would provide very different takes on *Beowulf*, notably Michael Alexander, to whose version I turn in the next chapter.

---

[42] See above, p. 111.

✦6✦

Michael Alexander:
Shadowing the Old English

The version of *Beowulf* by the British translator Michael Alexander appeared in 1973, when Alexander was in his early thirties.[1] He had studied English at Oxford, receiving his training in Old English from Christopher Tolkien, Bruce Mitchell and others, and had embarked upon what would be a successful – and wide-ranging – academic career. Alexander had published some original lyric poems in the early 1960s, eventually collected together in an elegant small volume published in 1978,[2] but most of his poetry has been translations from the Old English, among which his most signal achievement has been the translation of *Beowulf*. His career has been one that has integrated scholarship and art and this integration is reflected above all in his work on *Beowulf*. His translation of the poem proved extremely popular, staying continuously in print until it was recently reissued in a new revised edition. Alexander points out that his *Beowulf* and an earlier volume of translations, *The Earliest English Poems*, have between them sold more than half a million copies over the years.[3]

Among British verse translations of *Beowulf* of the second half of the twentieth century, Alexander's version is highlighted in the present chapter as being not only the most popular and the one used most for teaching purposes but also, in my view, as a particularly interesting and enabling translation, reading well in its own right while bringing a lively sense of the poetry of the original poem to the modern reader. A verse translation by Kevin Crossley-Holland, to be discussed in Chapter 8, had come out a few years before Alexander's (1968),[4] and it too has maintained a steady, if lesser, popularity over a period of decades.

---

[1] Alexander, trans. *Beowulf: A Verse Translation*. In references to Alexander's *Beowulf* herein, line numbers refer to the 2001 revised edition (some of the lines in the original edition are miscounted).
[2] *Twelve Poems*; in a note prefacing the volume, Alexander reports that the poems were written between 1960 and 1963.
[3] *Beowulf*, revised ed., p. xi.
[4] Crossley-Holland, trans., *Beowulf*.

In the later twentieth century British readers of verse translations came to *Beowulf* through these two versions, or they made use of certain of the plethora of American translations produced in the period.

Like other translators whose versions of *Beowulf* we are considering, Alexander had already published translations of Old English poetry by the time he produced his rendering of the epic poem, having brought out his collection *The Earliest English Poems*, mentioned above, in 1966.[5] *The Earliest English Poems* had included selections from *Beowulf*, four passages amounting to 152 lines in all, which are lightly, but interestingly, reworked in the *Beowulf* volume in a way that reflects Alexander's developing approach to his task as a translator of Old English poetry.[6] He would go on to produce a further volume of translations from Old English, *Old English Riddles from the Exeter Book* (1980), and he has continued to have a close relationship with Old English poetry throughout his career and to think about issues involved in its translation.[7] In 1995 he brought out an edition of *Beowulf* in the original Old English, in the Penguin English Poets series,[8] and he has produced new editions of his books of translations, not only *Beowulf* (in 2001) but also *The Earliest English Poems* (in 1977 and 1991; revised and expanded as *The First Poems in English* in 2008) and *Old English Riddles* (in 2005), introducing a small number (about forty) of minor rephrasings in the revised edition of his *Beowulf* translation in the light of revisions of the text of the poem as presented in recent editions of it, including his own.[9] The editions he had used for his own translation of *Beowulf* were those by Klaeber and Wrenn.[10]

Alexander's study of poetry has been by no means confined to Old English. In the present context it is particularly relevant to mention his book on Ezra Pound, *The Poetic Achievement of Ezra Pound*, published in 1979. This book shows Alexander to be a perceptive critic of Pound's poetry in general and of his 'The Seafarer' in particular, a poem that had a profound influence on his own practice as a translator of Old English poetry, stimulating him indeed to take up translating Old English in the first place.[11]

---

[5] *The Earliest English Poems*.
[6] In the 1991 edition he adds a fourth passage, of forty-five lines, identical to the corresponding passage in his *Beowulf*.
[7] *Old English Riddles from the Exeter Book*; a number of his translations of riddles had appeared earlier in *The Earliest English Poems* and elsewhere; with reference to criticism of Old English literature, note especially his *Old English Literature*; on issues in translation, see the section 'Translating *Beowulf*', in the revised (2001) edition of the Beowulf translation, pp. liii–lvi, and 'Old English Poetry into Modern English Verse' ('Translating *Beowulf*' draws in part on this article).
[8] *Beowulf: A Glossed Text*.
[9] See 'Preface' to his revised translation, p. xi.
[10] See the bibliography to the 1973 edition of his *Beowulf* translation.
[11] Alexander, *The Poetic Achievement of Ezra Pound*; on Pound's 'The Seafarer', see especially pp. 66–79. Concerning the influence of 'The Seafarer' on himself, Alexander writes, 'As an undergraduate student of Old English, I was aroused to emulate Pound's translation and

Alexander's Approach to Translating Old English Poetry

Alexander's approach in his translation of *Beowulf* is diametrically opposed to that of Raffel, who had striven to recreate the Old English work as a modern poem in a natural-sounding modern idiom. *Beowulf* is not a modern English poem and Alexander wishes to convey a sense of its alterity in his translation. He is conscious that *Beowulf* comes from a culture very different from our own and conscious too that the quality and 'feel' of Old English verse is not like that of more recent poetic traditions. He does not work to minimize the differentness of *Beowulf* or to accommodate it to modern experience but instead, in line with the Schleiermacherian principle of moving the reader towards the original (see above, pp. 7–8), seeks to give the reader something of the experience of this different kind of poetry, while at the same time producing a verse that itself works as poetry and sustaining it for over three thousand lines. As he had written in *The Earliest English Poems*, 'the first aim in translating a living poem from a language which happens to be unknown into one's own language is to produce something with art in it, something which lives'.[12] This is a Scylla-and-Charybdis-type task – remaining faithful to the poetry of *Beowulf* while at the same time producing 'something with art in it, something that lives'. Like all our poetic translators, Alexander is insistent about the imperative that the translation must 'live'.

The alterity of *Beowulf*

Not only is the poetic language of *Beowulf* different from that of Modern English, indeed, but, as we saw earlier in this book, in its original Anglo-Saxon context it is also to be seen as unlike the language of ordinary speech and unlike writing in prose. There is a kind of double alterity at play for the modern reader in approaching *Beowulf*, since the language is twice removed from that of modern experience. As Alexander is well aware, the language of *Beowulf* is not the 'natural' language of Old English speech or prose but belongs to a special, poetic, register: it is heightened, highly wrought and 'artificial', and it is also formulaic. Old English poetry has its own metre, of course, which is unlike that of later literary periods, but it also has its own syntax, style and diction. Alexander himself had referred, in *The Earliest English Poems*, to the 'word-hoard' of Old English poetry as amounting to 'almost a language within a language'[13] and he had pointed out that 'the diction of the poems was traditional and archaic even at the time they were written down'.[14]

inscribed my version of the Old English poem "The Ruin", "to E.P." (*The Poetic Achievement*, p. 66; on his translation 'The Ruin', see further below).
[12] *The Earliest English Poems*, p. 22; 3rd ed., p. xxiii.
[13] *The Earliest English Poems*, p. 11; 3rd ed., p. xii.
[14] *The Earliest English Poems*, p. 23; 3rd ed., p. xxiv.

In his 1973 Introduction to his *Beowulf* Alexander reports that his translation 'began as an attempt to catch in modern English some of that sense of masterful power communicated by the verses of the original Old English poem'.[15] He is specific about the poetic qualities of *Beowulf* and other Old English poems that contribute to this 'masterful power', identifying in particular indirectness and metaphor as 'endemic in the poetic style',[16] viewing parallelism, antithesis and variation as characteristic of Old English,[17] and, with particular reference to *Beowulf*, drawing attention to the 'denseness and allusiveness [...] chiefly created by diction';[18] he also highlights the oral dimension of Old English poetry, insisting that '*Beowulf* was not written to be readable but to be listened to'.[19] For Alexander, the poetry of *Beowulf* is intricate and crafted and we can see him carefully responding to these perceived qualities in his translation.

An imitative approach

Alexander's approach is strongly imitative, not only in metre but also in syntax, style and diction. In his essay 'Old English Poetry into Modern English Verse' he writes, 'Translating form as well as meaning involves the translator in shadowing the syntactic and stylistic conventions of Old English verse composition.'[20] This 'shadowing' is a risky strategy given the foreignness of Old English style to Modern English, with the possibility that the translation might end up as quaint and/or unintelligible, like those ridiculed by Edwin Morgan. Raffel was daring in reconceiving the poetry of *Beowulf* in a different idiom; Alexander is daring in incorporating its style into modern verse. Far from following the Raffelian approach of 'leaving the original behind', he adopts a literary language that takes over as much as it can from the Old English. He does not aim by any means at a word-for-word translation but transfers key features of Old English poetic style and expression into the heightened and somewhat stylized register he has devised. He sticks as rigorously as possible to Old English metre, allowing himself less flexibility in his deployment of this metre than do most other translators, including Morgan and Raffel. As he had written in *The Earliest English Poems*, 'My aim, therefore, has been to keep to the original metre as far as possible and at all times to give a faithful impression of its vigour'; he adds, 'I have been more careful to achieve a correct stress-pattern than to keep the alliteration absolutely

---

[15] *Beowulf*, p. 9; in reappropriating this sentence in the revised ed. (in a different context), he slightly changes the wording: 'This translation began with the desire to catch in modern English some of the mastery of the Old English verse of the original' (p. lii).
[16] *Beowulf*, p. 43; in the revised edition he reworks this, referring to 'the elaborate unstraightforwardness with which the expected is disguised' (p. xlix).
[17] *Beowulf*, p. 45; revised ed., p. xlix.
[18] *Beowulf*, p. 46; revised ed., p. xlix.
[19] *Beowulf*, p. 49; revised ed., p. lvi.
[20] 'Old English Poetry into Modern English Verse', p. 71.

regular', though it is noticeable that the rules of alliteration too are more strictly adhered to in Alexander's version than in most other translations.[21] Alexander's stricter interpretation of the rules of Old English metre places considerable constraint on his freedom of expression (and increases the unfeasibility of word-for-word translation) but this technical constraint also stimulates him to some of his most striking renderings of the Old English.

Alexander seeks in his translation to give his readers a sense of the character of Old English poetry and of the pleasure of reading/hearing it, including the pleasure to be derived from that alien concept for the reader of modern poetry, formulaic language. In this context, judgement is strongly called for on the part of the translator, if the imperative of producing artful and living poetry in Modern English is also to be fulfilled. In my view Alexander's translation does succeed to a remarkable degree, guided by his sensitivity to the potential and richness of Modern English as well as his appreciation of the qualities of Old English. Not everything works in the translation but, more than those of most other translators, Alexander's version gives a sense of what it is like to read Old English poetry in the original. And his version comes across not as an exercise in clever literary reconstruction or eccentric imitation but as, for the most part, an engaging – and (appropriately) clever – poetic creation, high-sounding and articulate.

Alexander, Pound and Old English poetry

Alexander has defined poetic translation as 'an attempt to offer an equivalent poem to those who cannot read the original'.[22] In his translations in *The Earliest English Poems*, written over a period of some years, we see him working towards refining a register that provides an acceptable 'equivalent' to that of Old English. He began his translation of Old English poetry very much under the influence of Ezra Pound, to whom he dedicated *The Earliest English Poems*. It was Pound's famous translation of *The Seafarer*, which Alexander regarded as giving 'far and away the most concentrated impression of Anglo-Saxon poetry', that prompted him to translate Old English poems in the first place, 'fired by its example'.[23] Pound's 'The Seafarer' taught him that it was possible excitingly to convey the feel of Old English poetry in Modern English and showed him some possible techniques for doing so. Alexander writes that as he began translating he followed the aim of Pound, which was 'to re-create the impression the poem made upon him, using an archaic register and approximating to the verse-form of the original',[24] and indeed in the first poem in *The Earliest English Poems*, 'The

---

21 *The Earliest English Poems*, p. 22; 3rd ed., p. xxiv.
22 *Beowulf*, revised ed., p. lvi; on 'equivalence', see also Barnstone, *The Poetics of Translation*, pp. 233–6 and *passim*.
23 *Beowulf*, p. 23; see also 'Old English Poetry into Modern English Verse', p. 70.
24 'Old English Poetry into Modern English Verse', p. 70.

Ruin',[25] the foreignizing example of Pound is very much in evidence. Alexander's translation begins,

> Well-wrought this wall: Wierds broke it.
> The stronghold burst. [...]
> Snapped rooftrees, towers fallen,
> the work of Giants, the stonesmiths,
> mouldereth.

In its insistent half-line structure, its deployment of the obsolete Old English word *Wierds*, its imitation of *burston*, 'fell apart' (line 2 in the original), its invention of the unusual Old-English-like compound *rooftree* (the Old English has *hrofas*, 'roofs', line 3), its use of the archaic present tense form *-eth* and its clipped syntax, with verbs omitted, this is a very Poundian if not a very subtle way of translating Old English. It is very much in the style of the opening lines of Pound's 'The Seafarer':

> May I, for my own self, song's truth reckon,
> Journey's jargon, how I in harsh days
> Hardship endured oft.
> Bitter breast-cares have I abided,
> Known on my keel many a care's hold,
> And dire sea-surge, and there I oft spent
> Narrow night-watch nigh the ship's head
> While she tossed close to cliffs.[26]

In Alexander, as in Pound, we get a thrilling sound impression of Old English poetry but the verse comes across as strange and cumbersomely inarticulate, in striking contrast to Old English poetry itself. And certainly the idea of maintaining this kind of mannered intensity for over three thousand lines would not provide an acceptable 'equivalent' to *Beowulf*.

Vigour and intensity are apparent throughout *The Earliest English Poems*, not least in Alexander's bold version of *The Seafarer*, which is free in its treatment of the Old English original, though much closer to the sense of that original than is Pound's version. And unlike Pound, Alexander doesn't edit out the Christian final third of the poem and its other Christian references (though, in common with some other translators and editors, he leaves out the last twenty-two lines, which are in a number of places notoriously opaque in meaning and textually corrupt).[27] As Lawrence Venuti points out, Pound by his editing and revising of the received poem paradoxically domesticates it to modernist (individualist as opposed to communal Christian) values, despite the foreignizing translation

---

[25] For the Old English text, see *ASPR* III, 227–8.
[26] Pound, 'The Seafarer from the Anglo-Saxon'.
[27] In his third edition of *The Earliest English* Poems and in *The First Poems in English* Alexander supplies a prose translation of these lines, as he does for the second half of *The Dream of the Rood*, which was not translated in the 1966 version.

strategy that he uncompromisingly adopts.[28] John Corbett speaks of the 'creative interpretation and selection' by means of which Pound is able to 'refashion both the source-culture and his own'.[29] It should also be mentioned that Pound's exclusion of Christian elements was in line with a still-influential critical approach to the poem at the time, one that reflected the romantic scholarly desire that Eric Stanley refers to as 'the search for Anglo-Saxon paganism'.[30] Alexander, by contrast, preserves the original poem's tension between Christian and secular ideals.

The muscular quality and denseness of Alexander's writing in his translation of *The Seafarer* are illustrated in passages such as that (corresponding to the Pound passage quoted above) at the beginning of the poem describing the speaker's life at sea, in which the hardship of the life is conveyed by verse that is rhythmically tense, and insistent in its plosive alliteration:

> This tale I frame shall be found to tally:
> the history is of myself. Sitting day-long
> at an oar's end clenched against clinging sorrow,
> breast-drought I have borne, and bitterness too.
> I have coursed my keel through care-halls without end
> over furled foam, I forward in the bows
> through the narrowing night, numb, watching
> for the cliffs we beat along.

In more lyrical (and rather less plosive) mood the life of the seafarer is contrasted with that of one

> whose life has run
> sweet in the burgs, no banished man,
> but well-seen at wine-round.

The use of obsolete words and obsolete meanings, as *burg* in this passage from 'The Seafarer', is particularly pronounced in *The Earliest English Poems*. Alexander even begins his translation of *The Dream of the Rood* and one of the riddles with 'Hwaet'.[31]

[28] See Venuti, *The Translator's Invisibility*, pp. 34–6; see also Bassnett, *Translation Studies*, p. 97.
[29] Corbett, 'The Seafarer', p. 160.
[30] Stanley, *The Search for Anglo-Saxon Paganism*. Writing in 1915, leading Anglo-Saxonist Ernst Sieper declared of *The Seafarer*, 'In the first half of the poem we have true poetry which will at once move every perceptive reader. In the second half we have pious talk which is not the product of artistic necessity but the result of a desire to instruct and convert' (Sieper, *Die altenglishe Elegie*, p. 191; quoted by Stanley, *The Search for Anglo-Saxon Paganism*, p. 55); and his view is very much that reflected in Pound's treatment of the part of *The Seafarer* that he translated when Sieper goes on to say, 'I regard as interpolations all those passages in the older elegies in which *dryhten* refers to the Christian God' (Sieper, *Die altenglische Elegie*, p. 194; Stanley, *The Search*, p. 55).
[31] He changes *Hwaet!* to *Listen!* in *The First Poems in English* at the beginning of his translation of *The Dream of the Rood* (but still retains Hwaet! in his translation of Riddle 79).

He glosses in the Introduction to the book a number of Old English words he has used 'neat', including *Wierd*, *burg* and *Hwæt* but also *aetheling*, *byrnie*, *cynn*, *scop* and *weard*. Alexander argues that the life of a word 'comes from its root, and that the occasional use of a word in its original sense is one of the duties as well as one of the prerogatives of a poet', adding (defensively?), 'One has to risk making mistakes.'[32]

Experience, and possibly feedback, taught him to tone down his use of obsolete and archaic words, but not to drop them altogether. Recognizing that 'certain archaisms [. . .] are no longer generally practicable',[33] he develops a more reserved register in later poems in the same volume, with fewer curiosities. He continues to refine his style in *Beowulf*, a poem that makes additional demands on the translator because of its sheer length: 'An archaism which draws attention to itself', notes Alexander, 'might work with a short, fragmentary, and indeed ruinous text like *The Ruin*. But translation from Old English cannot take too many thanes in dreary byrnies. Words such as "mouldereth" remained at the bottom of my word-hoard.'[34] Still, in *Beowulf* he maintains a stylized and highly 'poetic' register, reflective of, or 'equivalent' to, the distinctive voice of the original poem, and he continues to draw widely upon 'ancient or half-forgotten words',[35] where he deems their use appropriate.

Alexander's earliest translations are strongly influenced by Pound, as we have seen. His style is not obviously Poundian in *Beowulf*, in which, as he had increasingly done in *The Earliest English Poems*, he pays much more attention to sense and moderates his use of archaic language, compound-clogged diction and clipped syntax. However, the underlying influence and inspiration of Pound remains in that Alexander seeks to imitate the effect of the Old English verse form and is drawn to reflecting the language and rhythm of the original as closely as he can, and though he moderates his practice in *Beowulf* he still follows elements of the example of Pound in key ways.

Alexander regarded Pound's 'The Seafarer' as 'the most powerful realization of Old English poetry we are ever likely to have'.[36] He was far from uncritical of Pound's poem, however, coming to see it as a deeply flawed and curious piece of writing, 'fantastically archaic', as he puts it in *The Achievement of Ezra Pound*, and 'a late sport of the Saxonizing school of Morris, Barnes, Hopkins and Hardy'.[37] Alexander has a much more sophisticated appreciation of Old English poetry than Pound had, and he is at once delighted and exasperated by his master's translation, celebrating its verve but also drawing attention to its errors, distor-

---

[32] *The Earliest English Poems*, p. 23; 3rd ed., p. xxiv.
[33] Ibid.
[34] 'Old English Poetry into Modern English Verse', p. 72.
[35] *The Earliest English Poems*, p. 23; 3rd ed., p. xxiv.
[36] *The Poetic Achievement of Ezra Pound*, p. 78.
[37] *The Poetic Achievement*, p. 70.

tions and incoherence, and finding it 'brilliant, stimulating, inaccurate, misleadingly heathen and at times rather loud'.[38]

Despite his criticisms of it, Alexander insists that 'the sound of "The Seafarer" is an authentic if new kind of translation'[39] (he wonders, however, whether 'adaptation' or 'imitation' might be better words to describe what Pound does in it, rather than 'translation'[40]) and he is able to preserve essential aspects of Pound's technique in his own work, while avoiding violating the sense of the original in the blatant way that Pound does. His deployment of 'ancient or half-forgotten words', for example, is something for which he has seen the blueprint in Pound's more extravagant practice. He speaks of Pound 'transferring' words from Old to Modern English and achieving dynamic effects: 'The motive is perhaps a magical one', he writes, 'that the virtue of the word should survive.'[41] This recalls Alexander's justification for his own use of 'ancient or half-forgotten words' in his Introduction to *The Earliest English Poems*: 'it is that an old word tensed and tuned in a strict form, can still be made to yield its *virtù*.'[42] He continues to make – more sparing but still evident – use of such words in his *Beowulf*.

Offering an Equivalent Poem to Those who Cannot Read the Original

Alexander sets out in his translation of *Beowulf* to write poetry that works convincingly as modern English, poetry that is 'living', but that also gives an enabling impression of what the Old English poem he is translating is like, not only in sense but in sound and style. The register that he has evolved is a heightened and somewhat stylized form of modern English verse, elevated in tone, 'poetic' in expression and showing a taste for rare and unusual vocabulary. It is modern English verse inflected by features derived from or somehow suggestive of Old English poetic practice. Alexander's heightening and stylization of Modern English is characteristic of his whole approach to the translation, being particularly in evidence in his treatment of syntax and of diction and rhetorical features.

Syntax

Apposition and variation are among the most distinctive features of Old English poetry. These features are difficult to transfer successfully into Modern English because of the constrictions of present-day syntax and word order but they are features that Alexander makes considerable use of in the heightened register

---

38   *The Poetic Achievement*, p. 78.
39   *The Poetic Achievement*, p. 75.
40   Ibid.
41   *The Poetic Achievement*, pp. 74–5.
42   *The Earliest Poems in English*, p. 23; 3rd ed., p. xxiv.

adopted in his translation of *Beowulf*. His deployment of appositive phrases ranges from single or double instances of variation, imitating the corresponding half-line-based structures of the original, as in

> Lord Hrothgar
> sat silent then, the strong man mourned,
> the glorious king, (lines 128–30)

or

> torment sat
> on the Friend of the Scyldings, fierce sorrows
> and woes of every kind, (lines 146–8)

to longer sequences, such as

> hoping that their lord's son would live and in ripeness
> assume the kingdom, the care of his people,
> the hoard and the stronghold, the storehouse of heroes,
> the Scylding homeland, (lines 909–12)

and sequences interrupted by other material, as in

> until One began
> – the king had grown grey in the guardianship of the land –
> to put forth his power in the pitch-black night-times
> – the hoard-guarding *Dragon* of a high barrow
> raised above the moor. (lines 2207–11)

In general Alexander seeks to imitate the syntax of the Old English narrative, which can be abrupt as well as intricate and is often cumulative and in which verbs are predominantly in the indicative mood. He resorts only relatively rarely, for example, to present-participle phrases of the kind favoured by Raffel as a way of structuring narrative detail. Instances of present-participle phrases in Alexander are *before mounting his bed* (line 676), *his hopes swelling* (line 731), *her maidens following* (line 923) and *sweeping forward* (line 2955). Alexander also follows, and indeed extends, the Old English practice of making statements in a negative form, a variety of understatement, as in *Not easily did I survive* (line 1654; Old English *Ic þæt unsofte ealdre gedigde*, line 1655, 'Not easily did I preserve my life'), *it is no secret* (line 2920; Old English *ac wæs wide cuð*, line 2923, 'but it was widely known') and *it was not a petty mound* (line 3135; Old English *ad [. . .] unwaclicne*, line 3138, 'a pyre not feeble'), and he adopts and again extends the *Beowulf* poet's fondness for epithets and indeed nouns in *un-*, having internalized this Old English stylistic trait. Examples of *un-* epithets are *unshrinking officer* (line 287; Old English *ombeht unforht*, 'unafraid officer'), *this unlovely one* (line 433; Old English *se æglæca*, 'the terrible being'), *undoomed* (lines 573, 2290; Old English *unfægne*, lines 573, 2291, 'not doomed to die'), *unblinking watch* (line 708; Old English *wæccende*, 'watching, awake'), *an unlovely light* (line 727; Old English *leoht unfæger*, 'un-fair light'), *unfriendly fingers* (line 748; Old English *feond mid folme*, 'the enemy with his fingers'), *unanxious for his life* (line 1441; Old English *nalles for ealdre mearn*, line 1442, 'he did not worry at all about his life'), *unloved ones* (line 2860; Old English *unleofe*, line 2863, 'ones not loved'). Nouns in *un-*, a stylized usage in Modern English, are *unfriendliness* (line 549; Old English *wið laðum*, line 550, 'against the hostile one') and *unwisdom* (line 1733; Old English *unsnyttrum*, line 1734, 'lack of wisdom').

Another Old English syntactic feature that Alexander makes use of is asyndetic coordination, as in

> High over head they hoisted and fixed
> a gold *signum*; gave him to the flood,
> let the seas take him, (lines 46–8)

though he does insert one *and* here, not in the original,[43] and does supply conjunctions in many places throughout the translation, as in *and it is said that no boat was ever more bravely fitted out* (line 38), where the corresponding Old English is asyndetic: *Ne hyrde ic cymlicor ceol gegyrwan*, 'I have not heard of a ship more splendidly prepared.' Asyndetic coordination is common in Alexander, however, and he also normally preserves from the Old English formulations in the first-person singular of the kind *I have heard* (line 61, etc.) and *as I heard* (line 73, etc.), but he also varies his treatment of such Old English formulas, as can be seen from our last quotation, *and it is said that no boat was ever more bravely fitted out*.

As well as taking over features of Old English style, Alexander also makes widespread use of other (non-Old English) syntactical strategies that serve to distance his writing from the discourse of ordinary speech and that contribute to his heightened register. His syntax has a poetic feel about it. Most notably in this respect, Alexander cultivates poetic inversion of normal word order. Such inversion takes the form of displacement of the object to before the verb, as in *the warrior king / he would seek* (lines 198–9), *God they thanked* (line 227), *success she wished him* (line 653) and *no rings he gave me* (line 1718), and also the displacement of adverbial and adjectival material, as in *when late was born* (line 55), *empty then stood* (line 144), *we'll at night play* (line 683) and *you yesternight enjoyed* (line 955). Some inversions also involve stylized word usages, as in *to Hrothgar I would [. . .] unfold a plan* (lines 277–8, a usage of *would* that is archaic or literary) and *if he undaunted be* (line 572, in which the subjunctive *be* occurs, no longer current in normal speech), and inversion can also involve the use of literary/archaic tense forms, as in *then did the heroes [. . .] salute each other* (lines 652–3), where normal Modern English would require 'then the heroes saluted each other', and *(they) sat not down* (line 562) and *the world's palace / fell not to the ground* (lines 772–3), where the normal verb forms would be 'did not sit' and 'did not fall'. At line 543,

---

43 Cf. the Old English *Þa gyt him asetton segen gyldenne / heah ofer heafod, letton holm beran, / geafon on garsecg* (lines 47–9a), 'Then yet they set a golden standard high over his head, let the sea bear him, gave him to the ocean'.

Alexander omits the verb altogether in a poetic ellipsis (again with a special usage of *would*): *He could not away from me; nor would I from him.*

And Alexander's syntax is also notable for its marked deployment of impersonal forms, which contributes to the formality of the expression and conveys a sense of categorical authority in what is being said. Thus, *It is by glorious action / that a man comes by honour in any people* (lines 24–5), *It was with pain that the powerful spirit / [. . .] endured that time* (lines 85–6), *It was not remarked then* (line 137), *It is with loyal and true intention that we come* (line 267), and so on. Formality of expression is particularly evident in the speeches, which of course are very carefully worded in the original. In Alexander's translation Beowulf's first speech begins with typical stylized formality: *We here are come from the country of the Geats* (line 260, with archaic use of the verb *to be* in the periphrastic perfect, as well as displacement of the adverb). An extreme example of such formality of expression is to be found in the Latin-sounding syntax of *your suddenly resolved seeking out* (line 1986), where the utterance ends up being unnecessarily cumbersome. Better judged in my view is the resonant opening to one of Beowulf's speeches before he fights the dragon:

> Many were the struggles I survived in youth
> in times of danger; I do not forget them. (lines 2423–4)

Wielding words: diction and rhetorical features

Alexander's vocabulary includes words that are archaic and/or poetic and words taken straight from Old English vocabulary even though they are now obsolete. In the first category, which includes non-obsolete Old English words but also ones of other derivation, are words like *adventured*, used transitively to mean 'imperilled, risked (him)' (line 44), *vaunting*, used adjectivally in *(he) vaunting spoke* (line 341), *fleet*, as a verb meaning 'move swiftly' (line 162), *foe* (line 510, and *foeman*, line 1151), *oft* (line 572), *whelms* (line 581), *targe* (line 655), *plaint* (line 786), *eldritch* (line 806), *yesternight* (line 955), *hasped* (line 975), *lindens* (line 1242, etc.), *whither* (line 1330), *hart* (line 1367), *wreathèd* (line 1380), *drake*, for dragon (*sea-drakes*, line 1452; *fire-drake*, line 2685 etc.; *earth-drake*, line 2712, etc.), *O*, exclamation (line 1651, etc.), *doom* (line 2140: *my doom was not yet*), *meed* (line 2145), *lambent* (line 2153), *bills*, for swords (line 2201), *thee* (line 2247), *worm*, meaning 'serpent' (line 2306, etc.). Alexander's use of the literary word *dingles* (of unknown origin but not Old English) in association with *sea* (*the dingles of the sea*, line 564, translating *sægrunde neah*, 'near the sea-bottom') suggests the specific influence of Auden's poem 'The Wanderer', which begins 'Doom is dark and deeper than a sea-dingle' (cf. also line 1393, *in any dingle of the sea*; Old English *on gyfenes grund*, line 1394, 'at the bottom of the sea').[44] Alexander also wields the Old English words *wield* and *Wielder* (lines 17, 30, etc.), which are not obsolete

---

[44] Auden, 'The Wanderer', in *The English Auden*, ed. Mendelson, pp. 55–6.

but are very much stylized usages, and he uses *limbs* to refer to tree-limbs (line 96) in the alliterating phrase *limbs and leaves* (translating directly *leomum ond leafum*, 'branches and leaves'), a more mannered metaphorical usage today than it would have been in Old English. Similarly, he mirrors the original in using *winters* in the sense 'years' (lines 1723, 3047), an Old English usage but one also found in later literary tradition. Adverbial *all of* in the phrase *all of dragon skins* (line 2087, describing Grendel's glove) is also a literary formulation.

Words taken straight from Old English are *atheling* (line 20, etc.; at line 20 the Old English has *guma*, 'man', not *æðeling*), *Weird*, though unlike in *The Earliest English Poems* Alexander does not use the older spelling *wierd* (line 477, etc.; Old English *wyrd*),[45] *battle-rune*, with *rune* meaning 'counsel' or 'words' (line 501; Old English, *beadurune*, 'hostile utterance'), *sell*, meaning 'give' (line 1371; Old English *seleð*, 'will give'), *bite*, meaning 'cut, penetrate' with reference to weapons (line 1522: Old English *bitan*), *stool* in its Old English sense of 'chair, seat', in *gift-stool* (lines 2326, etc.; Old English *gifstol/bregostol*, 'gift-seat/ruler-seat').

Alexander's diction is also characterized by the sheer range of the vocabulary drawn upon, from rare and recondite words to other kinds of specialized and stylized vocabulary. Stylized usages include such formulations as *all kinds misbegotten* (line 110), *the current sea* (line 297), *at hall* (line 836) and *lapped in flesh* (line 2421); we have already seen Hrothgar *mounting* his bed, rather than just getting into it (line 676). Examples of rare words, or rare meanings, are *catches*, meaning 'tricks' (*his nasty catches*, line 683; *sudden catches*, line 738), *shrilled* as a transitive verb (*shrilled terror*, line 784), *unexceptioned* (line 1096), *upwellings* (line 1492), *heft*, meaning 'weight, strain' (line 1910), *healed* (*with gold*), meaning 'covered' (line 2254), *casque*, for helmet (line 2970), as well as the Latin word *signum* (line 47). Romance-derived terms are in evidence, such as *gallant* (line 340), *liegeman* (line 1992), *guerdon* (line 2144) and *fealty* (line 2282), and Latin-derived (via French) abstract nouns are also frequent, such as *disparagement* (line 1048), *alleviation* (line 1989) and *endowment* (line 2180); also Latin-derived, and rather prosaic, is *manufacture* (line 1442). And Alexander draws upon nautical usage when he uses *unshipped* (line 51), *hoisted / and belayed* (lines 1903–4) and refers to ships by means of the feminine pronoun (line 37, etc.).

The translation also makes widespread use of compound words, another aspect of Alexander's imitation of Old English poetic style. Some of his compounds are exact calques of the Old English, others being inventions on Old English principles. Thus he shadows the Old English in translating *folccwen* as *folk-queen* (line 641) and *gifstol* as *gift-stool* (line 2326; at line 167, however, he translates *gifstol* as 'treasure-throne'), and he also uses the analogous formation *folk-king* (line 2592, translating *se ðe ær folce weold*, line 2595, 'who had formerly ruled the people'), here adopting a compound, *folccyning*, that occurs elsewhere in *Beowulf* (lines 2733 and 2873, translated respectively by Alexander in these instances as *ruler*

---

[45] He also uses *weird* uncapitalized (line 1056), meaning a fated event, as opposed to the personification of Fate.

and *the king of our people*, not *folk-king*), but the form *folk-founder* (line 31) is Alexander's own invention (translating *landfruma*, 'leader of the land'). Other such calques, among many, include *whale-road* (line 10; Old English, *hronrade*), *out-eager* (line 33; Old English *utfus*; cf. also *death-eager*, line 2417, translating *wælfus*), *wife-love* (line 2045; Old English *wiflufan*) and *blood-smoke* (line 2658; Old English *wælrec*).

Many of Alexander's compounds are unremarkable, like *body-armour* (line 40), *mead-hall* (line 68, etc.) and *word-hoard* (line 259), these again often being exact or close translations of the Old English, and they can sometimes sound quite lame, as in *after-inheritor* (line 2728; Old English *yrfeweard*, line 2731, 'guardian of the inheritance'). Others, however, present carefully constructed and sharply focused images, amplifying the sense of the Old English: examples are *scathing steel-thresh* (line 597; Old English *atole ecgþræce*, line 596, 'terrible sword-edge-attack') – *thresh* prompted by the sound of *þræce* –, *war-taste* (line 2045; Old English *wigbealu*, line 2046, 'evil of war'), *death-taken* (line 2119, converting the Old English indicative statement *deað fornam*, 'death took [him] away'; this is varied as the more archaic-sounding *death-rapt* at line 2234, the Old English again having *deað fornam*, line 2236), *twisted tangle-thing* (line 2558; Old English *hringbogan*, line 2561, 'coiled creature'). Among Alexander's more striking compounds is the curious *battle-dwarfing* (helmet) (line 2152; Old English *heaðosteapne*, line 2153, 'towering in battle'), the meaning of which is unclear. An example of a tripartite compound is *wine-supper-hall* (line 771), which spells out more fully (if unnecessarily?) the meaning of Old English *winsele*, 'wine-hall'. Many of the compounds are archaic-sounding even when they are Alexander's own inventions: *in warspite* (line 548; Old English *heaðogrim*, 'fierce in battle'), *life's faring-forth* (line 2468; Old English *þa he of life gewat*, line 2471, 'when he departed from life'), etc.

And Alexander also works to give a sense of the formulaic diction of the Old English. We have already noted his use of recurrent first-person phrases such as *as I heard*. Formulaic-sounding expressions are found throughout the translation, many of them closely rendering phrases in the original but many also generated by Alexander, who has to some extent internalized the 'grammar' of Old English systems. Thus at lines 342 and 404 we get the epithet *hard under helmet*, calquing *heard under helme*; at line 2536, however, Alexander varies his translation of *heard under helme* to *brave beneath helmet*, and at line 2638 he uses an analogous phrase, *keen under helmet*, where there is no corresponding formula in the Old English, which reads *hwate helmberend* (line 2642), 'brave helmet bearers'. Similarly, his formulaic-sounding phrase at line 428 *Shield of the South Danes* is not a literal translation of the Old English, which has *brego Beorht-Dena* (line 427), 'lord of the Bright-Danes' – and indeed a phrase meaning 'Shield of the South Danes' occurs nowhere else in the original either – but instead is generated from Alexander's application of principles derived from relevant Old English formula systems, in accordance with the requirements of alliteration; *Helmet of the Scyldings* some lines later, however (line 456), is a direct verbal equivalent to the Old English *helm Scyldinga*.

One context in which the formulaic quality of Alexander's writing is particularly in evidence is at the introduction of speeches, where he assiduously follows the Old English in using variants of the one-line verbal structure consisting of name (or other identifier) followed by speech-verb in the first half-line, followed in the second half-line by a descriptive appositional phrase, often but not always giving the paternal lineage of the speaker:[46] *Then Hrothgar spoke, the Helmet of the Scyldings* (line 456; Old English *Hroðgar maþelode,   helm Scyldinga*), *Then Unferth spoke, the son of Edgelaf* (line 499; Old English *Unferð maþelode,   Ecglafes bearn*), *Then Beowulf spoke, son of Edgetheow* (line 529; Old English *Beowulf maþelode,   bearn Ecgþeowes*), and so on. Alexander supplies a sense of narrative continuity by inserting *then* in these instances but his strategy is to adopt the formal Old English pattern rather than seeking more original ways of signalling the beginning of a speech. There are other ways of introducing speeches both in *Beowulf* itself and in Alexander's translation, of course, but Alexander is happy to take his lead from the original rather than seeking to add variety.

In his use of formulaic-sounding language, as in other aspects of his diction, Alexander cultivates a register that is removed from normal modern usage, aiming at the same time, however, not to alienate the reader by sounding either too peculiar or too repetitiously trite. Craft and judgement help him mostly to succeed in this purpose, qualities also evident in his treatment of the rhetorical features of the original.

Understatement, reflective of Old English poetic style, is a notable feature of Alexander's mode. We have already noted his fondness for negative statements and *un-* words and might also mention his frequent use of *little* to provide understatement: for example, *little was the hurt* (line 1944; Old English *hio leodbealewa læs gefremede*, line 1946, 'she caused fewer harms to the people'), *there was little cause* (line 2992; Old English *ne ðorfte him*, line 2995, 'he did not need to'). In these cases Alexander reworks the litotes of the original, as he does also with *hardly* at line 2352, *that was hardly the least* (Old English *No þæt læsest wæs*, line 2354, 'That was not at all the least'); at line 2860, however, it is he who supplies the litotes: *with little joy at heart* (Old English *sarigferð*, line 2862, 'sad-hearted').

Another characteristic of Old English poetry that Alexander transmits is the use of grim irony. Taking his lead from the Old English, he refers to Grendel as a *new hall-thane* at Heorot (line 140), translating *healðegenes* (line 142); Beowulf in a passage of sustained irony exclaims that in his swimming-match with Breca the monsters of the deep *sat not down / to dine* on him (lines 562–3), reflecting the Old English's *symbel ymbsæton* (preceded by a negative) (line 564), 'sat round at the banquet'; in similar vein, Beowulf is described as the *guest* (line 1544) of

---

[46] A variant of this in the Old English allows an adverbial insertion in the second half-line, delaying the appositional phrase until the first half of the next line, as in *Weard maþelode, ðær on wicge sæt, / ombeht unforht* (lines 286–7a), 'The watchman spoke, where he sat on his horse, an officer unafraid'.

Grendel's mother in the scene of their fight, picking up on the Old English image of Beowulf as a *selegyst* (line 1545), 'hall-guest'.

Indirectness, careful expression and mannered phrasing are other features of Old English style that Alexander imitates, particularly in speeches, as we have seen. Indirectness is a feature of Old English poetic imagery, including in kennings (to be discussed further in the next section), and here again Alexander provides his own instances as well as passing on those of the original, as at lines 437–8, in which he refers to the *shielding / yellow board*, i.e., the shield, where the corresponding Old English *sidne scyld, / geolorand to guþe*, 'the broad shield, the yellow shield to the battle', is more direct, having in fact two explicit nouns for shield.

Consonant with his heightened register, from time to time Alexander fashions rhetorical patterns of balance, repetition and wordplay, usually prompted by verbal figures in the Old English. Such patterns include antithesis, as in *night's table-laughter turned to morning's / lamentation* (lines 127–8), this being a free and alert reworking of *Þa wæs æfter wiste wop up ahafen, / micel morgensweg* (lines 128–9a), 'then after the feast lamentation was raised up, a great morning-cry'; and he also deploys balanced phrases and longer sequences. An example of a balanced longer sequence is *he never before and never after / harder luck nor hall-guards found* (lines 718–19; Old English *næfre he on aldordagum ær ne siþðan / heardran hæle, healðegnas fand*, 'he never found in the days of his life, before or since, hall-thegns with harder fortune'), in which Alexander builds on the balanced phrasing of the Old English, creating a second pairing in the zeugma of *harder luck nor hall-guards* and rhetorically delaying the verb until the end of the sentence.

Balanced phrases often involve word-pairs, as *hater and hated* (line 440; Old English *lað wið laþum*, 'enemy against enemy'), *friend or foe* (line 510; Old English *ne leof ne lað*, line 511, 'neither loved nor hated'), *never before and never after* (line 718; Old English *ær ne siþðan*, 'before nor since'), *string and song* (line 1062, slightly varying the Old English *sang ond sweg*, line 1063, 'song and sound'), *kinsman and kinsman* (line 1978; Old English *mæg wið mæge*, 'kinsman to kinsman'). The phrase *treasures and trappings* (line 41) is analogous to these examples but is not taken from the Old English (which has *madma mænigo*, 'a multitude of treasures'). The high-flown triplet *too cruel a feud, / too long, too hard* (lines 132–3) does go back directly to the Old English, translating *to strang, / lað ond longsum* (cf. too the variant at lines 191–2).

The mode is predominantly declarative, with the rhetorical figure of exclamation much in evidence, particularly in speeches but also in narrative, in keeping with the lofty tone that Alexander confidently adopts in imitation of the original poem: *What a banquet that was!* (line 1231; Old English *Þær wæs symbla cyst*, line 1232, 'There was the best of banquets'), *What a nation they were!* (line 1249; Old English *wæs seo þeod tilu*, line 1250, 'that was a good people'), *ample was his spirit!* (line 1811; Old English *þæt wæs modig secg*, line 1812, 'that was a brave man'); a verbless example is *a cheerless wood!* (line 1415; Old English *wynleasne wudu*, line 1416, 'a joyless wood').

Imagery and sound

As noted above, Alexander's translation preserves something of the indirectness of expression that is one of the characteristics of Old English poetic style. The indirectness of Old English poetry is seen most obviously, perhaps, in that poetry's use of kennings. Other translators make sparing use of kennings or substitute more direct forms of expression for them but Alexander prefers to transmit the Old English trait and indeed to introduce his own original instances of it. Some examples closely translating the Old English are *over swan's riding*, i.e., 'over the sea' (line 199; Old English *ofer swanrade*, line 200), *sound-wood*, i.e., 'ship' (line 207; Old English *sundwudu*, line 208), *battle-flame*, i.e., 'sword' (line 1522; Old English *beadoleoma*, line 1523), *hammers' legacy*, i.e., 'sword' (line 2825; Old English *homera lafe*, line 2829), *iron shower*, i.e., 'shower of arrows' (line 3113; Old English *isernscure*, line 3116). In *A special sea-dress, a sail* (line 1903) Alexander follows the Old English (*merehrægla sum, / segl sale fæst*, lines 1905–6, 'a particular sea-garment, a sail made fast with rope') in providing a gloss for the kenning, as he does also in *the harp, / the joy-wood* (lines 2107–8; Old English *hearpan wynne, / gomenwudu grette*, 'the joy of the harp, greeted the joy-wood'); cf. also *harp-play, / glee-wood's gladness* (lines 2261–2; Old English *hearpan wyn, / gomen gleobeames*, lines 2262–3, 'the joy of the harp, the pleasure of the music-wood'). The kenning *over the salt-trails* (line 228; Old English *yplade*, 'wave-journey') is Alexander's own, as is the particular image in *strayer of the ocean*, i.e., 'ship' (line 1881; Old English *sægenga*, line 1882, 'sea-goer').

A particularly obscure kenning for crossing the sea is evident in *danced on the Spear-Man* (line 515; translating *glidon ofer garsecg*, 'glided over the spear-man'), in which Alexander adopts a cryptic Old English poetic usage, complicating it indeed by daringly translating *glidon*, literally 'glided, moved easily', as *danced*; in his commentary he provides a brief note on 'Spear-Man' meaning 'sea' (mentioning Neptune's trident as a possibly analogous image), but it is notable that rather than reducing the obscurity of the Old English in his translation, he embraces its obliqueness.

In some of these examples of kennings we see Alexander adding to the Old English, though drawing on 'Old English' techniques to do so. Generally it is in the area of imagery that some of his most creative touches are in evidence, amplifying or sharpening the original. His approach may be imitative and he does not seek to distract from the original or to impress with extraneous show, but Alexander is a writer of effective poetry and his perceptive treatment of imagery provides a key source of the interest and engagement that his writing produces in the reader.

He subtly amplifies the original when he writes that Heorot *bulks to the sky* (line 285; the Old English refers to it as being *on heahstede*, 'in a lofty place'), that a swimmer *whitened the ocean* (line 541; the Old English has him *flodyþum feor*, line 542, 'far on the flood-waves'), and that Wiglaf was *thrilled at the sight of the dragon's gold* (line 2755; in the Old English he simply saw, *geseah*, the gold, line 2756). He refers in a sharp image to *wind-picked moors* near Grendel's lair (line 1357; Old English *windige næssas*, line 1358, 'windy headlands') and to the dragon's chamber as the *womb of the earth* (line 3047; Old English *wið eorðan fæðm*, line 3049, 'in the earth's embrace'). At lines 1801–2 he alertly introduces a lyrical description of sunlight, saying that it *shook out above the shadows*, an image prompted by the Old English word *scacan* (line 1802), which means, however, not 'shake' but 'move quickly', and he describes vividly how the beasts of battle *bared the bodies of the slain* (line 3024), strengthening the Old English image in *reafode* (line 3027), 'plundered'.

In such vivid images, invariably combined with the play of sound, Alexander adds to the interest of the narrative, often by means of single short phrases – other examples are *his glut of slaughter* (line 124), the *loathsome snouts snickered by me* (line 559), (the dragon's) *hissing gust* (line 2555) – but also sustaining graphic descriptions over a number of lines, not least in passages of violent action. Sound and sense are inseparable in Alexander's graphic translation of the famous description of Grendel attacking a sleeping warrior in Heorot, relating how he

> Savagely tore at him,
> gnashed at his bone-joints, bolted huge gobbets,
> sucked at his veins, and had soon eaten
> all of the dead man, even down to his
> hands and feet. (lines 741–5)

Here the vigorousness of the imagery is reinforced by the urgency of the rhythm, the use of monosyllables and the plosive and hissing alliteration. In other places the mood, and the imagery, is gentler, as in the synaesthesia of the reference to the steward with the container of mead who *poured out its sweetness* (line 496); synaesthesia occurs in Old English poetry but not at the relevant point in *Beowulf*, which has *scencte scir wered*, 'poured out the shining drink'. The image of a successful man in Hrothgar's great speech of advice to Beowulf lyrically embellishes the original in the phrase *sweetly the world / swings to his will* (lines 1737–8), a deft modification of the Old English *him eal worold / wendað on willan* (lines 1738–9), 'for him all the world turns to his will', with the gentle rhythm swinging with the sense. An appealing piece of pleonasm on the part of Alexander comes in his mention of spring as *the weather of rainbows* (line 1135), where the Old English has *wuldortorhtan weder* (line 1136), 'gloriously bright weather'.

Thus though inspired by the Old English in his attitude to imagery, as in other respects, Alexander is also imaginative enough and skilled enough to free himself from slavish dependence on it. In subtly amplifying and sharpening the imagery of *Beowulf* he is making the poetry his own. Even when translating literally, however, as he often appears to be, he is still making the poetry his own.

The integration of imagery with the other aspects of poetic expression is carefully attended to. We have seen something of the vitality of Alexander's use of wordplay and rhetorical and grammatical patterning. Alliteration, which is structural, is handled with varying effects from the understated to the strongly percussive and its judiciously controlled use by Alexander avoids the danger of tiring the reader with excessive intrusiveness. Rhythm, though firmly based on an underlying Old English metrical structure, with emphatic caesura (after which new sense units often begin), is flexibly adapted to mood and content. We have already seen strongly rhythmical descriptions of violent action. A passage of dense imagery that combines urgency with sinisterness is that describing the return of the mortally wounded Grendel to his ghastly mere:

> The tarn was troubled; a terrible wave-thrash
> brimmed it, bubbling; black-mingled,
> the warm wound-blood welled upwards. (lines 846–8)

This translates

> Ðær wæs on blode   brim weallende;
> atol yða geswing   eal gemenged
> haton heolfre   heorodreore weol. (lines 847–9)

> [There the water was surging with blood; a terrible swirling of waves, all mingled with hot gore, it welled with battle-blood.]

Alexander's vivid translation is a heavily monosyllabic passage with lively sound effects including alliteration (predominantly plosive), tumbling rhythm, dense appositive phrasing and suggestive atmospheric description. *Tarn* is a topographically appropriate word in this context, *wave-thrash* brings life to the formulaic *yða geswing* (cf. also *one wave-thrasher*, line 1433; Old English *yðgewinnes*, line 1434), *well* picks up alertly on Old English *weallende* (cf. *upwellings*, line 1422; Old English *weol*) and *wound-blood* is an effective equivalent to *heorodreore*.

Elsewhere the rhythm may be smooth or 'swinging', and can have an iambic character, as in the suggestive passage describing the stag in the woods – *the hart that roams the heath, when hounds have pressed him* (line 1367) – or, also with anapestic elements, that describing the anxiety of Beowulf's warriors while he is fighting Grendel's mother: they are *staring at the pool with sickness at heart* (line 1602). Rhythmical variety inflects and enlivens the dominant four-stress metrical structure.

Two Passages for Consideration

Alexander's *Beowulf*, lines 1–11

> Attend!
> We have heard of the thriving of the throne of Denmark,
> how the folk-kings flourished in former days,
> how those royal athelings earned that glory.
>
> Was it not *Scyld Scefing* that shook the halls,
> took mead-benches, taught encroaching
> foes to fear him – who, found in childhood,
> lacked clothing? Yet he lived and prospered,
> grew in strength and stature under the heavens
> until the clans settled in the sea-coasts neighbouring
> over the whale-road all must obey him
> and give tribute. That was a king![47]

These opening lines establish the elevated and somewhat stylized register that Alexander adopts as his 'equivalent' to that of the original poem. This is an expressive kind of Modern English, fluent and forceful, but it is clearly not the language of everyday speech. The very opening word *Attend* suggests high formality, with perhaps epic overtones, and Alexander follows this up with the mannered alliterative phrase *the thriving of the throne of Denmark*, the Old English poetic compound *folk-kings* (imitating the corresponding Old English word *þeodcyninga*), the obsolete *athelings*, and towards the end the kenning *whale-road*, all of which are defamiliarizing for a modern reader and suggestive of a special poetic language. Other literary usages are *thriving* (as a noun), *flourish* (used of peoples' success), *foe*, and *must* as a past tense form; and *sea-coasts neighbouring over the whale-road* provides a carefully wrought poetic image of location (here Alexander transfers the 'neighbouring' of *ymbsittendra* from the people to the place where they live), as well as being rhythmically interesting. The metre is distinctive but, consonant with the elevated register, is mostly not obtrusive.

Though somewhat stylized the writing is notably restrained in this passage, in which the tone is one of admiration for the great deeds of the heroes of the past, emphatically but decorously expressed. The power of Scyld is brought out in the brisk sequence of active verbs applied to him – *shook, took, taught* – and in the reference to the passivity of the neighbouring tribes – *must obey, give tribute*. The description of the military exploits of Scyld is kept quite unspecific, however, with only the most understated reference to the violence and destructiveness that would have accompanied his conquests, and Alexander preserves the symbolically significant acts of taking mead-benches and giving tribute. In describing the feats of Scyld and the Danes the pace of the passage is steady and

---

[47] For the corresponding Old English lines, see p. 32, above. In his 2001 revision, Alexander makes one change to the translation of this passage, in the closing half-line, which reads *He was a good king!*

dignified, though building towards the concise climax of the exclamation at line 11. It is unhurried, with word and phrase pairings and other kinds of balance, as in the two *how* clauses in the first sentence and the pairs *lived and prospered*, *strength and stature* and *obey him and give tribute*.

The poetic register is self-consciously literary but unostentatious. Stylized usages are part of the register but much of the vocabulary here is fairly plain, with the majority of words indeed being monosyllabic. At the beginning of his career as a translator Alexander might have leapt to translate *weox under wolcnum* (line 7), 'grew under the heavens', as *waxed under the heavens* but here he selects the straightforward verb *grew* (he does use *wax* at line 1740, however, in a passage of heightened rhetoric, translating *weaxeð*). The single change that he makes to the translation in the 2001 revision has the effect of removing the one possible element of colloquialism in the passage: he changes *That was a king!* to the more understated *He was a good king!* (the latter being a more literal translation of *þæt wæs god cyning*). The compounds *folk-kings, mead-benches, sea-coasts* and *whale-road* are unspectacular, suggestive of a traditional word-hoard rather than of startling originality. Also suggestive of tradition is the inclusive first-person plural of the first sentence and the rhetorical question of the second, the latter assuming agreement from the imagined audience. It is too early in the poem for the reader to become attuned to a formulaic feel to the diction but later we will get echoes of some of the phrases used here – *folk-king, under the heavens, whale-road* – and *atheling* turns out to be a favourite word in the translation.

Alexander's version of these lines is faithful to the ideas of the original but quite free in its detail. In phrases like *shook the halls, taught encroaching tribes* and *lacked clothing* we see him filling out the imagery of the original. The syntax too is reworked: there is rearrangement of clauses in the opening lines, with two *how* clauses, and a rhetorical question is introduced in the second sentence (expressing in new terms the sense of the *Oft* of the original); later a *syððan*, 'since', clause (line 6) becomes a relative clause, and connective *ands* are inserted at lines 7 and 11. Despite these changes, however, Alexander manages to convey features of Old English poetic syntax. After the first sentence, sense-breaks tend to come with the caesura; though *ands* are inserted, asyndetic coordination is also in evidence (*shook* [. . .] took [. . .] taught; prospered, grew*), reflecting apposition in the Old English; the temporal development of the original is preserved, leading to the *until* (*oðþæt*) clause of the closing lines, with its delayed verbs; the narrative mode is direct and cumulative, working towards the concluding exclamation. This exclamation, as in the original, echoes that of the opening call to attention (*Attend!*; *Hwæt*), providing an enclosing pattern of unity to the passage overall. Structurally, Alexander's translation also preserves the clearly apparent tripartite organization of the Old English passage, with an opening generalization followed by a specific focus on Scyld and then a description of his success.

Alexander's treatment of the Old English passage is sensitive and assured. Unlike other translators, he gets into his stride straightaway, capturing the exclamatory but also dignified tone of the original and setting up the narrative in an engaging manner. He elides some details (*egsode eorlas*, line 6, 'he terrified the men'; *he þæs forfre gebad*, line 7, 'he experienced comfort for that') but conveys well both the general sense and the feel of the Old English passage. His writing here is accessible and attractive but also gives an excellent impression of qualities of the poetry of *Beowulf* itself and of that poem's alterity for the modern reader.

Alexander's *Beowulf*, lines 866–73

> Or a fellow of the king's,
> whose head was a storehouse of the storied verse,
> whose tongue gave gold to the language
> of the treasured repertory, wrought a new lay
> made in the measure. The man struck up,
> found the phrase, framed rightly
> the deed of Beowulf, drove the tale,
> rang word-changes.[48]

This is a lively descriptive passage in which Alexander gives a vivid impression of the art of the oral *scop*. In his own poetry here Alexander also works to reflect something of the artfulness that is apparent in the corresponding passage in *Beowulf*. His writing is rather more elaborate here than in the first extract, more insistent in its poetic effects. A number of striking images appear and there are some highly mannered word choices. These do not always hit the right note, perhaps, and some of them may be unnecessarily distracting. *Fellow* has possible misleading connotations of class and *repertory* of theatre, while *drove the tale* is surely an unenlightening metaphor; *fellow*, *repertory* and *drove* all supply the requisite alliteration but are strained choices in the context. The phrase *rang word-changes* provides a concise way to refer to poetic variation (and keeps close to Old English *wordum wrixlan*, 'exchange words') but perhaps suggests a mechanical process rather than a creative one; *made in the measure* relevantly captures associations of *soðe gebunden*, 'truly bound together', but (at least to my ear) is uncomfortably like 'made to measure'. The strong image of the oral poet's tongue giving gold to the language, Alexander's pleonastic addition, is attractive but it is also potentially confusing, since the language being referred to is that of the 'repertory', which is 'treasured' already.

In making use of these words and images Alexander's touch may be seen as less assured than in the first passage (and than in his general practice). The lines flow well, however, and succeed in presenting an engaging picture of the *scop*, getting across the key ideas of the orality, traditionality and technical skill of the *scop*'s art. As in the Old English, the passage is made up of two sense units, the first providing the narrative information and describing the art of the *scop* in general terms, the second elaborating on the qualities of the 'new lay' that

---

[48] For the corresponding Old English lines, see p. 37, above.

he composes about Beowulf. The passage is connected to the preceding narrative material by the conjunction *Or*, which is Alexander's deft response to the *Hwilum* [. . .] *hwilum*, 'At times . . . at times', formulation of the Old English. The syntax of the passage's two sentences is recast but still has something of the character of that of the original, notably in the positioning of sense-breaks at the caesura and in the use of apposition. The first sentence, as in the Old English, presents balanced descriptive material and has a delayed verb. Alexander enhances the element of balance here by ending the first two lines with *of* phrases, by having two appositive *whose* clauses and by introducing anaphora in *storehouse* and *storied*. The second sentence is made up of a series of five appositive phrases, reworking the three phrases (with supplementary material) of the Old English, two of which Old English phrases indeed are joined by *ond* rather than being in apposition.

Overall, the narrative sweeps along here, enlivened by the inclusion of interesting descriptive detail, which, as in the original, is impressionistic rather than precise in what it conveys about the features of Germanic poetry. As suggested above, some of Alexander's translation choices, particularly in positions of alliteration, appear rather strained here and these detract from what is otherwise an effective passage of verse. Even with these possible glitches, however, Alexander's version of these lines is attractive and gives a good sense of both the content and the 'flavour' of the corresponding passage in *Beowulf*. As in *Beowulf*, the passage is something of a set piece, as well as fitting in fluently to its larger narrative context.

Beowulf 'as Literature'

Alexander published his translation of *Beowulf* conscious of the reputation of the Old English poem at the time as 'a sort of dinosaur at the entrance hall of English Literature',[49] pored over by philologists and historians but generally disregarded as literature. It was taught as 'English language', not literature, in British universities, in a manner that many on the receiving end found uncongenial. It is worth quoting again Frank Kermode's experience of studying *Beowulf* at university:

> The interests of the teachers were exclusively philological and antiquarian. *Beowulf* provided them with a great variety of complicated scholarly problems, and it was in these that they wanted to involve their students. They rarely found it necessary or desirable to speak of *Beowulf* as a poem, and when they did so they were quite likely to say it was not a particularly good one.[50]

---

[49] See above, p. 104.
[50] Kermode, 'The Modern *Beowulf*', p. 2.

Alexander laments that, though some students acquired an unsatisfied curiosity about *Beowulf* as literature, 'Some of the mud that was so zealously slung at the old "crib and gobbet" approach seems to have stuck, very unfairly, to the image of the unoffending poem.'[51] Working in a British context, Alexander's aim was to rescue the unoffending poem for people interested in literature and in the history of English literature, to make the poetry of *Beowulf*, an unread classic standing 'at the beginning of our literature',[52] available to the general educated reader. He was bringing *Beowulf*, as a poem, into the modern reader's literary canon in a way that it had not been before. He accepts that *Beowulf* belongs in the English literary canon and is untroubled about the possible questions of ownership raised by his use of the term 'our literature'. As we shall see, such questions of ownership *were* troubling to Seamus Heaney.

In bringing *Beowulf*, as a poem, to the modern reader, Alexander insists that it is necessary to use verse rather than prose, questioning indeed 'whether a literal prose version of a verse epic is, properly, a translation.'[53] In his revised edition of the *Beowulf* translation he refers to poetic translation as 'an attempt to offer an equivalent poem to those who cannot read the original',[54] thereby making the original poem accessible to them. Edwin Morgan had sought to produce a *Beowulf* for his 'poetic co-readers and co-writers'. Alexander's aim is more democratic; he writes for a wider readership. This aim is reflected in the publication profile of his translation, which was very different from that of Morgan's. Morgan's translation was published originally in a small-scale poetry outlet but Alexander's was commissioned by the Penguin Classics series, which by the early 1970s had developed into a very successful enterprise that managed to combine prestige and high quality with low price and popularity. The whole ethos of the paperback publishing house Penguin Books, as fostered by the group's founder, Allen Lane, and espoused not least in the Penguin Classics division (which by the early 1970s had produced several hundred translations of 'classics'), was one that aimed 'to combine social and educative responsibility with commercial success'.[55]

Alexander's *The Earliest English Poems* had appeared under the auspices of the founding editor of Penguin Classics, E. V. Rieu, and, building on the popularity of that collection, *Beowulf* was commissioned by Betty Radice (who was to become Rieu's successor). As mentioned above, it became, along with the version by Kevin Crossley-Holland, the form in which most British readers came to know *Beowulf*, displacing Penguin's existing prose translation, by David Wright, itself a much-reprinted publication. In translating into prose, Wright was following the

---

[51] *Beowulf*, 'Introduction' to 1973 edition, p. 10.
[52] Ibid.
[53] *Beowulf*, 'Introduction' to 1973 edition, p. 49 (though later he qualified his opposition to prose translation of poetry: see above, p. 21).
[54] *Beowulf*, revised ed., p. lvi.
[55] MacKenzie, 'Lane, Sir Allen (1902–70)', p. 416.

general domesticating norm of Penguin Classics,[56] the example having been set by E. V. Rieu himself, whose prose *The Odyssey*, soon to be followed by *The Iliad*, had been the first title in the Penguin Classics series.[57] Alexander's translation of *Beowulf* fits well into this cultural context, though in its author's insistence in writing poetry and in his somewhat foreignizing approach it is clear that he is also transcending the educative remit of Rieu.[58]

Also indicative of Alexander's interest in appealing to a wider audience than Morgan is his care about the user-friendliness of his translation. There is a helpful introductory essay and in the translation itself Alexander provides (in the original 1973 edition) line-number spans for each page in the header of that page; the header for the right-hand page of each opening also gives a summarizing phrase describing the content of the opening, the left-hand header having the title *Beowulf* (in the revised edition instead of having line numbers in the header Alexander supplies them, in tens, along the side of the page). The text is divided into paragraphs but there are no sections or other divisions, headed or otherwise. Major names are given in italics at their first occurrence. Alexander provides explanatory notes (revised and expanded in the 2001 edition), along with a map, family trees and an annotated index of proper names. The appeal of the book is enhanced by the attractiveness of Penguin's design.

The sales figures of Alexander's *Beowulf*, in their hundreds of thousands, are one indication of the success of his enterprise. The translation is accessible but not reductive, and readers (and teachers) liked it. For the critic and the Anglo-Saxonist, Alexander's version, while lacking the flashes of brilliance seen in other versions and not always hitting the right note in its diction, must be regarded as highly successful. It is a thoughtful translation by a sensitive reader of Old English poetry, generally assured in its technique and lively and interesting in its manner, giving a vivid depiction of the poem's heroic world and of the seriousness of its concerns. Above all, it succeeds better than most other translations in conveying to the modern reader an enabling sense of what it is like to read *Beowulf* in the original today (we cannot, of course, experience what it would have been like for an Anglo-Saxon to read, or hear, *Beowulf*), while at the same time being written in convincing modern verse. In his *Beowulf* Alexander leaves the unsubtlety of Pound's 'The Seafarer' behind but continues to be inspired by his mentor's feel for essential qualities of the poetry of the Anglo-Saxons.

---

56 Wright, trans., *Beowulf: A Prose Translation*. An early example of a Penguin Classic with verse translated into verse was Helen Waddell's *Mediaeval Latin Lyrics*, originally published in 1929 but brought out in the Penguin Classics series in 1952. On Wright's version, see further above, pp. 21-3.

57 Rieu, trans., *Homer: The Odyssey* (1946); *Homer: The Iliad* (1950).

58 In Rieu's view, translation should be into 'contemporary but not too topical prose, readily intelligible to all' (Connell, 'Rieu, Emile Victor (1887–1972)', p. 964).

✦7✦

Seamus Heaney:
A Living Speech Raised to the Power of Verse

Seamus Heaney's translation of *Beowulf* was published in 1999 to a reception that was mostly very enthusiastic indeed. Attracting a level of interest unprecedented in recent times for a verse publication, the translation caught the imagination of modern readers, even having lengthy stints at the top of the best-seller lists in Britain and Ireland and in the United States. It was praised by poetry critics for its freshness and vigour, and, for the most part, Anglo-Saxon scholars approved of the translation too.[1] They hailed it as a sensitive and generally accurate rendering of the great Old English poem, based on good scholarship, and as a production which brought welcome public attention to *Beowulf* and to Old English literature more generally. Among dissenting voices have been those of Tom Shippey, who disapproves of what he refers to as Heaney's 'fashionable gestures towards post-colonialism and other anachronisms,'[2] and Loren C. Gruber, who objects that Heaney's Irish diction politicizes *Beowulf*, that his grammatical renderings sometimes lose the subtlety of the original and that his English diction 'is sometimes off.'[3] Michael Alexander, on the other hand, is full of praise for Heaney's translation. Sympathetically reviewing it in *The Observer*, he refers to Heaney as 'a generous poet [who] has brought back our own, in his own words'[4] (I will need to come back to that quotation, however). Enlightening recent (approving) considerations of the translation are those of Chris Jones,[5]

[1] See, for example, Phillips, 'Seamus Heaney's *Beowulf*'; Donoghue, 'The Philologer Poet: Seamus Heaney and the Translation of *Beowulf*'; Honegger and Müller, 'Re-forging the Ancestral Tongue – Seamus Heaney's New Translation of *Beowulf*'; Sauer and Milfull, 'Seamus Heaney: Ulster, Old English, and *Beowulf*'; Sauer, 'Heaneywulf, Liuzzawulf: Two Recent Translations of *Beowulf*. See also the shorter reviews by Stanley and Caie.
[2] Shippey, '*Beowulf*: A Verse Translation, Revised Edition by Michael Swanton', p. 91; see also Shippey's review of Heaney, '*Beowulf* for the Big-Voiced Scullions'.
[3] Gruber, '"So". So What? It's a Culture War. That's "Hwæt!"', p. 69. See also Howe, 'Scullionspeak'.
[4] Alexander, 'Cracking the Norse Code', p. 111.
[5] *Strange Likeness*, pp. 182–237.

who examines Heaney's *Beowulf* and his other Old English-influenced writings in the context of the wider picture of engagement with Old English poetry on the part of twentieth-century poets; Conor McCarthy,[6] who places Heaney's medieval-inspired works in the context of his oeuvre as a whole; and John D. Niles, who pays particular attention to Heaney's Ulster speech.[7]

Language and Poetry

'The living speech of the landscape I was born into'

The evident popularity of the translation with readers was a vindication of its writer's stated aim of making *Beowulf* available, in 'a fresh chance', to quote from Heaney's Introduction to the translation, to the readership of 'the global village of the third millennium'.[8] Heaney set out to make the early medieval poem accessible to such an audience, producing a strong narrative and writing with great directness and immediacy. What I wish to stress in the present discussion, however, is that despite its accessibility and popularity Heaney's translation, as he himself was very much aware in producing it, is in key respects a revolutionary one, which re-presents and re-positions *Beowulf* in a new cultural setting. For Heaney, writing as an Irish poet, translating *Beowulf* was not a matter of 'bringing back our own' in any simple sense, to refer to Alexander again (whom does Alexander's inclusive 'our own' refer to anyway?). Heaney's engagement with the poem is a more complex matter, raising issues of language and identity and of cultural connections, and the starting-point for an understanding of Heaney's approach to his translation must be an awareness of the complexity of his relationship to and interaction with the Old English poem. 'Our own' for Heaney would have to refer to his own cultural situatedness and also to the readership of the global village to whom he makes *Beowulf* available, transforming it in the process.

In addressing his audience of the global village, Heaney hones a kind of writing that is in one sense the antithesis of global. His translation is written in Standard English but a Standard English insistently inflected by the usage of the local speech area in which the poet grew up in the rural Ulster of the mid twentieth century. The language of the translation is a function of where Heaney is coming from, so to speak, and of how he sees himself as relating to the original poem and the world from which it comes. The *Beowulf* that modern readers get in Heaney's version is self-consciously different from the *Beowulf* constructed by traditional scholarship, and Heaney's stance in approaching the poem is distinctively different from that of other translators. The orientation of his translation

---

[6] McCarthy, *Seamus Heaney and Medieval Poetry*, pp. 86–126.
[7] Niles, 'Heaney's *Beowulf* Six Years Later'.
[8] Heaney, *Beowulf*, p. xiii.

might be (has been) said to be post-colonial,⁹ but it could also be seen as striving to be post-nationalist. Writing out of his own experience, Heaney gives us a new *Beowulf* in what he presents as self-consciously an appropriation of the Old English poem, in a kind of experiment in cultural transposition. In doing so he implicitly draws our attention to the fact that all realizations of *Beowulf* today, whether scholarly or creative, and whether they know it or not, are constructs, produced with reference to assumptions about 'our own'. He also reminds us that the experience of the translator shapes the translation.

Heaney has constructed something of a mythology of his relationship to *Beowulf*, a mythology which provides a desired justification of his approach to the translation. I think he was drawn to the idea of translating *Beowulf* and his instinct was to translate the poem as he did, and indeed this is the only way he could have translated it while remaining true to his own poetic idiom, but since he was profoundly changing the register of the venerable poem he needed some kind of rational licence for doing so. Thus, he writes of the 'little epiphany'¹⁰ of finding that the humble Ulster word *thole* is an inheritance from Old English. In a sense this recognition is a red herring, since it is perfectly possible to translate from languages with which one has no such personal identification (as Heaney does elsewhere, as in *The Burial at Thebes*); and anyway *thole* appears in other varieties of English as well ('northern' and Scots). But for Heaney *thole* and the like represent, in his romantic phrase, 'illumination by philology'.¹¹ They provide a rationale for his poetic approach, and politically they provide a way of breaking down what may be perceived as an Irish–English dichotomy. Such a perceived dichotomy is reflected in Heaney's statement, in a newspaper article published just before the translation of *Beowulf* came out, 'Before I set out to translate *Beowulf*, I had to persuade myself that I was born into its language and that its language was born into me.'¹² None of our other translators has such a problem with the idea of translating *Beowulf*.

Heaney's translation of *Beowulf* is a work of his mature years rather than, as in the case of other examples highlighted in this book, coming early in his poetic career. His relationship with *Beowulf* was a long-lasting one¹³ and his translation of it, done mostly in the 1990s (and based on the Wrenn–Bolton edition),¹⁴

9   See also Sauer and Milfull, 'Seamus Heaney: Ulster, Old English, and *Beowulf*, pp. 97–102.
10 Heaney, *Beowulf*, p. xxvi.
11 Ibid.; on Heaney's 'illumination by philology' in the wider context of Anglo-Saxon studies, see Lerer, *Error and the Academic Self*, pp. 94–101.
12 *The Sunday Times*, 26 July, 1998, Section 8, *Books*, 6.
13 Surveying the wider trajectory of Heaney's work, Chris Jones insists, 'Far from thinking of *Beowulf* as a discrete episode in the Heaney canon, a side-track, it deserves to be seen, like *Buile Suibhne* and Dante's *Divine Comedy*, as an aspect of Heaney's literary inheritance brought over into his corpus through a variety of refractions and rewritings over a considerable period of time' (*Strange Likeness*, p. 228).
14 Heaney had produced a translation of lines 26–52 of *Beowulf* in his 1987 collection *The Haw Lantern*, 'A Ship of Death' (p. 20). The copy of the Wrenn–Bolton (1973) edition used

had a long gestation period, its conception dating back ultimately to his first encounter with Anglo-Saxon poetry as a student at Queen's University, Belfast, in the 1960s, where he was taught by John Braidwood, a traditional philologist who had a special interest in the English language in Ulster. Through his studies Heaney came to see that direct connection between Old English and the dialect spoken in the part of rural Ulster in which he had been brought up. The dialect in question is Northern Hiberno-English, which is spoken across much of Ulster and persists in its more distinctive forms particularly in country areas and, as Heaney was observing as he grew up, in the language of older and less educated people.[15] The dialect is separate from but influenced by the neighbouring regional variety, Ulster Scots, and it also has elements derived from the Irish language (which had fallen into disuse in Heaney's area generations ago, as throughout most of the rest of Ulster).

Being struck by correspondences between Old English and his native vernacular form of English, Heaney came to connect *Beowulf* with his own language experience in a way that he had not expected, but seems to have needed to. He came to see that the language of *Beowulf* was in some immediate sense *his* language rather than being only an earlier form of the more prestigious language he was encountering in the wider world and in literature. This perception of connectedness was a 'little epiphany' to Heaney and he explains that it was this that led him to fashion the distinctive stylistic register of his translation, 'the note and pitch for the overall music of the work'.[16] Heaney's distinctive register is what makes his poem what it is and renders it so unlike other translations of the Old English original. Conor McCarthy puts it well when he says that 'what Heaney does is to write his own roots into this foundational work'.[17]

Now on purely linguistic grounds, Old English is just as closely related to any one modern regional variety as it is to any other. No particular dialect can really be seen as having a special authenticity in its relationship to Old English, whether Northern Hiberno-English or some other variety, even though some regional varieties might preserve features not found in others or in Standard English. What Heaney was responding to in coming to the understanding that his local vernacular was 'an historical heritage'[18] was not something absolute that differentiated his native dialect from others but related to a more personal narrative. It was the subjective recognition of the relevance of his own personal experience and identity to his engagement with the Old English poem, his inclu-

---

by Heaney for his translation is among his *Beowulf* archive materials donated by him to the Library of Queen's University, Belfast in 2003.

[15] Heaney, *Beowulf*, p. xxv. On Hiberno-English, see Hickey, *Irish English*; Filppula, *The Grammar of Irish English*; Dolan, *A Dictionary of Hiberno-English*.
[16] *Beowulf*, p. xxvi.
[17] McCarthy, *Seamus Heaney and Medieval Poetry*, p. 107.
[18] Heaney, *Beowulf*, p. xiv.

sion after all in what could have been regarded as alien to him.[19] He was not suggesting that his own variety of English was somehow purer or superior to others (he was, however, suggesting that it was not inferior).[20] In writing out of his own language experience Heaney was aligning himself, as he put it in that article published before his *Beowulf* came out, with those writers who in deploying regional varieties of English 'sing themselves and celebrate their local idiom as part of the polyphony that is English' (he mentions specifically Hugh MacDiarmid, Derek Walcott, Toni Morrison and Les Murray).[21]

Heaney had assumed *Beowulf* to be unrelated to his own language experience because of the hierarchical view of language that still underpinned traditional literary studies as he was growing up and because of the socially stigmatized status of non-standard forms of language, complicated in the Irish context of Heaney's own experience by considerations of language ownership and perceptions of colonialism. Heaney's approach takes the poem out of its perceived traditional context in the institution of English literature and relates it to a different kind of experience. It is an interesting fact, therefore, that the translation was commissioned by that bastion of the institution of English literature *The Norton Anthology of English Literature*.[22] In its latest (seventh) edition, Heaney's translation comes right at the beginning of the *Anthology* and, with its distinctive register, has the immediate effect of unsettling easy notions about the canon of English literature. I don't know whether the *Norton* editors bargained for such a radical and self-consciously political take on *Beowulf*.[23] They embraced it,[24] but Heaney's translation presents a challenging opening to the *Anthology*, making an impression on the reader much different from that of Talbot Donaldson's worthy prose version, which had appeared in earlier editions of the *Norton*.

---

[19] Cf. the discussion by Sauer and Milfull of Heaney's 'sentimental etymology' ('Seamus Heaney: Ulster, Old English, and *Beowulf*, p. 99).
[20] Shippey's criticism of Heaney in this respect is misplaced when he writes, 'If [Heaney] is under the impression that "Scullion-speak", as he calls it, somehow preserves a native purity which other and more effete dialects of English do not, then that is a delusion: an amiable delusion, maybe, for ancestral piety is to be admired, but a dangerous delusion' ('*Beowulf* for the Big-Voiced Scullions', p. 9).
[21] *The Sunday Times*, 26 July, 1998, Section 8, Books, 6.
[22] Abrams and Greenspan, ed., *The Norton Anthology of English Literature*.
[23] Heaney's 'political' response to *Beowulf* is also stressed by Heather O'Donoghue in her essay 'Heaney, *Beowulf* and the Medieval Literature of the North'; O'Donoghue writes there that '[Heaney's] appropriation of *Beowulf* – establishing its indivisible continuity with the present – is an act of literary and linguistic politics' (p. 205).
[24] Heaney's translation and its appropriateness for the *Norton Anthology* is discussed by one of the *Norton* period editors, Alfred David, in 'The Nationalities of *Beowulf*: Anglo-Saxon Attitudes': responding to the criticisms of Heaney's translation of Howe and Chickering, David writes, echoing Heaney's comments about the polyphony of English quoted above, 'While [Heaney's Ulsterisms] say "Made in Ireland", they also alert us to the multicultural and transnational nature of any translation and of the English language and *Beowulf* itself' (p. 7).

Because of its highly subjective take on the poem some users of the *Norton* are likely to find Heaney's translation inappropriate. Howell Chickering, reviewing Heaney's *Beowulf*, predicts that 'after its day in the sun' the translation will be assigned out of the *Norton Anthology* 'by foot-soldiering non-specialists teaching required survey courses'.[25] He could be right. Heaney himself seems to have worried about the extent of the idiosyncrasy of his approach to *Beowulf* in the context of writing for a *Norton* readership. Chris Jones explains how he toned down some of his 'Irishisms' as he worked on successive drafts of the translation.[26] The idiosyncrasy of the published version is still clearly evident, however.[27]

Among the features that commentators have found most distinctive about Heaney's translation of *Beowulf* is his deployment of dialect words that belong to the vocabulary of his native Hiberno-English variety of English. This deployment is indeed a distinctive, if perhaps overstated, feature of the translation: as Jones points out, Heaney's use of Irish vocabulary is actually quite limited, relatively speaking.[28] But his deployment of dialect vocabulary should be seen as part of a larger picture. It is the overall register rather than simply these individual instances which gives the translation its character. Heaney is remembering and cherishing the language he heard in his youth, though many of the dialect words and usages in his *Beowulf* are still widely heard today in ordinary speech in Ulster. Examples of 'everyday' current dialect words are *tholed*, 'suffered' (line 14) (interestingly, Heaney never takes the option of using this verb as a direct translation of Old English *þolian*, which occurs five times in *Beowulf*), *stook*, 'upright bundle of sheaves' (line 329), *mizzle*, 'drizzle' (line 596), *session* (line 767), referring to an entertaining occasion (from Irish *seissiún*), *hirpling*, 'walking with difficulty, limping' (line 975),[29] *blather*, 'idle chatter, nonsense' (line 980), *wean*, 'child, wee one' (line 2433), *hoke*, 'dig' (line 3027). Other dialect words that Heaney deploys have gone out of normal use, as traditional ways of life have changed, but the

---

[25] Chickering, 'Beowulf and Heaneywulf', p. 177; Chickering suggests that most readers of the *Norton* will find aspects of Heaney's language incomprehensible, especially since his 'Introduction' is not printed in this edition (p. 177). Note also Des O'Rawe's observation that Heaney's use of Ulster colloquialisms 'can confine the translation's relevance to the translator's oeuvre' (O'Rawe, 'The Poet as Translator', p. 182).

[26] Chris Jones, *Strange Likeness*, pp. 232–3. Jones reports, for example, 'At one stage the *gomela Scilding* ("old Scylding", l. 2105) whom Beowulf describes to Hygelac as performing poetry in Heorot was translated as "an old seanchaí". Queried by Helen Vendler as "too Irish?", the published version settles for "old reciter" (though Heaney retains several Irishisms also questioned by Vendler)' (p. 232). See also David, 'The Nationalities of *Beowulf*', pp. 5–7.

[27] Howe argues that Heaney 'sets out to make an Irish poem' ('Scullionspeak', pp. 35–6), a view cogently opposed by Joseph McGowan, 'Heaney, Cædmon, *Beowulf*'; see esp. p. 40, where McGowan takes issue with Howe's criticism ('Scullionspeak', p. 36) that Heaney attempts 'to graft himself onto the English literary tradition'.

[28] *Strange Likeness*, pp. 230–1; see also McCarthy, *Seamus Heaney and Medieval Poetry*, pp. 90–8.

[29] For Chickering, *hirpling* 'might well be a word from "Jabberwocky"' ('Beowulf and Heaneywulf', p. 167).

ones mentioned above are still familiar. *Gumption* (line 287), though not specifically a dialect word, is in very common use in Hiberno-English, and *scare* (line 2314: 'a hot glow / that scared everyone') is the normal word for 'frighten' (note also the Hiberno-English *scaresomely*, line 3041). Particular dialect usages of Standard English words are found in *So* (line 1) (used to introduce a topic), *cub* (line 13) (for a young boy: not, as might seem to be the case at first sight, an imaginative reworking of the neutral Old English word *geong*, 'young', on the part of Heaney but a very familiar application in rural speech communities in Ulster), *rigged (out)* (lines 779, 1472, 2056 and 2078) (used in reference to clothing), *right*, 'good, praiseworthy' (line 1250: 'They were a right people'), *reek* (used of smoke) (line 2661).

Translators make choices and in the case of Heaney's *Beowulf* the key choice that the translator made was not at the level of these individual words but was that of the register in which the work is cast. Heaney has written famously about the language of the 'big-voiced Scullions' of his boyhood locality that gave him not just the lexical items mentioned above but also 'the note and pitch for the overall music of the work'. This is a type of speech, immediately recognizable to those who share something of Heaney's linguistic origins, that combines dignity and solemnity of utterance with an unrhetorical-looking plainness and a cultivation of familiar idiomatic phrasing. In Heaney's representation of it, it is a masculine voice.[30]

Heaney's adopted register is based on the real language of ordinary people, or rather, more particularly, the real language of ordinary people as he remembers it from his youth. It is a language that is colloquial but at the same time measured, with its own decorum and formality. The vocabulary of this 'real language', reflective of a traditional way of life, is expressive but limited, with much use of stock phrases, which can be banal as well as apt. It does not go in for curiosities. Narration in this register is characterized by a lack of effusiveness that may remind one of the reserved style found in the Icelandic saga, with which it also shares a fondness for understatement and for gnomic expressions of conventional wisdom.

The language has much in common with that of other speech communities and is in most respects accessible, even if not fully transparent, to English speakers everywhere, especially since Heaney presents it in the grammar of Standard English. But though accessible the language is nonetheless specific – 'authentic' – in its cultural inflection and in its association with the world of

---

[30] Readers have been struck by this 'masculinity' of Heaney's narrative voice in his *Beowulf*; this voice corresponds to the masculinity of the heroic world but has been seen to have the effect of 'shackling' the more complex presentation of the female in the original poem. For Helen Phillips, it is 'Heaney's treatment of the females in *Beowulf* that is the most disappointing' (Phillips, 'Seamus Heaney's *Beowulf*, p. 275); see also Brearton, 'Heaney and the Feminine', p. 87. For a more sympathetic view of Heaney's presentation of females (especially Grendel's mother) in the translation, see McCarthy, *Seamus Heaney and Medieval Poetry*, pp.116–20.

speakers of Northern Hiberno-English. It is more thoroughly and consistently Irish than many commentators appreciate.[31]

Its association with the world of Irish-English speakers is the source of Heaney's striking cultivation of well-worn idioms and sayings in his translation, to which critics have taken exception.[32] Far from avoiding ready-made language, Heaney can be seen to favour it in many of his expressions, thereby calculatedly incorporating the prosaic into his poetry. The succession of colloquial everyday phrases is constant, including such stock items as the following (which occur both in the narrative and in speeches): *troubles they'd come through* (line 15), *hold the line* (line 24), *laid down the law* (line 29), *in full view* (line 77), *the killer instinct* (line 54), *a weather-eye* (line 143), *numb with grief* (line 234), *she flew like a bird* (line, 218, used of a ship, and with colloquial use of feminine gender for the ship), *unless I am mistaken* (line 249), *where you hail from* (line 254), *anyone with gumption* (line 287), *come ahead* (line 291), *sheer vanity* (line 509), *friend or foe* (line 511), *the pair of you* (line 511), *safe and sound* (lines 519, 1628 and 1998), *gave as good as I got* (line 561), *kith and kin* (lines 587, 1178 and 2479), *in fighting mood* (line 708), *he won't be long for this world* (line 973), *big talk* (line 979), *bad blood* (line 1104), *under a cloud* (line 1166), *dead and gone* (line 1309), *in the line of action* (line 1328), *not man enough* (line 1468), *in fine fettle* (line 1641), *alive and well* (line 1974), *on the prowl* (line 2211), *bore the brunt* (line 2318), *life from limb* (line 2423), *away you go* (line 2747), *bought and paid for* (line 2842), *the bane of his life* (line 2903). It is notable that many of these phrases, which tend to have strong rhythmical patterns, and often alliterate, consist of pairs of mostly monosyllabic words (many of the dialect words mentioned above are also monosyllables). Heaney is also happy to use colloquial contracted verb forms occasionally (*they'd* occurs at line 15, immediately after *they had* in line 14).

Such phrases are in general currency in English, of course, but Heaney knows them from the ordinary speech of his home area, where they provide the texture of a vernacular in which traditional forms of speech reflect a traditional outlook on life. It is their integral place in that vernacular that gives Heaney the confidence to make such widespread use of them in the translation of an epic poem, paying homage to the English of his home area of his formative years by doing so. Even more than in his deployment of dialect vocabulary in his translation of *Beowulf*, Heaney demonstrates the revolutionary nature of his approach in his domesticating cultivation of unglamorous, ostensibly unpoetic, language. To my mind, this conventional – formulaic – language, with which the dialect words are also integrated, is one of the most remarkable features of his translation.

---

[31] In this respect, Nicholas Howe's comment is somewhat misplaced when he writes, 'I think that the method would have been far more successful if Heaney had gone all the way and written a fully Ulsterized version of *Beowulf*, 'Scullionspeak', p. 36.
[32] Chickering finds that in his use of colloquialisms, 'clichés' (in which 'the problem lies with their jazzy tone') and Ulsterisms Heaney 'often unintentionally breaks his own decorum' of direct 'foursquare' writing ('Beowulf and Heaneywulf', p. 167), but this is to miss Heaney's attentiveness to register in his use of these features.

Through its use Heaney suggests communal experience, constructing a community that the masculine-gendered *Beowulf*ian first-person narrator can appropriately relate to, though it is a community different from the early Germanic community constructed in the original poem. Morgan and Raffel excise the first-person-plural pronoun at the beginning of the poem and they largely dispense with the formulaic use of the first-person-singular pronoun in their translations but Heaney keeps the communal *we* of the opening sentence and first-person-singular formulations appear three times in his first seventy-four lines alone.

'Raised to the power of verse'

Heaney's use of the Ulster vernacular in his *Beowulf* gives his writing directness and vitality and suggests a traditional kind of speech. The chosen register provides him with 'the note and pitch for the overall music of the work'. But to stick to it too literally would be to place significant limitations on what he could achieve in his translation: like the Scots of Morgan's 'The Auld Man's Coronach' discussed above,[33] this register, while it might have its strengths, necessarily lacks the ornateness, variation and verbal brilliance that the original Old English poem sustains. In fact, of course, Heaney's translation is not written in the language of ordinary speech, any more than *Beowulf* is, but presents a *version* of that language 'raised to the power of verse', as Heaney puts it.[34] It is raised to the power of verse not only by the metrical structure that Heaney elaborates, loosely modelled on that of the Old English, and the accompanying rhythmical play in and across the lines of verse, but also by the (unscullionlike) inventiveness of Heaney's expression, the richness of his vocabulary and the precision and alertness of his diction and imagery, which constantly surprise and delight – features, of course, well recognized in his poetry more generally.[35]

His dialect words include elements from ordinary speech but are not restricted to this; they also encompass the archaic and the recondite. Among the latter elements are the Scottish-Gaelic-derived word (via Scots) *bothies*, 'rough lodgings provided for a labourer by an employer' (line 140), and the historical term *bawn* (lines 523, 721, 1304 and 1920), from the Irish, referring to a walled enclosure which could be used for defensive purposes, a word that was particularly applied by the Irish to the enclosures of unwelcome settlers from Britain at the time of the Ulster plantation (thereby revealing disturbing connotations in Heaney's application of it to Heorot).[36] Suggestive of a past way of life, Heaney also uses

---

[33] See above, pp. 86–7.
[34] Heaney, *Beowulf*, p. xxii.
[35] On Heaney's use of combinations of dialect and other registers of English in his *Beowulf* translation, see also Finlay, 'Putting a Bawn into *Beowulf*'; Finlay writes of the 'mixed diction' (p. 141) evident in the translation.
[36] Conor McCarthy also reminds us that the word *bawn* has resonances with Heaney's own biography, since 'Mossbawn' is the name of the farm he grew up on; as McCarthy comments, 'the inclusion of the word "bawn" in the *Beowulf* translation writes not just Irish colonial

the Irish-derived Hiberno-English word *keshes*, 'makeshift roads across peat bogs' (line 1359), which is not in ordinary Ulster vocabulary today. The (Anglo-Saxon) term *howe* (line 2774), 'hollow', unfamiliar to most potential readers of the translation, is now also unusual even in Ulster, as is *graith* (lines 324 and 2988), ultimately from Old Norse, meaning 'equipment', used particularly with reference to the harness and trappings of a horse.[37] *Steadings*, too, 'farm buildings' (line 2462), has an archaic ring to it.[38]

One of Heaney's gifts as a poet is his ability to search out rare and interesting words – non-Hiberno-English examples in *Beowulf* are the literary-sounding *reavers* (not the Scots form *reivers*), 'robbers' (line 163) (where the straightforward noun *robbers* would have supplied the alliteration as well as the sense), *boltered*, 'matted [with blood]' (line 419),[39] *slathered*, 'moved in a sliding manner' (line 1607), and *gorget*, 'throat armour' (line 2172). It is important to note that some of the Irish words are also of this recherché type. The noun *brehon* (line 1457), referring to a judge in early Ireland, would not have been known to speakers of Heaney's local dialect; this is Irish but is a learned literary word.[40] *Sept*, 'clan, tribal group' (line 1674), also has more learned connotations.[41]

Heaney's language presents a combination of the ordinary and prosaic and, to borrow one of his own metaphors in the poem, the 'far-fetched':

> Far-fetched treasures
> were piled upon him, and precious gear. (lines 36–7)

The 'far-fetched' includes Hiberno-English and non-Hiberno-English elements, from the past and from elsewhere, integrated into the dominant register, which is itself a marked and reflective one, despite its apparent spontaneity and directness. On the ordinary and prosaic side, as well as colloquial words and phrases of the kind already mentioned, such unglamorous expressions as *battle-equipment* (line 232), *hawser* (line 302), *arbitrate* (line 1106), *cache* (lines 1223, 3051) and *reconnoitre* (line 2402) are in evidence, some of which sound almost like technical terms. Heaney also makes use of Latinate-sounding vocabulary in places, as in *unremitting humiliations* (line 830) and *unaccustomed anxiety* (line 2332), and also of romance vocabulary, as in *their gallant escort* (line 312), *the priceless torque* (line

---

history but also Heaney's personal history into the poem' (*Seamus Heaney and Medieval Poetry*, p. 107).

[37] Cf. Michael Alexander's use of *harness* in his translation, at line 323, etc.

[38] On these and other Ulster words used in Heaney's *Beowulf*, see McAfee, ed., *A Concise Ulster Dictionary*, s. v.

[39] Cf. Shakespeare, *Macbeth*, 4.1.123: 'For the blood-bolter'd Banquo smiles upon me'.

[40] On *brehon*, see Dolan, *A Dictionary of Hiberno-English*, s. v. Chris Jones notes that *brehon* is found in medieval and early Modern English (from Irish *brithem*) and suggests that it is 'a site of cultural contestation' (*Strange Likeness*, p. 231).

[41] See Dolan, *A Dictionary of Hiberno-English*, s. v. At one stage Heaney also intended to use *sept* at line 9, settling in the end for *clan*: see Chris Jones, *Strange Likeness*, p. 232; Jones comments (ibid.), 'Perhaps it seemed too early to force such an oblique Irish word on his international English-speaking audience in the opening lines of the poem.'

2173) and *a masterpiece of filigree* (line 2769); an expression that combines the romance with the Germanic and also has the Hiberno-Irish suffix *-some* is *He was utterly valiant and venturesome* (line 898).

Through this combination of different types of vocabulary, Heaney, displaying thoughtfulness about language at every level, in effect creates a distinctive literary language with which to render, and appropriate, the Old English epic, making his version of it unmistakably a Heaney poem. He does so in a way that 'celebrates his local idiom' (see above, p. 165) but also extends and enriches it. As Heaney had written, in a different context, in *Preoccupations*, 'The secret of being a poet [. . .] lies in the summoning of the energies of words. But my quest for definition [. . .] is conducted in the living speech of the landscape I was born into.'[42]

Aspects of the Art of Heaney's *Beowulf*

In this section of my discussion of Seamus Heaney's translation I wish to focus on some characteristic features of Heaney's response to *Beowulf*, before going on later in the chapter to consider in particular what he does with the two illustrative passages from the poem analysed in Chapter 2.

Sound and sense

One of the most insistent features of the diction of *Beowulf* is the deployment of compound words. These can be routine in nature, to the point of banality, but are often richly suggestive and arresting; as we have noticed, many of the compounds in *Beowulf* are *hapax legomena*, words that are found only once in the corpus. Heaney's use of compound words can be traced back to his earliest work and is particularly evident in and after *North* (1975),[43] but such words appear with particular frequency in his *Beowulf*, where their widespread cultivation is prompted by the example of the Old English poem. They include such routine formulations as *mead-benches* (line 5), literally translating *meodo-setla*, and *the grey-haired treasure-giver* (line 607), closely following *sinces brytta, / gamol-feax* (*Beowulf*, lines 607–8), but more often they are imaginative coinages presenting highly expressive images, more sharply focused than those of the Old English poem with its tendency to generalize and universalize rather than to empha-

---

42 Heaney, *Preoccupations: Selected Prose, 1968–78*, p. 37.
43 Examples from *Death of a Naturalist* include *nimble-swimming* (p. 3), *crow-black* (p. 18), *candle-tongues* (p. 29); *Door into the Dark* has, for example, *grass-dust* (p. 14), *white-pronged* (p. 20), *milk-limbed* (p. 23) and the Anglo-Saxon-looking *bone-hooped* (p. 30); in relation to *bone-hooped*, cf. Old English *bancofa, banfæt, banhring, banhus, banloca*, all of which occur in *Beowulf* (lines 1445, 1116, 1567, 2508, 818, respectively). On compounding in *North* and later collections, see Chris Jones, *Strange Likeness*, pp. 224–5; see also Heather O'Donoghue, 'Heaney, *Beowulf* and the Medieval Literature of the North', pp. 203–4; O'Donoghue notes that Heaney's practice in using compounds 'chimes with the Old English' (p. 203).

size specificity. Among the most striking of Heaney's coinages are *ring-whorled* [prow] (lines 32, 1131), translating *hringedstefna(n)*, literally 'ringed-prow', in which Heaney contributes the suggestive *whorled* to the synecdochic image;[44] *far-fetched* [treasures] (line 36), where the Old English expression is the vaguer '[treasures] from distant ways' (*of feorwegum*, line 37); *wall-stead* (line 75), translating *folc-stede* (literally 'folk-stead'; *Beowulf*, line 76): in *wall-stead* Heaney's coinage picks up on the *-stede* part of the original Old English compound and combines this with 'wall' to produce an Old-English-looking compound (though *weallstede* is not in fact recorded): familiar lexical elements are combined here, as elsewhere, to suggest something unfamiliar, with overtones, perhaps, of Ulster experience (*stead* being part of the dialect vocabulary). The word *wall-stead* occurs again at line 146 in a phrase added by Heaney, expanding on *husa selest*, 'the best of houses'.

At line 216 Heaney's *wood-wreathed* [ship] presents an alert refinement of the Old English *wudu bundenne*, 'wood bound together' (cf. also *a lapped prow loping over currents* [line 1910], translating *bundenstefna   ofer brimstreamas*, 'a bound prow over the sea-streams'), dispensing here with the synecdoche; *head-clearing* [voice] (line 497) is a sharper image than the Old English *hador*, 'bright, clear-sounding [minstrel]'; *wound-slurry* (line 848), rendering *heorodreore*, 'battle-blood' (*Beowulf*, line 849), provides a startling image through the unlikely combination of straightforward words, an image that recasts that of boiling and surging (*haton heolfre   heoro-dreore weol*, 'with hot gore it boiled with battle-blood') in the original; at line 1209 with *the frothing wave-vat* Heaney introduces a compound imitating the Old English's kenning for the sea, *ofer yða ful*, 'over the cup of the waves' (*Beowulf*, line 1208) but adds the descriptive (and clarifying) epithet *frothing*; at line 1800 *gold-shingled and gabled*, rendering *geap ond goldfah*, 'broad(?-)gabled) and adorned with gold', particularizes the image in an alliterating phrase alluding to the custom, common in Ulster, of decorating the plaster on the outside of houses with shingles, and daringly transferring this idea to the gold decoration of the hall Heorot; in *his feud-callused hand* (line 2488) Heaney compresses into a single image the more discursive metonymic expression of the Old English, *hond gemunde / fæhðo genoge*, 'his hand remembered feuds enough' (lines 2488–9), adding the vivid image of *calloused*.

In these and very many other examples we see Heaney coming up with strikingly focused images based on compound words, sharpening or particularizing the sense of the Old English, often to powerful effect. They are images not taken over directly from the Old English but represent a technique prompted by the Old English; they are the product of an inventiveness in compounding that strikes an Anglo-Saxonist as very *Beowulfian*, though one is struck by the fact that Heaney's compounds, like those of Morgan, tend to be much more precise in their imagery than those of the original poem.

---

[44] In Heaney's earlier version of this passage, published originally in *The Haw Lantern*, he has *ring-necked* instead of *ring-whorled* (*The Haw Lantern*, p. 20, 'A Ship of Death').

Heaney also shows great precision of imagery in many of the descriptive simplex words he employs. These words range from the ordinary to the rare but what is distinctive about Heaney's deployment of them is that 'summoning of the energies of words' that for him is the mark of the poet. The words themselves may be arresting but it is often the context in which he uses them that makes them so. Thus we find in the description of the Creation a *gleaming plain girdled with waters* (line 93), corresponding to the Old English *wlitebeorhtne wang, swa wæter bebugeð*, 'brightly beautiful plain which water surrounds': the specific metaphor of *girdled* provides a precise and apt extension of the Old English image. The reference at line 276 to *this corpse-maker mongering death* draws upon a specialized usage of *monger* (a verb) and startlingly combines this with *death*, applying it to Grendel; this vivid noun phrase employs arresting imagery to recast the sense and grammar of the original – *eaweð þurh egsan   uncuðne nið, / hynðu ond hrafyl*, 'manifests through terror the unknown malice, humiliation and slaughter' (lines 276–7a); it collapses into a single concrete image the abstract cumulation of the Old English formulation. Another such example is *slick with slaughter* (line 487), used of Heorot after the attacks of Grendel, which creates a startlingly unexpected alliterating combination, rendering more specific the Old English *blode bestymed, / [. . .] heorodreore*, 'soaked with blood, with battle-gore' (lines 486b–7a).

At line 447, in the phrase *gorged and bloodied* Heaney detaches into two vivid epithets the single descriptive phrase of the original, *dreore fahne*, 'stained with blood' (with its employment of the poetic word *dreor*, 'blood [especially dripping or flowing]'); similar word pairings are found *in ringing and singing* (lines 1521–2), used of the sound of Beowulf's sword striking Grendel's mother (here with rhyme rather than alliteration linking the two words), where the Old English develops a metaphor at greater length, through personification: *hringmæl agol / grædig guðleoð*, 'the ring-patterned one [the sword] sang out, greedy, a battle song' (lines 1521b–2a); and note too the expressive *slather and thaw* (line 1607), used of melting ice, for the straightforward Old English *wanian*, 'dwindle'. Other examples of intensification of description through the use of (often alliterating) doublets occur at line 756, where Beowulf declares that Grendel *had never been clamped and cornered like this*, a graphic condensation of the Old English's understated abstract reference to Grendel's *drohtoð*, 'situation': *ne wæs his drohtoð þær / swylce he on ealderdagum   ær gemete*, 'his situation there was not such as he encountered before in the days of his life' (lines 756b–7).

Another alliterating doublet used by Heaney is *hasped and hooped* (line 975), along with *hooped and hasped* (line 1451). This combination imaginatively brings together two archaic verbs, *hasp*, 'confine, imprison', and *hoop*, 'fasten round (as) with hoops', that Heaney has garnered from literary sources.[45] *Hasped and hooped* occurs in a description by Beowulf of the injured Grendel:

---

[45] Cf. Shakespeare, *The Winter's Tale*, 4.4.431: 'Or hoop his body more with thy embraces'; *hasped* also occurs in Alexander's translation (line 975).

> He is hasped and hooped and hirpling with pain,
> limping and looped in it. (lines 975–6)

This cumulative passage has, mostly monosyllabic, verbs of a recherché kind (note also the participle *looped*, another archaic usage, meaning 'held in a loop', and the dialect word *hirpling*), which provide insistent alliteration and an appropriately stumbling rhythm, to produce a graphic descriptive image of Grendel's injury. Again the Old English is much less specific, employing emotive personification but not presenting a physical image: *ac hyne sar hafað / in niðgripe nearwe befongen, / balwon bendum,* 'but pain has seized him tightly in its malicious grip, its deadly bindings' (lines 975b–7a).

The phrase *hooped and hasped* occurs, in a literal application, in a description of Beowulf's helmet: *princely headgear hooped and hasped* (line 1451), where it corresponds to the Old English *befongen freawrasnum,* 'encompassed with splendid bands'.

Such instances of Heaney constantly surprising the reader with his exciting phrasing, as he remakes in precise and graphic terms the imagery of the *Beowulf* poet, could easily be multiplied: a couple of examples using dialect vocabulary are *making a mizzle of his blood* (line 596), used of the violence of battle (the Old English [line 597] has the more abstract *atole ecgþræce,* 'terrible violent attack'), and *how he hoked and ate* (line 3027), used of the raven feeding on the slain (where the Old English has the less explicit, but chilling, *hu him æt æte speow,* 'how he succeeded at the meal').

Heaney is particularly attracted to the net and sewing/weaving metaphors that he finds widely used in the original poem with reference to mailed armour, consistently rendering these through imagery of 'webbing'. He writes at lines 404–5 of the *webbed links that the smith had woven, / the fine-forged mesh of his gleaming mail-shirt,* greatly developing in this vigorous descriptive passage, with its alliterative and rhythmical patterning of stressed monosyllables, the Old English image *on him byrne scan, / searonet seowed smiþes orþancum,* 'on him his corslet shone, a battle-net knit together by the skills of the smith' (lines 405b–6). At lines 1888–9 his image of the warriors *dressed in the web / of their chain-mail and war-shirts,* translating *hringnet bæron, / locene leoðosyrcan,* 'they wore their ringed-nets [armour], their interwoven body-corslets' (lines 1889b–90a), picks up on similar associations of 'net'. And at lines 2260 and 2615, respectively, Heaney has *webbed mail* and *webbed chain-mail,* in what amounts to a set, quasi-formulaic, rendering of the Old English terms *byrnan hring,* 'ring[-mail] of the corslet', and *hringde byrnan,* 'ringed corslet'.

Such is the association in Heaney's mind between mail-coats and webbing that he even introduces the image in references to armour where it does not occur in the original. At line 453 he refers to *this breast-webbing that Weland fashioned,* translating *beaduscruda betst, þæt mine breost wereð, / [. . .] Welandes geweorc,* 'the best of war-garments, that protects my breast, [. . .] the work of Weland' (lines 453–5). Here, prompted perhaps by *breost* and by the recollection of terms like *breostnet* (*Beowulf*, line 1548), he develops the 'clothing' image of the original, adding the 'web' metaphor. Similarly, at line 1443 the metaphor of *fine-webbed mail* is Heaney's addition: the original has the straightforward compound noun *herebyrne*, 'war-corslet'.

A sense of physicality and concreteness is a key feature of many of the images I have been referring to. This sense is achieved not by the imagery alone, however, or by the particular evocative words that Heaney has deployed, but by the words in the context of the rhythmical and aural dimension of the verse. We have perceived sound and rhythm to be central qualities of the poetry of *Beowulf*; they are also central to the, different, poetry of Seamus Heaney, with its powerful aural dimension.[46] The vigorousness of Heaney's writing is apparent in lines of such immediacy as *blundering back with the butchered corpses* (line 125), describing Grendel's return to his home after attacking Heorot. This line combines insistent alliteration of plosives, particularly *b*, with strong imagery and an underlying rhythmical pattern that is distinctly dactylic; beside this the Old English – *mid þære wælfylle   wica neosan*, 'with his fill of slaughter [he went] to seek out his abode' (line 125) – looks almost tame. Heaney also strengthens the accompanying verb, having *rushed* (line 123) where the Old English has the neutral *gewat*, 'departed'.

Alliteration of plosives similarly gives a muscular quality to Beowulf's account to Hrothgar of his former exploits:

> They had seen me boltered in the blood of enemies
> When I battled and bound five beasts. (lines 419–20)

The Old English has *selfe ofersawon* [. . .] / *fah from feondum,   þær ic fife geband*, 'they themselves saw me stained from my enemies where I bound five'. Heaney presents a more graphic image of ferocity in battle, pursuing the meaning of Old English *fah*, 'stained', to highlight the bloodiness of the encounter and making use of the rare word *boltered*, recollected from Shakespeare's *Macbeth* (4.1.123), to present a vivid image of hair matted with blood.

At line 447 plosives again alliterate in another vigorous descriptive line, as Beowulf imagines Grendel returning home victorious: *as he goes to ground, gorged and bloodied*. This is a considerable expansion of the Old English *byreð blodig wæl*, 'he will carry the bloody corpse'. Adding the startling image of voraciousness of *gorged*, Heaney conveys the intense physicality of the Old English through

---

[46] Appreciation of the aural quality of Heaney's translation is reflected in the popularity of the audio CD version of the poem, with Heaney himself as the reader (*Beowulf*, read by Seamus Heaney). Hans Sauer, in his discussion of the use of Irish English in the translation, makes the interesting point that the Irish dimension of the language is more immediately and consistently evident in the recorded version, in which '[Heaney] reads it with a definite Irish English accent; in this spoken version the Irish background of his translation is, of course, marked much stronger and indicated much more continuously than in the printed version' ('Heaneywulf, Liuzzawulf', p. 342).

vivid epithets and heightened language, in one of what is a sequence of lines with strong rhythmical and alliterative structure. The shock of *gorged and bloodied* is enhanced by its juxtaposition to the idiomatic phrase 'goes to ground', a phrase that portrays Grendel as a wily animal.

At the climactic moment of the great scene of violent action between Beowulf and Grendel alliteration of plosives is again deployed by Heaney in his graphic description:

> The monster's whole
> body was in pain, a tremendous wound
> appeared on his shoulder. Sinews split
> and the bone-lappings burst. Beowulf was granted
> the glory of winning. (lines 814–18)

Here the predominant *b* alliteration, reinforced by that of *p*, is interwoven with *s* and *l* sounds, as the physicality of Grendel's wound is conveyed with increasing explicitness. At the centre of the sequence Heaney typically combines the vivid with the arcane in the coinage *bone-lappings* (cf. *lapped prow*, at line 1910). The corresponding description in the Old English is also unusually graphic at this point, especially in the image *seonowe onsprungon, / burston banlocan*, 'sinews sprang open, bones broke apart' (lines 817b–18a). In this highly wrought passage in the Old English the image comes at the centre of a sequence of seven consecutive lines of double alliteration (lines 814–20). If anything, however, Heaney's version is even more powerful.

Earlier Heaney had described the dismay of King Hrothgar at Grendel's attack: the king is *bewildered and stunned, staring aghast* (line 132). The modern version is highly dramatic, in contrast with the decorous grief of the original: *þolode ðryðswyð þegnsorge dreah*, 'the mighty one suffered, endured sorrow about his thegns' (line 131).[47] The rhythmical discordance of Heaney's line, with the stressed alliterating words starkly juxtaposed at the caesura, reflects the agitation of the Danish king. Such dissonance of rhythm and sound is exploited elsewhere in contexts of perturbation and conflict, one notable instance being *loathsome upthrows and overturnings* (line 847) (used of the waters of Grendel's mere),[48] where the Old English has the formulaic *atol yða geswing*, 'dire swirling of the waves'; here the unruly rhythm combines with an almost technical-sounding vocabulary. Another instance is provided by the stumbling phrase *unaccustomed anxiety and gloom* (line 2332) (used of Beowulf when he hears about the depredations of the dragon): the Old English has *breost innan weoll / þeostrum geþoncum, swa him geþywe ne wæs*, 'his breast surged within with dark thoughts, as was not

---

[47] It is notable that *þolode* does not trigger *tholed* in Heaney's translation; cf. also lines 283 (*endure*; Old English *þolað*, line 284), 831 (*undergo*; Old English *þolian*, line 832), 1525 (*gone through*; Old English *ðolode*, line 1525), 2500 (*shall last*; Old English *þolað*, line 2499). Heaney's use of the dialect word is considered rather than being an easy reflex of the Old English.

[48] Cf. Alexander's use of the suggestive term *upwellings* in his translation (line 1422).

customary for him' (lines 2331b–2); again Heaney's use of rhythm and sound sharpens the original's depiction of emotion.

The double stress pattern, set off by the pause of the caesura, that we have noted in line 132, had also been used in a line quoted earlier in our discussion, the predominantly monosyllabic *as he goes to ground, gorged and bloodied* (line 447), with its alliteration of plosives. Another example of the same pattern is at line 962, when Beowulf declares in a vigorous statement also consisting of stressed plosive monosyllables, *My plan was to pounce, pin him down*; the Old English has

> Ic hine hrædlice   heardan clammum
> on wælbedde   wriþan þohte. (lines 963–4)

[I intended to bind him quickly in hard grips on a bed of slaughter.]

The translation captures the urgency of the original but adds an element of dramatic vividness.

Sound and sharply focused imagery are also integrated purposefully in a different way in lyrical and elegiac passages in Heaney's translation. The sound-patterning and the smooth, iambic-like, rhythm of *they wept to heaven / and mourned under morning* (lines 128–9) combine with the suggestive coinage *under morning* to produce a concise expression of passive grief in the face of Grendel's predations in a linked pair of verb phrases, where the Old English has two appositive noun images in a sequence that more starkly contrasts joy and sorrow: *Þa wæs æfter wiste   wop up ahafen, / micel morgensweg*, 'Then after the feast weeping was raised up, a great sound/cry in the morning' (lines 128–9a). In an expressive passage later in the poem, Hrothgar's description of Grendel's mere is both lyrically expressive and filled with foreboding: *stormy weather makes clouds scud and the skies weep* (lines 1373–4); the personification is inherited from the Old English but Heaney adds the image of the clouds scudding in an inventive natural observation; the Old English has appositive phrases rather than smooth linking: *oð þæt lyft ðrysmaþ, / roderas reotað*, 'until the sky grows dark, clouds weep' (lines 1375b–6a). Another lyrical addition is to be seen in Heaney's phrase *silent flagons* in an evocation of human transience in the sequence *silent flagons, precious swords / eaten through with rust* (lines 3048–9), corresponding to *discas lagon   ond dyre swyrd, / omige þurhetone*, 'dishes lay there and precious swords, eaten through with rust' (lines 3048–9a). Here the metaphor *eaten through with rust* corresponds directly with the Old English but Heaney's insertion of the (transferred) epithet *silent* adds to the elegiac mood.

Though Heaney can draw upon iambic metrical patterns in lyrical passages (as elsewhere),[49] as in the description of Shield's (Scyld's)[50] mysterious origins –

---

[49] Cf. *began to work his evil in the world* (line 101), *whatever reply it pleases him to give* (line 355).
[50] Heaney uses modernized versions of the name *Shield Sheafson* and *Shielding* to bring out their etymology but otherwise preserves names as they appear in *Beowulf* itself; he does not

and launched him alone out over the waves (line 46) –, he generally prefers more complicated rhythmical effects. An excellent example is Beowulf's description of sunrise in his long speech to the insulting retainer Unferth:

> when morning light,
> scarfed in sun-dazzle, shines forth from the south
> and brings another daybreak to the world. (lines 604–6)

This renders

> siþþan morgenleoht
> ofer ylda bearn   oþre dogores,
> sunne sweglwered   suþan scineð. (lines 604b–6)

[when morning light over the children of men for another day, the sun clothed in brightness, shines from the south.]

Heaney's version begins and ends with a flowing iambic rhythm but interrupts this with the sequence of stressed syllables of *scarfed in sun-dazzle*, which is Hopkinsesque in its rhythm as well as in its diction. The adjective *scarfed* presents a more striking image than the generalized *-wered*, 'clothed', of the Old English, and one that plays on contradictory associations, as *scarf* and *sun* are not usually associated. *Sun-dazzle* too intensifies the imagery, developing the Old English's idea of the brightness of the sun. Heaney produces a lyrical rendering of a lyrical passage, using soft *s* sounds – no sign of alliteration of plosives here – and, as we have seen to be a consistent feature of his translation, crafting a sharper and more vivid image than the Old English, which is typical in its generalizing manner. The Old English stresses the wonder of the daily occurrence of sunrise, Heaney its beauty.

In the context of discussing aspects of sound and sense in Heaney's approach to translating *Beowulf*, one final feature that I wish to mention concerns his fondness for devising images and expressions suggested by the sound, not the meaning, of words in the original. Heaney is constantly being influenced by the sound associations of the language of the Old English poem.

An example of this construction of imagery and phrasing through sound association occurs in a passage discussed above where Heaney says that the Danes *wept to heaven* (line 128) in their distress about Grendel's attacks. The Christianizing reference to heaven is Heaney's addition but it has evidently been prompted by the word *ahafen* in the original poem (line 128), which sounds not unlike the Old English word *heofon*, and indeed Modern English *heaven*, but means 'raised up'. Another example comes at line 519, *He was cast up safe and sound one morning*, where *safe and sound* is a typical Heaney idiomatic phrase but does not have an equivalent in the Old English; just before this point, however, the Old English has the phrases *on sund* (line 512) and *æt sunde* (line 517), *sund* being a word for the sea, and it is evident that sound association has

follow Raffel in simplifying Old English names to make them look less alien.

influenced Heaney's phraseology. *Safe and sound* also appears at lines 1628 and 1998 (bearing out its sense of formulaic usage), where it translates the adjective *sundne*, 'sound'.

In another passage discussed earlier, *the decorated blade came down ringing / and singing on her head* (lines 1521–2), the rhyming phrase is stimulated by the Old English metaphor in *agol*, 'sang', but the first element of the doublet is suggested by sound association from *hring-*, 'metal ring', which is also the source of Heaney's adjective *decorated*.[51] Similarly, in the vigorous monosyllabic line with sprung rhythm effect, *slash of blade, blood-gush and death-qualms* (line 1939), translating *þæt hit sceadenmæl   scyran moste, / cwealmbealu cyðan*, 'that the ornamented sword should settle it, make known death-destruction' (lines 1939–40a), the second element of the arresting compound *death-qualms* is suggested by the sound association of *cwealm-*, which means not 'qualms' but 'death'. And at line 2081, *There was blood on his teeth, he was bloated and dangerous*, translating *bona blodigtoð,   bealewa gemyndig*, 'the bloody-toothed killer, mindful of evils' (line 2082), in which the adjectival phrase is recast as a finite clause, *bloated* recalls *bealewa*, 'evils, destruction', by sound association.[52]

Syntax and style

Attention to narrative is central to Heaney's approach in his translation of *Beowulf*. '[W]hat I was after first and foremost', he declares, 'was a narrative line that sounded as if it meant business and I was prepared to sacrifice other things in pursuit of this directness of utterance.'[53] As will be illustrated in the analyses of individual passages from the translation in the next section of this chapter, Heaney makes his 'narrative line' mean business by providing, like other translators, a firm sense of forward momentum and connectedness, using modern English syntactical structures to help him do so and inserting clear narrative links between and within sentences: *Afterwards* (line 12), *Then* (line 53), *So* (lines 67, 99, 115, etc.), *And soon* (line 76), and so on.

Directness of utterance is not quite what we find in *Beowulf* itself, however, especially in speeches. Heaney himself acknowledges, in the passage referred to above, that its narrative method is 'at times oblique',[54] and in focusing on directness of utterance in his translation he sacrifices some of the delicacy and indi-

---

51   Here Heaney startlingly appropriates the phrase 'ringing and singing' with its joyful religious connotations; he is also perhaps recalling Edwin Morgan's use of the phrase with reference to passages in translations of *Beowulf*, where Morgan says that 'the narrative must sparkle and the direct speech must ring and sing' (*Beowulf*, p. xxix).
52   Note also examples at lines 324, *graith*, prompted by *gryregeatwum*, 'fearsome equipment'; 497, *head-*, prompted by *hador*, 'clear'; 817, *lappings*, prompted by *-locan*, 'locks'; 1427, *slouching*, prompted by *swylce*, 'likewise'; 1754, *lent*, prompted by *læne*, 'transitory'; see also the discussion of lines 1–11, below, pp. 182–5.
53   Heaney, *Beowulf*, p. xxix.
54   *Beowulf*, p. xxvii.

rectness of the expression which the Old English manages to combine with a sense of weightiness and communal outlook. Heaney writes, 'What I have always loved [in *Beowulf*] was a kind of foursquareness about the utterance, a feeling of living inside a constantly indicative mood',[55] but, as Tom Shippey points out, the subjunctive is also central to the nuanced grammar of *Beowulf*, something that Heaney downplays. Referring to one particular 'subjunctive' passage in the poem, Shippey comments, 'Catching the tone of the subjunctive is hard in modern English, but it is a major part of the careful, prickly dignity of armed men in the heroic world'.[56] Heaney is right in his perception of 'foursquareness' in the style of *Beowulf*, in my view, but this quality is by no means the whole story of that style.[57]

Some of the key respects in which Heaney reworks, and simplifies, the narrative line of the original have been outlined by Helen Phillips, who writes, 'Eschewing much of the variation, syntactic repetition, and compounding of the original, and using Modern English syntax, less flexibly amenable to complicated patternings, [Heaney] transforms *Beowulf* into verse paragraphs that move rapidly and directly, with a diminution of the eddying, meditative quality of much of the original. It becomes more a tale of action.'[58]

Phillips rightly identifies here some of Heaney's ways of adapting the syntax and style of the original, ways that may also incidentally recall for us the practice of other (un-Heaney-like) translators we have looked at, but her remarks may give the impression that Heaney avoids Old English syntax and style more determinedly than is in fact the case. In writing in a modern poetic idiom he has to move away from Old English syntax and style, but what strikes me is the extent to which, in contrast to other translators, he is still able, in doing so, to reflect and suggest features of the original.

Compound words, for example, are not as all-pervasive as in *Beowulf* but they are still common in Heaney's version, some being unremarkable but some, as we have seen, having great expressiveness and originality; alliteration too, while more flexible than in *Beowulf* itself, is very pronounced in the translation; and although Heaney fashions sense units that extend beyond the half-line and makes much use of enjambment, his verse retains a strong sense of half-line structure, marked by short self-contained phrases. Many such short phrases stand out in apposition to other sentence elements in a manner that reflects the patterns of variation and repetition of *Beowulf*. Compared to the original, such features are considerably reduced in the translation, as Phillips points out, but they are still widespread, occurring at least every few lines, and they contribute crucially to Heaney's characteristic style. Among countless examples, appositive

[55] Ibid.
[56] Shippey, '*Beowulf* for the Big-Voiced Scullions', p. 9.
[57] Cf. Chickering's comment: 'I myself certainly wouldn't call the style of the original Old English "foursquare". It is both restrained and exuberant, often ironic, oblique, ceremonial, sometimes sententious' ('Beowulf and "Heaneywulf"', p. 164).
[58] Phillips, 'Seamus Heaney's *Beowulf*', p. 273.

structure based on short phrases is evident in the description of Shield's funeral ship as *ice-clad, outbound, a craft for a prince* (line 33); we see it too in the characterization of Halfdane as *heir [to Beow], / the great Halfdane [. . .] their elder and warlord [. . .] four times a father, this fighting prince* (lines 56–9), in which the descriptive phrases are entwined around the verb-based framework of the sentence; and we see it again in the sentence telling of Hrothgar's misery in the face of Grendel's attacks (in which the phrasal apposition is also enlivened through the use of enjambment):

> So that troubled time continued, woe
> that never stopped, steady affliction
> for Halfdane's son, too hard an ordeal. (lines 189–91)

An example of a sentence made up of appositive verb phrases, as well as having appositive adjectival material, is the following (on Beowulf's voyage to Denmark):

> Time went by, the boat was on the water,
> in close under the cliffs. (lines 210–11)

In these respects, Heaney's practice can be viewed as successfully reflecting features of the original poem. This is a point also suggested by Conor McCarthy, who discusses apposition at some length, declaring that 'In adding new [appositive, or 'stereoscopic'] layers to *Beowulf*, it's possible to argue that Heaney is working with, rather than against, the grain of the original poem.'[59]

Heaney's unusual and unexpected vocabulary choices, discussed above, may also be viewed as reflecting features of the original poem, corresponding in a sense to the special, mannered, vocabulary characteristic of *Beowulf*: *anathema* (line 110), *thresh* (line 227) and *appointment* (line 368) are varied examples (in addition to those given above) from the early pages of the translation. We have already seen that Heaney's overall register suggests something of the traditional, formulaic quality of Old English poetry.

Thus, Phillips's comments about Heaney's reworking of the syntax and style of the Old English poem to make it a tale of action need to be qualified by an appreciation of how much he has managed to take over from the Old English while at the same time writing in a modern poetic idiom. Even her point about Heaney transforming *Beowulf* into verse paragraphs does not necessarily point to a radical departure from Old English practice on his part, since the technique

---

59 McCarthy, *Seamus Heaney and Medieval Poetry*, p. 116; McCarthy also refers to Daniel Donoghue's discussion of Heaney's employment elsewhere in his work of 'something very close to *Beowulf*ian apposition' (ibid., referring to Donoghue, 'The Philologer Poet', p. 244); see also Chris Jones, *Strange Likeness*, pp. 215–16, Heather O'Donoghue, 'Heaney, *Beowulf* and the Medieval Literature of the North', p. 202.

of composition in verse paragraphs, or 'movements', has also been identified as characteristic of Old English poetry.⁶⁰

Two Passages for Consideration

Finally in the context of this consideration of Heaney's approach to translating *Beowulf*, let us look at his response to the two passages we have been considering in earlier chapters, the first eleven lines and the description of the oral poet at work (lines 867–74).⁶¹

Heaney's *Beowulf*, lines 1–11

So. The Spear-Danes in days gone by
and the kings who ruled them had courage and greatness.
We have heard of those princes' heroic campaigns.

There was Shield Sheafson, scourge of many tribes,
a wrecker of mead-benches, rampaging among foes.
This terror of the hall-troops had come far.
A foundling to start with, he would flourish later on
as his powers waxed and his worth was proved.
In the end each clan on the outlying coasts
beyond the whale-road had to yield to him
and begin to pay tribute. That was one good king.⁶²

The voice here is that of a participant in tradition and a secure transmitter of story from 'days gone by', speaking to and for the communal 'We' of the second sentence. The tradition that Heaney draws upon as his correlative to that of the original poem is based on the speech of his rural Ulster upbringing. It can be heard in the opening *So* and the colloquial exclamation at the end of our passage. This register is idiomatic but the tone is fittingly measured and dignified, the mode declarative. As befits the register, the three expansive sentences of the original are broken up into smaller units; the pattern of smaller, but carefully linked, sense units in Heaney's translation (with sentences here of two, one, two, one, two, and two and a half lines, respectively, before the final half-line exclamation) also has the effect of foregrounding narrative and clarifying relationships between events or circumstances, which are left unexpressed by the *Beowulf*ian appositive, additive style.

The three sentences of the original are broken up into smaller units but with a strong sense of consecutiveness between these units: *There was* (line 4) moves

---

⁶⁰ See especially Pasternack, *The Textuality of Old English Poetry*.
⁶¹ For another discussion of the opening lines of Heaney's translation, see Sauer and Milfull, 'Seamus Heaney: Ulster, Old English, and *Beowulf*, pp. 116–18.
⁶² For the corresponding Old English lines, see p. 32, above.

the narration from the general to the particular; *This* (line 6) specifies further, and *had come far* (also line 6) relates Shield's success to his earlier life; *to start with* and *later on* (line 7) emphasize narrative continuity; *as* (line 8) supplies a smooth syntactic transition; and *in the end* (line 9) provides a sense of conclusion, leading up to and justifying the closing exclamation. The idiomatic quality of some of these linking phrases is notable, contributing to the poem's distinctive register, evident too, of course, in the final half-line of the passage.

An unobtrusive alternation in sentence length is apparent, and the syntax is smooth, with a natural-sounding word order rather than one which attempts to reflect the mannered poetic syntax of the original. The syntax of *Beowulf* progresses through distinct, often abrupt, half-lines, with phrases in opposition or apposition to each other. Heaney has patterns of abrupt opposition/apposition elsewhere (often highlighted for the reader by means of the cues provided by colons and dashes) but here grammatical opposition is mostly replaced by joined phrases and clauses: in the first sentence *and* is used to link *the Spear-Danes* and their *kings*, where the Old English had them in apposition, and *and* also joins *courage* and *greatness*, which are grammatically separated in the original; *ands* are also introduced at lines 8 and 11. The second sentence, however, consists of a series of short appositional phrases.

Reflecting Old English metre, a caesura is clearly evident in most of Heaney's lines, breaking them into two half-lines, but some lines are continuous: in our passage line 3, *We have heard of those princes' heroic campaigns*, in which the possessive *princes'* unifies the line, lacks a discernible caesura; elsewhere the caesura may be light, as in line 9, *In the end each clan on the outlying coasts*, which indeed arguably divides into three rather than two. It is notable too that in this passage Heaney's preference is for end-stopped lines, which contribute to the sense of steadiness of narration and the measured tone.

In his flexible version of the Old English metre Heaney has alliteration in most lines, with the alliteration usually being supplied by the first stressed syllable of the second half-line, in line with Anglo-Saxon practice; in line 9, however, it is the last stressed syllable, *coasts*, that supplies the alliteration. Line 4, which has *sh* alliterating with *sk*, is irregular in Old English terms, as *sh* (spelt /sc/ in Old English) should alliterate only with *sh*: compare line 4 of *Beowulf*:

> Oft Scyld Scefing   sceaþena þreatum.
>
> [Often Scyld Scefing in troops of enemies.]

As well as structural alliteration, Heaney employs other alliterative effects. He does so within the line: line 1 has secondary *s* alliteration, as well as the structural *d* alliteration; line 8 has cross-alliteration of *w* and *p*. And these alliterative effects can also go across lines: in line 3 *campaigns* picks up on the *c* alliteration of the previous line; *foes* and *far* (lines 5 and 6, respectively) anticipate the *f* alliteration of line 7; *beyond* (line 10) has structural *y* alliteration in its stressed syllable but its first syllable also alliterates with that of *begin* in line 11 (which itself also bears structural *g* alliteration in its stressed syllable). Line 4 provides a rare example of double alliteration, with *s* occurring at the beginning of both stressed syllables of the first half-line as well as in the first stressed syllable of the second half-line; here, however, it is really the proper name Shield Sheafson that supplies the double alliteration (as in the original poem), rather than any particular inventiveness on the part of Heaney.

In its metrical technique, as in other aspects of its measured approach, Heaney's writing is restrained in this opening passage, as befits the restrained character of the corresponding lines of the original poem and the *Beowulf* poet's evocation in them of the ancient past and meditation on the steady passage of great events remembered from long ago. There is little sign of the startling play of sound and sense we have seen in other parts of Heaney's translation. This is still a highly crafted passage, however, and considerations of sound and sense are at the heart of Heaney's approach to translating it. Phrases are carefully composed, often made up of two elements linked grammatically and with balanced rhythm: *courage and greatness, a scourge of many tribes, A foundling to start with,* and *begin to pay tribute.* Some of these have a steady iambic base; indeed, in that last phrase, *and begin to pay tribute,* we see Heaney refining the sense of the original to produce the iambic effect: the Old English has the more abrupt *gomban gyldan,* 'to give tribute', but Heaney's *begin* (linked smoothly to the preceding line by *and,* the latter also introduced by Heaney) gives his line its steady rhythm, as well as suggesting a greater sense of continuity and gradual progress on the part of Shield than is found in the Old English at this point.

The violence that Shield's success depended on comes out in the reference to him as *scourge* and *terror,* though these do not present sharply focused images. More graphic is the line *a wrecker of mead-benches, rampaging among foes* (line 5), which makes Shield, founder of the Danish dynasty, into a destructive and disturbing warrior (even, perhaps, with overtones of Grendel about him). In the Old English, Scyld's taking away of the mead-benches of his enemies is a trope to express his conquest of them; it is not perhaps envisaged as a literal act. In Heaney's version it becomes a vivid image of Shield in action, reinforced by the portrayal of him as furiously uncontrolled, in *rampaging.* In the sudden eruption of this line Heaney disconcertingly suggests the ferocious violence that underpins warrior society, with its *heroic campaigns,* but he does so without allowing this perception to compromise the overall tone of our passage too much: the imagery is fierce here but the rhythm of the line, despite the double stress of *mead-benches,* is actually quite smooth. Complication enters the definition of *courage and greatness,* however.

Apart from *wrecker* (of mead-benches) and *rampaging,* the vocabulary of these opening lines of Heaney's translation is notably unspectacular, but though unspectacular it contributes a sense of dignity and formality which complements the idiomatic expressions mentioned above. In many instances the diction closely follows that of the original poem: the compound *mead-benches* is taken directly from the Old English, as is the kenning *whale-road;* unlike other translators,

Heaney translates *Gar-Dena* literally as *Spear-Danes*;[63] *waxed* and *worth* are also prompted by the Old English; *hall-troops* is Heaney's own invention (translating *eorlas*, 'men') but is grounded on the compounding technique of Old English; *clan* provides a suitable variant to *tribes*; *foes*, *waxed* and *yield* are archaic usages; the passage makes much use of abstract nouns, adopting thereby a *Beowulf*ian trait but extending it more widely: *terror* translates the verb *egsode*, 'terrified' (line 6), and *powers* is an expansion of *þah* (line 8), 'prospered', another verb.

As elsewhere, some of Heaney's lexical choices are prompted by the sound association of Old English words; *foundling* is suggested by *funden*, 'found', but translates *feasceaft*, 'destitute' (line 7); *yield* is suggested by *gyldan*, 'give', but translates *hyran*, 'obey' (line 10); *scourge* is similarly perhaps influenced by the sound of *sceaþena*, 'enemies' (line 4).

Generally, in these opening lines we see a microcosm of the features that characterize Heaney's translation but with less emphasis in this scene-setting sequence on incisiveness of imagery and arresting verbal effects than is the case later. Heaney adopts a lively and idiomatic register but introduces the poem in a suitably dignified way, establishing the seriousness of its concerns and the standing of its people. In doing so, he changes the structure and scale of the sentences but shows great respect to the diction of the original. And at least one line in the passage serves to problematize the values of the heroic world with its cultivation of ferocious violence.

Heaney's *Beowulf*, lines 866–73

The second of our passages is rather different in its content and in its approach. In this one Heaney presents his picture of the oral poet producing a new composition:

> Meanwhile, a thane
> of the king's household, a carrier of tales,
> a traditional singer deeply schooled
> in the lore of the past, linked a new theme
> to a strict metre. The man started
> to recite with skill, rehearsing Beowulf's
> triumphs and feats in well-fashioned lines,
> entwining his words.[64]

This smoothly flowing passage is notably unostentatious in its treatment of the Old English. It is respectful in tone and communicates a sense of appreciation of the art of the oral poet. In it we see Heaney at his least interventionist. His sentences here, for example, unlike in the previous passage discussed, are coter-

---

63 Liuzza has 'spear-Danes', with an explanatory footnote (*Beowulf: A New Verse Translation*, p. 53).
64 For the corresponding Old English lines, see p. 37, above.

minous with those of the original.[65] The second sentence is very much a development of the first and, as in the Old English, it begins in the middle of the line, thus enhancing the passage's sense of fluidity. The first sentence itself begins in the middle of the line and the second one ends in the middle of the line. The sense of fluidity in the passage is also contributed to by the use of enjambment, a feature of the original that Heaney reproduces here (at lines 868–9 and 869–70) but also extends (at lines 866–7 and 871–2), so that, although based, as is normal in his translation, on half-line sense units, Heaney's lines are predominantly run-on in this passage.

The first sentence reflects the cumulative nature of the corresponding Old English sentence, being structured as a descriptive sequence referring to the qualities of the *thane* as a poet, leading up to the verb phrase telling of this man's present action in composing a new poem, but the internal arrangement of this sentence is slightly different in Heaney's version: the Old English phrases *guma gilphlæden*, 'a man laden with eloquence', and *gidda gemyndig*, 'mindful of songs' (line 868), are combined in Heaney's single phrase *a carrier of tales* (Heaney's phrase alertly refashions the metaphor of *-hlæden*, 'laden'), and the relative clause of the Old English becomes an appositive phrase, *a traditional singer deeply schooled / in the lore of the past*. Heaney omits the reference to this poet devising new words (*word oþer fand*), substituting instead the idea of elaborating a new *theme* and applying the image of *linking* (Old English *gebunden*, 'bound', line 871) not to the words being bound together properly in the alliterative metre but to the coming together of theme and metre in the composed poem. In a parallel fashion, at the end of the second sentence Heaney reconceives *wordum wrixlan*, 'vary words', as *entwining his words*. Despite these minor changes of accent in highlighting the qualities of the poet, Heaney's passage remains faithful to the overall sense and spirit of the original, fastening above all on the central emphasis of the corresponding passage in the Old English, which is the theme of the traditionality of the poet's art.

The structure of the second sentence in the Old English rests on the verb *ongan*, 'began', followed by a sequence of three infinitives, the first linked to the second by *ond*, 'and', the third in apposition to the second. Heaney changes the second and third of these to participles, *rehearsing* and *entwining*, thus producing a slightly more varied sentence, but again he preserves the basic shape and extent of the Old English sentence. The phrase *triumphs and feats*, a balanced half-line unit of the kind we noted in the first passage, is an evocative expansion of the less precise Old English single word *sið*, 'experience'.

Triumphs and feats is more forthcoming than the Old English *sið* but it is still an unspecific phrase rather than being sharply definitive. Also unspecific are

---

[65] In earlier discussion I referred to these sentences as sense units, reflective of the punctuation of the Klaeber edition, which has a semi-colon rather than a full-stop in the middle of line 871. These sense units are presented as full sentences in the Wrenn–Bolton edition, the one used by Heaney.

the adverb phrases *with skill, in well-fashioned lines* and even *entwining his words*, though the latter, like *to a strict metre*, is slightly more instructive as a description of poetry.

Heaney conveys appropriately in this passage the sense of the Old English (which we have seen also to be unspecific in its description) and achieves across the two sentences a fluidity of narration that reinforces the onward sweep of the story. Narrative, as we have observed (see above, p. 179), is particularly emphasized in Heaney's *Beowulf*; it is one of the great strengths of the translation. The present passage provides an interesting illustration of this emphasis and of how Heaney produces it.

The passage is not such a set piece in Heaney's version as it is in *Beowulf* itself but Heaney's customary play of word and sound is in evidence, particularly in the elaboration of alliterative effects: secondary *t* alliteration is to be found across lines 867 and 868; secondary *s* alliteration is there in lines 868 and 871 (line 868 therefore having *t* and *s* alliteration as well as structural *d* alliteration); cross-alliteration (*st* and *m*) appears in the pivotal line 870; and there is secondary *w* alliteration across lines 872 and 873. As elsewhere, Heaney appears to be influenced in his choice of vocabulary by the sound associations of Old English words: *Hwilum*, 'at times' (*Beowulf*, line 867), prompts *Meanwhile* (line 866), and *start* (line 870) is perhaps influenced by *styrian*, 'relate' (*Beowulf*, line 872).

There are no examples in these lines of the kind of 'far-fetched' vocabulary we have noted elsewhere in the translation, and equally there is an absence of colloquial and idiomatic expressions. The phrase *deeply schooled / in the lore of the past* is the most striking in the passage, particularly in its utilization of the rich associations of *schooled* (there is no equivalent in the original poem), but even this is hardly colourful. Heaney's restrained rendering of the passage is such as not to distract from the key factor of the progress of the narrative and it may be seen too as conveying a sense of respect for the traditional poetry that is being described, keeping that poetry itself at the centre of attention. Heaney does not attempt to match here the virtuosity of the original but in his very restraint he expresses quiet admiration for the traditional poet at work. His adaptation of the Old English passage is artful, but unobtrusively so.

Conclusion

Whose *Beowulf* is it anyway? In his distinctive and untraditional approach to translating the poem Heaney presents a *Beowulf* for the postmodern age. Rather than 'giving us back our own', he is presenting *Beowulf* from a new angle, bringing out new possibilities in how the poem might be understood.

One way he does this is by complicating the domesticating versus foreignizing binary. Heaney 'domesticates' the poetry of *Beowulf* to 'the living speech of the landscape I was born into'. Thereby, paradoxically, he 'foreignizes' his translation for most inhabitants of the global village. For most readers Heaney's distinctive register, though accessible, will be a defamiliarizing one, evincing an element of alterity that reflects that of *Beowulf* itself. Alison Finlay makes a point akin to this when she writes of Heaney using Ulster language to bring out the 'strangeness' of *Beowulf*: 'Heaney exploits this strangeness, using the resources of his own provincial, non-standard linguistic heritage to decentre the poem further from the orthodox.'[66]

In significant ways Heaney's register, based on a localized form of Modern English 'raised to the power of verse', can also be seen as paralleling that of the Old English poem. Most notably in this latter respect, Heaney's language has a traditional feel that corresponds to the traditionality of Old English poetry, including a cultivation of what we have seen referred to as 'the aesthetics of the familiar';[67] in *Beowulf*, as in Heaney, traditional forms of speech reflect a traditional outlook on life and a communal perspective, though those in *Beowulf* are very different from those of rural Ulster. And in *Beowulf*, as in Heaney, the poet participates in a tradition but is also external to that tradition, having a wider perspective and a consciousness of his own apartness from it.

Other particular qualities I have identified in describing Heaney's chosen register are also characteristic of Old English poetry, including *Beowulf*. What could be more *Beowulf*ian than dignity and solemnity of utterance, understatement, gnomic expressions of conventional wisdom and familiar phrasing (we have seen that the very basis of the poetics of *Beowulf* is formulaic)? But the traditional language that *Beowulf* is composed in is a specifically poetic language, in the highest style available. It is ornate, conspicuously artificial, particularly in its elaborate use of variation and wordplay, and brilliantly inventive in its vocabulary. The traditional language that Heaney works with, on the other hand, is not a 'poetic' language, but Heaney transforms it into such through his masterful use of rhythm and sound, a use that might be viewed as analogous to that of the Old English poet; through his cultivation of variation and apposition; and through his 'summoning of the energies of words' – 'far-fetched' as well as mundane. The vocabulary of the *Beowulf* poet too stretches from the apparently banal to the thrillingly unexpected, as study of the words distinctive to the poem makes clear.

There are telling literary correspondences, then, between the *Beowulf* of Seamus Heaney and the original poem. It was his perception of such potential correspondences that enabled Heaney to translate the poem in the first place, appropriating it as he did so. The nature of the Heaney register is such that his narrative voice is necessarily more low key than that of *Beowulf* itself with its epic loftiness, and the world of his poem is necessarily smaller in scale, a world of farms, yards and 'bothies', populated by down-to-earth people rather than the grand world of heroic poetry. The resulting poem is lower in key and smaller in scale but is endowed with the vitality and directness of a genuinely

---

[66] Finlay, 'Putting a Bawn into *Beowulf*, p. 152.
[67] See above, p. 27.

personal work rather than being an exercise in excavating or preserving an interesting specimen from the ancient past. The preoccupation of producing poetry that lives has been a constant for the major translators of *Beowulf*, as it is for poetic translators in general. To quote Roy Liuzza, whose own fine translation of *Beowulf* will be discussed later, 'A translation is successful or not, not by virtue of its accuracy or fidelity to its indecipherable cause, but by how well it makes the poem seem like a living thing rather than a dead one.'[68] While I would argue that to a remarkable degree Heaney's *Beowulf* is faithful to essential features of the Old English poem, as defined by scholars and critics, it works because it is 'a living thing', transposed as it is to a fresh cultural context.

---

[68] Liuzza, 'Lost in Translation', p. 295; see also Howe, '*Beowulf* in the House of Dickens', pp. 434–5. Cf. also Edwin Morgan, 'the translator's duty is as much to speak to his own age as it is to represent the voice of a past age: these are, indeed, equal tasks' (*Beowulf*, p. xi).

✦8✦

Other Post-1950 Verse Translations

In addition to the four discussed in previous chapters, many other English-language verse translators have been busy on *Beowulf* in the past fifty years or so, particularly in America. Earlier in the book I noted the comment from the prose translator David Wright in 1957, 'Almost everyone has heard of *Beowulf*'.[1] That was overstating things then and would be today as well, but *Beowulf* – though not in the original language – is now known about more widely than at any time in the past. Recent film versions have brought it into popular culture, its association with the magic name of Tolkien has given it visibility, and the work of translators and adaptors in recent decades has introduced it to new audiences.[2] The version of Seamus Heaney has been especially popular but a wide range of other verse translations, some good, some not so good, have also found ready markets. The readiest market has been among students studying *Beowulf* in translation at university, but Heaney's version didn't get onto best-seller lists in the English-speaking world by being bought only by students. Other versions too have aimed to appeal well beyond the campus.

This chapter surveys briefly the Modern English Verse translations of *Beowulf* printed on both sides of the Atlantic in the last half-century or so,[3] other than those treated separately in other chapters, taking account of their historical circumstances and attending to their aims, their approaches to translating the Old English poem, and their poetic qualities. Aware that there are very contrasting kinds of translations among those published in the relevant period and that the translations have different ambitions, I will nonetheless venture to offer some critical assessment of the success of the translations, guided by consideration of their engagement with the poetry and poetics of *Beowulf* as well as their 'accu-

[1] Wright, *Beowulf*, p. 9.
[2] In a recent discussion of 'the future of *Beowulf*' two US college instructors attest, 'Many freshman students at our university sign up for the medieval section of the mandatory Western civilization course because of *Beowulf* (Momma and Powell, 'Death and Nostalgia: The Future of *Beowulf* in the Post-National Discipline of English', p. 1350).
[3] A number of separate online translations have also appeared, of varying degrees of academic respectability. For further details, see Syd Allen's comprehensive website www.beowulftranslations.net/.

racy'. The translations reviewed here are generally much better than those of the previous period (no great accolade in itself) and in their multifariousness they are testimony to the kinds of interest that *Beowulf* has engendered in the last couple of generations.

As well as the versions by Morgan, Raffel, Alexander and Heaney, more than twenty verse translations have been produced since 1950, the vast majority in America. Indeed, only four British verse translations have been published since that of Morgan, by Kevin Crossley-Holland, Michael Alexander, Paula Grant and Louis Rodrigues.[4] Of these, the last two made little impression but the first two appear to have satisfied the British market in the decades after their publication, with Alexander in particular being widely read and Crossley-Holland also maintaining a steady popularity. Since the appearance of Heaney's version they have lost their dominant position but they are still very much in circulation and both of them have appeared in new editions since Heaney's came out. As mentioned below, one verse version was recently published in Ireland – a 'performance' version – by the Australian actor and writer Felix Nobis.

The absence of other versions before Heaney may point to the perceived excellence of Crossley-Holland and Alexander but may also reflect a relative lack of interest in *Beowulf* in the wider culture of Britain and Ireland in the second half of the twentieth century. In the second half of the century *Beowulf* became one of the books 'most necessary for educated people to know' (to allude to King Alfred again), or perhaps 'to know about', but its status in the wider culture was fairly marginal for most of the period and creative people were not queuing up to produce new versions of it. And for the educated British and Irish readership that wanted access to *Beowulf* in verse translation there were the versions of Crossley-Holland and Alexander (two versions very different in their approach to translation), while the version by Raffel (different again) was also on the shelves of some bookshops. The appearance of Heaney's translation in 1999 may have contributed to changing perceptions of *Beowulf* in Britain and Ireland in recent years but we await further significant creative engagement with the poem.

Translations in Britain and Ireland

The version by **Kevin Crossley-Holland**, which has been in print ever since it first came out in 1968, continues to be popular as an accessible and attractive 'teaching' text for courses in which *Beowulf* is studied in translation, as well as appealing to the general reader.[5] Crossley-Holland has a traditional English-

---

[4] John Porter's translation, in his *Beowulf: Text and Translation*, looks like verse at first sight but is not a literary translation but rather a half-line by half-line gloss of the Old English text, which it accompanies in parallel-text fashion. A similar approach is adopted in the online version *Beowulf on Steorarume* (trans. Slade).
[5] Crossley-Holland, trans., *Beowulf*.

literary-history view of *Beowulf*, seeing it uncomplicatedly, as had earlier generations of commentators, as an originary English text, and he wishes to make this canonical work straightforwardly available to a new readership. For Crossley-Holland, *Beowulf* has an 'essentially English character' (as reflected in its 'out-and-out heroism, a dogged refusal to surrender, a love of the sea, an enjoyment of melancholy, nostalgia'), and in publishing his translation he sought to present *Beowulf* as a poem that 'has the power to stir us to the roots of our being; through it we can come to understand more about our origins; and thus achieve a deeper sense of perspective'.[6]

Though, like Morgan and Alexander, adopting a non-syllabic four-stress metre, Crossley-Holland contrasts with Morgan and Alexander in his approach to translation. In making the poem available to a new – general – readership he aims at fluency and naturalness and does not attempt to suggest the otherness of *Beowulf* or to convey the feel of its verse: this is very much the domesticating approach to translation. Alliteration is light and intermittent and there is an absence of a pronounced caesura, with pauses tending to come at the end of the line. Grammatical connectives and explanatory details are added, contributing to a sense of brisk and smoothly flowing narrative. In the 'Translator's Note' to the 1968 edition, Crossley-Holland writes, 'My diction inclines towards the formal, though it is certainly less formal than that of the *Beowulf* poet; it seemed to me important at this time to achieve a truly accessible version of the poem, that eschewed the use of archaisms, inverted word orders and all "poetic" language'.[7] In fact there are occasional examples in the translation of archaism and inversion, and colloquial forms are also introduced,[8] but the overall effect is unobtrusive and fairly plain, but with a dignified tone maintained throughout.

Crossley-Holland's version brings the story of *Beowulf* to a modern readership with directness and vigour and in a manner that also reflects its elegiac tone. The translation is astute and imaginative, with attractive touches such as Grendel occupying Heorot 'on cloudless nights' (line 167; Old English *sweartum nihtum*, 'dark nights'), or the mind of the Danish watchman being 'riddled with curiosity' (line 234; Old English *hine fyrwyt bræc*, 'curiosity pressed him'), but the style is often so subdued as to verge on the prosaic:

> So those warrior Danes lived joyful lives,
> in complete harmony, until the hellish fiend
> began to perpetrate base crimes. (lines 99–101)

To my mind a limitation of the translation is, as noted above, that it doesn't give a feel of the quality of the verse of the original poem. Crossley-Holland's

---

6 *Beowulf*, 'Translator's Note', p. xi (original 1968 edition).
7 Ibid.
8 Archaic usage includes references to 'shrithing' (line 162, etc.) and 'quaffing [beer/mead]' (line 480, etc.); examples of inverted word order are 'so did they cross the sea' (line 223), 'Thus was the lay sung' (line 1160); colloquialisms include 'not give them no for an answer' (line 367), 'asking for trouble' (line 425).

translation achieves its modest ambition well, however, and the 1999 edition in particular is user-friendly in its layout and in its inclusion of supplementary material. In the balancing act that the translator engages in, Crossley-Holland consciously leans towards the modern reader in his versification, seeking in an assimiliationist approach to present *Beowulf* as an accessible and unproblematic classic of English literary history.

The translation by **Paula Grant**, published in 1995,[9] is an eccentric one, which is in an archaizing form of free verse rather than, as claimed in its Introduction, in blank verse.[10] The translation is loose and inaccurate, reflective of an insecure grasp of the sense of the original, as in

> We have from Gardanes in yore days learned (line 1)

or

> When Scyld's fated hour drew near
> Awesome the voyage in Frean was. (lines 26–7)

Grant hints in her Introduction that she worked from Garmondsway's [sic] prose translation rather than the Old English. The translation's title, *Aldfrith's Beowulf*, proclaims its underlying premise, that *Beowulf* was composed by King Aldfrith of Northumbria.[11] Grant believes indeed that the Geats of the poem are not continental Scandinavians but Deiran Northumbrians.

The remaining, and most recent at time of writing, verse translation published in Britain is that by **Louis Rodrigues** (2002), in a free stress-based metre with light alliteration.[12] Presenting his version in a parallel-text (Old English–Modern English) format, Rodrigues has produced a serviceable enough translation in that he follows the sense of the Old English as closely as Modern English grammatical considerations will allow. In key respects the translation reads more like a work of the nineteenth century rather than the twenty-first, however. Particularly evident in the speeches, it has an archaizing diction:

> Art thou that Beowulf who strove with Breca,
> competed at swimming in the open sea?
> There ye two for pride tackled the waters,
> and ventured your lives in deep water
> for a foolish boast. (lines 506–10a)

This archaizing reflects Rodrigues's intention in his version, which he insists on calling a rendering rather than a translation, of attempting 'to transfer a very

---

[9] Grant, trans., *Aldfrith's Beowulf*.
[10] Grant, *Aldfrith's Beowulf*, p. 12.
[11] Beowulf had been linked with King Aldfrith and Northumbria by Albert C. Cook, 'The Possible Begetter of the Old English *Beowulf* and *Widsith*': Cook argued that the poem had been commissioned by Aldfrith, a view that has no support among scholars today.
[12] Rodrigues, trans., *Beowulf and the Fight at Finnsburh*.

old idiom into its nearest modern equivalent,[13] though the suggestion that the register adopted is the 'nearest modern equivalent' requires justification. Generally, Rodrigues's version seems pedestrian, with many of the translation choices recalling those of prose translators. The translation is accompanied by basic summarizing notes on selected passages.

In addition to the verse translations of *Beowulf* produced in Britain, an 'adaptation' of the poem was published in Ireland in 2000 by the Australian performer Felix Nobis.[14] Following in the footsteps of the British actor Julian Glover,[15] Nobis produced a verse version of *Beowulf* for theatrical performance, with which he successfully toured for several years. Unlike Glover, who used existing translations for his performance, chiefly Michael Alexander's, Nobis prepared his own 'performance translation', a version that emphasizes the oral dimension of the work: 'While I have remained faithful to [the] manuscript', writes Nobis in his Introduction, 'I admit that my translation is coloured by the greater goal of remaining faithful to the spirit of the poem as an oral, rather than written work.'[16]

As suits its primary function as a script for recitation, Nobis's version, which was praised by no less a luminary than Seamus Heaney,[17] has a strong aural quality and a gripping and urgent forward movement, while maintaining a dignified tone. It adopts a stress metre and is freely alliterating. As reflected in his own term 'adaptation' to describe it, Nobis's arresting version is not a translation of *Beowulf* in the narrower sense represented in the versions I have been concentrating on in this book but is rather a much abbreviated paraphrase. It is a reduced and reimagined version tailored for a new specific artistic purpose. It covers the whole story of *Beowulf* but at about 1200 lines it is not much more than a third of the length of the original poem, omitting whole episodes, speeches and digressions and insistently foregrounding storytelling, thereby successfully capturing a key element of *Beowulf* itself, though inevitably sacrificing others.[18]

---

13   From the back cover of Rodrigues's *Beowulf*.
14   Nobis, *Beowulf: An Adaptation*.
15   In the late 1980s and 1990s, Glover toured widely with his acclaimed performance of *Beowulf*, the text of which appears in his glossy publication *Beowulf*.
16   Nobis, *Beowulf*, p. viii.
17   Seamus Heaney: 'As a translator and narrator of the Beowulf story, Felix Nobis has found a style that is high but not inflated, true to the poetry of the original and enthralling to a contemporary audience' (quoted on the back cover of Nobis's book).
18   Contrast the performance version (in Old English) by Benjamin Bagsby mentioned below (p. 218), which covers only the fight with Grendel (lines 1–1062); the recitation of this part alone lasts one hour and forty minutes on the DVD recording of the show.

Meanwhile in America

In the past fifty years there was evidently a more lively interest in *Beowulf* in the United States, as reflected strikingly in the fact that eighteen American verse translations have appeared in print since Raffel's, and it is significant that Heaney's version too was commissioned in the first place by an American publisher (Norton); meanwhile Morgan, Crossley-Holland and Alexander have also been available to American readers. Until Heaney's version appeared it is difficult to identify translations that became widely accepted as 'standard' or definitive for Americans. Though many versions became favourites for particular users and have been much reprinted, none can be seen as having satisfied American readerships in the way that Crossley-Holland's and Alexander's ostensibly did in Britain and Ireland. Heaney's translation must now be by far the most widely used but it is not to everyone's taste and new translations continue to appear, catering for college courses and for interested general readers and various kinds of enthusiasts. Some older translations, such as those by Gummere and Garnett, are now cheaply available again as well.

The first American verse translation after Morgan was that of Raffel (1963, discussed in detail in an earlier chapter), which was followed a decade and a half later by the dual-language version of **Howell D. Chickering, Jr** (1977).[19] Raffel's version had been intended for audiences of students and general readers who would not be accessing the original poem. By contrast, Chickering's translation was not really meant to be free-standing at all but was to be used along with the Old English text by students working with the original. In what is a substantial scholarly volume, the translation appears in parallel-text format facing Chickering's critical text of the original poem, accompanied by a thorough introduction to *Beowulf*, a section on how to read the poem aloud and a comprehensive commentary of nearly one hundred pages covering literary and linguistic issues and background material, informed by Chickering's mastery (though sometimes an unwieldy mastery) of *Beowulf* scholarship. The translation is conceived of as one of 'two aids' (the other one being the commentary) by means of which the reader 'can experience [*Beowulf*'s] poetic power first hand'.[20]

In line with the ancillary function of the translation, Chickering sets out to provide in it 'the plain sense of the original', ignoring 'the alliteration and other audible features of the facing original'.[21] He adopts a four-stress line with a heavy caesura, employing some alliteration and assonance, though 'only sparingly', but he acknowledges in his preface, 'The translation has few other pretensions to literary form', and he explains that he has tried to keep the translation 'always one step lower in pitch than the original'.[22] Chickering is perhaps being overly

---

[19] Chickering, ed. and trans., *Beowulf: A Dual-Language Edition*.
[20] Chickering, *Beowulf*, p. ix.
[21] Chickering, *Beowulf*, p. x.
[22] Chickering, *Beowulf*, p. xi.

modest here, as his version is not without imaginative touches, but the translation is mostly not interesting or suggestive in itself. It generally sticks close to the original, which makes for a stilted effect, as in

> Many awful sins against mankind,
> the solitary fiend often committed,
> a fearsome shaming. (lines 164–6a)

It gives a reliable guide to the surface sense of the original and enables detailed study of that original but is not, and does not claim to be, a modern poem that lives. It is *Beowulf* that Chickering wishes the users of his book to read, not the translation.

One year later **Albert W. Haley, Jr**, brought out a version of *Beowulf* not as a study aid but with the more ambitious aim of representing the original as a free-standing modern poem.[23] Haley's translation, presented in a slim volume with no introductory or supplementary material, not even a preface, is fast-paced and studiously unornate and it adopts a register that is considerably less high-sounding than that of *Beowulf* itself. The translation is a paraphrase rather than a literal translation, with much syntactical recasting. According to the blurb on the book's cover,[24] the translation is the product of its author's insistence that 'a translation must be completely natural in the new language, and also be of the time and place of the original'. Haley puts the former principle into effect by eschewing Old English rhythms, alliterative patterns and other poetic devices, while the latter principle leads him, as the blurb puts it, to select 'words and expressions closely resembling those given in the original text'; random examples are *aethelings* (line 4), *midyard* (line 873), *glee-wood* (line 2486). The result is an uneasy combination of plain modern language –

> it entered into his mind that he should
> order men to put up a hall-building (lines 77–8) –

and discourse of a more distancing kind:

> Often Scyld Sceffing wrested mead-seats from
> troops of foemen and many tribes. (lines 5–6)

Haley's translation attracted no attention from Old English scholars and was not widely noticed elsewhere. Though relevant and interesting as an attempt to represent *Beowulf* in a new idiom its verse may be seen as too prosaic to engage convincingly with the poetry of the original.

---

[23] Haley, trans., *Beowulf*.
[24] The blurb is enthusiastically romantic and high-sounding in its appeal to the potential reader, employing a mannered register that contrasts with the relative restraint of the actual translation: 'Here is the saga of the glory hoarders, first sung to the harp in an age of ring bestowing, when battlemoody warriors competed in deeds story-worthy, and mead ran aplenty in the wide-doored halls.'

Stanley B. Greenfield, widely regarded as the major critic of Old English poetry of his generation, produced a translation of the poem in 1982. His intention in doing so is reflected in the title he chose for the translation, *A Readable Beowulf*. Greenfield elaborates on this intention in his Introduction, where he explains that he has set out to write a 'faithful' translation but wishes also to produce a work that is (echoing John Lennon), 'A Poem in its Own Write': 'I wanted it to "flow"', he says, 'I wanted it both modern and Old English in its poetic reflexes and sensibilities, delighting both the general reader and the Anglo-Saxon specialist'.[25] Greenfield's translation is indeed 'readable'; it is also one of the most attractive versions with regard to presentation and user-friendliness.[26]

Greenfield's version is, in line with what has been the dominant translation philosophy of the modern period, fluent and accessible, and it reliably though not slavishly transmits surface meaning. As his mode of translation, Greenfield adopts what he calls the principle of 'equivalency', as opposed to the more restricting method of 'imitation',[27] a principle that allows him to explore the possibilities of Modern English rather than always having to look over his shoulder towards Old English patterns but one that also works against the shock of the old. Greenfield's is a smooth translation, but smoothness is not generally what we find in *Beowulf*.

The chosen metre of the translation is a distinctive one, a form of syllabic verse, in which each line has nine syllables, with occasional allowance of eight- and ten-syllable lines, and each syllable notionally receives equal stress, as in the following lines, which also illustrate the relative freedom of the translation (there is nothing in the original corresponding directly to the suggestive *life's first dawn* and *breaking*):

> who launched him forth in his life's first dawn,
> a boy alone on the breaking waves. (lines 45–6)

In practice such lines are less unlike Old English ones than they might seem in theory.

As is also evident in these lines, Greenfield is flexible in his employment of alliteration. The verse form allows him to introduce a wide range of poetic effects without distracting from the flow of the narrative. He cultivates a pronounced caesura but makes much use of enjambment, ensuring a steady forward flow, also aided by the use of grammatical connectives – *so, thus, yet,* etc. He writes in a fairly formal register but a modern one, avoiding archaism, inversion of word order and obvious poeticisms. Especially in direct discourse, there is a strong sense of careful and precise wording, as in *Beowulf* itself, but the effect is some-

---

[25] Greenfield, *A Readable Beowulf*, p. 29.
[26] It is laid out in a broad-page format, with brief on-page explanatory notes (111 in all), marginal descriptive section-headings and running line-numbers, a number of illustrative line drawings (by Sarah Higley, in a plain modern style), supplementary information, and an authoritative introduction to *Beowulf* by Alain Renoir).
[27] Greenfield, *A Readable Beowulf*, p. 29.

what prosaic. As John D. Niles observes in his largely favourable assessment of Greenfield's translation, 'The virtues of syllabic meter are largely the virtues of good prose.'[28] Niles adds, 'syllabic verse tends to be marked by a certain taut quality, for the discipline of finding the right mathematics can lead to artful avoidance of the easy phrase.'[29]

Greenfield's version is 'readable' in the sense of being an easy and enjoyable read for a general audience; it is a version for reading, as is also reflected in visual cues on the page, such as the apostrophe in *kings'* in line 2, disambiguating the word's grammatical function – 'Indeed, we have heard of the Spear-Danes' glory / and their kings"(lines 1–2) – or the enclosing of *triumph* in inverted commas at line 532, to indicate irony. It also reads fluently aloud, being direct and unostentatious in style. The grandeur and elaborate artifice of the original poem are jettisoned in Greenfield's more modest refashioning, but the translation maintains a strong narrative. The translation is not as 'tepid' and 'limp', as Burton Raffel finds it, but Raffel is surely right in seeing it as the work of a scholar rather than a poet.[30]

Working at about the same time as Greenfield, **Marijane Osborn** produced a version that echoes some of the qualities of his translation. Osborn, stimulated by her evident passion for the poem, has been one of the most active promoters of *Beowulf* to a wider audience in recent decades and in 1983 she brought out her *Beowulf: A Verse Translation with Treasures of the Ancient North*, a book that is even more visually attractive than Greenfield's publication.[31] It is a rather *de-luxe*-looking volume in large format, with the text set out landscape and accompanied by a wealth of well-chosen line drawings and black-and-white photographs of artefacts. It was produced not as a cheap paperback for students to buy but very much as an artistic production to be savoured and enjoyed. There is a thoughtful Introduction by Fred C. Robinson to lend authority, but Osborn herself is a wise and eloquent commentator on the poem, as is evident here and elsewhere.

Osborn seeks to convey through her book a sense of the compelling splendour of *Beowulf* to an uninformed audience and does all that she can to make the poem appealing to such an audience and the reading of it a pleasurable experience. With regard to the translation itself, she declares her primary aim as being 'to achieve clarity in a resonant narrative verse that moves as freely as prose.'[32] She approximates her verse form to that of the original, adopting a four-stress imitative alliterative metre but not applying this so rigidly as to compromise her primary aim of clarity and freely moving narrative:

> The fall of night brought Grendel forth

[28] Niles, 'Rewriting *Beowulf*: The Task of Translation', p. 872.
[29] Ibid.
[30] Raffel, review of *A Readable Beowulf*, p. 93.
[31] Osborn, trans., *Beowulf: A Verse Translation with Treasures of the Ancient North*.
[32] Osborn, *Beowulf*, p. 126.

to see how the Danes, with drinking done,
had gone to rest in that gabled hall. (lines 115–17)

The metre does not impede the naturalness of style or distract from the narrative. And along with the fairly formal diction it lends dignity to the tone.

In line with the principles of clarity and freely moving narrative, Osborn adds names and explanatory details, avoids archaism (though she introduces some Old English words 'that have a technical meaning and give a flavor to the poem', e.g., *byrnie, atheling, shope* [should that not be *shop*, though?]),[33] adopts modern literary syntax, and is sparing in her use of compound words. In her section 'On Translating *Beowulf*' at the end of the book, she wonders if she has made *Beowulf* 'much too readable'.[34] Her aim is to transmit her sense of the attraction of the poem and to bring new readers to it but she does indeed bend over backwards in doing so, carrying out much of the hard work for the reader and reconstituting the poem in the process. She explains, for example, that she decided to translate *beot* not as 'boast' but, because of the negative connotations of 'boast' in modern culture, as 'pledge'; 'boast' would have been constructively defamiliarizing, however.[35] To aid the reader she italicizes the many passages in the poem that are not part of the immediate narrative; this facilitates reading but is highly interpretative and interventionist (and curiously it has the effect of foregrounding the perceived digressions).[36]

Like other translators, then, Osborn succeeds in making *Beowulf* readable, but at a cost, that of eliding a sense of the power of its poetry and of the otherness of its world. The otherness of *Beowulf* is brought out in the book's fine illustrations but the translation itself accommodates the poem to the experience of modern readers. In commenting on her approach Osborn expresses the hope that the translation 'is so transparent that one may pass through it into the world the poet envisaged, of an age before his own'.[37] All translations mediate, however, especially ones that are as obligingly domesticating as Osborn's.

1987 saw the publication of the translation of **Bernard F. Huppé**, the layout of which reflects Huppé's decided views of the structure of *Beowulf* and his Augustinian interpretation of its theme.[38] The translation sets out to provide 'a suggestion of the [Old English] metrical form in its simplest and loosest form' (with alliteration and a strong caesura),[39] and Huppé declares that the translation will be successful if it turns the reader 'to the labor of reading the original'.[40]

---

[33] Ibid.
[34] Ibid.
[35] Osborn, *Beowulf*, pp. 126–7.
[36] Osborn, *Beowulf*, pp. 127–8.
[37] Osborn, *Beowulf*, p. 128.
[38] Huppé, trans., *Beowulf: A New Translation*. Huppé's Augustinian reading is set out in detail in his book *The Hero in the Earthly City: A Reading of Beowulf*.
[39] Huppé, *Beowulf*, p. 27.
[40] Huppé, *Beowulf*, p. 29.

Huppé sees his translation as 'in accord with the aim of faithfulness',[41] but is by no means closely literal in his treatment:

> Hear the ancient tale that we are told
> of the great deeds of Danish kings,
> and their lordly lives of valor. (lines 1–3)

The translation, domesticating in approach, is the work of a scholar rather than a poet, but it is fairly vigorous in style.

Most of the translations of *Beowulf* discussed in this book adopt metrical structures based freely on the four-stress line of Old English poetry. As indicated by the title of her 1988 translation, *Beowulf: An Imitative Translation*, **Ruth Lehmann** goes further, setting herself the challenge of 'imitating' the Old English alliterative metre itself,[42] something that, as we have seen, S. B. Greenfield for one went out of his way not to do. In her own words, Lehmann seeks to be 'accurate in interpretation and keep to the alliterative meter'.[43] Though referring to her translation as 'more or less' imitative of Old English metre, arguing that '[a] more exact imitation is compromised by an effort not to distort modern English into something awkward and unintelligible',[44] in fact Lehmann applies the Old English rules to her verse in a strict way, certainly much more strictly than anything we have seen in this chapter so far. She allows herself somewhat greater leniency in her use of anacrusis (the introduction of unstressed syllables at the beginning of a verse) in verse-types A, D and E than is found in the original, but each of her half-lines is carefully based on one of the Sievers five types.

Lehmann's translation, last reprinted in 2000, is interesting as a scholarly exercise but does not work as a poem. Lehmann, a student of Old English metrics (I quoted from one of her articles in Chapter 2),[45] has the scholarly equipment to produce modern English verse using Old English metre but may be seen not to possess the poetic equipment to do so convincingly – perhaps no one could (as shown below, Frederick Rebsamen, a better poet than Lehmann, doesn't produce a satisfying imitative version either). She is far from creating poetry that lives. There are vigorous passages that suggest the excitement of the original but generally the translation comes across as stiff and stilted, with an abundance of unnatural-sounding expressions in evidence, as Lehmann struggles with the demands of the metre. This version is full of archaisms, a few examples being *forth-faring* (line 27, etc.), *weeds of battle* (line 39), *bills* (line 40), *foeman* (line 142), *fell* (adjective, line 193), *quaffed* (line 629), and mannered and curious usages, often also archaic-sounding and/or involving inversion, are ubiquitous;

---

[41] Huppé, *Beowulf*, p. 27.
[42] Lehmann, trans., *Beowulf: An Imitative Translation*.
[43] Lehmann, *Beowulf*, p. 17.
[44] Lehmann, *Beowulf*, p. 16.
[45] See above, p. 30, n. 12.

the following examples give a flavour: *thaneguards* (line 123), *Who may ye be, having armor?* (line 237), *Guard of the seashore / for a time am I* (lines 240–1), *Be our good tutor* (line 269), *naught but a child* (line 372), *A dangerous journey you dared swimming* (line 512). Clumsy and innaposite renderings distract and detract from the flow of the narrative: *not at all the less* (line 43), *had chosen choice fighting men* (line 205), *fearless official* (line 287), *delightful chorus* (line 611, referring to warriors in the hall). In the terms of her own reflections as referred to above, Lehmann's spirited translation is 'intelligible' but it does not consistently avoid being 'awkward'.

1990 saw the publication of **Raymond Tripp**'s highly idiosyncratic verse translation (with a flexible stress-based metre),[46] a translation that sets out to be as literal as possible and that reflects the approach to the poem and its interpretation outlined in Tripp's 1983 publication *More About the Fight with the Dragon*.[47] Tripp finds elaborate wordplay everywhere in *Beowulf*, even in words that look perfectly straightforward in meaning (as in the quotation below). His concentration on close translation and on multiple meaning at the lexical level is at the expense of overall tone and style, resulting in a register that is an uneasy combination of the formal, often specifically chivalric, and the colloquial, and an expression that seems heavy-handed and insensitive to the real subtlety and associative power of the language of *Beowulf*. The multiple meanings themselves mostly strain credulity to breaking point, and although Tripp insists that he wishes to bring out these multiple meanings, the one meaning that he tends not to give is the ostensibly obvious one. Thus, for example, the passage at the beginning of the poem which is usually (and correctly) interpreted as being about Scyld depriving his enemies of their mead-benches is rendered

> Often would a benchman among brawling men,
> At many a meeting shove Scyld Scefing aside,
> And bully the earl, as soon as his bounty was
> Found unforthcoming. (lines 4–7a)

Tripp's translation, which did not achieve wide circulation, might be viewed as refreshingly iconoclastic but it must be seen as presenting too much of a distorted image of *Beowulf* to be of benefit to the general reader or to be useful in the classroom.

---

[46] Tripp, trans., *Beowulf: An Edition and Literary Translation in Progress*. As Tripp explains in his Introduction, the translation is not based on any existing edition: 'the present translation returns to the manuscript and restores the text in many places, eliminating numerous editorial emendations and re-punctuation according to the new story which emerges' (p. i), but he does not provide an Old English text or any editorial discussion: hence, presumably, the *in Progress* of his title. The translation is accompanied by a short Introduction but no further supplementary material.

[47] Tripp, *More About the Fight with the Dragon: Beowulf 2208b–3182: Commentary, Edition, and Translation*. The translation of the corresponding part of the poem in Tripp's 1990 translation is considerably re-worded.

We have already looked at Marijane Osborn's 1983 translation of *Beowulf*. In 1990 Osborn was part of another high-production-value publication, one that presented the version of the poem by **Raymond Oliver**. This publication was *Beowulf: A Likeness*, a collaboration between Oliver, the designer Randolph Swearer and Osborn, the latter providing a seven-page essay, 'Imagining the Real World Setting of *Beowulf*'.⁴⁸ Here again we see *Beowulf* beautifully packaged and presented, and again there is an Introduction by Fred C. Robinson. *Beowulf: A Likeness* is a coffee-table-size volume on glossy art-paper, illustrated with black-and-white photographs (of artefacts and landscapes) and other images, with some use of blue in the illustrations; each page opening is conceived as a single unit, with generous margins on text pages and some pages having white print on black for dramatic effect while some have text printed on photographs. The book is designed as a visual experience.

I refer to Oliver's text as a version of the poem but in fact it is such in only the broadest of senses. This is not a direct translation but rather a reimagining and rewriting of the poem in new poetic terms, what Dryden would have referred to as an 'imitation'.⁴⁹ Howell Chickering compares it to John Gardner's *Grendel*: 'it is a new work of art, a literary experience in its own right, that takes great imaginative liberties with its parent text and yet also translates portions of it very closely'.⁵⁰ Oliver himself compares his approach to that of Malory in treating his French sources, which involved 'much adding, subtracting, and rearranging of large structural units as well as thorough rewording; it can be securely described neither as translation nor "imitation"'.⁵¹ In Oliver's case such an approach enables the introduction of new characters and narrative details and entails the simplification of what Robinson refers to in the Introduction as the 'spiritual climate' of the poem, 'free[ing] readers to turn their attention to other matters in the story which would have equal importance for an Anglo-Saxon and a modern audience'.⁵² Oliver uses a variety of metres, including rhyming stanzas and heroic couplets, and is not interested in producing a 'likeness' of the poetry of *Beowulf* itself.

The opening stanza of Oliver's *Beowulf* reads as follows:

> When Scyld the distant-father died of time,
> Old in winters, come to the end of deeds,
> His body being fresh as in his prime,
> Sweet as flowers newly mown in the meads,
> They wrapped it all in linden trimmed with gold,
> And otter-furs against the snowy cold. (lines 1–6)

---

48   Swearer, Oliver, trans., and Osborn, *Beowulf: A Likeness*; for Osborn's essay, see pp. 119–27.
49   For Dryden's classification of kinds of translation, see 'John Dryden: From the Preface to *Ovid's Epistles*'; on Dryden, see further below, p. 204.
50   Chickering, review of Mark Hudson, trans., *Beowulf*, and Swearer, Oliver and Osborn, *Beowulf: A Likeness*, p. 690.
51   *Beowulf: A Likeness*, p. 8.
52   Fred C. Robinson, 'Introduction', *Beowulf: A Likeness*, p. 5.

This is a thoughtful reworking and development of ideas prompted by the prologue of *Beowulf*; it is not a translation of the opening lines of the poem, however.

Oliver's poem overall is insightful and suggestive, bringing aspects of *Beowulf* vividly to life and exploring its silences. It is a living poem in its own right but must be viewed as a response to rather than a translation of the Anglo-Saxon poem in the narrow sense. And it is very partial in its interpretation of the original. It misleadingly implies that *Beowulf* comes from a world of crude experience: we have already noted Oliver's simplification of the religious dimension of the poem but he also elides the elaborate decorum of life at Heorot and the complexity of interaction between the warriors. As Kevin Kiernan notes, 'Oliver is not interested in the polished behavior of Hrothgar's royal thanes. In the loutish setting he creates, the complexities of Hunferth's character are simplified by crude insults, delivered in mock-heroic rhyming couplets.'[53] Oliver provides a provocative read but he is highly selective, and subjective, in his treatment, which is not intended to be seen as a faithful translation. Rather than being aimed at bringing the general reader to a knowledge of *Beowulf*, it would be best appreciated by readers who know the original poem already.

1990 also saw the publication of **Marc Hudson**'s verse translation of *Beowulf*, accompanied by an extensive and interesting 'Commentary' by him on issues in poetic translation in general and in the translation of *Beowulf* in particular, with reflection on his own practice.[54] Hudson's translation is flowing and dignified, generally restrained in tone and attentive to the meditative quality of *Beowulf*. Hudson refers to his version as paraphrase, picking up on Dryden's distinction between metaphrase (close literal translation), paraphrase ('translation with latitude', in Dryden's terms) and imitation ('taking only some general hints from the original', the approach adopted by Raymond Oliver, for example).[55] Hudson's translation sticks close to the general sense of the original but is strikingly free in expressing that sense, with many original touches and much recasting of imagery. Describing the first coming of Grendel, for example, Hudson writes,

> So that company of men lived in a circle
> of light, until one began,
> a fiend in hell, to work evil. (lines 99–101)

This follows the original literally, except for the imaginative recasting of the Old English *dreamum lifdon, / eadiglice*, 'lived in joys, happily' (lines 99–100), as 'lived in a circle / of light', conveying something of the associative depth of *dreamum*.

In his Commentary Hudson identifies the principles that provided a framework for his translation: 'The four-stress line, the diction of a higher note, the

---

[53] Kiernan, review of Swearer et al., *Beowulf: A Likeness*, p. 264.
[54] Hudson, trans., *Beowulf: A Translation and Commentary*.
[55] Hudson, *Beowulf*, pp. 16–18; see further 'John Dryden', in *The Translation Studies Reader*, ed. Venuti.

resolution of kennings into phrases, the fidelity to the rhetorical figures and to the contemplative character of the poem – these represent controlling biases that informed my choices, providing the work as a whole with a unity it would not have otherwise possessed.'[56] In applying these principles, Hudson sacrifices some of the excitement of the narrative of the original and eschews obvious virtuosity but he conveys the reflective quality of *Beowulf* effectively. He aims at a natural-sounding syntax, preserving the Old English feature of variation where he can do so, but only 'within the limits of Modern English syntax'.[57] He greatly reduces the number of compound words, though some striking ones are included, such as *edge-keeper* (Old English *mearcstapa*, 'traverser of the borderlands', line 103), *dawn-lament* (Old English *morgensweg*, 'cry in the morning', line 129) and *death-gear* (Old English *gryregeatwum*, 'terrifying equipment/war-gear', line 324), the latter being particularly arresting in the adjectival phrase, describing the Geatish warriors, 'beautiful in death-gear' (there is no equivalent to *beautiful* in the original).

In Hudson's version we see a poet engaging thoughtfully with the poetry of the original in a way that is also designed to appeal to the 'general' modern reader. The verse form itself is mostly unobtrusive, to the extent of being prose-like. The register is notably formal, with some limited use of archaic and poetic vocabulary (*whither*, line 163; *unto*, line 183; *whelming*, line 394; *blithe*, line 604), obscure words (*cumbered*, line 15; *falchion*, line 40; *jinked*, meaning 'jingled', line 227) and Old English terms (*aethelings*, line 118; *wyrd*, line 455; *scop*, line 496); *shape* and *Shaper* (from Old English *scyppan* and *Scyppend*) are used in a mannered way for 'create, make' and 'Creator'. There are some notably prosaic words, however (e.g., *recalcitrant*, line 137; *achievement*, line 857), and a few colloquialisms here and there (e.g., 'set the record straight', lines 532–3; 'belly up', line 565); 'just dessert' (line 423) is either distractingly clever or a mistake.

Hot on the heels of Hudson's version came the translation by **Frederick Rebsamen**, first published in 1991 and brought out again in 2004 in an 'updated' version.[58] Twenty years earlier Rebsamen had produced a prose adaptation of the story of *Beowulf*, narrated by the protagonist and incorporating much extra-textual material, including new scenes and lines from other Old English poems.[59] Rebsamen's verse translation is completely independent from the prose appropriation. It is a daring and vigorous piece of work in which, like Lehmann (whose version he doesn't know), he imitates the metre of Old English poetry as closely as possible, observing the rules of verse-type and alliteration. This is a constricting verse form for Modern English and even though Rebsamen's translation is very much a free paraphrase (far more so than is Hudson's version), metrical considerations dominate expression. The rhythm is abrupt, based insist-

---

56 Hudson, *Beowulf*, p. 61.
57 Hudson, *Beowulf*, p. 51.
58 Rebsamen, trans., *Beowulf: A Verse Translation*; *Beowulf: An Updated Verse Translation*.
59 Rebsamen, *Beowulf Is My Name and Selected Translations of Other Old English Poems*.

ently on half-line units (with strong caesura), and word order is affected by the demands of the metre and by the adoption of Old English syntactical structures. The diction is resolutely modern but is heightened by the frequent use of invented compound words (*goldgifts, anger-flames, swordswings, throne-battle* and *blood-minded* in one short sequence at lines 80–5), words based on Old English usage (*gleemen*, line 52; *Deemer*, line 187; *wyrd*, line 572, etc.), and new formations and extensions of modern words (*eagering*, line 535; *sleepened* [by sword-swings], line 567). The result of the combination of such features is a verse that is modern, strange and striking. This is no easy read in the tradition of the invisible translation.

A sense of the distinctiveness of Rebsamen's translation is suggested by its opening lines, which also provide a vivid illustration of the freedom with which he treats his source:

> Yes! We have heard   of years long vanished
> how Spear-Danes struck   sang victory-songs
> raised from a wasteland   walls of glory. (lines 1–3)

This is clearly a considerable rewriting of the first lines of *Beowulf*, with new imagery introduced and elements of contrast (*struck, wasteland*) adding to the passage's abruptness. The reader has to work at the syntax but the sense of ancient glory and excitement is unmistakable.

There are many exhilarating touches in the translation – 'bright bench-laughter borne to the rafters' (line 88) is just one example – but hammering intensity is relentless throughout and soon begins to wear. Rebsamen's poetry seems muscle-bound and in many places awkward, with expression frequently appearing dense to the point of opacity. The translation is bold in its strangeness but the strangeness overwhelms the poetry. Hampered particularly by the strictness of the chosen metre and by his unwieldy syntax, in the assessment of one reviewer, Rebsamen's version 'is a hybrid that is neither modern English poetry, nor in any way an accurate rendering of the Old English poem'.[60] In my own view, in his *Beowulf* Rebsamen does write modern English poetry which is idiosyncratic and in places interesting, but it is also limited. It is incapable of adequately sustaining the narrative of *Beowulf* over the expanse of the translation and is a blunt instrument for conveying the sophistication of the original's poetry.

In 1994 the translation of **E. L. Risden** appeared, aimed explicitly at a student readership; like other great works from the past, writes Risden, *Beowulf* 'deserves the attention of all students interested in literature'.[61] With this general readership in mind and perceiving that existing verse translations 'tend to sacrifice literal meaning for aesthetic value', Risden sets out to provide 'the most accurate translation possible, while maintaining readability and keeping in mind the

---

[60] Schipper, review of Rebsamen, *Beowulf: A Verse Translation*, p. 377.
[61] Risden, trans., *Beowulf: A Student's Edition*; quotation at p. xiii.

poet's technique and the concerns of interested readers approaching the poem for the first time.'[62] His artistic aspiration is limited to producing a translation that is 'not entirely unbeautiful'[63] and in this modest aim he succeeds, though, inevitably, little of the power of the original poem comes across. Risden writes in a style that is dignified but generally unobtrusive. As he puts it in his Introduction, echoing sentiments we have seen widely displayed by other translators, 'The translation should sound as though the poem has come from the past rather than from Main Street, but it shouldn't sound as though the translator is struggling to make it so.'[64] The verse is in a form of half-line alliterating metre, freely adapted by Risden from that of Old English in a manner that does not unduly constrict syntax or intelligibility.

The translation is generally accurate, though there are some lapses, and the decision not to capitalize 'god' (on the grounds that it is not capitalized in the original manuscript and that Risden doesn't 'feel comfortable asserting that [some references] defin[i]tely do not suggest Othin or perhaps both Christian and Germanic gods at once'[65]) is an eccentric one, and is contradicted by the capitalization of 'Almighty'. And although the style is generally unobtrusive the concern to suggest that the poem comes from the past can lead to curiousness of expression, as in

> Not at all was he less   provisioned with gifts,
> heirlooms of his people,   than they once did
> who sent him at birth   far over the sea,
> alone on the waves   when he was a child. (lines 43–6)

Here the litotes is overdone and the sentence ends up being ungrammatical.

Risden's version is in the tradition of readable *Beowulf*s catering for literature students, with somewhat heightened, and slightly archaizing, diction and dignified expression. It would soon be overtaken by other translations for students studying *Beowulf* in translation which, while similar in approach to Risden's, were more attractively packaged, offered more in the way of introductory and supplementary material and in some cases were more interesting stylistically.

At the other end of the spectrum is the version by **Richard M. Trask** (1998),[66] which sets out to follow the 'old rules' of metre, alliteration and compound poetic metaphor, seeing key aspects of Old English prosody as still operative in Modern English. 'Fortified with the conviction', writes Trask, 'that the kenning as well as alliteration is appropriate to, and at home in, Modern English, we proceed afresh to translate Old English verse into Modern English using the alliterative pattern, retaining as many compound poetic metaphors as we are able and

---

[62] *Beowulf*, pp. ii–iii.
[63] *Beowulf*, p. iii.
[64] *Beowulf*, p. iv.
[65] *Beowulf*, p. v.
[66] Trask, trans., *Beowulf and Judith: Two Heroes*.

perhaps even throwing in some of our own making.'⁶⁷ Aimed at students and the general reader, the translation sets out to take the reader to the original poem and succeeds in capturing aspects of its form but hardly of its vitality. It has some nicely creative touches and arresting phrases (and some misleading renderings⁶⁸), and it is far from bland, but, as is the case with other imitative translations, comes across as somewhat stilted and awkward:

> Behold! We from the Spear-Danes   in days of old
> found out the glory   of our folk-hero kings,
> how the princes   proved their courage. (lines 1–3)

The translation is printed interlinearly with an Old English text but is not a half-line for half-line gloss but a freer imitation of the lines of the original, with some syntactical adaptation.

One of the most vigorous recent translations is that by **Thomas Kennedy** (2001), a version in eight-syllable verse with varying patterns of stress within the line.⁶⁹ Kennedy eschews the use of alliterative metre, arguing that for a modern reader 'alliteration does not seem to be versification at all',⁷⁰ and adopts a less obtrusive verse form that nonetheless, with its short phrases, gives a strong sense of half-line units. Kennedy has the interesting idea of directly taking over the metaphorical language of the Old English into Modern English: 'A principal aim of this translation is to uncover the metaphorical texture of the Anglo-Saxon poetry, a texture sometimes obscured in the attempt to find modern equivalents.'⁷¹ The result is a strongly foreignizing translation that does succeed in conveying the shock of the old, though at the expense of producing a version that is too literal and consequently too curious to work as modern poetry. Kennedy's version reads not as a modern poem but as a self-consciously reconstructed Old English poem in Modern English, in which the Anglo-Saxon metaphorical language sounds stilted in its modern garb.

Kennedy's literalness is not primarily at the grammatical level, though he does reproduce the additive, appositive style of the original and imitates Old English in omitting articles before nouns. Rather Kennedy is particularly literal at the level of diction and metaphor. Thus we read that 'all those around sitting / over the whale path' (lines 9–10; echoing *ymbsittendra*, *Beowulf*, line 9) yielded tribute to Scyld; Scyld's retainers are 'journey comrades' (line 25; echoing *wilgesiþas*, *Beowulf*, line 23); God is the 'Helmet of Heaven' (line 172; cf. also Hrothgar as 'helmet of Scyldings', line 351, etc.); 'Care seethed in Healfdene's

---

⁶⁷ *Beowulf and Judith*, pp. 6–7.
⁶⁸ E. g., 'to him four male children [. . .] / woke into the world' (lines 59–60), where one of the children (*bearn*) is female; Grendel is a 'soulless man' (line 104) (there is nothing to warrant this in the Old English); 'bidding / to get some help   against the soul slayer' (lines 176–7), where it is the soul slayer (*gastbona*) that the Danes are praying to.
⁶⁹ Thomas C. Kennedy, trans., *Beowulf*.
⁷⁰ *Beowulf*, p. iv.
⁷¹ *Beowulf*, p. ii.

son' (line 179); and so on. In such renderings Kennedy brings out the metaphorical meaning of Old English phrases; he also uses Old English words and Old-English-derived words, closely following the phrasing of *Beowulf* itself: Scyld attacks 'scather gangs' (line 5), a *scather* being one who injures; Scyld 'waxed straight and strong under welkin' (line 8); God is 'Wielder of fame' (line 15); no one can say 'for sooth' (line 46) who received the cargo of Scyld's funeral ship. Other archaic/Old English usages, modelled on the language of the original, include *brim* (line 26), *weeds* (line 34), *wading* (line 210, 'going'), *one-fold* (line 244), *heap* (line 379, 'group'), *doom* (line 412, 'judgement'), *wyrd* (line 431, etc.), *cringe* (line 611, 'fall').

Such defamiliarizing language is accompanied in the translation by a marked use of inverted word order that looks highly artificial in Modern English, especially as articles are also omitted:

> Wielder of fame to child of Scyld
> world honor gave. (lines 15–16)

Elsewhere formulations that directly imitate the Old English can sound not only artificial but a bit wooden: 'Of mankind we are of the Geats' (line 248, literally translating *We synt gumcynnes Geata leode*, *Beowulf*, line 259), and 'We have, to the king of the Danes, / a great errand' (lines 259–60a, literally translating *Habbað we to þæm mæran   micel ærende*, *Beowulf*, line 270).

Like Rebsamen's, Kennedy's translation may be seen as lacking subtlety and in its adoption of Old English poetic patterns rather clunky. It is lightly abbreviating in its treatment of the original, simplifying and telescoping syntactical structures and, very occasionally, omitting details (such as the name of Scyld's son Beow/Beowulf at line 18 of the original), so that the total line-count of the translation is 3174, as compared to 3182 in the original. Some renderings might also raise scholarly eyebrows, for example *deeds of love* (line 22) for Old English *lofdædum* (*Beowulf*, line 24), 'deeds of praise'; *fearful garments* (line 3040) for *gryregeatwum* (*Beowulf*, line 324), 'fearsome war-gear'; and *Living alone was their reward* (line 106), a very free interpretation of *he him ðæs lean forgeald* (*Beowulf*, line 114), 'he gave them requital for that'.

At the other extreme from foreignizing translations like those of Rebsamen and Kennedy are the recent versions of Roy Liuzza, Alan Sullivan/Timothy Murphy and John McNamara. **Roy Liuzza**'s translation came out in 2000,[72] just after that of Seamus Heaney, and it was well received, even eliciting favourable comparison with Heaney's version. Frank Kermode considers that one could compare passages in the two versions line by line 'and say that Heaney wins some and loses some'.[73] Carolyne Larrington is of the view that 'Liuzza's imagination and ear rival Heaney's; in particular, *lifbysig* in line 966 is "squirming for

---

[72] Liuzza, trans., *Beowulf: A New Verse Translation*. Liuzza reflects on translation and on his own translation in '*Beowulf* in Translation – Problems and Possibilities'.
[73] Kermode, 'The Modern *Beowulf*, p. 11.

life", *gryrefahne*, line 2576, is "mottled horror", and in line 2829 *heaðoscearpe* is the onomatopoeic "battle-scarred shard".[74] Examples of such felicitous renderings could be multiplied.

As well as presenting his own version, Liuzza's volume is a resource pack for studying *Beowulf* and its translations. He includes specimens of other translations down the generations as well as invaluable supplementary material, the whole informed by scholarship of the highest quality and laid out attractively. The translation is fluent and unshowy. In Liuzza's view a translation is not a substitute or simulacrum of the original but 'in the end, a gesture towards an empty space where a text used to be': it is 'a suggestion'.[75]

In his Introduction to the translation Liuzza describes his approach to the poetry of *Beowulf*. He aims above all at 'fluency and precision', choosing a verse form that will enable him to achieve these goals:

> I have tried to write in a poetic idiom that is analogous to, not imitative of, the character of the original; the end result has been a translation that is quieter than most others. Each verse has four stresses, a medial pause, and alliteration, but these are by no means as marked as they are in the original, and on rare occasions are foregone altogether.[76]

The verse form gives structure to the narration but is not distracting; caesuras are not too pronounced, rhythm not too pounding, and alliteration is used for rhetorical and ornamental effect rather than structurally. Liuzza makes some use of Old English stylistic features such as apposition and compounding but sparingly and without generally straining his modern idiom.

His register is consistently fairly formal but also idiomatic. Like other aspects of the translation the diction is mostly natural-sounding and unostentatious, with little in the way of colloquialism (one example is 'They asked for trouble', line 423), no cultivation of the archaic (apart from the odd appearance of *hither*, *thence*, *unto* and the like) and only the occasional suggestion of stiffness: 'wielded speech' (line 30). Some phrases seem well worn (e.g., *billowing waves*, line 217; *crest of the waves*, line 471), which may be viewed as reflecting formulaic diction, and indeed formulaic phrases too are passed on (e.g., *Hrothgar spoke, protector of the Scyldings*, line 371, etc.; *hardy in his helmet*, line 341, etc.). In this context the occasional use of strange-looking compound words and Old English words (such as *byrnies*, *scop*, *wyrd*, glossed by means of footnotes) is particularly arresting.

Syntax, while allowing some apposition and interweaving of elements, is modern, with frequent substitution of grammatical subordination for parataxis and insertion of explanatory connectives, such as *and*, *but* and dashes, the latter as in (with *need* and *dire distress* also in apposition here):

---

[74] Larrington, review of R. M. Liuzza, *Beowulf: A New Verse Translation*, p. 247.
[75] Liuzza, *Beowulf*, p. 46.
[76] Liuzza, *Beowulf*, p. 47.

> whom God sent
> as a solace to the people – He saw their need,
> the dire distress they had endured. (lines 13b–15)

Liuzza's is a domesticating translation but with defamiliarizing touches every so often that in my view add an important dimension. Kermode picks up on this when he comments that 'Liuzza is more confident [than Heaney] in the strangeness of the literal', noting, for example, the 'odd' adjective *bone-adorned* (line 780) in Liuzza's description of Heorot.[77] Other striking compounds include *folk-stead* (line 76), *battle-minded* (line 306) and *sword-panic* (line 583), and I have already alluded to the introduction of Old English words. Heaney it isn't – Liuzza himself writes modestly, 'My own version was not produced with any great pretensions to poetic beauty, or with the kind of profound wrestling with the poetic tradition that Heaney offers'[78] – but the translation admirably fulfils Liuzza's objectives of fluency and precision. Understandably, it (and its supplementary material) is popular with students and instructors, and it is likely to remain so in the years ahead.

The translation by **Alan Sullivan and Timothy Murphy** (2004) is in a volume of the same kind as Liuzza's, but one that provides even more supplementary material, clearly aimed at the beginning student.[79] It includes plot summary, a table of dates, detailed textual annotation, translations of Latin contextual material and translations of extracts from a wide range of poetry and prose in Old English and Old Norse; there are also extracts from a number of previous translations of *Beowulf* (from Turner to Lehmann). The book presents an attractive and convenient package, making life easy for students with no background in Anglo-Saxon literature who are studying *Beowulf* in translation.

The translation also makes life easy for the reader. Written in an imitative metre that is not overly strict, it is freer in its treatment of the sense of the original than that of Liuzza, with considerable restructuring of syntax and recasting of expression, as illustrated by the opening three lines:

> So! The Spear-Danes in days of old
> were led by lords famed for their forays.
> We learned of those princes' power and prowess.

Explanatory and descriptive additions are inserted (*'brusquely* brandished / spear-haft in hand', lines 205–6; *'envious* Unferth', line 444; 'their *elk*-horned hall', line 698; etc.); formulaic language largely dispensed with, and compound words are few and far between, though there are some examples (*soul-slayer*, line 155; *wave-courser*, line 173; *man-scather*, line 639; etc.).

The register is rather formal, with a modern diction punctuated by 'near-archaisms' (*fell affliction*, line 130; *helms*, line 271; *couched with his queen*, line 595; *sojourn to* [sic] *Hell*, line 721; *fire-drake*, line 2376; etc.), rare words (*fulmar*, line

---

77 Kermode, 'The Modern *Beowulf*', p. 11.
78 '*Beowulf* in Translation', p. 24.
79 Sullivan and Murphy, trans., *Beowulf*.

190; *berm*, line 196; *thews*, line 386; etc.) and Old English terms (*byrnies*, *scop*, glossed). With regard to such unusual lexical choices the translators declare that they have taken their cues from Tolkien's practice in his fantasy writing.[80] The resulting diction can appear quaintly mannered and curious: *World's Warder*, line 25; *bevy of devils*, line 677; *Folk-leaders fared*, line 748; and so on.

There are many nice touches in the translation but plenty of wrong notes too: 'raising the rafters' at line 68 sounds more like having a good time than building a hall; 'I knew him once' (line 333) refers more naturally to acquaintance with an adult rather than a child; 'whose gilded gables he knew at a glance' (line 642) suggests that Grendel had to quickly make sure that he was approaching Heorot and not somewhere else; and there are also plenty of questionable translations: 'fair dealing', for example, at line 22, for *lof-dædum*, 'praiseworthy deeds' (*Beowulf*, line 24); 'whose word held his land whole' (line 71), for *se þe his wordes geweald wide hæfde*, 'who widely had power of/by his word' (*Beowulf*, line 79); 'spell' (line 776) for *spel*, 'tale' (*Beowulf*, line 873). And lexical choices often seem distractingly dictated by the requirements of alliteration: obtrusive-looking words invariably occur in stressed alliterating positions (*beach*, line 26; *Baltic*, line 44; *fulmar*, line 190; *berm*, line 196; etc.).

Sullivan and Murphy present the story of *Beowulf* in a lively and fast-paced way. In the process, like other translators, they sacrifice the possibility of conveying much of a feeling of the poetry of the original. Reflective of the pace of the narrative is the fact that this is a translation of *Beowulf* of 2800 lines, not the expected 3182 – not because the translators have left chunks out but because they speed on so swiftly. The passage corresponding to the prologue consists of 47 lines (not 52), that corresponding to fitt 1 has 54 lines (not 62), that corresponding to fitt 2 63 lines (not 74), and so on.

Also aimed at students is the version by **John McNamara** (2005), which appears in a concise volume in the Barnes and Noble Classics series.[81] This book has an Introduction helpful to beginning students, stressing the importance of the Germanic oral tradition to the poetry of *Beowulf*, and the translation is accompanied by short explanatory notes and glosses of particular words. There is a brief section at the end presenting some well-chosen comments on *Beowulf*, from Conybeare to Tolkien, and there is a three-page survey of creative works inspired by the poem. The translation is accurate, intelligent and readable, in a four-stress metre with caesura and extensive use of alliteration and a formal but largely natural-sounding register. It attempts to strike a balance between the domesticating and foreignizing approaches, though tending more towards the former. The balance comes out in a sentence like

> Then was Beow of the Scyldings a beloved king
> for a long time, in the town-forts of the people,
> famed among the folk – his father had passed on. (lines 53–5)

[80] Sullivan and Murphy, *Beowulf*, p. xix.
[81] McNamara, trans., *Beowulf: A New Translation with Introduction and Notes*.

Here we have inversion in the opening phrase, an imitative compound in *town-forts* and a formulaic-sounding alliterative phrase in *famed among the folk*, which are all heightening effects, but the vocabulary is otherwise that of ordinary speech and the closing half-line presents a well-worn modern euphemism for 'died'. McNamara would not claim to be a great poet but his nicely produced book is well positioned to cater for the *Beowulf*-in-translation college market.

The most recent verse translations of *Beowulf* at time of writing are the contrasting versions of Martin Puhvel and Dick Ringler, published in 2006 and 2007, respectively. **Martin Puhvel**'s accessible and unshowy translation, 'intended primarily for readers who possess no, or limited, knowledge of Anglo-Saxon and are thus unable to enjoy the great poem in its original language',[82] is accompanied by a succinct scholarly Introduction and explanatory and interpretative notes and comments, as well as maps, genealogies and a glossary of proper names; Puhvel shows particular interest in matters of legendary history and mythology.

Written in a flexible imitative metre, the translation is a sound, if perhaps unexciting, version that flows well, presenting a clear narrative line while keeping close to the sense of the original. It succeeds, through the use of apposition and other Old-English-like syntactical patterns, in suggesting something of the 'austere terseness and concentrated impact'[83] of the original. Puhvel cultivates a dignified but fairly plain register, in which an elevated tone finds expression through the use of formal, though mostly unornate, language, with much deployment of rhetorical inversion, often with a touch of the archaic about it (*On his pledge he reneged not*, line 82; *until empty stood / the best of buildings*, lines 149–50). There is some stilted phrasing in the translation (*started to utter a speech of contention*, line 498; *much vexed was he with the venture of Beowulf*, line 499), but well-chosen imaginative renderings are also much in evidence (*thoughts of hell / haunted their minds*, lines 181–2, for *helle gemundon / in modsefan*, lines 179–80, 'they thought of hell in their minds'; *Then he laughed in his heart*, line 720, for *Þa his mod ahlog*, line 730, 'Then his mind laughed/exulted'). The translation may be seen as catering particularly for courses that have an interest in studying folkloristic and legendary aspects of *Beowulf*.

The last translation to be noticed here, that of **Dick Ringler**,[84] is also one of the most interesting. As the title of the translation, *Beowulf: A New Translation for Oral Delivery*, proclaims, this is a version for reading aloud, and indeed audio-recordings of oral renditions of Ringler's text are available on CD and online (the full performances of these lasting some three hours).[85] Ringler's translation is preceded by a substantial Introduction (more than one hundred pages) focusing particularly on the poetry of *Beowulf* and the perceived themes of the poem, and the volume also includes translations of three other Old English

---

82 Puhvel, trans., *Beowulf: A Verse Translation and Introduction*; quotation from p. vii.
83 Puhvel, *Beowulf*, p. v.
84 Ringler, *Beowulf: A New Translation for Oral Delivery*.
85 See bibliography below, under 'Ringler', for details.

poems, 'The Fight at Finnsburg', 'A Meditation' (the poem usually referred to as *The Wanderer*) and 'Deor', and a glossary of proper names. Thus it incorporates useful material for studying *Beowulf* (though no annotation or commentary); Ringler's underlying purpose, however, is to present a version of the poem that people today will enjoy orally.

For his translation Ringler adopts a strict form of Old English metre, thus producing a version that gives a strong sense of the sound patterns of the original poetry. In formatting his text on the page he reverts to the nineteenth-century practice of arranging the verse in short lines (half-lines), intending thereby to emphasize the rhythmic independence of each verse-unit. Though this arrangement downplays the linking together of pairs of half-lines, as Ringler declares, 'it also encourages a more fluent and fast-moving reading of the text than the line-by-line layout'.[86]

It is a considerable achievement of Ringler's that despite the constrictions of a metre so ostensibly unsuited to the resources of present-day English the translation reads excellently as convincing narrative verse. Ringler has to sacrifice the intricacy of style of the original and much of its formulaic dimension but his vigorous translation strikingly transmits the rhythm of Old English poetry while effecting a mode of expression that is mostly neither stilted nor strained. Part of the secret here is that Ringler allows himself latitude in his treatment of the sense of the Old English: the translation is free and incorporates judicious pleonasm rather than sticking literally to the surface meaning of the original. The language is formal and decorous but natural-sounding. It conspicuously lacks the archaizing tendencies of many other modern translations and eschews interference with normal Modern English word order.

Ringler's translation lacks the flashes of poetic brilliance we have seen particularly in the versions by Morgan and Alexander but it is lively throughout and has many imaginative touches, not least in additions which expand on the sense of the original: thus, in one short passage, Grendel approaches the 'silent hall' (line 231), he goes 'shambling home / with his shameful spoil' (lines 248–9), his destruction is visible 'in the grey / light of morning' (lines 251–2), and, as a result, Hrothgar

> sat bowed with grief,
> dazed by the dreadful
> death of his friends. (lines 260–2)

The latter clause is a free rendering of the more restrained, and more formulaic, Old English

---

[86] Ringler, *Beowulf*, p. cii. As Ringler also points out (pp. ci–cii), his layout also enables readers visually to distinguish 'normal' verses from the occasional light and heavy verses which the translation takes over from the original. Light verses (which have only one stressed syllable) are indented, and heavy verses (which have three stressed syallables) are set out as beginning further to the left on the page, beyond the 'normal' verse margin.

unbliðe sæt,
þolode ðryðswyð, þegnsorge dreah. (lines 130b–1)

[literally: he sat joyless, the powerful one suffered, endured sorrow for his friends.]

Ringler's register is different from that of the Old English and his language is more graphically descriptive. There is significant losing as well as gaining in evidence in the translation but it presents a compelling and accessible narrative, and it is rich in sound effects, rather than being tiresomely repetitive in its rhythm, a fault of other imitative versions.

Conclusion

These translations, increasing throughout the period in the frequency of their appearance, tell a story of widespread interest in *Beowulf* particularly on the American side of the Atlantic Ocean and of a desire to make the poem available to new general readers and to provide access to it in forms helpful to those studying it in translation. Clearly, it is the latter group that many of the translations are targeted at, and in general the translations for student use have got more attractive in appearance as time has gone on, with the incarnation of the Heaney translation in the Norton Critical Editions series also conforming to this pattern. Another group of *Beowulf* versions belongs to the 'beautiful book' variety. These are more expensive publications, in which the translation is accompanied by art work and photographs, the whole ensemble making the poem look good and offering a pleasing aesthetic experience; the recent illustrated version of the Heaney translation edited by John D. Niles also comes into this category.[87] A final group is made up of translations and adaptations that are essentially poetic engagements with *Beowulf* aimed in the first place at the general reader or the reader of poetry, in the tradition of Edwin Morgan. The groups are not discrete, however, and some versions cater for more than one type of reader. American editions of the version by Heaney, for example, are aimed at all three markets.

In the versions surveyed we see translators being fascinated and challenged by *Beowulf* and responding to it creatively in different ways. The sheer variety of responses to *Beowulf* among our translators is striking, though they operate within familiar theoretical parameters with regard to register, literalness and their degree of foreignness/domestication. Some versions may be seen to work better than others but overall there is an impression of vitality and imagination in them that is to be applauded. None of them provides the last word on the poem, of course, and we can expect new versions to continue to appear in the future. One translation that has not yet been published is that by the American poet/scholar Stephen Glosecki, completed just before his tragically early death

---

[87] Heaney, trans., *Beowulf: An Illustrated Edition*, ed. Niles.

in 2007. Published portions of the translation attest to its muscular imitative and emphatically foreignizing style.[88]

Some literary people still find *Beowulf* irrelevant or are suspicious of its long-standing canonical status (I referred to Terry Eagleton's view in a previous chapter [p. 72]) but it is no longer really the 'dinosaur' at the beginning of English literature that it was when Michael Alexander or Frank Kermode were studying it, a philological text that bored or irritated most students. Since those days the story of *Beowulf* has been brought accessibly by the translations we have been looking at to new readers not necessarily aware of its inherited canonical status or its academic history. Some of these versions give little sense of the poetry of *Beowulf* or little sense of what it is like to read it in Old English, but even they may encourage some people to experience the poem in the original.

Meanwhile in the academic world *Beowulf* has begun to be reimagined in recent decades, entering more than in the past into the mainstream of contemporary critical concerns. Its identity as a patriarchal English monolith has fragmented and scholars are now engaging with it intellectually from a wide range of critical positions. Some of the most interesting approaches were brought together recently in an anthology of essays edited by Eileen Joy and Mary Ramsey,[89] but this does not cover the full range of 'new angles' on *Beowulf*; among the most interesting areas of study has been that concerned with the history of the scholarship of the poem and of its reception in the modern period, to which I hope the present book will make a small contribution.

At the intersection of the academic and the literary stand the verse translators of *Beowulf*, the best of whom bring the poem to life for modern readers and stimulate us to think about it in new ways.

---

[88] Passages from *Beowulf* translated by Glosecki were published in *Birmingham Poetry Review* (Fall–Winter 1999 and Fall–Winter 2000). See further Glosecki, 'Skalded Epic (Make it Old)', in which he reflects about working on translating *Beowulf* and includes his version of lines 2444–71.

[89] Joy and Ramsey, *The Postmodern Beowulf*.

Epilogue

A veritable industry of popular *Beowulf* adaptations and spin-offs has been in evidence in recent years, bringing our hero to life on the page, on the stage, on the cinema/television screen, and on the computer/game-console screen. *Beowulf* has made it into popular culture at last.[1] There is supposed to be no such thing as bad publicity, and so this unprecedented popular attention to the story of *Beowulf* and its hero should be taken as good news for the poem. The new versions of *Beowulf* may even eventually bring some people to the poem itself, curious to sample the original.

There have been notable adaptations of the *Beowulf* story in novelistic form, by Frederick Rebsamen, John Gardner and Michael Crichton, all three of these dating from the 1970s.[2] Rebsamen's *Beowulf Is My Name* takes the form of a retelling of the story in the voice of Beowulf himself, who speaks from an imagined position outside his life and is thus able to include his own death in the narration; this appropriation fills in details about Beowulf and his story which are not given in the poem and includes additional narrative and descriptive material derived from other sources and from the imagination of the adaptor. Gardner's *Grendel* relates the story from the point of view of the monster Grendel, who becomes a conflicted anti-hero, suffering anguish in his hostility to humankind. Crichton in *Eaters of the Dead* cleverly recasts central elements of the story of *Beowulf* and combines them with the narrative of a real tenth-century documentary source chronicling the travels of the Arab Ibn Fadlan among the Norse Rus, with non-fiction merging imperceptibly into fiction and the conceit reinforced by the inclusion of a battery of invented (as well as some genuine) scholarly footnotes; Crichton reported his alarm on returning to the novel some years

---

[1] On popular adaptations and appropriations, see George, *Beowulf: A Reader's Guide to Essential Criticism*, pp. 115–49 (George is particularly interesting on film versions), and Clark and Perkins, ed., *Medieval Culture and the Modern Imagination*.

[2] Rebsamen, *Beowulf Is My Name, and Selected Translations of Other Old English Poems*; Gardner, *Grendel*; Crichton, *Eaters of the Dead*.

later on finding that he could not be certain whether some passages in it were real or made up.³

These novelistic adaptations are now approaching forty years old, but the latter two are still in print and *Eaters of the Dead* was given a new lease of life when it was made into a popular film in 1999, one of a number of filmic versions of the *Beowulf* story to have appeared in recent years.⁴ The most high profile of the *Beowulf* films, the 2007 version directed by Robert Zemeckis, also spawned a glossy picture book⁵ and a computer game (of what is called the 'hack and slash' variety, targeted primarily at young males), and indeed in its flattening 'performance-capture' animation format Zemeckis's film itself has something of the appearance of a computer game. Meanwhile, comic-book and graphic novel versions of *Beowulf* have also been produced⁶ and there has been a steady flow of prose retellings,⁷ and at least one verse retelling, aimed at children.⁸

'One-man' stage performances of *Beowulf* in Modern English verse (presenting abridged versions of the whole poem) were put on in the late 1980s and early 1990s by Julian Glover and in the late 1990s and early 2000s by Felix Nobis,⁹ and Benjamin Bagsby has produced an original-language performance version of *Beowulf*'s fight with Grendel and its aftermath, in which Bagsby accompanies himself on Anglo-Saxon harp; on the DVD recording of a 2006 performance of the recitation a serviceable prose subtitle-translation is provided.¹⁰ And stage musical adaptations of *Beowulf* have also appeared, most notably a full-scale opera by Los Angeles Opera (the latter based on Gardner's *Grendel* rather than *Beowulf* itself).¹¹

---

3   'While I was writing, I felt that I was drawing the line between fact and fiction clearly. [...] But within a few years, I could no longer be certain which passages were real, and which were made up', Crichton, 'A Factual Note', p. 185.
4   *The 13th Warrior*, directed by John McTiernan (1999); note also *Beowulf*, directed by Graham Baker (1999); *Beowulf and Grendel*, directed by Sturla Gunnarsson (2005); *Beowulf*, directed by Robert Zemeckis (2007); *Outlander*, directed by Howard McCain (2008); and the animated films *Grendel Grendel Grendel*, directed by Alexander Stitt (1980; based on John Gardner's novel), and *Beowulf*, directed by Yuri Kulakov (1998).
5   Vaz and Starkey, *The Art of Beowulf*.
6   *Beowulf*, drawn by Michael Uslan and Ricardo Villamonte; *Beowulf*, drawn by Gerry Bingham; *The Collected Beowulf*, drawn by Gareth Hinds; *Beowulf*, written by Stefan Petrucha, drawn by Kody Chamberlain; another spin-off from the Zemeckis movie is the graphic novel *Beowulf*, written by Chris Ryall, drawn by Gabriel Rodriguez.
7   Of these the most enduring has been Sutcliff, *Beowulf: Dragonslayer* (first published 1961); see also Morpurgo, *Beowulf*; Hicks, *Beowulf*.
8   Serraillier, *Beowulf the Warrior*.
9   See above, p. 195.
10 Bagsby, *Beowulf*.
11 See the review of the 2006 Los Angeles Opera production *Grendel: Transcendence of the Great Big Bad*, by Lisa Oliver, 'Beyond *Beowulf*: Los Angeles Opera Brings *Grendel* to the Stage' (Oliver also refers to other musical adaptations).

It is modern verse translations, however, that have been the main focus of attention throughout this book. We noted the beginnings of the verse translation of *Beowulf* in the period when the poem first came into modern consciousness, the nineteenth century, in which only the version by William Morris stood out from the attempts of scholars and aficionados as a serious poetic engagement with the Anglo-Saxon epic, though Morris's treatment of the poem was too strange and uncompromising for most readers. We identified the version of Edwin Morgan as the first major poetic translation of the twentieth century and examined a number of important and influential translations produced in the sixty years since Morgan, highlighting particularly those by Burton Raffel, Michael Alexander and Seamus Heaney but surveying also the range of disparate versions produced by other writers in the same period, a range that reflects the enduring artistic appeal of *Beowulf* and reflects also contending ideas about translation current at the time, and indeed still current today.

In concluding this discussion, it should be observed that Michael Alexander's Penguin Classics translation was not his only version of *Beowulf*. To complete my survey of verse versions, I include here the text of Alexander's '*Beowulf* Reduced':[12]

> There was once a hero called Scyld
> Whose descendant decided to build
>   A magnificent hall
>   With seating for all,
> But some of his best friends got killed.
>
> A visitor, Beowulf the Geat,
> Whose strength was surprisingly great,
>   De-armed the De-mon,
>   Then beheaded its Mum,
> A yet more remarkable feat.
>
> Much later a dragon awoke,
> Sent Beowulf's hall up in smoke.
>   So his fifty-not out
>   Was all up the spout –
> But he killed it, then died. What a bloke!

'Ðær wæs Beowulfes / mærðo mæned' (*Beowulf*, lines 856b–7a), 'There Beowulf's glory was related'.

---

12 Alexander, '*Beowulf* Reduced'. Cf. also the 26-line Maurice Sagoff version in rhyming couplets in his *ShrinkLits: Seventy of the World's Towering Classics Cut Down to Size* (pp. 20–1): 'Monster Grendel's tastes are plainish, / Breakfast? Just a couple Danish [...]'.

Bibliography

Editions, translations, facsimiles, appropriations

Abrams, M. H., and Stephen Greenblatt, ed., *The Norton Anthology of English Literature*, 7th ed., 2 vols (New York: W. W. Norton, 2000); I, 1–465, 'The Middle Ages', ed. Alfred David and E. Talbot Donaldson
Alexander, Michael, trans., *The Earliest English Poems* (Harmondsworth: Penguin, 1966; 2nd ed., 1977; 3rd ed., London, 1991; parallel text edition, Berkeley and Los Angeles, CA: University of California Press, 1970); revised and expanded (with a new introduction) as *The First Poems in English* (London: Penguin, 2008)
——, trans., *Beowulf: A Verse Translation* (Harmondsworth: Penguin, 1973; revised ed., London, 2001)
——, *Twelve Poems* (London: Agenda Editions, 1978)
——, trans., *Old English Riddles from the Exeter Book*, Poetica 11 (London: Anvil Press Poetry, 1980), revised as *Old English Riddles* (2005)
——, ed., *Beowulf: A Glossed Text* (London: Penguin, 1995; revised ed., 2000)
——, 'Beowulf Reduced', *Agenda* 37.4 (2000), p. 84
Amis, Kingsley, *Collected Poems 1944–1979* (London: Hutchinson, 1979)
Arnold, Thomas, ed. and trans., *Beowulf, a Heroic Poem of the Eighth Century, with a Translation, Notes, and Appendix* (London: Longmans Green, 1876)
Bagsby, Benjamin, *Beowulf* (New York: Charles Morrow Productions, 2006)
Baker, Graham, director, *Beowulf* (Capitol Films, 1999)
Bingham, Gerry, graphic artist, *Beowulf* (First Comics Inc., 1984)
Botkine, L., trans., *Beowulf, Épopée Anglo-Saxonne* (Le Havre: Lepelletier, 1877)
Bradley, S. A. J., trans., *Anglo-Saxon Poetry: An Anthology of Old English Poems in Prose Translation, with Introduction and Headnotes* (London: Dent, 1982)
Carson, Ciaran, trans., *The Inferno of Dante Alighieri: A New Translation* (London: Granta, 2002)
Chickering, Howell D., Jr, ed. and trans., *Beowulf: A Dual-Language Edition* (New York: Anchor Books, 1977)
Child, Clarence G., trans., *Beowulf and the Finnesburh Fragment* (Boston, MA: Houghton Mifflin, 1904)
Conybeare, John Josias, trans., *Illustrations of Anglo-Saxon Poetry*, ed. William Daniel Conybeare (London: Harding and Lepard, 1826)

Crichton, Michael, *Eaters of the Dead: The Manuscript of Ibn Fadlan, Relating His Experiences with the Northmen in A.D. 992* (New York: Ballantine Books, 1976; reissued with 'A Factual Note' [dated 1992], London: Arrow Books, 1997)

Crossley-Holland, Kevin, trans., *Beowulf*, with an introduction by Bruce Mitchell, with drawings by Brigitte Hanf (London: Macmillan, 1968); translation also published in Kevin Crossley-Holland, trans., *The Anglo-Saxon World: An Anthology* (Woodbridge: Boydell Press, 1982; Oxford and New York: Oxford University Press, 1984, pp. 74–154); also as Kevin Crossley-Holland, trans., *Beowulf; The Fight at Finnsburh*, edited with an introduction and notes by Heather O'Donoghue (Oxford and New York: Oxford University Press, 1999)

Donaldson, E. Talbot, trans., *Beowulf: A New Prose Translation* (New York: W. W. Norton, 1966)

Earle, John, trans., *The Deeds of Beowulf, Done into Modern Prose* (Oxford: Clarendon Press, 1892)

Ettmüller, Ludwig, trans., *Beowulf. Heldengedicht des achten Jahrhunderts. Zum ersten Male aus dem Angelsächsischen in das Neuhochdeutsche stabreimend übersetzt* (Zurich: Meyer and Zeller, 1840)

——, ed., *Carmen de Beovulfi Gautarum regis rebus praeclare gestis atque interitu, quale fuerit ante quam in manus interpolatoris, monachi Vestsaxonici, inciderat* (Zurich: Zürcher and Fürrer, 1875)

Gardner, John, *Grendel* (New York: Ballantine Books, 1971)

Garmonsway, G. N., and Jacqueline Simpson, trans., *Beowulf and its Analogues*, including 'Archaeology and Beowulf' by Hilda Ellis Davidson (London: Dent, 1968)

Garnett, James M., trans., *Beowulf: An Anglo-Saxon Poem, and The Fight at Finnsburh* (Boston, MA: Ginn, Heath and Co., 1882; 2nd ed., 1885)

Glosecki, Stephen, trans., 'Selections from *Beowulf*, *Birmingham Poetry Review* 21 (Fall–Winter 1999), 15–18, and 23 (Fall–Winter 2000), 9–15

Glover, Julian, ed., *Beowulf*, illustrated by Shiela Mackie, introduced by Magnus Magnusson (Stroud: Sutton Publishing, 2005; first published 1987)

Grant, Paula, trans., *Aldfrith's Beowulf* (Felinfach: Llanerch Publishers, 1995)

Greenfield, Stanley B., trans., *A Readable Beowulf: The Old English Epic Newly Translated*, with an introduction by Alain Renoir (Carbondale and Edwardsville, IL: Southern Illinois University Press, 1982)

Grein, C. W. M., trans., '*Beowulf*, in his *Dichtungen der Angelsachsen* (Göttingen: Georg H. Wigand, 1857), pp. 222–308; revised and published separately as *Beowulf* (Kassel: Georg H. Wigand, 1883)

——, trans., *Bibliothek der angelsächsischen Poesie, stabreimend übersetzt*, 2 vols (Göttingen: Georg H. Wigand, 1857–8)

——, ed., *Beovulf nebst den Fragmenten Finnsburg und Valdere* (Kassel and Göttingen: Georg H. Wigand, 1867)

Grion, Guisto, trans., '*Beovulf*: poema epico anglosassone del vii secolo', *Atti della Real Accademia lucchese di scienze, lettere ed arte* 22 (1883), 197–379

Grundtvig, Nic. Fred. Sev., trans., *Bjowulfs Drape. Et Gothisk Helde-digt fra forrige Aar-tusinde af Angel-Saxisk paa Danske Riim* (Copenhagen: A. Seidelin, 1820)

Gummere, Francis B., trans., *The Oldest English Epic: Beowulf, Finnsburg, Waldere, Deor, Widsith, and the German Hildebrand* (New York: Macmillan, 1909); *Beowulf* translation also published as Francis B. Gummere, trans., *Beowulf*, Harvard Classics 49.1 (New York: P. F. Collier & Son, 1910); Francis B. Gummere, trans., *Beowulf* (Lawrence, KS: Digireads.com, 2005); Francis B. Gummere, trans., *Beowulf: In Old English and New English*, ed. James H. Ford (El Paso, TX: El Paso Norte Press, 2005)

Gunnarsson, Sturla, director, *Beowulf and Grendel* (The Film Works, Eurasia Motion Pictures and Goodweird, 2005)

Haley, Albert W., Jr, trans., *Beowulf* (Boston, MA: Branden Press, 1978)

Hall, John Lesslie, trans., *Beowulf, an Anglo-Saxon Poem, Translated from the Heyne-Socin Text* (Boston, MA: D. C. Heath, 1892)

Hall, John. R. Clark, trans., *Beowulf and the Finnesburg Fragment*, revised edition, revised by C. L. Wrenn, with Prefatory Remarks by J. R. R. Tolkien (London: George Allen & Unwin, 1950; original ed., *Beowulf and the Fight at Finnsburg* [London: Swan Sonnenschein, 1901])

——, trans., *Beowulf: A Metrical Translation into Modern English* (Cambridge: Cambridge University Press, 1914)

Heaney, Seamus, *Death of a Naturalist* (London: Faber, 1966)

——, *Door into the Dark* (London: Faber, 1969)

——, *North* (London: Faber, 1975)

——, *Preoccupations: Selected Prose, 1968–78* (London: Faber, 1984)

——, *The Haw Lantern* (London: Faber, 1987)

——, trans., *Beowulf* (London: Faber, 1999); also published as Seamus Heaney, trans., *Beowulf: A New Verse Translation*, Bilingual Edition (New York: Farrar, Straus & Giroux, 2000; New York: W. W. Norton, 2001; London: Faber, 2007); Seamus Heaney, trans., 'Beowulf, in *The Norton Anthology of English Literature*, ed. Abrams and Greenblatt, I, 29–99 (does not contain Heaney's 'Introduction'); Seamus Heaney, trans., Daniel Donoghue, ed., *Beowulf: A Verse Translation: Authoritative Text, Contexts, Criticism*, Norton Critical Edition (New York: W. W. Norton, 2002); Seamus Heaney, trans., ed. John D. Niles, *Beowulf: An Illustrated Edition* (New York: W. W. Norton, 2007); *Beowulf*, read by Seamus Heaney (Penguin Audiobooks, 2000)

Heyne, Moritz, ed., *Beowulf. Mit ausführlichem Glossar* (Paderborn: Ferdinand Schöningh, 1863)

——, trans., *Beowulf. Angelsächsisches Heldengedicht* (Paderborn: Ferdinand Schöningh, 1863)

Hicks, Penelope, *Beowulf* (London: Kingfisher, 2007)

Hill, Geoffrey, *Mercian Hymns* (London: André Deutsch, 1971)

Hinds, Gareth, graphic artist, *The Collected Beowulf* (The Comic.com, 2000)

Holder, Alfred, ed., *Beowulf*, 2 vols: I: *Abdruck der Handschrift im British Museum*; II: *Berichtigter Text mit knappen Apparat und Wörterbuch* (Freiburg im Breslau: J. C. B. Mohr, 1881, 1884)

Holthausen, Ferdinand, ed., *Beowulf nebst dem Finnsburg-Bruchstück*, 2 vols (Heidelberg: Winter, 1905–6)

Hudson, Marc, trans., *Beowulf: A Translation and Commentary* (Lewisburg, PA: Bucknell University Press/London and Toronto: Associated University Presses, 1990)

Huppé, Bernard F., trans., *Beowulf: A New Translation* (Binghamton, NY: Center for Medieval and Reniassance Studies, 1987)

Jack, George, ed., *Beowulf: A Student Edition* (Oxford: Clarendon Press, 1994)

Kemble, John M., ed., *The Anglo-Saxon Poems of Beowulf, the Travellers Song, and the Battle of Finnesburh* (London: William Pickering, 1833); 2nd ed., ed. and trans., 2 vols: I (1835); II, *A Translation of the Anglo-Saxon Poem of Beowulf, with a Copious Glossary, Preface and Philological Notes* (1837)

Kennedy, Charles W., trans., *Beowulf: The Oldest English Epic, Translated into Alliterative Verse, with a Critical Introduction* (New York: Oxford University Press, 1940)

Kennedy, Thomas C., trans., *Beowulf* (Leawood, KS: Leathers Publishing, 2001)

Kiernan, Kevin, ed., *Electronic Beowulf*, 2 CD-ROMs (London: British Library, 1999)

Klaeber, Fr., ed., *Beowulf and the Fight at Finnsburg*, 3rd ed., with First and Second Supplements (Boston, MA: D. C. Heath, 1950; 3rd ed. originally published 1936)

——, ed., *Klaeber's Beowulf and The Fight at Finnsburg*, 4th ed., ed. R. D. Fulk, Robert E. Bjork and John D. Niles (Toronto: University of Toronto Press, 2008)

Krapp, George Philip, and Elliott Van Kirk Dobbie, ed., *The Anglo-Saxon Poetic Records*, 5 vols (London and New York: Columbia University Press, 1931–53): I, *The Junius Manuscript*, ed. George Philip Krapp (1931); II, *The Vercelli Book*, ed. George Philip Krapp (1932); III, *The Exeter Book*, ed. George Philip Krapp and Elliott Van Kirk Dobbie (1936); IV, *Beowulf and Judith*, ed. Elliott Van Kirk Dobbie (1953); V, *The Paris Psalter and the Meters of Boethius*, ed. George Philip Krapp (1932); VI, *The Anglo-Saxon Minor Poems*, ed. Elliott Van Kirk Dobbie (1942)

Kulakov, Yuri, director, *Beowulf* (S4C, 1998)

Lehmann, Ruth P. M., trans., *Beowulf: An Imitative Translation* (Austin, TX: University of Texas Press, 1988)

Leo, Heinrich, ed., *Altsächsische und angelsächsische Sprachproben* (Halle: Eduard Anton, 1838)

——, ed., *Beowulf, das älteste deutsche, in angelsächsischer Mundart erhaltene, Heldengedicht* (Halle: Eduard Anton, 1839)

Liuzza, R. M., trans., *Beowulf: A New Verse Translation* (Peterborough, Ontario: Broadview Press, 2000)
[Longfellow, Henry Wadsworth,] 'Anglo-Saxon Literature', *North American Review* 17 (1838), 90–134; reprinted in his *Poets and Poetry of Europe* (Philadelphia: Cary & Hart, 1845) [contains a verse translation of lines 189–257 of *Beowulf*, also printed in Longfellow, *The Poetical Works*, pp. 739–40]
Longfellow, Henry Wadsworth, *The Poetical Works of Henry Wadsworth Longfellow* (London: Oxford University Press, 1910)
Lumsden, H. W., trans., *Beowulf, an Old English Poem, Translated into Modern Rhymes* (London: C. Kegan Paul, 1881)
McCain, Howard, director, *Outlander* (Weinstein Company, 2008)
McNamara, John, trans., *Beowulf: A New Translation with Introduction and Notes* (New York: Barnes and Noble, 2005)
McTiernan, John, director, *The 13th Warrior* (Touchstone Pictures, 1999)
Mendelson, Edward, ed., *The English Auden: Poems, Essays and Dramatic Writings 1927–1939* (London: Faber, 1977)
Mitchell, Bruce, and Fred C. Robinson, ed., *Beowulf: An Edition, With Relevant Shorter Texts* (Oxford: Blackwell, 1998)
Morgan, Edwin, trans., *Beowulf: A Verse Translation into Modern English* (Aldington, Kent: Hand and Flower Press, 1952; reprinted Manchester: Carcanet Press, 2002)
——, 'Auld Man's Coronach', *The Glasgow Herald*, 8 August, 1953, p. 3
——, *Themes on a Variation* (Manchester: Carcanet Press, 1988)
——, *Collected Poems* (Manchester: Carcanet Press, 1990)
——, *Nothing is Not Giving Messages: Reflections on Work and Life*, ed. Hamish Whyte (Edinburgh: Polygon, 1990)
Morpurgo, Michael, *Beowulf* (London: Walker Books, 2007)
Morris, William, *The Collected Works of William Morris*, 24 vols (London: Longmans, Green and Co., 1910–15)
——, trans., *The Aeneids of Virgil, The Collected Works of William Morris*, XI
——, and Eiríkr Magnússon, trans., *Grettis Saga: The Story of Grettir the Strong*, in *The Collected Works of William Morris*, VII, xxxvii–279
——, and Eiríkr Magnússon, trans., *Völsunga Saga: The Story of the Volsungs and the Niblungs, with Certain Songs from the Elder Edda*, in *The Collected Works of William Morris*, VII, 281–490
——, and Eiríkr Magnússon, trans., *The Song of Atli*, in *The Collected Works of William Morris*, VII, 446–57
——, and Alfred J. Wyatt, trans., *The Tale of Beowulf, Sometime King of the Weder Geats* (Hammersmith: Kelmscott, 1895)
Nobis, Felix, trans., *Beowulf: An Adaptation* (Cork: Bradshaw Books, 2000)
Osborn, Marijane, trans., *Beowulf: A Verse Translation with Treasures of the Ancient North*, with an introduction by Fred C. Robinson (Berkeley and Los Angeles, CA: University of California Press, 1983)

Petrucha, Stefan, and Kody Chamberlain, graphic artist, *Beowulf* (HarperTrophy, 2007)

Porter, John, trans., *Beowulf: Text and Translation* (Hockwold-cum-Wilton: Anglo-Saxon Books, 1991)

Pound, Ezra, 'The Seafarer from the Anglo-Saxon', in his *Personae* (London: Elkin Mathews, 1909), pp. 64–6; also in his *Selected Poems* (London: Faber, 1948), pp. 18–21

Puhvel, Martin, trans., *Beowulf: A Verse Translation and Introduction* (Lanham, MD: University Press of America, 2006)

Raffel, Burton, trans., *Poems from the Old English*, foreword by Robert P. Creed (Lincoln, NE: University of Nebraska Press, 1960; 2nd [enlarged] ed., 1964)

——, trans., *Beowulf: A New Translation* (New York: New American Library, 1963; reprinted New York: Signet Classics, 1999)

——, trans., *Poems and Prose from the Old English*, ed. Alexandra H. Olsen and Burton Raffel, introductions by Alexandra H. Olsen (New Haven, CT: Yale University Press, 1998)

Rebsamen, Frederick, trans., *Beowulf: A Verse Translation* (New York: HarperCollins, 1991); revised as Frederick Rebsamen, trans., *Beowulf: An Updated Verse Translation* (New York: Perennial Classics, 2004)

—— (Frederick R. Rebsamen), *Beowulf Is My Name, and Selected Translations of Other Old English Poems* (San Francisco, CA: Rinehart Press, 1971)

Ricks, Christopher, ed., *The Poems of Tennyson*, 2nd ed., 3 vols (London: Longman, 1987; first ed. 1969)

Rieu, E. V., trans., *Homer: The Odyssey* (Harmondsworth: Penguin, 1946)

——, trans., *Homer: The Iliad* (Harmondsworth: Penguin, 1950)

Ringler, Dick, trans., *Beowulf: A New Translation for Oral Delivery* (Indianapolis, IN: Hackett Publishing, 2007); performance CD, *Beowulf: The Complete Story: A Drama* (Nemo Productions, 2006); streamed sound file of Ringler reading entire text available at http://digital.library.wisc.edu/1711.dl/Literature.RinglBeowulf

Risden, E. L., trans., *Beowulf: A Student's Edition* (Albany, NY: Whitston Publishing Company, 1994)

Rodrigues, Louis J., trans., *Beowulf and the Fight at Finnsburh: A Modern English Verse Rendering* (London: Runetree Press, 2002)

Rosenthal, Eliot (score), Julie Taymor (production and libretto), J. D. McClatchy (libretto), *Grendel: Transcendence of the Great Big Bad* (Los Angeles Opera production, 2006)

Ryall, Chris, and Gabriel Rodriguez, graphic artist, *Beowulf* (San Diego, CA: IDW Publishing, 2007)

Sagoff, Maurice, *ShrinkLits: Seventy of the World's Towering Classics Cut Down to Size*, revised ed. (New York: Workman Publishing, 1980)

Serraillier, Ian, *Beowulf the Warrior* (Oxford: Oxford University Press, 1954)

Simons, L., trans., *Béowulf, Angelsaksisch Volksepos vertaald in stafrijm en met inleidung en aanteekeningen* (Ghent: A. Siffer, 1896)

Simrock, Karl, trans., *Beowulf. Das älteste deutsche Epos* (Stuttgart and Augsburg: Cotta'scher Verlag, 1859)

Slade, Benjamin, ed. and trans., *Beowulf on Steorarume (Beowulf in Cyberspace): A New Critical Edition of the Text*, www.heorot.dk (2002)

Smith, William, ed., *Choice Specimens of English Literature*, selected by Thomas B. Shaw (London: John Murray, 1864)

Stitt, Alexander, director, *Grendel Grendel Grendel* (distributed by Family Home Entertainment, 1980)

Sullivan, Alan, and Timothy Murphy, trans., *Beowulf*, ed. Sarah M. Anderson (New York: Pearson, 2004)

Sutcliff, Rosemary, *Beowulf: Dragonslayer* (London: Red Fox, 2001; first published 1961)

Swearer, Randolph, Raymond Oliver, trans., and Marijane Osborn, *Beowulf: A Likeness* (New Haven, CT, and London: Yale University Press, 1990)

Thorkelín, Grímur Jónsson, ed. and trans., *De Danorum rebus gestis seculi III & IV: Poëma Danicum dialecto Anglosaxonica* (Copenhagen: Th. E. Rangel, 1815)

Thorpe, Benjamin, ed. and trans., *The Anglo-Saxon Poems of Beowulf, The Scôp or Gleeman's Tale, and The Fight at Finnesburg* (Oxford: John Henry Parker, 1855)

Tinker, Chauncey Brewster, trans., *Beowulf, Translated out of the Old English* (New York: Newson, 1902)

Tolkien, J. R. R., ed. and trans., *Finn and Hengest: The Fragment and the Episode*, ed. Alan Bliss (London: George Allen and Unwin, 1982)

Trask, Richard M., trans., *Beowulf and Judith: Two Heroes* (Lanham, MD: University Press of America, 1998)

Tripp, Raymond P., Jr, trans., *Beowulf: An Edition and Literary Translation in Progress* (Denver, CO: Society for New Language Study, 1990)

Uslan, Michael, and Ricardo Villamonte, graphic artist, *Beowulf* (DC Comics, 1975)

Vaz, Mark Cotta, and Steve Starkey, *The Art of Beowulf* (San Francisco, CA: Chronicle Books, 2007)

von Wolzogen, Hans, trans., *Beovulf (Bärwelf). Das älteste deutsche Heldengedicht* (Leipzig: Philipp Reclam, 1872)

Wackerbarth, A. Diedrich, trans., *Beowulf, an Epic Poem Translated from the Anglo-Saxon into English Verse* (London: William Pickering, 1849)

Waddell, Helen, trans., *Mediaeval Latin Lyrics* (Harmondsworth: Penguin, 1952)

Waterhouse, Mary E., trans., *Beowulf in Modern English: A Translation in Blank Verse* (Cambridge: Bowes and Bowes, 1949)

Wickberg, Rudolf, trans., *Beowulf, en fornengelsk hjeltedikt* (Westervik: C. O. Ekblad, 1889)

Wrenn, C. L., ed., *Beowulf With the Finnesburg Fragment*, 3rd ed., revised W. F. Bolton (London: Harrap, 1973; original ed. 1953; revised ed. Exeter: University of Exeter Press, 1997)

Wright, David, trans., *Beowulf: A Prose Translation with an Introduction* (Harmondsworth: Penguin, 1957)
Zemeckis, Robert, director, *Beowulf* (Warner Bros Pictures, 2007)

Secondary literature

Aitken, A. J., 'Scottish Speech: A Historical View with Special Reference to the Standard English of Scotland', in *Languages of Scotland*, ed. A. J. Aitken and Tom McArthur (Edinburgh: Chambers, 1979), pp. 85–118

Alexander, Michael, *The Poetic Achievement of Ezra Pound* (London: Faber, 1979)

——, *Old English Literature* (London: Macmillan, 1983); revised as *A History of Old English Literature* (Peterborough, Ontario: Broadview Press, 2002)

——, 'Tennyson's "Battle of Brunanburh"', *Tennyson Research Bulletin* 4.4 (1985), 151–61

—— (M. J. Alexander), 'Old English Poetry into Modern English Verse', *Translation and Literature* 3 (1994), 69–75

——, 'Cracking the Norse Code' (review of Seamus Heaney's *Beowulf*), *The Observer*, 26 September, 1999, p. 111

Allen, Syd, '*Beowulf* Translations.net', www.beowulftranslations.net/

Arnold, Matthew, *On Translating Homer: Three Lectures Given at Oxford* (London: Longman, Green, Longman and Roberts, 1861)

Barnstone, Willis, *The Poetics of Translation: History, Theory, Practice* (New Haven, CT, and London: Yale University Press)

Bassnett, Susan, *Translation Studies* (London and New York, 1980)

Bäuml, Franz H., 'Varieties and Consequences of Medieval Literacy and Illiteracy', *Speculum* 55 (1980), 237–65

Benjamin, Walter, 'The Task of the Translator', trans. Harry Zohn, in *The Translation Studies Reader*, ed. Venuti, pp. 75–85 [originally published as 'Die Aufgabe der Übersetzung' as the foreword to Benjamin's translation of Charles Baudelaire's *Tableaux parisiens* (Heidelberg: R. Weissbach, 1923)]

Bernstein, R. B., *Thomas Jefferson* (New York: Oxford University Press, 2003)

Bessinger, Jess B., Jr, and Robert F. Yeager, ed., *Approaches to Teaching Beowulf*, Approaches to Teaching Masterpieces of World Literature 4 (New York: Modern Language Association of America, 1984)

Bjork, Robert E., 'Grímur Jónsson Thorkelin's Preface to the First Edition of *Beowulf*, *Scandinavian Studies* 68 (1996), 291–320

——, and John D. Niles, ed., *A Beowulf Handbook* (Lincoln, NE: University of Nebraska Press; Exeter: University of Exeter Press, 1997)

——, and Anita Obermeier, 'Date, Provenance, Author, Audiences', in *A Beowulf Handbook*, ed. Bjork and Niles, pp. 13–34

Bliss, Alan J., *The Metre of Beowulf*, revised ed. (Oxford: Blackwell, 1967)

Blockley, Mary, *Aspects of Old English Poetic Syntax: Where Clauses Begin* (Urbana and Chicago, IL: University of Illinois Press, 2001)

Boenig, Robert, 'The Importance of Morris's *Beowulf*', *Journal of the William Morris Society* 12 (1997), 7–13

Bolter, Jay David, and Richard Grusin, *Remediation: Understanding New Media* (Cambridge, MA: MIT Press, 2000)

Bonjour, Adrien, *The Digressions in Beowulf* (Oxford: Blackwell, 1950)

Bradley, Henry, '*Beowulf*', *Encyclopædia Britannica*, 11th ed. (London: Encyclopædia Britannica, 1910), III, 758–61

Brearton, Fran, 'Heaney and the Feminine', in *The Cambridge Companion to Seamus Heaney*, ed. Bernard O'Donoghue, pp. 73–91

Brodeur, Arthur G., *The Art of Beowulf* (Berkeley and Los Angeles, CA: University of California Press, 1959)

Brooke, Stopford A., *The History of Early English Literature, being the History of English Poetry from its Beginnings to the Accession of King Alfred*, 2 vols (London: Macmillan, 1892)

——, *English Literature from the Beginning to the Conquest* (London: Macmillan, 1898)

Brophy, Brigid, Michael Levey and Charles Osborne, *Fifty Works of English Literature We Could Do Without* (London: Rapp and Carroll, 1967)

Caie, Graham, '*Beowulf* – Dinosaur, Monster or Visionary Poem?', *European English Messenger* 10.2 (2001), 68–70

Cavill, Paul, 'Christianity and Theology in *Beowulf*', in *The Christian Tradition in Anglo-Saxon England: Approaches to Current Scholarship and Teaching*, ed. Paul Cavill (Cambridge: D. S. Brewer, 2004), pp. 15–39

Chase, Colin, ed., *The Dating of Beowulf* (Toronto: University of Toronto Press, 1981; reissued 1997, with an afterword by Nicholas Howe)

Chickering, Howell, review of Marc Hudson, trans., *Beowulf*, and Randolph Swearer, Raymond Oliver and Marijane Osborn, *Beowulf: A Likeness*, *Speculum* 67 (1992), 689–94

——, 'Beowulf and Heaneywulf', *Kenyon Review* 24.1 (2002), 160–78

Clark, David, and Nicholas Perkins, ed., *Anglo-Saxon Culture and the Modern Imagination* (Cambridge: D. S. Brewer, 2010)

Clemoes, Peter, *Interactions of Thought and Language in Old English Poetry*, CSASE 12 (Cambridge: Cambridge University Press, 1995)

Colley, Linda, *Britons: Forging the Nation 1707–1837*, revised ed. (New Haven, CT, and London: Yale University Press, 2005; first ed. 1992)

Connell, P. J., 'Rieu, Emile Victor (1887–1972)', *The Oxford Dictionary of National Biography*, ed. Matthew and Harrison, XLVI, 963–4

Cook, Albert C., 'The Possible Begetter of the Old English *Beowulf* and *Widsith*', *Transactions of the Connecticut Academy of Arts and Sciences* 25 (1921–2), 281–346

Cooley, Franklin D., 'Early Danish Criticism of *Beowulf*', *English Literary History* 7 (1940), 45–67

Corbett, John, 'The *Seafarer*, Visibility and the Translation of a West Saxon Elegy into English and Scots', *Translation and Literature* 10 (2001), 157–73

Crane, John Kenny, '"To Thwack or Be Thwacked": An Evaluation of Available Translations and Editions of *Beowulf*', *College English* 32 (1970–1), 321–40

Creed, Robert P., '"... Wél-hwelć Gecwæþ ..."': The Singer as Architect', *Tennessee Studies in Literature* 11 (1966), 131–43

Cunningham, Valentine, 'Thou Art Translated: Bible Translating, Heretic Reading and Cultural Transformation', in *Metamorphosis: Structures of Cultural Transformations*, ed. Jürgen Schlaeger, REAL: Yearbook of Research in English and American Literature 20 (Tübingen: Gunter Narr, 2005), pp. 113–27

——, 'Interlinearversitility, or, The Anxieties of Translating', unpublished lecture (April 2006)

David, Alfred, 'The Nationalities of *Beowulf*: Anglo-Saxon Attitudes', in *Beowulf in Our Time: Teaching Beowulf in Translation*, ed. Ramsey, pp. 3–21

Davis, Kathleen, *Deconstruction and Translation* (Manchester: St Jerome Publishing, 2001)

D'Israeli, I., *Amenities of Literature, Consisting of Sketches and Characters of English Literature*, 3 vols (London: Edward Moxon, 1841); revised ed., Isaac Disraeli, *Amenities of Literature, Consisting of Sketches and Characters of English Literature*, ed. B. Disraeli, 2 vols (London: Routledge, Warnes and Routledge, 1859)

Dolan, Terence Patrick, ed., *A Dictionary of Hiberno-English: The Irish Use of English*, 2nd ed. (Dublin: Gill and Macmillan, 2004)

Donoghue, Daniel, 'Word Order and Poetic Style: Auxiliary and Verbal in *The Metres of Boethius*', *Anglo-Saxon England* 15 (1987), 169–96

——, 'The Philologer Poet: Seamus Heaney and the Translation of *Beowulf*', in *Beowulf: A Verse Translation*, trans. Heaney, ed. Donoghue, pp. 237–47; reprinted, with revisions, from *Harvard Review* 19 (2000), 12–21

Dryden, John, 'John Dryden: From the Preface to *Ovid's Epistles*', in *The Translation Studies Reader*, ed. Venuti, pp. 38–42

Eagleton, Terry, 'Hasped and Hooped and Hirpling: Heaney Conquers *Beowulf*', *London Review of Books*, 11 November, 1999, p. 16

Eco, Umberto, *Mouse or Rat? Translation as Negotiation* (London: Weidenfeld and Nicholson, 2003)

Eliason, Norman E., 'The "Improvised Lay" in *Beowulf*', *Philological Quarterly* 31 (1952), 171–9

F. L. E., 'Obituary, Francis Diedrich Wackerbarth', *Monthly Notices of the Royal Astronomical Society* 45 (1885), 200–3

Filppula, Markku, *A Grammar of Irish English* (London: Routledge, 1999)

Finlay, Alison, 'Putting a Bawn into *Beowulf*', in *Seamus Heaney: Poet, Critic, Translator*, ed. Ashby Bland Crowder and Jason David Hall (Basingstoke: Palgrave Macmillan, 2007), pp. 136–54

Fjalldal, Magnús, 'To Fall by Ambition – Grímur Thorkelín and his *Beowulf* Edition', *Neophilologus* 92 (2008), 321–32

Foys, Martin K., *Virtually Anglo-Saxon: Old Media, New Media, and Early Medieval Studies in the Late Age of Print* (Gainesville, FL: University Press of Florida, 2007)

Frank, Roberta, 'Sharing Words with *Beowulf*', in *Intertexts: Studies in Early Insular Culture Presented to Paul E. Szarmach*, ed. Virginia Blanton and Helene Scheck, MRTS 334 (Tempe, AZ: Arizona Center for Medieval and Renaissance Studies, 2008), pp. 3–15

——, 'A Scandal in Toronto: The Dating of *Beowulf* a Quarter Century On', *Speculum* 84 (2007), 843–64

Frantzen, Allen J., *Desire for Origins: New Language, Old English, and Teaching the Tradition* (New Brunswick, NJ, and London: Rutgers University Press, 1991)

——, and John D. Niles, ed., *Anglo-Saxonism and the Construction of Social Identity* (Gainesville, FL: University Press of Florida, 1997)

—— (Allen Frantzen), 'By the Numbers: Anglo-Saxon Scholarship at the Century's End', in *A Companion to Anglo-Saxon Literature*, ed. Pulsiano and Treharne, pp. 472–95

Fulk, R. D., ed., *Interpretations of Beowulf: A Critical Anthology* (Bloomington and Indianapolis, IN: University of Indiana Press, 1991)

—— (Robert D. Fulk), 'The Textual Criticism of Frederick Klaeber's *Beowulf*, in *Constructing Nations, Reconstructing Myth*, ed. Wawn, pp. 131–53

Garmonsway, G. N., review of Charles W. Kennedy, *Beowulf: The Oldest English Epic, Translated into Alliterative Verse*, *The Year's Work in English Studies* 21 (1940), 34

George, Jodi-Anne, *Beowulf: A Reader's Guide to Essential Criticism* (Basingstoke: Palgrave Macmillan, 2010)

Girvan, Ritchie, *Beowulf and the Seventh Century: Language and Content* (London: Methuen, 1935; reprinted 1971, with a new chapter by Rupert Bruce-Mitford)

Glosecki, Stephen, 'Skalded Epic (Make it Old)', in *Beowulf in Our Time*, ed. Ramsey, pp. 41–66 (an earlier version of this had appeared in *PN Review* 22.5 [2000], 52–5)

Greenfield, Stanley B., and Fred C. Robinson, *A Bibliography of Publications on Old English Literature to the End of 1972* (Toronto: University of Toronto Press, 1980)

Gregson, Ian, 'Edwin Morgan's Metamorphoses', *English* 39 (1990), 149–64

Gruber, Loren C., '"So". So What? It's a Culture War. That's "Hwæt!"', In *Geardagum* 23 (2002), 67–84

Gummere, Francis B., 'The Translation of *Beowulf*, and the Relations of Ancient and Modern English Verse', *American Journal of Philology* 7 (1886), 46–78

Haarder, Andreas, *Beowulf: The Appeal of a Poem* (Copenhagen: Akademisk Forlag, 1975)

Hall, J. R., 'The First Two Editions of *Beowulf*, Thorkelin's (1815) and Kemble's (1833)', in *The Editing of Old English: Papers from the 1990 Manchester Conference*, ed. D. G. Scragg and Paul E. Szarmach (Woodbridge and Rochester, NY: D. S. Brewer, 1994), pp. 239–50

———, 'Mid-Nineteenth-Century American Anglo-Saxonism: The Question of Language', in *Anglo-Saxonism and the Construction of Social Identity*, ed. Frantzen and Niles, pp. 133–56

———, 'Anglo-Saxon Studies in the Nineteenth Century: England, Denmark, America', in *A Companion to Anglo-Saxon Literature*, ed. Pulsiano and Treharne, pp. 434–54

Hauer, Stanley R., 'Thomas Jefferson and the Anglo-Saxon Language', *PMLA* 98 (1983), 879–98

Henderson, Ebenezer, *Iceland; or the Journal of a Residence in that Island during the Years 1814 and 1815*, 2 vols (Edinburgh: Oliphant, Waugh and Innes, 1818)

Hickey, Raymond, *Irish English* (Cambridge: Cambridge University Press, 2007)

Hill, John, '*Beowulf* Editions for the Ancestors: Cultural Genealogy and Power in the Claims of Nineteenth-Century English and American Editors and Translators', in *Constructing Nations, Reconstructing Myth*, ed. Wawn, pp. 53–69

———, 'Translating Social Speech and Gesture in *Beowulf*', in *Beowulf in Our Time: Teaching Beowulf in Translation*, ed. Ramsey, pp. 67–79

Honegger, Thomas, and Sabine Müller, 'Re-forging the Ancestral Tongue – Seamus Heaney's New Translation of *Beowulf*', in *Fäschen Faux Fakes*, ed. Thomas Honegger, Thomas Hunkeler and Sylvie Jeanneret (Bern: Peter Lang, 2000), pp. 133–48

Horsman, Reginald, *Race and Manifest Destiny: The Origins of American Racial Anglo-Saxonism* (Cambridge, MA: Harvard University Press, 1981)

Howe, Nicholas, *Migration and Mythmaking in Anglo-Saxon England* (New Haven, CT, and London: Yale University Press, 1989)

———, 'Scullionspeak', *The New Republic* 222.9 (2000), 32-7

———, '*Beowulf* in the House of Dickens', in *Latin Learning and English Lore*, ed. O'Brien O'Keeffe and Orchard, I, 421-39

Howlett, David, *British Books in Biblical Style* (Dublin: Four Courts Press, 1997)

Hunter, Fred, 'Morley, Henry (1822-1894)', in *The Oxford Dictionary of National Biography*, ed. Matthew and Harrison, XXXIX, 222-3

Huppé, Bernard F., *The Hero in the Earthly City: A Reading of Beowulf*, MRTS 33 (Binghampton, NY: State University of New York Press, 1984)

Irving, Edward B., Jr, 'Reviews of Recent Translations', *Yearbook of Comparative and General Literature* 15 (1966), 67-70

———, *A Reading of Beowulf* (New Haven, CT, and London: Yale University Press, 1968)

———, *Rereading Beowulf* (Philadelphia: University of Pennsylvania Press, 1989)

———, 'Christian and Pagan Elements', in *A Beowulf Handbook*, ed. Bjork and Niles, pp. 175-92

———, 'The Charge of the Light Brigade: Tennyson's *Battle of Brunanburh*', in *Literary Appropriations of the Anglo-Saxons*, ed. Donald Scragg and Carole Weinberg, CSASE 29 (Cambridge: Cambridge University Press, 2000), pp. 174-93

Jones, Charles, *The English Language in Scotland: An Introduction to Scots* (Edinburgh: Tuckwell, 2002)
——, ed., *The Edinburgh History of the Scots Language* (Edinburgh: Edinburgh University Press, 1997)
Jones, Chris, 'Edwin Morgan in Conversation', *PN Review* 31.2 (2004), 47–51
——, 'Edwin Morgan', in *British Writers: Supplement IX*, ed. Jay Parini (New York: Charles Scribner's Sons, 2004), pp. 157–70
——, *Strange Likeness: The Use of Old English in Twentieth-Century Poetry* (Oxford: Oxford University Press, 2006)
——, 'The Reception of William Morris's *Beowulf*, in *Writing on the Image: Reading William Morris*, ed. David Latham (Toronto: University of Toronto Press, 2007), pp. 197–208
Joy, Eileen A., and Mary K. Ramsey, ed., *The Postmodern Beowulf: A Critical Casebook* (Morgantown, WV: West Virginia University Press, 2006)
——, 'Introduction: Liquid *Beowulf*, in *The Postmodern Beowulf*, ed. Joy and Ramsey, pp. xxix–lxvii
Kemble, John Mitchell, *The Saxons in England: A History of the English Commonwealth till the Period of the Norman Conquest*, 2 vols (London: Longman, Brown, Green and Longmans, 1849)
Ker, W. P., *The Dark Ages* (Edinburgh: Blackwood, 1904)
Kermode, Frank, 'The Modern *Beowulf*, in Frank Kermode, *Pleasing Myself: From Beowulf to Philip Roth* (London: Penguin, 2001), pp. 1–12
Kiernan, Kevin S., review of Swearer et al. *Beowulf: A Likeness*, *Envoi* 3.1 (1991), 263–6
Kimbel, Ben, 'Mr. Morgan's *Beowulf*: C–', *Poetry* 83 (1953–4), 44–8
Klaeber, Fr., 'Die christlichen Elemente im *Beowulf*', *Anglia* 35 (1911), 111–36, 249–70, 453–83; 36 (1912), 169–99; trans. Paul Battles, *The Christian Elements in Beowulf*, Old English Newsletter Subsidia 24 (Kalamazoo, MI: Medieval Institute, Western Michigan University, 1996)
Kliman, Bernice W., 'Teaching *Beowulf* in Translation to Undergraduates', in *Approaches to Teaching Beowulf*, ed. Bessinger and Yeager, pp. 61–4
Lapidge, Michael, 'The Archetype of *Beowulf*', *Anglo-Saxon England* 29 (2000), 5–41
Larrington, Carolyn, review of R. M. Liuzza, *Beowulf: A New Verse Translation*, *RES*, New Series 52 (2001), 246–8
Lehmann, Ruth P., 'Broken Cadences in *Beowulf*', *English Studies* 56 (1975), 1–13
——, 'Contrasting Rhythms of Old English and New English', in *Linguistic and Literary Studies in Honor of Archibald A. Hill, Vol. IV*, ed. Mohammad Ali Jazayery et al., Trends in Linguistics, Studies and Monographs 10 (Berlin and New York: Mouton de Gruyter, 1979), pp. 121–6
Lerer, Seth, *Error and the Academic Self: The Scholarly Imagination, Medieval to Modern* (New York: Columbia University Press, 2002)
Lindsay, Jack, *William Morris: His Life and Work* (London: Constable, 1975)

Liuzza, R. M., 'Lost in Translation: Some Versions of *Beowulf* in the Nineteenth Century', *English Studies* 83 (2002), 281–95

——, '*Beowulf* in Translation – Problems and Possibilities', in *Beowulf in Our Time: Teaching Beowulf in Translation*, ed. Ramsey, pp. 23–40

——, 'Scribes of the Mind: Editing Old English, in Theory and in Practice', in *The Power of Words: Anglo-Saxon Studies Presented to Donald G. Scragg on his Seventieth Birthday*, ed. Hugh Magennis and Jonathan Wilcox, Medieval European Studies 8 (Morgantown, WV: West Virginia University Press, 2006), pp. 243–77

Lumianski, R. M., review of Mary E. Waterhouse, trans., *Beowulf in Modern English*, *JEGP* 50 (1951), 247–8

MacCarthy, Fiona, *William Morris: A Life for our Time* (New York: Alfred A. Knopf, 1995)

MacDougall, Hugh A., *Racial Myth in English History: Trojans, Teutons, and Anglo-Saxons* (Montreal: Harvard House; Hanover, NH: University Press of New England, 1982)

MacKenzie, Raymond N., 'Lane, Sir Allen (1902–70)', in *The Oxford Dictionary of National Biography*, ed. Matthew and Harrison, XXXII, 415–17

Magennis, Hugh, 'Audience(s), Reception, Literacy', in *A Companion to Anglo-Saxon Literature*, ed. Pulsiano and Treharne, pp. 84–101

——, 'Germanic Legend and Old English Heroic Poetry', in *A Companion to Medieval Poetry*, ed. Corinne Saunders (Chichester: Wiley-Blackwell, 2010), pp. 85–100

——, 'Translating *Beowulf*: Edwin Morgan and Seamus Heaney', in *Modern Scottish and Irish Poetry*, ed. Peter Mackay, Edna Longley and Fran Brearton (Cambridge: Cambridge University Press, 2011), pp. 147–60

Matthew, H. C. G., and B. Harrison, ed., *The Oxford Dictionary of National Biography, in Association with The British Academy, From the Earliest Times to the Year 2000*, 60 vols (Oxford, Oxford University Press, 2004)

McAfee, C. I., ed., *A Concise Ulster Dictionary* (Oxford: Oxford University Press, 1996)

McCarra, Kevin, 'Edwin Morgan: Lives and Work', in *About Edwin Morgan*, ed. Robert Crawford and Hamish Whyte (Edinburgh: Edinburgh University Press, 1990), pp. 1–9

McCarthy, Conor, *Seamus Heaney and Medieval Poetry* (Cambridge: D. S. Brewer, 2008)

McGillivray, Murray, 'Towards a Post-Critical Edition: Theory, Hypertext, and the Presentation of Middle English Works', *Text* 7 (1994), 175–99

McGowan, Joseph, 'Heaney, Cædmon, *Beowulf*, *New Hibernia Review* 6.2 (2002), 25–42

Mitchell, Bruce, 'The Dangers of Disguise: Old English Texts in Modern Punctuation', *RES* 31 (1980), 385–413

——, *Old English Syntax*, 2 vols (Oxford: Clarendon Press, 1985)

——, '*Apo koinou* in Old English Poetry?', *NM* 100 (1999), 477–97

Momma, H., *The Composition of Old English Poetry*, CSASE 20 (Cambridge: Cambridge University Press, 1997)
—— (Haruko Momma), and Michael Powell, 'Death and Nostalgia: The Future of *Beowulf* in the Post-National Discipline of English', *Literature Compass* 4 (2007), 1345–53
Morgan, Edwin, 'Dunbar and the Language of Poetry', *Essays in Criticism* 2.2 (1952), 138–57
——, 'The Beatnik in the Kailyard', *New Saltire* 3 (1962), 65
[Morley, Henry,] 'A Primitive Old Epic', *Household Words* 17 (1857–8), 459–64
Morley, Henry, *English Writers*, I, Part 1, *Celts and Anglo-Saxons; with an Introductory Sketch of the Four Periods of English Literature* (London: Chapman and Hall, 1867)
——, *Sketches of Longer Works in English Verse and Prose* (London: Cassell, Petter, Galpin & Co., n.d.)
Nicholson, Colin, *Edwin Morgan: Inventions of Modernity* (Manchester: Manchester University Press, 2002)
Niles, John D., *Beowulf: The Poem and its Tradition* (Cambridge, MA, and London: Harvard University Press, 1983)
——, 'Rewriting *Beowulf*: The Task of Translation', *College English* 55 (1993), 858–78
——, 'Introduction: *Beowulf*, Truth, and Meaning', in *A Beowulf Handbook*, ed. Bjork and Niles, pp. 1–12
——, 'Reconceiving *Beowulf*: Poetry as Social Praxis', *College English* 61 (1998), 143–66
——, *Old English Heroic Poems and the Social Life of Texts*, Studies in the Early Middle Ages 20 (Turnhout: Brepols, 2007)
——, 'Heaney's *Beowulf* Six Years Later', in his *Old English Heroic Poems and the Social Life of Texts*, pp. 325–53
Nolan, Barbara, and Morton W. Bloomfield, '*Beotword, gilpcwidas*, and the *gilphlædan* Scop of *Beowulf*, *JEGP* 79 (1980), 499–516
O'Brien O'Keeffe, Katherine, *Visible Song: Transitional Literacy in Old English Verse*, CSASE 4 (Cambridge: Cambridge University Press, 1990)
——, and Andy Orchard, ed., *Latin Learning and English Lore: Studies in Anglo-Saxon Literature for Michael Lapidge*, 2 vols (Toronto: University of Toronto Press, 2005)
O'Donoghue, Bernard, ed., *The Cambridge Companion to Seamus Heaney* (Cambridge: Cambridge University Press, 2009)
O'Donoghue, Heather, 'Heaney, *Beowulf* and the Medieval Literature of the North', in *The Cambridge Companion to Seamus Heaney*, ed. Bernard O'Donoghue, pp. 192–205
Oliver, Lisa, 'Beyond *Beowulf*: Los Angeles Opera Brings *Grendel* to the Stage', *Medieval Academy News* 156 (Winter 2006), 9
Ong, Walter J., *Orality and Literacy: The Technologizing of the Word* (London and New York: Routledge, 1982)

O'Rawe, Des, 'The Poet as Translator', *The Irish Review* 27 (2001), 180–3

Orchard, Andy, 'Oral Tradition', in *Reading Old English Texts*, ed. Katherine O'Brien O'Keeffe (Cambridge: Cambridge University Press, 1997), pp. 101–23

——, *A Critical Companion to Beowulf* (Cambridge: D. S. Brewer, 2003)

Osborn, Marijane, 'Translations, Versions, Illustrations', in *A Beowulf Handbook*, ed. Bjork and Niles, pp. 341–72

Palmer, D. J., *The Rise of English Studies: An Account of the Study of English Language and Literature from its Origins to the Making of the Oxford English School* (London: Oxford University Press, 1965)

Pasternack, Carol Braun, *The Textuality of Old English Poetry*, CSASE 13 (Cambridge: Cambridge University Press, 1995)

Payne, Richard, 'The Rediscovery of Old English Poetry in the English Literary Tradition', in *Anglo-Saxon Scholarship: The First Three Centuries*, ed. Carl Berkhout and Milton McC. Gatch (Boston, MA: G. K. Hall, 1982), pp. 149–66

Phillips, Helen, 'Seamus Heaney's *Beowulf*, in *The Art of Seamus Heaney*, ed. Tony Curtis (Dublin: Wolfhound Press, 2001), pp. 265–85

Prickett, Stephen, *Words and The Word: Language, Poetics and Biblical Interpretation* (Cambridge: Cambridge University Press, 1986)

Pulsiano, Phillip, and Elaine Treharne, ed., *A Companion to Anglo-Saxon Literature* (Oxford: Blackwell, 2001)

Quirk, Randolph, 'Dasent, Morris and Principles of Translation', *Saga-Book of the Viking Society for Northern Research* 14 (1953–5), 64–77

Raffel, Burton, review of Edwin Morgan, trans., *Beowulf*, *College English* 24 (1962–3), p. 587

——, 'On Translating *Beowulf*, *Yale Review* 54 (1964–5), 532–52; reprinted in his *The Forked Tongue*, pp. 58–70

——, *The Forked Tongue: A Study of the Translation Process* (The Hague: Mouton, 1971)

——, review of S. B. Greenfield, *A Readable Beowulf*, *In Geardagum* 5 (1983), 91–6

——, *The Art of Translating Poetry* (University Park, PA: Pennsylvania State University Press, 1988)

——, 'Translating Medieval European Poetry', in *The Craft of Translation*, ed. John Biguenet and Rainer Schulte (Chicago: University of Chicago Press, 1989), pp. 28–53

Ramsey, Mary K., ed., *Beowulf in Our Time: Teaching Beowulf in Translation*, Old English Newsletter Subsidia 31 (Kalamazoo, MI: The Medieval Institute, Western Michigan University, 2002)

Raw, Barbara C., *The Art and Background of Old English Poetry* (London: Arnold, 1978)

Rexroth, Kenneth, 'Classics Revisited – IV: *Beowulf*, *Saturday Review*, 10 April, 1968, p. 27

Ricks, Christopher, *Tennyson* (New York: Macmillan, 1972)

Robinson, Douglas, *Translation and Taboo* (DeKalb, IL: Northern Illinois University Press, 1996)
Robinson, Fred C., *Beowulf and the Appositive Style* (Knoxville, TN: University of Tennessee Press, 1985)
——, 'Ezra Pound and the Old English Translational Tradition', in his *The Tomb of Beowulf and Other Essays on Old English* (Oxford: Blackwell, 1993), pp. 259–74
——, '*Mise en page* in Old English Manuscripts and Printed Texts', in *Latin Learning and English Lore*, ed. O'Brien O'Keeffe and Orchard, II, 363–75
Robinson, Mairi, ed., *The Concise Scots Dictionary* (London: Chambers, 1996)
Rypins, Stanley, review of Mary E. Waterhouse, trans., *Beowulf in Modern English*, *Speculum* 26 (1951), 420–1
Sauer, Hans, 'Heaneywulf, Liuzzawulf: Two Recent Translations of *Beowulf*', in *Of Remembraunce the Keye: Medieval Literature and its Impact through the Ages: Festschrift for Karl Heinze Göller on the Occasion of his 80th Birthday*, ed. Uwe Böker, in collaboration with Dieter A. Berger and Noel Harold Kaylor, Jr (Frankfurt: Peter Lang, 2004), pp. 331–47
——, and Inge B. Milfull, 'Seamus Heaney: Ulster, Old English, and *Beowulf*', in *Bookmarks from the Past: Studies in Early English Language and Literature in Honour of Helmut Gneuss*, ed. Lucia Kornexl and Ursula Lenke, Münster Universitätsschriften, Texte und Untersuchungen zur Englischen Philologie 30 (Frankfurt: Peter Lang, 2003), pp. 81–141
Scannell, J. N., review of Mary E. Waterhouse, trans., *Beowulf in Modern English*, *Modern Language Review* 46 (1951), 300–1
Schipper, William, review of Frederick Rebsamen, *Beowulf: A Verse Translation*, *Anglia* 113 (1995), 377–9
Schleiermacher, Friedrich, 'On the Different Methods of Translating' ['Ueber die verschiedenen Methoden des Uebersetzens', 1813], trans. Susan Bernofsky, in *The Translation Studies Reader*, ed. Venuti, pp. 43–63
Scragg, Donald G., 'The Nature of Old English Verse', in *The Cambridge Companion to Old English Literature*, ed. Malcolm Godden and Michael Lapidge (Cambridge: Cambridge University Press, 1991), pp. 55–70
Shippey, Thomas A., 'Structure and Unity', in *A Beowulf Handbook*, ed. Bjork and Niles, pp. 149–74
—— (T. A. Shippey), and Andreas Haarder, ed., *Beowulf: The Critical Heritage* (London and New York: Routledge, 1998)
—— (T. A. Shippey), 'Introduction', in *Beowulf: The Critical Heritage*, ed. Shippey and Haarder, pp. 1–74
—— (Tom Shippey), '*Beowulf* for the Big-Voiced Scullions', *Times Literary Supplement* (1 October, 1999), 9–10
—— (Tom Shippey), '*Beowulf: A Verse Translation*, Revised Edition by Michael Swanton', in *The Wider Scope of English: Papers in English Language and Literature from the Bamburg Conference of the International Association of University Professors of English*, ed. Herbert Grabes and Wolfgang Vierekm, Bamberger

Beiträge zur Englischen Sprachwissenschaft 51 (Frankfurt: Peter Lang, 2006), pp. 87–91

Shklovsky, Viktor, 'Art as Technique', trans. Lee T. Lemon and Marion J. Reiss, in *Literary Theory: An Anthology*, ed. Julie Rivkin and Michael Ryan (Oxford: Blackwell, 1998), pp. 17–23

Short, Douglas D., 'Translations of *Beowulf*', in *Approaches to Teaching Beowulf*, ed. Bessinger and Yeager, pp. 7–14

Sieper, Ernst, *Die altenglishe Elegie* (Strassburg: K. J. Trübner, 1915)

Sievers, Eduard, 'Zur Rhythmik des germanischen Alliterationverses', *Beiträge zur Geschichte der deutschen Sprache und Literatur* 10 (1885), 209–314, 451–545

Simpson, John A., and Edmund S. C. Weiner, ed., *Oxford English Dictionary*, 2nd ed., 20 vols (Oxford: Oxford University Press, 1989)

[Smith, J.,] 'Editor's Choice', *Poetry Review* 54 (1963), 107–8

Stanley, Eric, 'Translation from Old English: "The Garbaging War-Hawk", or, The Literal Materials from Which the Reader Can Re-create the Poem', in *Acts of Interpretation*, ed. Mary J. Carruthers and Elizabeth D. Kirk (Norman, Oklahoma: University of Oklahoma Press, 1982), pp. 67–101

—— (Eric G. Stanley), *The Search for Anglo-Saxon Paganism* (Cambridge: D. S. Brewer, 1975); reprinted with unchanged pagination in Eric Gerald Stanley, *Imagining the Anglo-Saxon Past: The Search for Anglo-Saxon Paganism and Anglo-Saxon Trial by Jury* (Cambridge: D. S. Brewer, 2000), pp. 1–110

—— (E. G. Stanley), 'SEAMUS HEANEY (trans.), *Beowulf*, *Notes & Queries* 245 (2000), 346–8

Stanton, Robert, *The Culture of Translation in Anglo-Saxon England* (Cambridge: D. S. Brewer, 2002)

Staver, Ruth Johnston, *A Companion to Beowulf* (Westport, CT, and London: Greenwood Press, 2005)

Steiner, George, *After Babel: Aspects of Language and Translation* (Oxford: Oxford University Press, 1973; 3rd ed., 1998)

Storms, G., review of Mary E. Waterhouse, trans., *Beowulf in Modern English*, *English Studies* 32 (1951), 141

Swannell, J. N., 'William Morris as an Interpreter of Old Norse', *Saga-Book of the Viking Society for Northern Research* 15 (1961), 365–82

[Taylor, William,] *The Monthly Review* 81 (1816), 516–23

ten Brink, Bernhard, *History of English Literature*, I, *To Wyclif*, trans. H. M. Kennedy (London: George Bell and Sons, 1883); original ed., B. ten Brink, *Geschichte der englischen Litteratur*, I, *Bis zu Wiclifs Auftreten* (Berlin: Oppenheim, 1877)

Thompson, Ewa M., *Russian Formalism and Anglo-American New Criticism: A Comparative Study* (The Hague and Paris: Mouton, 1971)

Tilling, P. M., 'William Morris's Translation of *Beowulf*: Studies in his Vocabulary', *Occasional Papers in Linguistics and Language Learning* 8 (1981), 163–75

Tinker, Chauncey Brewster, *The Translations of Beowulf: A Critical Bibliography*, with an updated bibliography by Marijane Osborn and a new foreword by Fred

C. Robinson (Hamden, CT: Archon Books, 1974; original ed., Yale Studies in English 16 [New Haven, CT: Yale University Press], 1903)

Tolkien, J. R. R., 'Beowulf: The Monsters and the Critics', Proceedings of the British Academy 22 (1936), 245–95; widely reprinted

——, 'Prefatory Remarks on Prose Translation of "Beowulf"', in J. R. Clark Hall, trans., Beowulf and the Finnesburg Fragment, revised ed., pp. i–xliii; reprinted as 'On Translating Beowulf', in J. R. R. Tolkien, The Monsters and the Critics and Other Essays, ed. Christopher Tolkien (London: George Allen & Unwin, 1983), pp. 49–71

Tripp, Raymond P., Jr, More About the Fight with the Dragon: Beowulf 2208b–3182: Commentary, Edition, and Translation (Lanham, MD: University Press of America, 1983)

Turner, Sharon, The History of the Anglo-Saxons: Comprising the History of England from the Earliest Period to the Norman Conquest, 4 vols (London: Longman, Hurst, Rees and Orme, 1799–1805); 2nd ed., 2 vols (London: Longman, Hurst, Rees and Orme, 1807); 3rd ed., 3 vols (London: Longman, Hurst, Rees, Orme and Brown, 1820); further editions down to 7th ed., 3 vols (London: Longman, Brown, Green and Longmans, 1852)

Tyler, Elizabeth M., Old English Poetics: The Aesthetics of the Familiar in Anglo-Saxon England (York: York Medieval Press, 2006)

VanHoosier-Carey, Gregory A., 'Byrhthoth in Dixie: The Emergence of Anglo-Saxon Studies in the Postbellum South', in Anglo-Saxonism and the Construction of Social Identity, ed. Frantzen and Niles, pp. 157–72

Venuti, Lawrence, The Translator's Invisibility: A History of Translation (London and New York: Routledge, 1995)

——, The Scandals of Translation: Towards an Ethics of Difference (London and New York: Routledge, 1998)

——, ed., The Translation Studies Reader, 2nd ed. (New York and London: Routledge, 2001)

Wanley, Humphrey, Librorum Veterum Septentrionalium, qui in Angliae Bibliothecis extant, nec non multorum Veterum Codicum Septentrionalium alibi extantium Catalogus Historico-Criticus . . . , Vol. II in George Hickes, Linguarum Vett. Septentrionalium Thesaurus Grammatico-Criticus et Archaeologicus, 2 vols (Oxford, 1703–5)

[Watts, Theodore], review of William Morris and Alfred J. Wyatt, trans., The Tale of Beowulf, in William Morris: The Critical Heritage, ed. Peter Faulkner (London and Boston, MA: Routledge and Kegan Paul, 1973), pp. 385–7; reprinted from The Athenaeum, 10 August, 1895, no. 3537, 181–2

Wawn, Andrew, ed., with Graham Johnson and John Walter, Constructing Nations, Reconstructing Myth: Essays in Honour of T. A. Shippey, Making the Middle Ages 9 (Turnhout: Brepols, 2007)

Webb, R. K., 'Brooke, Stopford Augustus (1832–1916)', in The Oxford Dictionary of National Biography, ed. Matthew and Harrison, VII, 914–16

Young, Robert J. C., The Idea of English Ethnicity (Oxford: Blackwell, 2008)

Index

Alexander, Michael 3, 21–2, 105, 135–59, 161
Beowulf 6, 135–59, 219
'*Beowulf* Reduced' 219
'The Ruin' 139–40
'The Seafarer' 140–1
alienation 9, 11
alliteration 10, 29, 31, 35, 36, 37, 57, 71, 76, 88, 95, 111, 130, 139, 173, 175–6, 183–4, 187, 193, 198
Amis, Kingsley 105
amplification 123–4, 125–7, 131, 152
Anglo-Saxonism 72
apposition 33, 55, 143–4, 180, 181, 186
archaism, archaizing 4, 10, 16–17, 24, 51–2, 56, 59, 61, 66, 71, 78, 82–3, 92, 140, 142, 169, 194, 201
Arnold, Thomas, *Beowulf* 24, 52
audience *See* readership/audience
aural effects 29–32, 37–8, 95, 112–13, 152–3, 173–9, 183–4, 187

Bagsby, Benjamin, performance version 218
Bradley, S. A. J., *Beowulf* 20–1
Braidwood, John 164
Brooke, Stopford 54–5, 64–5, 68–9
Brophy, Brigid 105

canon, literary 3, 5, 86, 158, 193
Carson, Ciaran 9, 13
Chickering, Howell D., Jr, *Beowulf* 196–7
Child, C. G. 52, 71
children's versions 218
colloquialism 17, 22, 155, 167, 168–9, 170, 182, 187, 193, 202, 205, 210

compound words 31, 55, 90–1, 96–7, 147–8, 155, 171–2, 180
Conybeare, John Josias 48–50, 62–3
Crane, J. K. 75–6, 77, 107, 133
Creed, R. P. 119, 132, 133
Crichton, Michael, *Eaters of the Dead* 217–18
Crossley-Holland, Kevin, *Beowulf* 135, 192–4

defamiliarization 9, 188, 209, 211
Dickens, Charles 63
diction 4, 11, 24, 35, 38, 55, 57, 59, 89, 119–20, 128, 137, 146–51, 171–2, 193, 206
Disraeli, Benjamin 49, 63
D'Israeli/Disraeli, Isaac 49, 62, 63, 67–8
domesticating translation 7–13, 22–3, 87, 122, 131–4, 168, 187–8, 194, 200, 201, 211
Dunbar, William 88
Donaldson, E. Talbot, *Beowulf* 23, 133, 165
Dryden, John 7, 203, 204

Eagleton, Terry 72
Earle, John, *Beowulf* 24, 52
Eco, Umberto 3
editions 12–13, 43–4, 50–1, 74
enjambment 89, 95, 113, 131, 180, 182, 198

film versions 218
fluency 8, 20, 49, 67, 103, 130, 154, 198, 210–11
foreignizing translation 7–13, 54, 57, 137, 187–8, 208

formulaic language 3, 21, 35–6, 148, 155, 168–9, 181

Gardner, John, *Grendel* 217
Garmonsway, G. N., *Beowulf* 20, 21
Garnett, James, *Beowulf* 55–6, 70
Girvan, Ritchie 85
Glosecki, Stephen 215–16
Glover, Julian, performance version 218
grammar 4, 31–2, 38, 89, 104
Grant, Paula, *Beowulf* 194
graphic novel versions 218
Greenfield, S. B., *A Readable Beowulf* 11, 198–9
Grundtvig, N. F. S. 47, 50
Gummere, Francis, *Beowulf* 71

Haley, Albert W., *Beowulf* 197
Hall, John Lesslie, *Beowulf* 56–7, 70
Hall, John R. Clark 65, 68
  Beowulf (prose) 15–17, 23–4, 52, 65
  Beowulf (verse) 65–6
Heaney, Seamus 28, 105, 161–89, 195
  Beowulf 6, 161–89, 191, 215, 219
  'Bone Dreams' 29
  North 171
  Preoccupations 171
Henderson, Ebenezer 48
Heyne, Moritz 51
heroic world 28, 38, 159
Hiberno-English 161–71, 182, 188
Hopkins, Gerard Manley 84
Hudson, Marc, *Beowulf* 204–5
Huppé, Bernard F., *Beowulf* 200–1

imagery 35–6, 38, 94, 96–7, 101, 119–20, 125–7, 151–3, 171–9

Jefferson, Thomas 69

Keats, John, 'On First Looking into Chapman's Homer' 25

Kemble, John Mitchell 13–15, 44, 50–2, 70
  Beowulf translation 51–2
Kennedy, Charles W., *Beowulf* 76–7
Kennedy, Thomas, *Beowulf* 208–9
kenning 36, 150, 151, 172
Kermode, Frank 74, 157, 209
Klaeber, Fr. 74–5

Lehmann, Ruth, *Beowulf* 201–2
Leo, Heinrich 67
Liuzza, Roy, *Beowulf* 6, 209–11
Longfellow, Henry Wadsworth 69–70, 71–2

Madden, Frederic 50, 67
manuscript 28, 42
McDiarmid, Hugh 86
McNamara, John, *Beowulf* 212–13
medievalizing 1, 9, 10, 57, 60, 61, 83
metre 4, 29, 36–7, 38, 112
  syllabic 4, 48–9, 52–4, 77–9, 83, 138–9, 198
  stress-based 4, 54–6, 57, 76, 83–4, 87, 88, 110–11, 154, 169, 183, 193, 196, 199–200, 201, 202, 204, 205, 207, 210, 211, 212, 214
Morgan, Edwin 58, 77, 78, 81–108, 109, 158, 169
  Beowulf 3, 81–108, 133, 215, 219
  'The Auld Man's Coronach' 86–7, 169
Morley, Henry 63–4, 68
Morris, William 57–62
  Aeneids 60–1
  Beowulf 9–11, 57–62, 81, 83, 219
  Grettis Saga 59–60
  Song of Atli 60
  Völsunga Saga 59
Murphy, Timothy *See* Sullivan, Alan, and Timothy Murphy, *Beowulf*

nationalism 46, 47, 66–72, 85–6
negotiation 3, 84

Nobis, Felix, performance version 195, 218
Norton Anthology of English Literature 5, 6, 23, 133, 165

Old English poetry See poetics, Old English
Oliver, Raymond, *Beowulf* 203–4
orality 27, 30–1, 138
Osborn, Marijane 44, 58, 199–200, 203
  Beowulf 199–200

parallelism 33, 102
Penguin Books 21, 158–9
perceptions 5–6, 14–15, 17, 22, 27, 43, 46–8, 49, 51, 53, 62–75, 82, 104–6, 137–8, 139–43, 157–9, 163–5, 192–3, 194, 195, 202, 204, 216, 217–19
philology 50–1, 69, 74, 84–5, 104–5, 157–8, 163
pleonasm 111, 125, 131, 156
poetics, Old English 27–37, 44, 188
Pound, Ezra 136
  'The Seafarer' 9, 12, 136, 139–43, 159
  prose translation 13–24, 51–2, 54, 158–9
Puhvel, Martin, *Beowulf* 213
punctuation 12, 17, 29, 33, 97, 102, 104, 128, 183, 210

Raffel, Burton 107, 109–34, 137, 199
  Beowulf 6, 109–34, 196, 219
race 67, 68–9, 71
readership/audience 11, 71, 75, 84–6, 87, 106, 112, 131–4, 158–9, 162, 187–8, 196, 199, 205, 208, 213, 215
Rebsamen, Frederick
  Beowulf 205–6
  Beowulf Is My Name 205, 217
register 3–4, 17, 39, 81, 93, 103, 128, 131, 137, 139, 142, 143–4, 149–51, 154–5, 163, 164, 181, 188, 210, 211–12, 213, 215
repetition 31, 93, 150, 180

Rieu, E. V. 21, 158–9
Ringler, Dick, *Beowulf* 213–15
Risden, E. L., *Beowulf* 206–7
Ritson, Joseph 42
Rodrigues, Louis, *Beowulf* 194–5

Saxonism 51
Schleiermacher, F. E. 7–8, 132
scop 30–1, 156
Scots 85–7, 164, (Ulster) 169
Shklovsky, Viktor 9
Sullivan, Alan, and Timothy Murphy, *Beowulf* 211–12
synonyms 29, 34
syntax 24, 31–2, 34, 55, 78, 97–100, 101–2, 104, 113–19, 127–8, 130–1, 143–6, 155, 156–7, 179–83, 185–6, 210–11

Taylor, William 66
ten Brink, Bernhard 64–5
Tennyson, Alfred Lord 62–3
Thorkelín, Grímur Jónsson 42, 43–7, 48, 66–7
  Beowulf translation 43–7
Thorpe, Benjamin, *Beowulf* 15, 50, 52, 64
Tinker, Chauncey B. 24
  Beowulf 24, 52, 71
Tolkien, J. R. R. 15–16, 17–19, 73–4, 105
  'Finnsburh Episode' 18–19
tradition 27–9, 30–7, 98–100, 129–30, 155, 156, 169, 181, 182, 187, 188
translation theory 2–25, 54–62, 75–6, 81–5, 109–11, 137–43, 162–9, 197, 204–5, 210
Trask, Richard M., *Beowulf* 207–8
Tripp, Raymond, *Beowulf* 202
Turner, Sharon, 47–8, 50, 51, 63, 66, 67

Ulster English 161–71, 172, 182, 188

variation 31, 38, 96, 143, 180
Venuti, Lawrence 7–8, 11–12, 140–1
vocabulary 29, 31, 36, 91, 92, 93–5, 96–7, 101, 146–8, 155, 156, 166–71, 181, 184–5, 187

Wackerbarth, Diedrich A. 43, 52–3, 68
   Beowulf 9–10, 52–3
Wanley, Humphrey 42
Waterhouse, Mary, *Beowulf* 77–9
Wharton, Thomas 42–3
word order 31–2, 34, 35, 91, 92, 145–6, 209
Wrenn, C. L. 15, 16–17
Wright, David 21–4
   Beowulf 9, 22–2, 75, 158
Wyatt, A. J. 10

www.ingramcontent.com/pod-product-compliance
Lightning Source LLC
Chambersburg PA
CBHW070759230426
43665CB00017B/2420